Pierre-Esprit
RADISSON

Martin Fournier

Pierre-Esprit
RADISSON
Merchant Adventurer

1636 - 1710

SEPTENTRION

Les éditions du Septentrion wishes to thank the Canada Council for the Arts and the Société de développement des entreprises culturelles du Québec (SODEC) for the support of its publishing program, as well as the Government of Quebec for its tax credit program for book publishing. We are also grateful for financial support received from the Government of Canada trough the Book Publishing Industry Development Program (BPIDP).

The translation was realized with the financial support of the SODEC.

Cover: P. J. Bainbrigge, *Rapids on the Ottawa River above Iron Decharge,* c. 1836-1842, detail, NAC C-11795.

Copy editing: Joan Irving

Graphic Design: Dynagram

Cover Design: Folio infographie

Translated from the French by Mary E. Brennan-Ricard
Original French edition © 2001 Les éditions du Septentrion
English edition © 2002 Les éditions du Septentrion

Les éditions du Septentrion
1300, av. Maguire
Sillery (Québec)
G1T 1Z3

Diffusion:
McGill-Queen's University Press

Legal Deposit – 3rd quarter 2002
National Library of Canada
ISBN 2-89448-328-7

Table of Contents

Rediscovering Radisson

Reasons for a new biography

This new biography of Radisson fills a gap in the French language since thus far mainly English-speaking historians have studied this explorer and French coureur de bois, referring for the most part to English-language narratives. The first historians to examine the six travel narratives, discovered in London, England, by the archivist Gedeon D. Scull, then published for the first time at Boston, in 1885,[1] wanted above all to indicate where and when Radisson and Des Groseilliers had first reached, between 1645 and 1685, such points in America as Lake Superior, the Mississippi River and Hudson's Bay. They attached little importance to Radisson as an individual as he had no social status and little education and was guilty of national inconstancies as much towards France as towards England. At a later time, English-Canadian historians took a closer look at the roles of explorer and tradesman of the two brothers-in-law, but without making any real attempt to understand and evaluate their many changes of allegeance or to probe

---

1. The six voyages all appeared in English with a later discovery of French versions of the fifth and sixth narratives written in 1684 and 1685, the first four having been produced around 1667-1668. A virtually insolvable polemic exists about the language of the first four narratives: did Radisson write them directly in the form we know, in faulty English, or was his original French narrative translated by someone else? I believe that Radisson participated in the English-language version of his first four narratives (Fournier, 1996: 18-24); however, I am unable to prove this. I will return to the actual writing of these narratives in chapter 7.

their motivations (Guillet, 1997: 7-12). Then in 1943, the American historian Grace Lee Nute produced the most exhaustive biography of these two
coureurs de bois (Nute, 1943).

At the same time in Québec, such celebrated historians as François-Xavier
Garneau and Lionel Groulx were speaking of Radisson as an ignoble traitor to
the French nation, a debauched adventurer; this radical opinion impeded until quite recently Québec historians from carefully scrutinizing Radisson's narrative.[2] All the same, we now realize that the six travel narratives Radisson has
left us represent a reliable source of exceptional value and that the time has come
for French readers to rediscover one of the most fascinating figures in the history of New France (Guillet, 1997); (Heidenreich, 1997); (Warkentin, 1993,
1996a, 1996b); (Wykoff, 1995).

Radisson's narratives

When we compare Radisson's narratives to other well recognized sources
such as the *Jesuit Relations*, the *Correspondance* of Marie de l'Incarnation
and the testimony of Nicolas Perrot, or if we link them to existing anthro-
pological and ethnographic findings about the Iroquois and the other
Amerindian nations Radisson knew, we note the relevance of his account
on a great many subjects (Delage, 1991, l985); (Richter, 1992); (Vecsey, 1983);
(Viau, 1997); (White, 1991).[3] At that time, everything indicated Radisson's

---

2. To the extent that Marcel Trudel elected to retrace the itinerary of his voyages turning to the *Jesuit Relations* rather than consulting Radisson's own account. Trudel's *Histoire
de la Nouvelle-France* (History of New France), contains 14 references to the Jesuits and only
one to Radisson (Trudel, 1983a).

3. In America, my principal sources for verifying, evaluating or completing Radisson's
narratives are the Dutch archives assembled by Jameson, the narratives of the Jesuits and of
Marie de l'Incarnation (who knew Des Groseilliers well) and the writings of three voyagers,
contemporaries of Radisson who traded with the Indians, Pierre Boucher, Nicolas Perrot and
Cavalier de la Salle. In Europe, I relied mostly on British sources: the archives of the Hudson's
Bay Company and of the Royal Society and the Diary of Samuel Pepys provide much pertinent information about the people, the values and the customs prevalent in the various
milieux that Radisson frequented in England. In France, little is known about the circles and
the people Radisson knew; a few documents from administrators on appointment in France
or in New France or from individuals at the Court of Louis XIV enable me to pinpoint the
reasons why Radisson encountered difficulties in his native land. I used a facsimile of the first
edition of Radisson's travel narratives to analyse the first four of these. The references (Ra:
25) (Ra: 100) are always taken from the first transcription and publication by Gedeon Skull
in 1885 (Radisson, [1885] 1943).

desire to be recognized as a percipient and reliable informer-witness; one good example is the long letter he wrote from Grenada to his French patron to advise him about the naval expedition to the West Indies in 1678 in which he participated. Using rather clumsy French, Radisson gives an exact account of the salient events, thereby enabling the commission of inquiry appointed by Louis XIV to look into that failed expedition and make an exhaustive report (Nute, 1943: 303-308); (Roncière, 1934); (Saint-Yves, 1899); (Sue, 1845).

Further on we will see that in London, towards 1667, Radisson was encouraged to speak openly about what he had experienced in America so as to satisfy the curiosity of a small group of persons who attached importance to the detailed and abundant information he could provide about this new continent and its inhabitants. The first part of Radisson's tale – the first four travel narratives – represent a very reliable testimony: Radisson recounts his memories and reveals how he interprets and builds his persona using his past experiences. This text, not intended for publication, depicts a relatively private Radisson who is flattered by others' interest in his exploits. In telling his own story, Radisson enjoys great liberty, at times expressing his opinion directly, so that his comments, observations and the very personal tenor of his writings affirm his individuality. In brief, the first four narratives of Radisson's voyage contain numerous passages where the author reflects on his past in a personal manner, all the while pursuing a simple strategic objective: he wants to prove to the English that he is competent and has a keen sense of responsibility, hoping they will invest in the Hudson's Bay fur-trade project which he and Des Groseilliers are anxious to undertake.

Radisson wrote two other travel narratives in 1684 and 1685, in completely different circumstances. These last two narratives let us discover another aspect of his personality as he had just led two successive expeditions to the Nelson River (western shore of Hudson's Bay) to set up a trading post. Radisson depicts himself in these texts as a dignified Englishman, efficient and responsible, and we see him fight to keep his position in the respectable and prosperous enterprise that he had helped found: the Hudson's Bay Company. It is clear that this new "persona" corresponds to what Radisson hoped to become in England and to same extent probably did – a gentleman.

In their entirety, Radisson's narratives constitute a full and complete document providing detailed information about his reactions, his opinions, his preferences and even about the strategies he pursued to achieve social integration. It was thus possible to write the biography of a well-rounded individual, one who acts and reacts with his heart and his mind in the changing environments which influence him and to which he sought to adapt himself and integrate in, from those of France to New France, then to the Iroquois nation, the Great Lakes, Hudson's Bay, New England and finally, England. I also wanted to provide a detailed account of Radisson's momentous existence from a more than simply logical perspective, since his life is a tissue of unexpected, sudden reversals of fortune marked by many, and at times, disconcerting changes. And so, I have sought to accompany him through the hazards and inconsistencies of his complex existence, attempting to identify the individuals, the milieux and the prevailing cultures that nourished his adventures and offered him certain possibilities while setting him limitations. In short, I have attempted to understand the conjuncture of wills, needs and circumstances that might render intelligible the highly eventful existence of this extraordinary cultural Métis.

CHAPTER 1

The First Voyage:
Radisson Becomes an Iroquois

His birth and early years

No one knows exactly where or when Radisson was born for his baptismal certificate has never been found. The most explicit documents suggest he was born in Paris in the parish of Saint-Sulpice, probably in 1636 (Trudel, 1983, Jetté, 1983, and J. Radisson, 1996).[1] Since Marie de l'Incarnation (to whom the Jesuits had given this information) qualifies Radisson as a "jeune homme" (young man) in a letter of 1658 (Marie de l'Incarnation, 1971: 603), several historians have tended to make him as young as possible, but a careful reading of the Jesuit writings reveals that, for them, a young man may easily be beyond the age of twenty; for example, they speak of their yoeman, Guillaume Couture, as a young man when he is twenty-six years old (Roy, 1884: 13 and 31); they also mention in their journal "a young man of twenty" and "a young boy, 21 years of age, named Jean Chicot" (Casgrain and Laverdière, 1892: 153); (St-Arnaud, 1998: 93). Radisson himself subscribes to the same perception when he speaks of "a young man of twenty-

---

1. As to the place, several authors had retained the hypothesis of Saint-Malo, his mother's place of birth (Skull, 1943, and Adams, 1961), or Avignon, birth place of his father (Nute, 1943, and Warkentin, 1996), but one of Radisson's marriage contracts and that of his sister Françoise indicate that they were both from the parish of Saint-Sulpice, in Paris. As for the date of birth, I refer to the ages that Radisson declared in the 1681 census in New France and in an English-language affidavit of 1697, which give, respectively, 1636 and 1640 as the year of birth.

five" (Ra: 113). And so, it may be concluded that the young man of whom the Jesuits speak would likely be in his twenties. The fact that Radisson took part in an Iroquois war expedition in 1653 despite the misgivings of his adoptive mother who judged him too inexperienced and that fifteen was the minimum age for a young Iroquois to participate in such an expedition (Viau, 1994: 38 and 74), suggest that the year 1636 offers a realistic compromise between the numerous indications of Radisson's youthful age and the traces of his relative maturity: ostensibly, Radisson would have arrived at Trois-Rivières at the age of fifteen, would have participated in a fighting expedition along with ten or more Iroquois at age seventeen and been part of the Jesuit expedition of 1657 to the Onnontague Iroquois at the age of twenty-one. Such evaluation seems more in line with the spirit of independence and the feats of physical prowess that Radisson describes in his first two travel narratives.

The young Frenchman first tread upon the soil of the New France in spring 1651. It is not known if he arrived alone or was accompanied by his sister Élisabeth, but it is certain that he joined his half sister Marguerite Hayet, and his sister Françoise in Trois-Rivières, where the former was married to Jean Véron, called Grandmesnil, and the latter remained a spinster (Trudel, 1983, and Jetté, 1983). During the first year Radisson spent at Trois-Rivières, he most certainly mixed with the many Algonquins who lived in close rapport with the French inhabitants. He learned something of their language and became familiar with their customs; he also hunted, since at the time of his capture, he describes himself as a skillful and experienced hunter. These are the only particulars we have about Radisson's first year in Canada and we know even less about his early years in France, except for one interesting detail. When Radisson describes his first weeks of captivity among the Iroquois, he notes that, in the space of six weeks, he learned more about the Iroquois customs than he would have done in France in six months (Ra: 40), thereby indicating that he was already in contact with the Amerindian world before he left France, most likely through correspondence with his sisters or with other persons in the colony.[2]

---

2. Ms Germaine Warkentin, who has undertaken a critical edition of Radisson's narrative, links what we know about Radisson's early years to the typical training provided in that era by a commercial milieu. He received basic schooling, learning to read and write; then towards age 15, he was sent to serve his practical apprenticeship among his family's business associates. For example, he served in the entourage of Marguerite Hayet, his half-sister, a resident of Trois-Rivières, who was married to a fur trader (maintenance staff).

New France during the 1650s

When the French returned to colonize New France in 1632, after the conquest of Québec by the Kirke brothers and her retrocession to France by the King of England, the Jesuits began in earnest their missionary work in this new territory. With the support of the early Governors, they constituted until about 1660 the backbone of institutional power in a still sparsely developed colony (Beaulieu, 1992: 39). The economy of New France was then based on the fur trade, which operated solely in a close association with the Amerindians and, since the Jesuits conducted their missionary work among these same Amerindians, the two activities, conversion and commerce, soon became complementary (Delâge, 1985: 129); (Beaulieu, 1992: 38). The Jesuits were assisted by a few interpreters and experienced traders, as well as by a number of "donnés"[3] (yoemen) and servants who rapidly became indispensable partners and even competitors, at first in commercial dealings with the Amerindians, then, because of the influence of money, in political power-sharing within the colony (Horguelin, 1997). Nonetheless, the Jesuits were able to remain for a long time at the center of the political, military and commercial networks of alliance with the Amerindians, be these friends or enemies of the French (Beaulieu, 1992: 6).

The years 1648-1649 marked a turning point in the history of New France, when repeated Iroquois attacks forced the Jesuits to burn their main logistical base in the Great Lakes territory, the Sainte-Marie-des-Hurons mission, then leave the Huron territory; these attacks also decimated the Huron and their immediate allies who were poorly armed, divided and ultimately defenseless (Delâge, 1985: 223-229). A few alternatives remained to the Huron, recently converted to Catholicism by the Jesuits: they could flee to the south or to the west of their ancestral territory or take refuge at Québec (several hundred did reach that destination), or else accept death or, at best, servitude at the hands of their Iroquois captors (Viau, 1994: 110 and 196). The Iroquois would offer large-scale adoption, by entire villages or clans, to those Huron who had not converted. In a few months, the major fur-trading network that the Huron had set up on the base of their own secular trade network was dismembered. The shock waves provoked by the

---

3. Lay persons who gave their services totally to the Jesuits by virtue of a written contract committing them to celibacy and to pursuing the interests of the Society of Jesus, notably ahead of their own.

dispersion around 1650 of the Huron and of the other nations allied with the French in the Lakes Ontario, Erie and Huron regions struck a mighty blow to the French colony. Trois-Rivières, Montréal and Québec were harassed continuously, at times almost coming under siege by the Iroquois who had resolved, ostensibly, either to become by force the main trading partners of the French, or else to literally cast them out of the fur trade and out of America (Beaulieu, 1992: 130-132, and Jennings, 1984: 56-57). For the Amerindians who had taken refuge in the west, far from the supply sources in European goods that had become objects of power and covetousness among the warring or competitive nations, the situation was, to say the least, uneasy (Jennings, 1984: 7 and 85, and Viau, 1994: 63 to 65).

Between 1650 and 1665, New France endured sustained guerilla warfare on the part of the Iroquois. Since the colony depended on commercial and military relations with its native partners to prosper or even merely to survive, the French sought desperately to restore commercial ties with the nations forced to retreat to the western shores of the Great Lakes, and to protect the privileged alliance they enjoyed with the Algonquins and the Huron who continued to participate actively in defending the French establishments in the Saint Lawrence valley (Campeau, 1996: 335-342, 628-635 and 726); (Beaulieu, 1992: 165-175).

First capture and adoption

Radisson speaks explicitly about the climate of mounting tension that reigned in Trois-Rivières in 1652. He indicates that the French were at war against a savage nation called Iroquois, at the time so strong and so feared that virtually no one dared leave his cabin or his house without risking capture or death (Ra: 25). Despite such perilous conditions, when spring came, Radisson decided to leave on a hunting expedition with two companions. Perhaps the Iroquois menace had not yet materialized that year or else the three young people really showed great temerity, as Radisson intimates (Ra: 26); in any case, they apparently left the village of Trois-Rivières on an April morning to hunt the game fowl abundant at that time of the year (Ra: 25 and 32). Shortly afterwards, they were told by a farmer that the Iroquois were prowling in the vicinity. This information made them more vigilant and, when they had seized a first catch, one of Radisson's companions wanted to return to the safety of Trois-Rivières but Radisson disagreed calling him a coward and a quarrel broke out; then the group separated.

Radisson continued hunting on his own and only headed back at the end of the day to find his two companions dead, lying naked near the shore, riddled with bullet holes and scalped (Ra: 27-28). Then he made out not far from there, but obscured by reeds, the heads of some twenty Iroquois who rushed at him shrieking. Radisson shot his two rifles in their direction, but to no avail; they flung him to the ground, seized his guns and dragged him forcibly to their encampment, without harming him but after making sure that no Algonquin was tracking them. The Iroquois then set about preparing their repast after which they combed and greased Radisson's hair, also covering his face with a reddish paint (Ra: 29-30).

Terrorized, Radisson was unable to eat the half-rotten meat that his captors gave him; but he did manage to swallow a few scraps of meat they had boiled separately and dredged in a bit of flour. Apparently, Radisson was unaware that the red colour they had applied to his face meant that he had already been chosen as a candidate for adoption (Viau, 1994: 159); he would thus not be tortured or brutalized for the moment. His being chosen by the Iroquois can be explained. Since adoptees were intended to replace a deceased family member and could in time enjoy the same status and the same esteem as the dead person, it was important that the candidate for adoption prove his worth (Jameson, 1909: 180); (Viau, 1994: 42). The courage Radisson had shown in distancing himself alone from Trois-Rivières no doubt pleased his ravishers who had likely been observing him well before his capture, as was their habit. Moreover, the fact that Radisson had made a good catch must have greatly increased his chances of adoption since a talent for hunting was essential to the Amerindian communities for their survival (Viau, 1994: 23 and 29).

The night following his capture, Radisson dreamt he was drinking beer in the company of a Jesuit, which made him hope he would get out alive. Although he remained terrorized for some time, tied up as he was beside the scalps of his two companions in the canoe that was carrying him to Iroquois country, Radisson was no less encouraged by the benevolent attitude of his captors. He regained confidence gradually and attempted as far as possible to make up to them; they in turn encouraged his attempts and even taught him a few words of their language. After three days of feasting and hunting, the Iroquois bands who had assembled between Trois-Rivières and the mouth of the Richelieu each headed home. In due course, Radisson's captor and official guard handed him a paddle rather than tying him up. Radisson then began paddling energetically, but when he had lathered up a sweat, his guard took away his paddle; Radisson refused to rest and insisted energetically that he be given back the paddle, until his guard agreed to do so, this time showing him how to conserve his energy (Ra: 32-33).

The attention accorded Radisson did not mean that his fate was definitively sealed. For example, the care his captors paid to his food reflected on the habit the Iroquois had of carefully nourishing their captives so that, on their return to the village, the obvious vigor of the prisoners would bear witness to the strength and courage of their captors (Richter, 1983: 529); (Viau, 1994: 151). That Radisson later viewed himself in a mirror, his body painted half red, half black, would indicate that his captors were hesitating as to his ultimate fate (Ra: 34) (St-Arnaud, 1998: 143). Happily, he had little understanding of the Iroquois' behavior, for the growing confidence he was developing towards them as to his probable fate seems to have encouraged his reaching out to them – a misunderstanding that likely served him well (Viau, 1994: 146).

When they met up with another band, on the Richelieu River, Radisson's "brother" – to wit, his guard, the person responsible for bringing him home to the village (Viau, 1994: 150) – warned him that a member of that band wanted to molest him. Radisson took the bull by the horns showing the young Iroquois more attention and interest than he did towards any other, offering him a piece of roasted meat covered with a bit of salt and flour; this gesture was appreciated and may have avoided him receiving the intended blows. The Iroquois then taught him to yell as they did, which Radisson imitated without difficulty as he already knew the similar shriek of the Algonquins. He also sang for them in French, to the particular amusement of the Amerindians who had come to enjoy the melodious European strains. Then one morning, awake before the others and untrameled, he began romping about the shore... for a moment, he thought of escaping, but decided not to attempt the adventure alone. Later, when the band were certain of his docility, one of them offered him a knife, which Radisson was able to keep for the rest of the voyage. That same day, in the canoe, his guard and "brother" allowed him to shoot a rifle at a deer which had ventured out of the woods: another sign of trust (Ra: 33 to 35).

A first incident occurred when the group arrived at a fishing camp, not far from the village where Radisson was to be adopted. Someone struck him immediately upon his arrival but, when his "brother" indicated to him to strike back, a very roisterous battle ensued between the two young men, a fight which apparently Radisson won. All at once, several members of his band surrounded him, congratulating him and offering him food; again they combed and greased his hair. Then, an Iroquois whom Radisson thought he had wounded at the time of his capture came to him not to exact revenge as he feared, but on the contrary to show him his esteem, his solidarity, also calling him "my brother" and offering him a full box of red paint (Ra: 37). The following day, on their arrival in the village, Radisson escaped the beating that the Iroquois traditionally reserved for their prisoners since his adoptive mother, a kindly old woman, took him directly into her hut. Afterwards, several elders came to claim him but his mother was able to make a strong case for keeping him and she succeeded in convincing the elders to leave him in her care, without any further formality. From that point on, Radisson was able to stay with his adoptive mother's family where he was well treated (Ra: 38-39).

During the following five or six weeks, his mother encouraged him to develop relationships with other young men in the village who became his hunting and sporting companions (Ra: 39). This attitude confirmed that Radisson was indeed destined for adoption, in other words for full and complete integration in the Iroquois community since the captives who had no status other than that of "slaves" had to remain in an exclusive relationship with their captor (Viau, 1994: 185). Radisson wrote that during those few weeks, he no longer thought about his country of origin, taking advantage of a pleasant existence without much restriction or any responsibility. Just before his adoption banquet, which took place the sixth week after his arrival in the village, his mother asked him if he was French. Radisson replied no that he was one of their nation, an Iroquois, naturally to the great pleasure of his adoptive mother (Ra: 40).

Radisson did write that he already felt Iroquois at that juncture but also that he was troubled as to his identity (Ra: 40). However, it is quite true that there was no other acceptable reply to his adoptive mother's query if he wished to avoid death. In fact, after that initial period of six weeks, Radisson's adaptation still appeared to be fragile since he attempted to escape at the first opportunity, shortly after his adoption banquet, when he went on a hunting expedition some distance from the village with three Iroquois companions. An Algonquin they had met by chance in the bush offered to help him return to Trois-Rivières; Radisson accepted the offer with little enthusiasm since they had first to assassinate the three Iroquois "who had never harmed me," he comments (Ra: 43). After nightfall, the two fugitives each killed a sleeping Iroquois using their axes and the third was disposed of with a shotgun

(Ra: 43-44). Then they went under cover for fourteen days, travelling only at night by canoe until they reached Lake Saint-Pierre close to Trois-Rivières. The Algonquin now wanted them to cover the last distance by day but Radisson remembered how well the Iroquois patrolled the territory and although he felt that the adventure would be too dangerous, he failed to convince his companion to wait until night. So he let him leave alone; then fearing the Algonquin would abandon him entirely, and that he would be unable to handle the canoe on his own or that all might think him a coward, he caught up to the Algonquin and together they hastened their canoe towards Trois-Rivières. Unfortunately, the Iroquois, just as he feared, were indeed waiting in ambush on the Saint-Lawrence and the pair were intercepted; the Algonquin was killed and Radisson recaptured when the two attempted to reach the shore to flee into the bush (Ra: 42-47).

This second capture was terrible yet decisive for Radisson. This time he would be forced to endure torture, but during the fifteen months he subsequently spent in intimate rapport with the Iroquois, he would acquire extensive knowledge of their customs and capabilities. To better understand the nature and scope of such forced adaptation, we must examine the situation of the Iroquois and take a look at their culture during the 1650s.

Renewal of a traditional society

Like the Mahican, their neighbors, who had seen Dutch boats journey up the Hudson River as early as 1610, the Iroquois first wondered if these strangers were gods, men or, indeed, animals. They believed that the Europeans were arriving from another world governed by different gods for otherwise, the Amerindians opined, they too would know how to build the great ships they now saw and they would also be able to repel the diseases which merely indisposed the white peoples while decimating the native populations (Jameson 1909: 178 and 293); (Merwick, 1990: 110).

Although it is difficult to evaluate with exactitude the nature, number or recurrence of the many losses and acquisitions that transformed the Iroquois customs and culture between 1610 and 1650, thanks to the regular contacts they had with their Dutch neighbors of Fort Orange, it is essential to note some of these transformations. What is most significant about the specific Iroquois culture are the conditions that define the particular period during which Radisson lived among them. Radisson witnessed a highly agitated period, a time when the Iroquois with great assurance had decided to counter the epidemics and the military and cultural shocks that were destabilizing them and to assure by all possible means their nation's future and far-reaching influence (Viau, 1994: 12 and 74). This climate reigned in the village where Radisson lived in 1652-1653, immediately following the major victories the Iroquois had won in the Great Lakes region. The five Iroquois nations, and particularly the Mohawk who had captured and adopted Radisson, were certain of their overwhelming superiority.[4] During the period from approximately 1645 to 1665, the Iroquois by force of arms dominated the entire northeast of America, driving out or slaughtering the Huron, Petun, Neutral, Eries and Susquehannocks, along with a large number of Algonquins who were forced to leave their ancestral territories in the Saint-Lawrence, Ottawa, Great Lakes, and even so far as the Saguenay, regions. This supremacy destroyed the existing geopolitical balance, forcing a great number of nations to ally with the Europeans in order to obtain arms and munitions (White, 1991: 24) – a major dynamic revealed by Radisson in his first four narratives.

The frenzy animating his village coupled with his own desire to become a full-fledged member of the Iroquois communtiy motivated Radisson's decision to become a warrior.[5] Without actually realizing it, he thereby contributed to the Iroquois' overriding project, namely "to establish a single nation and a single land" with the other Amerindian nations who would comply with their rules and be governed by them. This last was reported by Father Jogues who, having also been captured by the Mohawk in 1643, was attentive to their discussions and wrote that as far he could tell the Iroquois intended to seize all the Huron, killing the most influential of their number along with many others so as to form a single people in a united territory (BRH, 1930: 48).

---

4. Jennings speaks of the Iroquois will to constitute an empire: "The Iroquois thought themselves the wisest of Indians, pointing to their League as evidence, and thus rationalized their role of hegemony over other tribes" (Jennings, 1984: 94). See also Jameson, (1909: 176). Viau mentions the Iroquois domination over all the other Iroquois tribes between 1650 and 1675 (Viau, 1994: 73).

5. Participation in a war party was a benchmark episode in an Iroquois youth's development and later success in battle [while increasing] the young man's stature in his clan and village (Richter, 1983: 530).

Although Father Jogues held a partisan point of view, since at that time the Jesuits were working to establish a veritable Catholic stronghold in the Huron territory, against the will of the Iroquois and of certain Huron, he nonetheless aptly described what would happen, once firearms began to take hold in America (Jennings, 1984: 112).

The New Holland colony

Despite strict orders to maintain neutrality, which the Dutch West Indies Company had given its representatives in America, those colonists who founded the Orange settlement on the Hudson River in 1626 sided with the Mahican, the enemy nation of the Mohawk, and suffered a bitter defeat. The Dutch were forced to retreat for a time to Manhatte (today New York), for their safety, and when they returned to Orange, lured by the castor pelts the Iroquois could provide in abundance, they condemned the actions of their former representative, seeking a privileged alliance at that point with the Mohawk who dominated the region and were ever anxious to obtain abundant supplies of European goods (Bogaert, 1988: XVII); (Merwick, 1990: 7 and 10; (Jennings, 1984: 53). The situation remained strained for several years, with the Iroquois frequently killing cattle and also burning a Dutch ship near Orange (Beaulieu, 1992: 109); (Merwick, 1990: 32). But the wide community of interest uniting the two parties and the concentrated efforts of both groups to overcome their differences finally resulted in a strong alliance between the Dutch at Orange and the Mohawk, an alliance confirmed by a first official treaty in 1643 (Jennings, 1984: 71 and 53).

A single document remains about these efforts at union, a short, informed narrative written by one Van den Bogaert who visited the Iroquois in the winter of 1634-1635 to revive the agreement of understanding that had once existed between the Dutch and the Iroquois and to revitalize lethargic trade relations (Bogaert, 1988: XIX and 13); (Beaulieu, 1992: 110-119). According to Bogaert, a few Frenchmen who understood the language and customs of the Iroquois had preceded him by several weeks, offering them presents and proposing a commercial alliance between the Iroquois, the French and their Amerindian allies. The negotiation undertaken by Bogaert was rendered all the more difficult because of his sketchy knowledge of the language, the fact that he brought no presents and that he had no mandate to conclude a definitive agreement with the Iroquois (Bogaert, 1988: 13 and 16). The latter pressured Bogaert to lower the price of the Dutch goods, insisting that he grant them parity with the advantageous trading conditions supposedly accorded them by the French (Bogaert, 1988: 13). But above all else, they promised the Dutch to trade exclusively with them if they agreed to their demands in regard to rates of exchange (Bogaert, 1988: 16).

This document also sheds light on various other aspects of the atmosphere that prevailed among the Iroquois. The lively curiosity Bogaert inspired during his visit to two populous Mohawk villages indicated that few white men had as yet spent time in Iroquois territory (Bogaert, 1988: 7 and 9). The warm welcome he received almost everywhere he went also showed the strong desire of many Iroquois to deal with the Dutch (Bogaert, 1988: 7, 19 and 22); yet, a cold reception on the part of one local chief confirmed that not everyone agreed as to how to react to the white men and their technologies (Bogaert, 1988: 21). Finally, Bogaert's narrative tells, of the keen interest the Iroquois now had in firearms. On several occasions they prevailed upon Bogaert to fire a musket shot, but most often he refused (Bogaert, 1988: 10, 12 and 22); only on three occasions, two at his own initiative, did Bogaert shoot his rifle into the air. He did so to mark the arrival of the new year (Bogaert: 14), to celebrate the end of negotiations between the Iroquois and himself – at that time firing three shots in answer to the three "Ho!" of acknowledgement shouted out by the Iroquois chiefs – and the last time when Bogaert left the village where the negotiations had taken place, to satisfy his hosts who had exhorted him to shoot his rifle. Each time Bogaert discharged his rifle, the Iroquois manifested unbridled excitement but no great fear; they were already enthralled by firearms and would quickly learn how to use them.

The Dutch-Iroquois alliance and firearms

The proximity of the Dutch post of Fort Orange located, according to the sites of the native villages, within only three, four or five days on foot, seems to have been a boon for these Iroquois (Jameson, 1909: 178 and 404); (Ra: 81). Even though the Mohawk were obliged to endure as many epidemics as the other Indians, their regular contacts with the Dutch seem not to have worsened the situation. The very fact that they were the first to procure firearms – they already possessed between three and four hundred muskets in 1643 (Viau, 1994: 58); (BRH, 1930: 48) – represented an obvious advantage. In any case, the majority of historians are certain of that advantage... moreover, since a researcher has expressed doubts about the efficacy of the rudimentary firearms of the XVIIth century, when these are compared with the traditional weaponry of the Amerindians, it is expedient to explain how the early acquisition of firearms would have given the Iroquois a considerable advantage.[6]

This advantage seems all the more obvious in that the Amerindians did not have to *abandon* any of their traditional weapons in favor of firearms; these *completed* the native arsenal, offering them a greater choice of strategies, renewed power and a greater impact on their adversaries (Viau, 1994: 66 and 165). Firearms enabled them to weaken the enemy at the moment of attack, wounding and destabilizing him at the outset, a technique already favored by the Iroquois who excelled in leaping out at their enemies, while shrieking furiously (Viau, 1994: 129-130). Guns also allowed them to recapture distant runaways and pierce the wooden shields that were soon to be abandoned; in addition, they fortified the ambushes that the Iroquois laid along the waterways to intercept canoes carrying furs or trade goods (Viau, 1994: 61 and 66). Most certainly, after the major Iroquois offensives, during the 1650s, the rival nations everywhere sought and clamored to obtain firearms, at times urgently, at times menacingly (Jennings, 1984: 80-81 and 102); (Jameson, 1909: 368). As to the psychological advantage that researchers concede to firearms, this fails to explain why all the Europeans and, it appears, all the Indians who had the opportunity, also hunted using rifles (Ra: 198). Moreover, the psychological advantage was always short-lived, and rather than returning exclusively to their traditional weaponry once the amazement had passed, the Amerindians continued to travel incredible distances to obtain shotguns and ammunition.

Even though certain tests carried out in the XXth century are not fully conclusive, the widespread use of and demand for firearms by the Amerindians and the Europeans of the XVIIth century confirm that they greatly appreciated the efficacy and power of even the most rudimentary iron weapons. Radisson's narrative concurs with this finding: he affirms that the acquisition of such weapons and firearms gave many Amerindians a strong motivation to ally with the Europeans and to trade with them over the years

---

6. Given, Brian J. (1994), *A Most Pernicious Thing. Gun Trading and Native Warfare in the Early Contact Period*, Carleton University Press, Ottawa, 138 pages. See also Viau, (1994: 60 et 62), for a brief discussion about a preceding article by Given: "The Iroquois Wars and Native Firearms," in Musée National de l'Homme, Collection Mercure, File 78, Ottawa 1981, pp. 84-91.

1650-1660, even if firearms occupied but a marginal place in the Amerindian arsenal. Yet, how did the Mohawk manage to obtain massive supplies of firearms before the other indigenous nations? The answer merits a brief discussion.

Life at Rensselaerwyck

The village of Rensselaerwyck that surrounded Fort Orange itself contained forty or so houses in 1644. Artisans and farmers resided there along with a small garrison and representatives of the company who lived inside the fort (Merwick, 1990: 9 and 37-38); (Jameson, 1909: 262). Since Rensselaerwyck farmers never had better than mediocre crops and the artisans few opportunities to work, it was only after the end in 1639 of the fur-trade monopoly exercised by the West Indies Company that the tiny village could develop (Merwick, 1990: 38 and 132-133). To feed his family, a farmer had to work his land all year round or trade a few beaver pelts with the Iroquois... It was no surprise that the desire to engage in trade soon transformed the occupation of the residents and enticed a growing number of individuals anxious to make an easy profit.

With the arrival of the future governor Van Corlaer at Fort Orange, towards 1638, relations between the Dutch and the Mohawk intensified.[7] On the one hand, the Dutch had agreed to sell firearms to the Iroquois who, for their part, exchanged their pelts only with the Dutch, while warring against the French and their allies. An official document of the West Indies Company provides an explanation for the rapid development in the firearms trade:

> the inhabitants of Rensselaerwyck, numbering as many tradesmen as other individuals, realized that the Mohawk wanted above all to procure rifles, that certain of their number had already gotten some from the English, and because they were ready to pay as much as twenty beavers for a rifle or as high as ten or twelve "guilders" for a pound of gunpowder, they came in greater numbers [to Orange], ... well supplied in rifles purchased at ordinary prices, thereby making considerable profits (Jameson, 1909: 272-273).

---

7. Van Corlaer developed extensive and strong alliances with the Iroquois (Jennings, 1984: 167). The testimony of a Protestant missionary confirms the friendly relations between the Dutch and the Iroquois in the 1640s: "Though they are so very cruel to their enemies, they are very friendly to us, and we have no dread of them. We go with them into the woods, we meet with each other, sometimes at an hour or two's walk from any houses, and think no more about it than as if we met with a Christian" (Jameson, 1909: 175 (Megapolensis)).

Company representatives also sold rifles to the Mohawk, who quickly became very powerful thanks to Dutch firearms. The Iroquois multiplied their raids on the Saint-Lawrence[8] and imposed their will on the nations living near the Hudson River, who often had to pay them tribute. In cooperation with the Dutch, they soon assumed the politico-military "management" of the entire region, to the advantage of both partners in this ever more solid and exclusive alliance.[9] Many Amerindian nations were penalized by this alliance including, to a lesser extent, the four other Iroquois nations who endured more limited access to firearms and Dutch goods and had to tolerate the often cavalier attitude of the Mohawk (Jennings, 1984: 57). The very severe repression that the Dutch imposed on the hostile tribes of the Manhatte region, who sought in 1643-1644 to safeguard their political autonomy and to free their lands from European appropriation, illustrates this dynamic. The Dutch massacred close to one thousand Indians but this act remained without retaliation thanks to the ongoing support of the Mohawk who exercised a tight control over other recalcitrant tribes in the region (Jameson, 1909: 172, 234, 263 and 275-284).

However, the West Indies Company judged that the bellicose attitude adopted by the director Kieft on that occasion was dangerous, in view of the growing number of firearms in Iroquois hands and the small number of Dutch inhabitants in the colony. The Company thus replaced Kieft by a new director in 1647 and asked him expressly to end the trade of firearms with the Mohawk (Jameson, 1909: 287). Despite the death penalty with which the new director Stuyvesant menaced the inhabitants of Rensselaerwyck, he failed, since the Iroquois threatened to retaliate against the Dutch because they feared losing their dominant position if they lacked rifles and ammunition. According to Company representatives in Orange, it was impossible to eradicate the arms trade since all the inhabitants of Rensselaerwyck were in the habit of offering the Iroquois many favors and

---

8. "Our Mahakas [Mohawk] carry on great wars against the Indians in Canada, on the river Saint Lawrence, and take many captives, and sometimes there are French Christians among them. Last year, our Indians got a great booty from the French on the River Saint Lawrence, and took three Frenchmen, one of whom was a Jesuit (Father Jogues)" (Jameson, 1909: 175 (Megapolensis)).

9. "The alliance was strictly a two-party affair. Its functions appear to have been to provide arms to the Mohawk, to repress the rebellious tribes of New Netherland, to damage New France, and to insure the delivery of furs to Fort Orange" (Jennings, 1984: 57).

privileges such as inviting them to their table, spreading the cloth before them, offering them wine and other such treats so that they would prefer trading their furs with them rather than with their neighbor.[10] This excessive courtesy turned against the inhabitants of Rensselaerwyck when they sought to interrupt the sale of firearms. The Iroquois who heretofore had only to demand rifles to get them often reacted with anger and threatened them (Jameson, 1909: 273-274).[11]

The control that the director Stuyvesant had over the Company's activities in New Netherland, the heavy taxes he imposed on the inhabitants, indeed his unfortunate habit of "seizing" the cargoes of foreign ships passing through Manhatte, had resulted in an anemic economy and provoked much discontent in the small Dutch colony (Jameson, 1909: 287 and 345-346). Opposition to Stuyvesant soon developed to the extent that a number of employees sent a memoir to Holland denouncing his tyrannical attitude. This opposition is significant in that the employee memoir and another prepared in Stuyvesant's defense at his own request both confirm that a contreband in firearms was flourishing for everybody involved (Jameson, 1909: 345).[12]

The power of the Mohawk thus continued to grow and in collaboration with the remaining four Iroquois nations they won several other major victories against a number of enemy nations, both near at hand and far away. Towards 1650-1655, their power and appetite for war reached fever pitch. Radisson witnessed the proud, even arrogant attitude they adopted towards the Dutch settlers who were not well protected – those living in small groups,

---

10. "This liberty (liberty to trade that all the inhabitants had obtained) was soon perverted to a great abuse. For everyone thought that now the time had come to make his fortune, withdrew himself from his comrade, as if holding him suspect and the enemy of his gains, and sought communication with the Indians from whom it appeared his profit was to be derived" (Jameson, 1909: 273-274).

11. Rumors confirmed by Radisson: "after that their heads had sufficiently danced, they begin to talke to warre against the hollanders" (Ra: 78). See also (Jennings, 1984: 103).

12. The opposing parties affirmed that Stuyvesant sold large quantities of firearms whereas the latter maintained that he respected the Company's authorization to sell arms parcimoniously, to avoid infuriating the Iroquois (Jameson, 1909: 345 and 369). However, the correspondence exchanged in 1648 between Stuyvesant and the Direction of the Company in the Netherlands confirms the opponents' point of view, namely that Stuyvesant agreed to massive sales of firearms in 1648: 400 rifles which the Iroquois used to launch a decisive attack against the Huron nation, in the spring of 1649 (Jennings, 1984: 99-100).

at some distance from the Fort. An altercation, described by Radisson, further shows the insolence of these Iroquois warriors, who were intoxicated by their resounding military successes:

> The next day we arrived in a small brough [borough] of the hollanders, where we masters them, without that those beere-bellies had the courage to frowne att us. [...] we with violence took the meat out of their potts [...] we take and eat what we gett. For drinking of their wine we weare good fellowes. So much that they [the Iroquois] fought with swords among themselves without the least offer of any misdeed to me. (Ra: 79)

The nature of convergent interests and restricting complementarities that I have attempted here to underscore in describing the formation of the close partnership between the Iroquois and the Dutch, and how the interactive influences create, in a game of mutual adjustments and successive actions-reactions, a specific historical situation, or event, is precisely what I want to show about Radisson: how his talents and his temperament along with the sociocultural environments and particular circumstances that he came to know combine to create his personality and ultimately to determine his destiny.[13]

Second capture and integration of Radisson

After the Iroquois had captured him a second time and treated him harshly throughout the voyage back to the village from which he had fled, Radisson knew that he must show great courage; and so with determination, he prepared to run the gauntlet, treatment normallyinflicted on all prisoners upon their arrival. He realized that those who showed signs of hesitation would be judged as cowards and subjected to the cruellest treatment (Ra: 47-50). But he was fortunate enough to avoid for a second time that which he describes as being the very image of hell on earth (Ra: 50), since his adoptive parents immediately removed him from the cluster of Huron captives and took him to their hut, where his father began calling him insane and an

---

13. This issue is considered in the perspective offered by Richard White in his *Middle Ground*. "(In the) study of Indian-White relations, I found that no sharp distinctions between Indian and White worlds could be drawn (...) history (...) during the horrible years of the mid and late seventeenth century is a history of perceptions, of attempts to make sense, of attempts to create coherence from shattered parts" (White, 1991: X1 and 2).

enemy. Still bound hand and foot, Radisson tried to speak with assurance, giving his father the somewhat revised version of murdering the three Iroquois and of his voyage to the outskirts of Trois-Rivières, a version he had recounted shortly after his second capture and in which he placed full responsibility for the murders on the Algonquin who accompanied him (Ra: 51). Even though he spoke more in Huron than in Iroquois (his adoptive mother was a Huron), Radisson managed to convince his parents to open negotiations so that he might avoid the vengeance the victims' families were entitled to exact.[14] However, at that very moment, several armed men arrived insisting that Radisson be conducted to the scaffold where ten other Huron prisoners were waiting for the villagers to begin torturing them.

Torture

The Iroquois torture sought to appease the tormented souls of those who had suffered a violent death, in war or by accident. For the captives, their torture provided an opportunity for them to prove their strength and courage, their endurance to pain. In this way, torture could be the last exploit of a valiant warrior, or his ultimate debasement if he failed to overcome his suffering and remain stoic. Finally, in regard to candidates for adoption, torture represented the destruction of their former identity and their entrance by fire into the Iroquois community, where they replaced a deceased person. The suffering that Radisson endured and later described in detail provides a means to assess the ultimate test that the Iroquois torture constituted for those obliged to confront it, while providing a good idea of the impact of this traumatic ritual on the subsequent integration of certain captives in the community (Viau, 1994: 40-42, 226-268).

A band of children began by throwing tiny arrows at the prisoners. After this, Radisson had four fingernails torn from his hands and was made to sing; then he was led into a hut where a woman told her child to cut off one his fingers, using a stone knife; the child was not strong enough to succeed and cut only the flesh surrounding the bone, before drinking the blood that flowed from the wound. Radisson was then left alone for an entire night,

---

14. A regular practice consisted in offering presents to compensate for an insult or even a murder, to avoid having the cycle of vengeance eliminate all candidates for adoption, or even fell certain influential community members who might have perpetrated a grave injustice (Viau, 1994: 36 and 97).

unable to sleep, as he was too feverish and in pain, while at the same time – but without his knowing it – his adoptive parents were pursuing negotiations and attempting to compensate by presents the assassination of the three Iroquois: a gesture that reflected the esteem, indeed the affection, that his parents had apparently developed for him. The minor tortures – in the Iroquois context – that Radisson had endured thus far may be explained by the fact that no one could execute a prisoner before his fate had been decided by his "owner", that is before the end of the negotiations for the redemption, or not, of his liberty (Viau, 1994: 163).

The next morning, Radisson was led again to the scaffold where his mother joined him to encourage him to remain "cheerfull" for he was not to die. This comfort was short-lived as an old man sat down beside him to smoke three consecutive pipes of tobacco, with Radisson's thumb thrust well down into the bowl of the pipe (my thumb swelled up and my flesh and nail became like charcoal) (Ra: 56). Fortunately, Radisson could count on the presence of his mother or his father near him on the scaffold; they encouraged him and, at times, brought him food. Then a young warrior inflicted the day's worst torture on him by piercing his foot with a red-hot dagger. It is probable that the outcome of the negotiations depended in part on how he faced the pain of torture; Radisson had to remain stoic if he hoped to survive. The intervention of an unusual torturer seems to confirm this necessity; another young warrior attached Radisson's leg to his own, then had a red-hot poker brought to him that he placed between their two legs before beginning to sing, as if nothing was happening, despite the burn he was inflicting on himself. Luckily, writes Radisson, "the poker was out on my side, and did no other effect then bourne my skin" (Ra: 57); he was therefore again able to contain the pain and remain "cheerful" despite his exhaustion.

Shortly afterwards, Radisson was led into a hut where about sixty elders had gathered to smoke and talk. He writes that he did not know if he was dead or alive after three days of sporadic torture. His adoptive brother appeared wearing several porcelaine wampun necklets, then his father entered followed by some twenty other prisoners. After several pronouncements, three prisoners were executed by axe blows and all the others were released. His adoptive father then launched into a lengthy and passionate harangue. When his mother joined them, she sang and danced before letting a porcelaine necklet fall to the middle of the area, and placing another around Radisson's neck. After this, she left the scene... His brother also sang and went out, followed by his father too left the scene... Radisson remained alone, and perturbed, in the company of the elders who were still deliberating his case. He later wrote that he thought all his parents' presents, songs and pronouncements had been of no use (Ra: 59). Finally, the hut was opened on all sides and, in the words of Radisson, two thousand persons attended the conclusion of the affair. His entire family was once again present. His father made a final pronouncement and threw at the feet of an old man the porcelaine necklet that Radisson wore about his neck, then cut the ties still binding Radisson and asked him to stand. Radisson describes this moment passionately: "the joy that I received att that time was incomparable, for suddenly all my paines and griefs ceased, not feeling the least paine. He bids me be merry, makes me sing, to wich I consented with all my heart" (Ra: 60).

Through the terrifying trauma of torture, the Iroquois had stripped Radisson of his former identity; now they welcomed him into the very heart of their society, as a member of one of their families, as one of their own. A particular term used by the Iroquois to qualify the integration of an individual by torture and adoption can be translated to signify a *disarticulated body whose limbs have been scattered* (Viau, 1994: 185 and 210). Radisson would long remember – or at least until he wrote his story, some fifteen years later – the boundless gratitude that he felt towards his adoptive parents, who having supported him without reserve most certainly saved his life. This feeling appears to have superseded any attachment to his biological parents, whom Radisson never mentions; yet, when he speaks of his Iroquois parents, giving a brief account of their life and praising their qualities (Ra: 63), Radisson feels so indebted to them that he tries subsequently to be worthy of their confidence and affection, seeking to achieve full integration into his new community.[15] In reality, the trauma of torture and the feelings of gratitude towards his adoptive parents seem to have provoked in him, for a time, a profound ambiguity over his identity and life projects. Initially, Radisson was shattered by suffering and fear, then he was overcome by joy and soon he would also be very encouraged by the *success* of his Iroquois integration, which he gradually discovered promised him the

---

15. Finally, seeing myselfe in the former condition as before, I constituted as long as my father and fortune would permitt mee to live there. (...) The desire that I had to make me beloved, for the assurance of my life made me resolve to offer myselfe for to serve, and to make party with them (in other words, participate in a military expedition)." (Ra: 61)

possibility of tangible social advantages based on his ability to become a "good" Iroquois.

This first radical upheaval in Radisson's life most certainly facilitated the numerous adaptations he subsequently underwent, for the passage from the French culture to the Iroquois culture would require of him a thorough, far-reaching and ongoing apprenticeship now that he wanted to become an Iroquois warrior, in order to honor his adoptive parents and take his place in the Mohawk community.

"Doe as they doe"[16]

The wounds Radisson endured during torture healed swiftly thanks to his mother's care. Once his foot was fully recovered and he was again able to move about, Radisson realized that his situation in the community seemed not to have suffered from the serious error he had committed, and that he had been fully pardoned (Ra: 61). But as he became aware of the bellicose atmosphere that reigned in the village,[17] Radisson soon realized that he had to participate in one of the war expeditions under preparation in the community. Fearing that his father did not fully trust him, he waited for his humor to improve, then, as he had done with his mother earlier on, asked him who he was. His father told him he was an Iroquois like himself and so Radisson replied: "Lett, me revenge (then), (...) my kindred (...), that you shall know I am your son, worthy to bear that title that you gave me when you adopted me" (Ra: 62). Warming to his adoptive son's proposals, the father agreed without hesitation that Radisson should go to war with one of his (real) sons, who was then preparing to confront the Erie nation.[18]

---

16. (Ra: 85).

17. "Daily there weare military feasts for the South nations, and others for the Algonquins and for the French;" Radisson discovered this bellicose atmosphere within the context of his adoptive family: "In those feasts my father heaves up the hatchet against the Algonquins. (...) Every night never failes to instruct and encourage the young age to take armes" (Ra: 61).

18. Although the place and the area where Radisson and his 10 Iroquois companions did battle remains conjectural, William Wykoff's detailed analysis of that part of Radisson's narrative indicates the probability that the expedition journeyed to the Erie (or Cat) nation's territory, south of the extreme western shore of Lake Erie and as far away as the Ohio River basin (Wykoff, 1995: 15-45).

A small group of ten persons, including Radisson, set out before the arrival of spring. The expedition was headed by a young brave aged 20, the group's captain, who had promised Radisson's father to watch over his two sons. When crossing Iroquois territory, the young warriors carried only their rifles, while "slaves" looked after their equipment; but as soon as the expedition left Iroquois country, Radisson and the others had to carry it themselves.[19]

A journey of ten days on foot and four days by canoe brought them to a great lake, still under ice – Lake Erie – where an unseasonably low temperature immobilized them for fifteen days. Then, they navigated on this "sweet see" for six days, paddling up river over a distance of forty leagues. They hid their canoes and set out again on foot during five days, crossing a desolate region and several small rivers and, finally, reached a place where they planned to confront their enemies. They erected a small fort, the captain demanding their utter silence, "which I observed strictly" (Ra: 67); then, after nightfall they explored the vicinity. The following day, Radisson and the youngest member of the group were sent to reconnoitre the shoreline of a small river while the rest of the party set out to locate a village they believed to be nearby. Already, Radisson had noted a number of Iroquois practices: their ability to construct in succession a number of elm-bark canoes, which they left behind to facilitate retreat; their parsimonious use of corn flour, which they ate only in the absence of game or fish; their knowledge of the territory as well as their endurance, discipline and discretion, upon arriving in enemy territory.

Having spotted two women on the opposite shore of a small lake they had reached and deciding for safety's sake not to attack them (on Radisson's recommendation), the two young men found they were unable to return to the fort before nightfall; they slept where they were, under pouring rain and without any provisions. The next day, when they caught up with their worried companions, they related the presence of the people they had spotted; then the entire group headed towards the small lake. There they discovered five men and four women fishing and, after a brief reconnaissance by the captain, attacked them: "like starved doggs or wolves devoured those

---

19. These slaves were prisoners who had been spared for their ability to work hard. Their masters could at any time execute them or elect to integrate them in their family, if they were satisfied with their behavior (Viau, 1994: 267).

poor creatures who in a moment weare massacred" (Ra: 71). Then, two of Radisson's companions killed an old woman and two children, whom they had found in a shelter. The small troup was satisfied with the twelve scalps they had taken: each could bring back at least one battle trophy and a few spoils. Finally, they came upon the village they were looking for and hid belly-to-ground in the underbrush. They were able to eat the fish they had seized from the fishers but had nothing to drink; and so they had the audacity to send one of their number in search of water right inside the village. Several small groups heading out to cut wood or work in the fields were allowed to pass, until, in the evening, four men and three women found them, forcing them to attack. In the melee, four Eries were killed and four others taken prisoner while some others fled, shouting the alarm. Radisson and his companions were obliged to get away as fast as they could. After a full night on the run, the two women were executed because they slowed down the group. The band continued to retreat for a full day before finding the right spot to hide and reorganize. They interrogated the two prisoners, but no one understood their language (Ra: 68-72).

Radisson next describes summarily, and somewhat confusedly, a period of six weeks during which he and his companions prowled about the area without encountering anyone. Hunger finally forced them to eat their prisoners.[20] Shortly after, they encountered a group of about thirty men and women and began to do battle with them: "They fought and defended themselves lustily; but (...) our guns were a terrour to them, and made them give over" (Ra: 73). Only the youngest Iroquois was wounded, although hideously, and so his companions burned him alive (Viau, 1994: 90). For the next two days the ten survivors fled on foot, almost without stopping, until they reached the canoes they had left behind: "without resting, or eating or drinking all the time, saveing (except for) a litle stagg's meate" (Ra: 74). They brought three prisoners with them and the booty seized from the battle – corn, deer skins, pipes and tobacco, various garments, bows and arrows....

Part of the return journey was made at night, often across violent and treacherous rapids, with the group hiding and resting by day. When at last they reached an area they considered to be safe, Radisson and his companions spent several days hunting and fishing, putting in an ample

---

20. "Hunger forced us to kill our Prisoners, who weare chargeable in eating our food, *for want of wich have eaten the flesh*" (Ra: 73). The italics in Radisson's text are always mine.

supply of food. Two women who had fled from the Iroquois territory were intercepted and again made prisoners. They next crossed a very hilly region where they were forced to make difficult portages, while guarding the five prisoners. Then they had to construct new canoes as the ones in use were in danger of sinking under their loads. Upon arriving in Iroquois territory, where they were on safe ground, they divided up the scalps and prisoners. Every man received two the scalps, but Radisson and his brother each took a prisoner, indicating their more active part in the battles where they were able to impose their will on the others (Ra: 75). Nearby the village where their arrival had been announced, several women, including Radisson's two sisters, came to meet the group, to welcome with joy and praise the small but victorious expedition (Ra: 73-76).

The entire expedition probably took about five months, during which time Radisson learned to sleep under any condition, to eat whatever was at hand, to cover considerable distances in snowshoes, in a canoe, on foot or running. He also learned to find his way in uncharted areas, to build canoes and portage under difficult conditions, to travel by night across all sorts of terrain – solid or watery – to recognize signs of the enemy, to remain immobile throughout hours of ambush, to fight hand-to-hand, to kill, to scalp, and even to eat human flesh. He learned the habits and battle strategies of the Iroquois. He also noted the indispensable solidarity of a small band of warriors whose survival depended on sharing and constant mutual assistance. Above all, he learned not to question his companions' cultural habits, for he realized that he depended entirely on them, particularly at the start of the expedition. Finally, after his return Radisson discovered exactly what constituted success and glory in Iroquois country. The story of this expedition further reveals the esprit de corps that Radisson recalled when writing his narrative, a rediscovered feeling he tried to relay by using, almost exclusively, the pronoun "we," making no distinction between himself and his companions during battles, journeys and decision-making. Rarely in this episode does he try to stand out or to dissociate himself from his comrades; they stand together, from start to finish.[21]

---

21. Warfare thus dramatically promoted group cohesion and demonstrated to the Iroquois their superiority over their enemies: (Richter, 1983: 534) "public opinion (...) also contributed to fighting Iroquois wars (...) a social phenomenon of solidarity, integration and community identification" (Viau, 1994: 102-103).

Radisson regains his individuality and use of the pronoun "I" once back in the village, when describing the presents he distributes and the welcome he receives. This is the time for an even greater integration in the Iroquois community for now Radisson sees the possibility of taking on a social role outside the restricted family circle.[22] Radisson immediately offers his sisters the two scalps he is carrying and to each he gives six deerskins. They accompany his return offering him myriad considerations and soon: "a multitude of people came to meate us with great exclamations, (..) biding me to be cheerfull and qualifying me *dodcon*, that is, devil, being of great veneration in that country to those that shew any vallour" (Ra: 77). To his mother, present amid the throng, Radisson offers two beavers pelts full of bear fat and another full of moose fat; he also gives her his prisoner, thereby indicating that he has learned how to make himself appreciated by his parents and his fellow Iroquois.

The next day, Radisson received his wages for the multiple spoils he had brought back to the village; these were porcelaine necklets and various other ornaments that he was careful thereafter to wear regularly.[23] The necklets attested to his victories and were proof of his courage in combat, which, in time, could also confer power and authority on him in the community as a war chief; that function was open only to the bravest and most valiant, those who had proved their superior qualities during successful war expeditions (Viau, 1994: 99). This wider social recognition finally enabled Radisson to trade at Fort Orange in the company of a number of Mohawk warriors and hunters who visited the fort regularly – a mark of trust they had refused him until that time.

Second rupture at Fort Orange

Radisson's account of his brief stay in Rensselaerwyck concurs with what Dutch sources relate: "the 4th day we come to the fort of Orange, where we weare well received, or rather our Castors, every one courting us; and was nothing but pruins and reasins and tobacco plentifully, and all for ho, ho,

---

22. "Warriors did in fact reap great social rewards" (Richter, 1983: 530). "War therefore represented a means of valorization common to Iroquois Societies" (Viau, 1994: 265).

23. "as the whole nation tooke me for proud, having allways great care to be garnished with porcelaine" (Ra: 82). Viau explains that since Iroquois societies were warlike, exhibitionism was essential to their self-definition, an indication to others that they were the best (Viau, 1994: 115).

wich is thanks" (Ra: 79). But, a French soldier thought he recognized a European under Radisson's red paint and Iroquois garb and asked him if he was a foreigner; Radisson answered no at first but the soldier insisted, swearing and repeating his question, this time in French; stupefied, Radisson then replied in French, eliciting a strong reaction from the soldier who embraced him and cried out loudly in every direction, capturing the attention of a group of Flemings and Frenchmen (probably Huguenots) who offered him food and alcohol, but, more particularly, help to escape from the Iroquois. Radisson also met with the Governor of Orange who offered to buy back his liberty at any price. Radisson relates that he refused all these offers. Why?...

It is difficult to elucidate the specific motives which might explain Radisson's conduct at this juncture, since he himself seems unable to do so, some fifteen years later. He speaks at the same time of destiny, love for his Iroquois parents and of the independence he wanted to conserve in regard to the Governor of Orange, adding that he preferred to wait for a better chance to escape and to go directly to New France, or again that he had to atone for the many sins which he had committed among the Iroquois before regaining his liberty (Ra: 79 to 81). I shall formulate here a few additional hypotheses more in accord with a contemporary understanding of the psychological impact of torture, as well as of the influence which the individual's cultural network can bring to bear on any event.

Thanks to his battle exploits, Radisson was enjoying a social status and an esteem he had probably never known in France or New France, owing to his youth. Furthermore, he knew the Iroquois culture well enough to at least sense that his exploits could lead to his acquiring an even more advantageous position if he played his cards carefully. The boundless attention accorded to him probably went to Radisson's head, and for the rest of his life he would seek the recognition of his peers without ever forgetting the traumatic impact of having endured torture, the latter having provoked a profound rupture in his identity. On this point, contemporary studies are unanimous: "destroying an old and forging a new identity are surely the end goals of torture" (Jacques, 1994: 96).[24] It is also quite probable that Radisson had a strong feeling of belonging to the Iroquois community after his torture in

---

24. "Captivity (for the Iroquois) may be seen as a particular process during which time the prisoner (...) is broken then recomposed to become the object of another signification" (Viau, 1994: 269). Fundamentally, all methods of torture have one point in common: "Tor-

that to the destructuring effects of physical suffering and the fear of death was added a lively sense of gratitude towards his adoptive parents, who had not only saved his life but had also assisted him *during* the torture, especially at the most horrible moments. This is when the help accorded to the torture victim provokes feelings of gratitude even towards his torturer – and even if that individual offers only limited succor – so desperately does the helpless victim seek aid of any sort at all (Amnesty International, 1974: 56).

In the Iroquois perspective – mirrored by Radisson for over a year as he did not meet a single whiteman during his entire stay in Iroquois country, prior to arriving at Fort Orange – he had managed to properly identify and apply with success an effective strategy for social insertion that seems to have assured him esteem and safety within the Iroquois community. Radisson must have realized that once he became a good Iroquois in the eyes of his abductors, he had nothing further to fear. And yet when Radisson renewed contact with the Europeans and in the same breath revived memories, ties and occidental references, he was quite unable in a few short hours to reconcile two contradictory perceptions: his recent confidence that now he could enjoy a normal and happy existence among the Iroquois against that of the Europeans at Fort Orange who, believing Radisson to be in great danger, were insisting on delivering him from a situation he persisted in viewing as enviable. Ultimately, most likely out of fear and a growing uncertainty, Radisson elected to return to the Mohawk village with his Iroquois companions.

However, on his return he was able to view his situation from an entirely different standpoint. No doubt the highly critical opinion of many Rensselaerwyck inhabitants forced Radisson to reassess his actual situation and his attachment to another, earlier-lived culture still alive within him, one that precluded him from viewing his present situation as enviable. Indeed, he soon bitterly regretted his return to the Mohawk village and decided to

---

ture is any institutional mechanism, no matter the methods utilized, by means of which the victim's beliefs and convictions are totally destroyed in order to divest him of all the elements that constitute his persona;" "Torture, by destructuring the victim's conscience, attempts to destabilize all his references (...) thereby shattering his identity and his battery of certitudes, convictions, associations, ties of affection, even his beliefs" (Jacques, 1994: 107). Of further note is the recent research on the extreme pain of certain gravely afflicted individuals (persons with bone cancer for example) who fear that surrendering to their agony will lead to their losing the awareness of being human.

attempt a second escape: "I could be att no safty among such a nation full of reveng" he writes, adding that "if in case the ffrench & the algonquins defeat(s) the troup of theirs then what spite they will have will reveng it on my boanes"[25] (Ra: 81).

Radisson made a firm decision to abandon the Iroquois because he no longer felt safe among them; moreover, he wanted to recover his full freedom (Ra: 81) but not because he scorned or detested the Iroquois. Quite the opposite, he would keep many good memories of his time among them, going as far as to confess to his English readers that he "loved those poore people entirely well" (Ra: 87).

Now that he had resolved to flee once again, Radisson had to master the troubling emotions that had returned to plague him. For to attempt an escape meant again exposing himself to capture, the gauntlet, torture and, ultimately, death (Ra: 81-82). Moreover, Radisson had to prepare himself mentally before undertaking the adventure: "putting away all feare & apprehension, I constituted to deliver meselfe from their hands at what ever rate it would come too. (…) he that is of a good resolution must be of strong hopes of what he undertakes" (Ra: 82). He decided to arm himself only with an axe and to carry no valuable object; in this way he could pretend to have lost his way if he were found in the woods. And so, he awaited the right moment, and gathering his courage, feigned one day going out to hunt; then he struck out through the woods towards Fort Orange. After running for two days with only a short night's rest, Radisson reached the outlying habitations of Rensselaerwyck and found safe refuge under the roof of a man and a woman with whom he promised to trade all his beavers on their assurance they would inform no other Iroquois of his presence. He then addressed a short message to the Governor of Orange which the man was to relay while Radisson remained hidden in their abode, in the company of the woman who made advances to him to better assure the transaction he had promised

---

25. "I was not 1.5 dayes retourned, but that nature itselfe reproached me to leade such a life, remembering the sweet behaviour and mildnesse of the french, & considered with meselfe what end should I expect of such a barbarous nation, enemy to God and to man" (Ra: 81). Radisson was right to fear a reversal in the situation as this was possible at such a difficult juncture, especially as he was likely aware of the narrow margin of manoever he had at Fort Orange concerning the conduct he had been forced to assume: "if those who were adopted… killed" (Richter, 1983: 533).

them; but the terrified Radisson repulsed her.[26] Finally, four men came to deliver him – among them the much-vaunted French soldier – and they conducted him "disguised" in European clothing to Fort Orange where he remained some three days before descending the Hudson to Manhatte, from where he set sail for Holland, and France. He would return to New France in the summer of 1654.

26. "she shews me good countenance as much as she could, hoping of a better imaginary profit by me. Shee asked me if we had so much libertie with the ffrench women to lye with them as they; but I had no desire to doe anything, seeing myselfe so insnared att death's door" (Ra: 84).

CHAPTER 2

A Man and History

S INCE WE KNOW NOTHING ABOUT RADISSON'S CHILDHOOD, his family milieu or
his education in France, his sojourn of over a year among the Iroquois,
as he describes it in the first travel narrative, is an excellent introduction to
the man and to the career he will soon undertake, that of coureur de bois. A
certain constancy in his behavior and in his reactions appears as of this first
voyage and will persist until the final narratives, some twenty years later;
this characteristic sheds greater light on specific aspects Radisson's personality.

In the earliest narratives, the young Radisson is already skillful in
hunting and fighting, and as a warrior; he also appears strong and
determined, traits which must on the whole reflect reality, otherwise he
could never have explored, lived in the bush, forged durable relations with
the Amerindians and achieved the commercial successes he enjoyed in many
countries, over so long a time.[1] Radisson also describes himself as a young
naïf, irresponsible, easily influenced, even fearful; this seems natural enough
when he admits fearing torture and running the gauntlet but less so when
he confesses having been terrorized by a strange creature that in reality
neither he nor his young Iroquois companion had ever encountered.[2] He
also depicts himself as a courageous warrior, but only after the rigorous
apprenticeship he underwent on a guerilla expedition with his Iroquois
companions.

---

1. Radisson died in London in 1710, at about age 75.
2. "That beast (...) felled down into our boat (...). There is the question who was most
fearfull? As for me, I quaked" (Ra: 69).

Radisson is a clever storyteller who knows how to render with precision various subtleties of perception depending on the age at which he had his adventures and taking into consideration the cultures surrounding him at a given time. This is why it was so compelling, so tempting to rely almost solely on Radisson's narrative when recounting his adaptation to life among the Iroquois. However, even though the first narrative appears highly factual in light of the documentation available, it is important to be wary of Radisson and not always take his remarks literally. Quite to the contrary. For his narrative talents allowed him to take certain liberties in regard to the events he recounts and, in particular, to their chronology, the whole arranged to better impress English-speaking readers for whom his stories were intended.

The analysis of several prevarications that Radisson openly discloses to his readers, in his first four narratives, reveals that his *skill at arranging things to his own advantage* likely consisted of a minimal distortion of the events, which he sought to "doctor" as simply as possible to leave him a way out while best serving his own interests.[3]

For example, Radisson gives two versions of the murder, immediately before his first escape, of the three Iroquois accompanying him. Firstly, he gives his English readers the "true" version, in which he participates in the killings: "having struck him with the axe blade, I was unable to withdraw it easily because it was so deeply embedded in his head (Ra: 39-40), a highly precise version which seems perfectly credible... Then Radisson relates how he explains the same events to his adoptive Iroquois parents in the hope of saving his life. The two versions are identical except for one crucial detail: in the presence of the Iroquois, Radisson alleges that his Algonquin accomplice having left them beforehand returned to commit the three murders single-handedly while he and the others were sleeping, waking him only after the fact to take him away with him. We realize that he is not trying to concoct a high-flown story but only to *arrange* the facts, making sure that the false version remains simple and well put together, thus easy to recount and to defend, in the end, to avoid being caught in a far-fetched story.

---

3. According to Montaigne, the liar's main problem is to preserve over time the same version of the events he recounts: "Over a period of time it simply becomes too hard to keep one's lies in mind and in order. It followed that 'anyone who does not feel sufficiently strong in memory should not muddle with lying'. Ultimately, liars revealed themselves by the diversity of their accounts; truth-tellers by the simplicity of theirs" (Shapin, 1994: 79).

Radisson simply relies on the real facts that he knows well, thereby enhancing his powers of persuasion. This minimal arrangement of actual events seems to arise from the art of misrepresentation on which Radisson relied in all situations throughout his lifetime, for reasons of efficacity and prudence.[4]

A few clarifications about Radisson's voyages and travel narratives

It is widely accepted that Radisson's brother-in-law, Des Groseilliers, was one of the two Frenchmen mandated by Governor Lauson in 1654 to re-store trade relations with the Amerindians of the Great Lakes (Campeau, 1996: 891-893). It is certain that Radisson did not participate in this voyage, even though he tells of having accompanied Des Groseilliers, since he signed two notorized documents in Québec in 1655 and we know that Des Groseilliers did not return to Montréal until August 1656.[5] Moreover, in a passage of his third narrative, Radisson reveals that another Frenchman, not himself, accompanied Des Groseilliers in 1654.[6] He also modified in like fashion the chronology of the first four voyages to present all his personal experiences and those of Des Groseilliers in a single long, joint episode, one that is more compact, more exciting and better structured, in-

---

4. Another falsehood reveals Radisson's propensity for "sticking" as far as possible to actual facts. On the journey to the Jesuit mission of Gannentaha, Radisson encountered nine Mohawk Iroquois who recognized him and asked him how and why he had left them. He replied that he had returned to Trois-Rivières through the woods in the space of 12 days (Ra: 113), or in the same way and almost within the same time frame as when he had escaped with the Algonquin (14 days instead of 12) (Ra: 44-45). In the context of the palavers which the Amerindians so enjoyed (Radisson had to spend several hours in the company of these Mohawk) (Ra: 114), it was essential that his story be credible and easy to relate in detail; indeed, the Jesuit Father Millet recounts that when the Indians are asked for news of their nation, they answer with stories that at times last the entire night (quoted in St-Arnaud, 1998: 100).

5. ANQ, clerk of the notary Guillaume Audouart (1634-1663), dated 2 November 1655, 7 and 15 November 1655, and 13 February 1656, three dates that in fact do appear on the second document. But no matter the actual date on which Radisson signed that act, Des Groseilliers was as yet in the Great Lakes region in the company of another Frenchman who remains anomymous.

6. "I found my brother who the yeare before came back from the lake of the Hurrons with other french" (Ra: 134). For a detailed discussion of this passage and of Radisson's non-participation in the voyage of 1654-1656, see my preceding book (Fournier, 1996: 69-75).

deed more convincing, as it is based on real events, albeit constructed differently. It is likely that Des Groseilliers and Radisson had agreed to present their experiences in this way well before Radisson committed the story to paper, for example, when they went to New England, where they had only the scope of their knowledge and their common realizations to convince the Bostonians to finance their trading project at Hudson's Bay.

Despite these strategic modifications, Radisson's narrative matches available complementary documents and, more importantly, provides precise details about the many events, customs, impressions, emotions and thoughts that he recounts or describes.[7]

Radisson's first four narratives offer a more spontaneous, more concrete testimony than those of the Jesuits or the administrators on appointment in the colony. His perception of the Amerindians, in particular, is most favorable compared to those of other educated authors of the XVIIth century and his concept of the world, albeit subjective, remains untramelled, centered totally on discovery and animated by a lively curiosity. Radisson observes and describes in detail a reality that he had to take on face value to survive on foreign terrain and to profit without delay from his many apprenticeships and discoveries. The information provided by his first four narratives complements other sources of the period which are much more clearly integrated in a social order, in a missionary contingent in an essentially European political project. For his part, Radisson took to America like a fish to water up until he decided to return to make a career and settle down in Europe, after 1665. For example, he declares his affection for the Amerindians he came to know: "I began to love my new parents that weare so good & so favourable to me" (Ra: 80); he also feels affection for the

---

7. Another example: the third year (fictional) of Des Groseilliers' voyage to Lakes Michigan and Superior in 1654-1656, rather than the two years that this journey actually took, is reduced to fifteen lines, or less than 1% of the thirty-eight pages that make up the narrative. The content is also very sketchy: Radisson hunted all summer long while Des Groseilliers amassed provisions of corn and wheat; they passed the winter enjoying good relations with their Amerindian hosts; they sent ambassadors to neighboring nations and Des Groseilliers took sick, then recovered (Ra: 158-159). End of story. The "triviality" of that year goes unnoticed amid the density of the rest of the narrative, just as a conjurer skillfully shifts the attention of an audience to better hide his manipulations. Everything indicates that Radisson tried to relate rigorously what he had experienced, to alter events as little as possible, as a careful examination of another passage of his narratives, presented in chapter IV, confirms.

immense territory of America: "we went along the coasts, which are more delightfull and wounderous, for it's nature that made it so pleasant to the eye, the sperit, and the belly" (Ra: 189). Radisson's testimony provides a glimpse of what so many other trappers and French coureurs de bois of the XVIIth century experienced, including those who wrote nothing and had no involvement whatsoever in the political and missionary projects of the elite, who left us most of the writings extant about New France.

During the XVIIth century, hundreds of Frenchmen would go on trading and hunting expeditions with the Amerindians, even at times accompanying them on the warpath to take revenge against the Iroquois; they went before, the explorers holding official mandates inside the continent and they assisted the missionaries. And yet, we know virtually nothing about these people, nothing about the motivations and the preferences that drove them to plunge into the untamed American landscape accompanied by Indians. Radisson's testimony allows us a familiarity with these trappers by describing for us the most intimate aspects of their existence, such as the joys and difficulties of their voyages, their exchanges with the Amerindians and many other details about their adaptation to primitive living.

A sketch of the young Radisson

Radisson was a good orator; thanks to his words and his demeanor, he was able to save his own life and convince his Iroquois captors of his firm desire to integrate in their society (Ra: 51 and 61-63). Later on, he managed to persuade a goodly number of Amerindian chiefs to become his allies at Lake Superior and at Hudson's Bay. He also exercised his talents with the Europeans, gaining the confidence of his brother-in-law Des Groseilliers (Ra: 134) and convincing first Bostonian then English investors to support the trading project that the two brothers-in-law would attempt to accomplish together at Hudson's Bay after 1660, despite the efforts and sacrifices such an undertaking might require (Ra: 243).

Radisson seemed remarkably attentive to happenings around him; one might call him adaptable, as if he possesses the ability to integrate in any group dynamic, whatever the values, objectives or attitudes. The milieu might be Iroquois or Jesuit, French or English, he finds the right tone and the appropriate manner to forge relations with certain members of that group. With the Iroquois, for example, he first won the appreciation of his

parents as a good son, then his companions as an able warrior, and finally
as a valuable and esteemed "member of the community," one who is
included without restriction in their trading activities.

An obvious paradox defines one of the more remarkable traits of
Radisson's personality; his great temerity was tempored by an equal measure
of caution. Despite his proven audacity, Radisson does take a number of
precautions, such as when he arrives for the first time at the western
extremity of Lake Superior with Des Groseilliers, in the midst of several
thousand Amerindians (Ra: 26, 82, 196-198), or when he makes his second
escape; he also peppers his story with numerous comments about prudence
and safety. This marriage of audacity and prudence explains his successes
and his very long career.

Contrary to the reputation often ascribed to him, Radisson is a faithful
man, insofar as the relations that he fosters with his "patron" or with his
partners work to his advantage. He respects the authority of the Jesuits
during the expedition to Gannentaha; he supports Des Groseilliers, without
reservation, and follows him everywhere during fifteen consecutive years;
and he will maintain solid and lasting ties with certain associates of the
Hudson's Bay Company despite the ensuing disavantages. Without being as
independent as Des Groseilliers, who on several occasions broke the ties he
had developed with his superiors, Radisson remains autonomous and
abruptly changes allegiance when his interests so dictate, as in 1684, when
he returned to England a second time.

Radisson's voracious curiosity pushes him ceaselessly forward, he always
seems ready for adventure, always open to the influence of the people and
the milieux with whom he associates. He agrees to transform himself
without fear of losing himself or his way. His association with the
Amerindians changed forever his perception of reality and his conduct. Des
Groseilliers fostered ambition in him along with a sense of effort and
organization. His stay in England revealed new capacities to him, ones that
his long narrative clearly underscores. Finally, his sojourn in France
encouraged him to complete his education and consolidated his sense of
the social hierarchy. The virtually uninterrupted adaptations that Radisson
achieves are noteworthy for the enthusiasm with which he seems to
undertake them, as well as for their significance and frequency, and finally,
because they seem to occur without crisis or difficulty, in an almost natural
fashion.

After the radical adaptation that Radisson experienced among the Iroquois and his subsequent readaptation to Europe and to New France, the "young man" whom the Jesuits engage in 1657 seems to have had no difficulty finding in himself a strong "ego," a center which the eventual changes in languages, mentalities, objectives and customs scarcely trouble at all.

1. The Routes of Radisson's First Two Expeditions

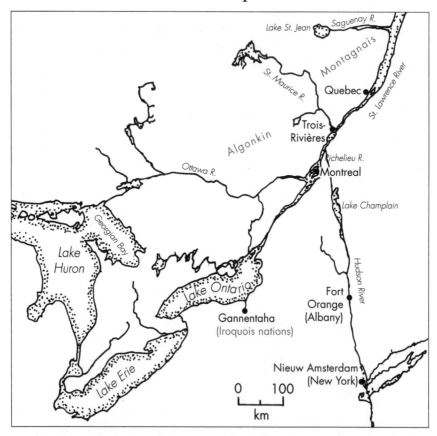

During his first expedition, Radisson describes how he was captured by Iroquois near Trois-Rivières in the spring of 1652, then taken to the Mohawk nation near Fort Orange (present day Albany, New York State). He then traveled with the Mohawk to a region southwest of Lake Erie, engaged in fighting, and left via Fort Orange and Nieuw Amsterdam (present day New York). During his second expedition, in 1657, he departed from Montréal and followed the St. Lawrence River to Lake Gannentaha, located south of Lake Ontario, among the Onondaga Iroquois. He remained in this region less than a year and returned to Montréal by the same route.

CHAPTER 3

Second Voyage: Mediator and Cultural Métis

R ADISSON WRITES ABOUT HIS MEETING with the Jesuit Father Poncet at Fort Orange, shortly before his return to Europe, recalling that the Jesuit made him "a great offer" (Ra: 85). In all likelihood Poncet would have invited him to join in the Jesuit missionairies' journeys across America since Radisson participated in two of their expeditions after his return to New France, in the summer of 1654.

Radisson's second narrative relates the voyage and the ten-month stay he made in 1657-1658 at Gannentaha, in the territory of the Onondaga Iroquois who lived at the heart of the Confederation of the Five Iroquois Nations; the second narrative also reveals that by that time Radisson's French identity had already undergone a major transformation.

Radisson returns to Iroquois territory[1]

A series of long and arduous negotiations between the French, the Iroquois and the Huron, who had taken refuge on the Île d'Orléans, resulted in a joint Franco-Huron-Iroquois expedition, in 1657. The Iroquois wanted to repatriate a group of Huron refugees from the Île d'Orléans to the Onondaga, while the French were anxious to move reinforcements and provisions to the mission founded the preceding year at Gannentaha. In the course of

---

1. To recount and assess this voyage, I have relied mostly on Radisson's testimony. But virtually all the facts – dates, time spans, succession of events and actual events – paralleled the version of the Jesuit Paul Ragueneau (JR, 44: 68-76); (JR, 44: 172-182); (JR, 44: 184-196); (JR, 44: 212-216); (Ra: 86-134).

this voyage, Radisson, with his knowledge of the Iroquois language and customs, enhanced the value of the French promises of alliance by paddling, portaging, hunting and fishing, as well as by parleying and feasting with the natives. The presence of a few other Frenchmen who, like Radisson and the Jesuit Father Paul Ragueneau, were accustomed to life in the woods must have earned them all a certain respect on the part of the Iroquois, who kept their own counsel as to their responsibilities as guides on this expedition.

The French and the Huron were compelled to assemble in Montréal to await their arrival. For various reasons, the expedition took time getting under way; in fact, shortly after the departure, some thirty Iroquois left the main contingent to do battle on the Saint Lawrence against the Huron and Algonquins who were not protected by the fragile peace negotiated between the French and the Iroquois (Beaulieu, 1992: 207-208). Then ten Frenchmen had to bring back to Montréal part of the Jesuits' load which the Iroquois had left behind on the shore (the canoes being overloaded, Radisson opines). Finally, four Huron took off without warning towards Montréal, suspecting an Iroquois trap (Ra: 97-99). The definitive expedition thus numbered the Jesuit Father Ragueneau, the Jesuit Brother Leboesme, Radisson and four other French trappers, eight or nine Huron warriors and several groups of ten or more Huron women and children that some fifty Onondaga and Seneca Iroquois were guiding back to their territory, south of Lake Ontario (Ra: 97-98); (JR, 44: 68); (Campeau, 1983: 33).

Seven days after the group left Montreal an unexpected and dramatic incident occurred when they set up evening camp on a small island in the middle of the river.

At the end of the day, when the expedition halted to encamp for the night, an Iroquois captain assassinated a Huron by striking him in the back of the head with an axe. After having offered a few empty words of assurance and comfort to appease the other, now terrified Huron, a goodly number of Iroquois leapt from the bush and using axes or knives killed all the warriors, save perhaps one, who according to Radisson, would be able to relate the incident. The Huron women and children were spared, as were the French, but for Father Ragueneau the deception was acute since he lost face while also losing many of his protégés, as this brutal act perpetrated by the Iroquois violated the terms of the peace he himself had negotiated with them. The Iroquois rapidly held a council to explain their actions to the Jesuit and to reassure him as to the fate they reserved for the French. Then Ragueneau and two Iroquois managed to convince the others, who had seized their weapons and were prepared to defend their lives at any cost, that they had nothing to fear (Ra: 102). At that point, all were invited to a feast in which Radisson participated. Then, Ragueneau held his own council to present to the Iroquois a three-tiered pact: he offered a first porcelaine necklet (wampum) to have them cease hostilities and to ensure that the friendship between the Iroquois and the French held firm; next, a second necklet was produced to ensure that the Huron women and children would be well treated, taken to Iroquois territory and adopted as their own; and finally, a third necklet was offered so that the voyage might continue without mishap until they reached Iroquois territory (Ra: 102); (JR, 44: 74-76). The Iroquois accepted the three proposals.

After that incident, Radisson relates that he soon lagged behind the rest of the expedition, remaining alone for six weeks in the company of four Iroquois – three men and one woman – in two separate canoes (Ra: 103). In this part of his narrative, he divulges his thoughts on the relations he has forged with his companions and on himself. The passages reveal his level of adaptation to Indian life and depict certain intimate aspects of his personality.

The Indianization of Radisson

During the six weeks he remains alone with the four Iroquois, Radisson will have several disputes with his canoeing companion, whom he describes as a young man, taller and better built than himself, but also a childish individual, younger than he is (Ra: 103-104). They will quarrel and scuffle ceaselessly; he goes on to say that although the others took pleasure in watching them fight, they hastened to separate them if either of the two seized a blade or a rifle (Ra: 103-104); they also delighted in hunting more for the sport than out of necessity, playfully going as far as to attach bells to the ears of deer; Radisson speaks of their amusement at seeing other deer running away to avoid a belled companion (Ra: 104). But Radisson also mentions feeling great solitude during such a long separation from the other Frenchmen; he notes that his spirits were particularly low as he missed the forthright conversations he enjoyed with his compatriots and would have had them accompany him on all his voyages (Ra: 103). Here is ample proof of Radisson's love for the spoken word.

The expedition had gotten off to a bad start. Then, when Radisson and his four Iroquois companions discovered a tree on the river bank with an effigy carved into its bark of six hanging men, each with his servered head lying at his feet, fear seized hold of Radisson who was sure that this presaged the murder of the six French members of the expedition, particularly since one of the men represented in effigy had short hair like Father Ragueneau. His companions assured him that he would not die, that he was in no danger, but anxiety gnawed at Radisson, who felt that since the Iroquois had shown such great treachery he ought not to believe their mollifying words and promises (Ra: 108). To calm himself, he reflected on the fact that the Iroquois would have to spare him if only until they reached their home territory, but he had great difficulty concealing his worst apprehensions. His canoeing companion then beached their craft on the shore: "He (…) takes his gunne, charges it, and goes into the wood. I was in feare (…). I remembered how the poore Hurron was served so a litle before in his boat and in like manner." The Iroquois made him a sign to remain silent, pointing to an eagle whose feathers he coveted, but Radisson was careful to protect himself by squatting like a monkey, seizing his gun without the other noticing his action, but keeping him in sight out of fear; then all of a sudden, his companion shot and killed the eagle (Ra: 109).

Briefly reassured, Radisson and his canoeing companion joined the other three Iroquois who were setting up camp for the night on the opposite shore. Radisson then observed a very disturbing incident, in view of the deep-rooted habits of sharing that characterized Amerindian ways: "One tooke my gunne, the other a little bondle of mine. I was surprised att this. Then they asked me my powder and shott, and opened my bagge, began to partage my combs and other things that I had" (Ra: 109). He could only let them do as they pleased and "submit to the strongest" but he felt overtaken by a mounting fright that he could no longer control... Radisson sought refuge for a moment near the woman whose fearful glances only troubled him all the more. Then he agreed to return to mid-river with an ailing Indian who was in the other canoe; but when the latter told him to jump into the water and gather some shellfish, Radisson, who had been careful to bring along his gun despite his companions' sarcastic remarks, and who was still terrified, refused categorically, fearing that his Iroquois companion wanted to drown him. When at last he resigned himself, he jumped in and was able to gather in the shallow water the shellfish which would be their supper, taking care to attach himself to the canoe.

On returning to shore, the forced sharing continued: "He putts on my shirt on his back, takes a knif and cutts a medail that hung to my necke. (...)

I thought every foot he was to cutt my troat" (Ra: 111). Exhausted by the terror that assailed him, Radisson again sat down close to the woman who tried to reassure him, telling him that she and her husband were fond of him and that they intended to welcome him to their home, once they had returned. They would also compensate him later on for what they were taking now, as a sign of alliance. To further reassure him, she gave him back his shirt, along with a blanket and convinced him to sleep: "And so I decided to receive the fatal blow asleep rather than awake, because I believed I could never make an escape" (Ra: 111). The following day, on waking, his fears had completely disappeared, but he still had to endure his companions' sarcastic remarks.[2]

In this passage, Radisson gives a detailed analysis of the fear he had been unable to control at the time and that he still had difficulty explaining, several years later. He attempts to communicate clearly that singular episode in his life, perhaps to further his own reflections or to rid himself of a bad memory, as contemporary psychiatry suggests. In this way, Radisson was trying to understand himself and to fully clarify his life experience for others, as well as to disclose all the know-how he had accumulated in his lifetime, a part of which concerned his inner nature. The precision of this short episode permits our reading it with reference to contempory research on torture.

The long-term impact of torture

The feeling of isolation represents one of the greatest agonies of torture.[3] And, since Radisson had fallen behind the other Frenchmen, he was suffering from feelings of isolation. Helplessness is another agony of torture, which renders even sharper the intensity of pain because torture is above all an "instrument of subjugation" and "the pain of the person under torture signifies the power of the torturer" (Jacques, 1994: 98). And so, when his fear became uncontrollable, Radisson gave in to subjugation by the Iroquois. A climate of death surrounded the expedition and the Iroquois' words of en-

---

2. "That morning they rendered all my things againe, & filled my bagge with victualls. (...) Some laughed att me afterwards for my feares wherein I was, which I more & more hoped for better intertainment" (Ra: 111).

3. "Because of the intense pain and its repetition, in a situation of being removed or cut off from all affective contact with loved ones (...) the victim is entirely focused on the present moment and on his efforts to survive" (Jacques, 1994: 98-99).

couragement and soothing promises rang false in the ears of Radisson, who had witnessed the Huron being assassinated before his very eyes, despite similar fine promises. So Radisson felt isolated, powerless and in grave danger of death. He found himself in a situation similar to that of his torture and it is not surprising that he was again overcome by a great fear, since "the type of behavior learned under torture (such as expressing great terror) can suddenly reappear" several years later (Amnesty International, 1974: 67).

The extreme physical pain endured under torture may therefore leave lasting psychological effects that are difficult for torture victims to overcome. There is little evidence of the impact of Iroquois methods of torture on their *Amerindian* captives, who were prepared from childhood for such an eventuality, but the considerable precautions that surrounded Radisson's second escape, his unflagging distrust of the Mohawk (Ra: 87) and the description he gives of the panic that had seized him indicate that even a strong and courageous European could remain marked by such a trauma.

To understand the murder of the Huron warriors and the institution of a Jesuit mission in Iroquois country, among those so recently made enemies, as well as to properly represent the geopolitical embroilment in which Radisson was involved during his stay at Gannentaha, it is necessary to take a brief look back.

A geopolitical upheaval and Amerindian rivalries

Thanks to their privileged alliance with the Dutch, the Iroquois became powerful and drove out of their territory most of the nations of the Saint-Lawrence, the Ottawa and of the Great Lakes, Ontario, Erie and Huron. The exiles were assembled particularly in the region located at the confluence of Lakes Michigan, Huron and Superior, in the vicinity of Sault Sainte-Marie, Michilimakimac and of Green Bay (western area of Lake Michigan) (Delage, 1985: 157); (Beaulieu, 1992: 165). Subsequently, the refugees spread out more to the south and to the west, where for many years their influx provoked confrontations, fresh conflicts and new alliances (Delage, 1985: 162-163).

Despite the scale of their victories, the Iroquois pursued their offensives with the same intensity until the end of the 1650s. In the north, they attacked the Amerindian allies of the French; to the west, they launched fresh raids as far as Lake Superior; in the south, they fought in vain against the Susquehanocks who were well armed by the Swedes of the Delaware region, and so they concentrated their aggressions on the purveyors of the furs of the Susquehanocks, the Eries, whom they completely annihilated within two or three years (JR, 44: 192); (Beaulieu, 1992: 218 and 249-250); (Jennings, 1984: 102-105); (Delâge, 1985: 159-160); (Campeau, 1996: 880).

The first peace negotiations that the Iroquois undertook with the French and with the Huron who had taken refuge at Québec, in 1653, sought among other objectives to permit the concentraton of the Iroquois military effort against the Susquehannocks and the Eries, by concluding a truce and, where possible, by obtaining firearms from the French (Beaulieu, 1992: 183-184); (Delâge, 1985: 160, 237). But this reconciliation continued well after the Iroquois victory against the Eries because the four "superior" Iroquois nations, reassembled round the Onondaga, took advantage of the situation (Beaulieu, 1992: 20 and 131-132); (Jennings, 1984: 104-106). The Onondaga sought to restablilize the Iroquois League by circumventing the far too exclusive association between the Dutch and the Mohawk, the latter of whom risked losing considerable power if an important part of the commerce of the four superior Iroquois nations was henceforth conducted with the French, and not, by their intervention, with the Dutch. Recurrent tensions between 1645 and 1667[4] thus disrupted on several occasions the relations between the Mohawk and the four other nations in the League (Jennings, 1984: 104-106); (Beaulieu, 1992: 178, 226-227); (Marie de l'Incarnation, 1971: 583-584). Without actually destroying the Iroquois League, these internal divisions did leave the French a sufficient margin of manoever for them to avoid disaster and gradually reestablish a situation that would remain extremely precarious.

Iroquois power and a climate of dissension

Encouraged by their decisive victories in the Great Lakes and by the virtual disappearance of commercial competition, the Five Iroquois Nations imposed military domination over the entire north-east of North America. But the extremely rapid expansion of their territory, their power and their

---

4. As of 1647, the Onondaga, the Oneida, the Cayuaga and the Seneca spoke of peace with the French, while the Mohawk continued to attack them. According to Father Jogues, the superior nations feared at the time that "the Hiroquois Annieronon, (...) who are intolerable even to their allies, might become too strong, and in time, tyrannize them" (JR, 33: 122); (Beaulieu, 1992: 161).

commerce, along with the massive adoptions and the transformation of ideologies that supported such expansion – particularly the practices of large-scale trade – destabilized their society and almost led it to a point of rupture (Richter, 1983: 540); (Jennings, 1984: 106, 109); (Beaulieu, 1992: 163, 176, 178, 183 and 234); (Campeau, 1983: 23). The sudden disappearance of several civil and military leaders, because of fatal epidemics and incessant conflicts, accentuated this instability. The choice of certain Iroquois to ally with the French rather than drive them out of the Saint Lawrence region, as well as the reprisal that the Algonquin populations who had fled west were then preparing and the internal dissensions, would reduce the power and influence of the Iroquois to much more modest dimensions when French military reinforcements arrived, in 1667, and more appreciably, after 1701, when the Great Peace signed at Montréal confirmed the final victory of the Algonquin nations of the Great Lakes over their age-old enemies, the Iroquois. Henceforth, the Iroquois would be active in commercial, diplomatic and military capacities over a considerably smaller region on the southwestern periphery of their traditional territory and to the south of Lake Ontario (Richter, 1983: 554-559); (White, 1991: 175, 188-189, 235).

A French waltz, Huron sighs and an Algonquin resurgence

The Mohawk, just as obstinately as the Onondaga, were desirous of repatriating the Huron who had taken refuge at Québec in the hope of neutralizing them definitively (Richter, 1983: 541); (Campeau, 1983: 13-18 and 28-29) (Beaulieu: 1992: 187, 189, 192-194 and 228). It had become clear that the Huron presence amidst the French represented an asset to commercial and military plans, since they were the traditional allies of the Algonquin nations of the Great Lakes region and were thus well acquainted with not only the trade routes and warpaths used by the Iroquois but also their military techniques.[5]

---

5. The Huron refugees of Québec whom the Mohawk repatriated in 1657 were ill-treated, according to Father Lemoyne who spent the winter of 1657-1658 among them: "they are treated like slaves. The husband is separated from his wife; the children, from their fathers and mothers. In short, they are used like beasts of burden by these savages" (JR, 44: 204); (Campeau, 1983: 20).

As early as 1653, seven representatives of several Algonquin nations that were former neighbours of the Huron, the Petun and the Neutral, all of whom had fled west, prepared to recommence trading with the French and to fight the Iroquois once again (JR, 38: 180). And so, the following year, some one hundred Petun and Ottawa warriors transporting a load of furs travelled to Montréal to acquire a few French goods (JR, 41: 78), most certainly firearms, in that time of widespread conflict (Campeau, 1996: 382, 384). Taking advantage of the relative peace then reigning with the Iroquois, Governor Lauson mandated Médard Chouart, called Des Groseilliers, and one other Frenchman, who remains anonymous, to accompany these Amerindians as far as the Great Lakes and once there to reorganize the trading network.[6] However, at that point, the French were playing a double game: while they attempted to reanimate the traditional alliance with their Algonquin partners of the Great Lakes, Governor Lauson and the Jesuits decided to acquiesce to the insistent demands of the Iroquois and so they stopped sustaining the Huron and Algonquins residing in the colony.

Several historians opine that the French had no choice, given the disastrous economic situation and military deficiency of New France; clearly, there was a need to gain time (Jennings, 1984: 104 and 95-96); (Campeau, 1983: 17-18); (Beaulieu, 1992: 231-232). But New France risked a great deal if she alienated in any lasting way the nations of the Great Lakes who until then had supported the French, supplying them with furs, even if some felt that perhaps these Amerindians were no longer able to resist the Iroquois; for the moment, it was obvious that the worst threat to the colony was the resumption of Iroquois attacks. The French therefore decided in favor of ambivalence and dissimulation,[7] a strategy not unlike that practiced by the Iroquois, with whom they now sought to strike an alliance by establishing a mission on their territory.

The Jesuits were at the heart of these delicate peace negotiations (Beaulieu, 1992: 214-218, 249-250). The traditional allies of the French – who were suspicious, and rightly so, of the Iroquois' intentions concerning them (Marie de

---

6. "To allow two Frenchmen (Des Groseilliers and an unknown companion) to return with the native canoe brigade to their country" (Heidenreich, 1997: 105-106).

7. Concerning the prickly issue of the Huron on the Île d'Orléans, in 1653, "the French adopted an extremely ambivalent attitude;" and in 1654, "Lauzon and the Jesuits were to adopt a two-tiered policy in regard to that question, namely to accept the departure of the Huron under Iroquois control, but also to try to delay same" (Beaulieu, 1992: 192-194).

l'Incarnation, 1971: 542-550) – soon realized that Governor Lauson and the Jesuits now attached more importance to making peace with the Iroquois than to maintaining a solid alliance with them (Beaulieu: 1992: 191-192).[8] The new French policy had its first dramatic consequence in the summer of 1656, when the Mohawk carried out a raid on the Huron who had taken refuge on the Île d'Orléans, killing a number of warriors and capturing several groups of ten or more individuals whom they paraded in full view of Québec and Trois-Rivières without the French reacting or even complaining (Beaulieu, 1992: 228-231). The Huron would long remember that rupture in the alliance they had contracted with the French several decades earlier when they had come to the very heart of the French colony seeking refuge and assistance (Beaulieu, 1992: 228-232).[9]

This major "about-face" in French military and commercial policies was to be of short duration.

Gannentaha, more at stake than a new mission

Lauson and the Jesuits were pursuing objectives other than simply opening a new mission when they sent out some fifty Frenchmen to build a fort in the Onondaga territory. They also hoped to facilitate a reopening of the Great Lakes trade routes and to develop the fur trade with the Iroquois (Beaulieu, 1992: 201, 203, 251). Marie de l'Incarnation confirms the commercial potential of the site: "from morning to night the Fathers' dwelling was always full of people because of the immensity of the surrounding Iroquois territory" (Marie de l'Incarnation, 1971: 602); (see also Beaulieu, 1992: 233). For the Onondaga, the French settling in their territory also afforded certain advantages. At the height of the tensions between the

---

8. In November 1653, the Governor of Trois-Rivières imprisoned the Huron who had killed two Mahicans accompanying the Mohawk ambassadors. Lauson offered presents to the Mohawk in compensation for these murders, affirming that "no matter what the Huron and the Algonquins do, Onontio wishes to keep the peace" with them (Beaulieu, 1992: 187). In 1655, Lauson had agreed in secret with the Mohawk that outside a certain area, apparently quite restricted, they could hunt down all the Huron and Algonquins they desired without risking French reprisal (Beaulieu, 1992: 207-208).

9. Some thirty years later, when Nicolas Perrot was voyaging in the Great Lakes region, the Huron reminded him of the incident: "They will always remember" he wrote "(...) how the French did so very little to oppose the Iroquois, when at a time of peace, they captured them on the Île d'Orléans and paraded them in canoes in full sight of Québec and Trois-Rivières" (Perrot, quoted in Beaulieu: 232).

Mohawk and the Onondaga, firearms and the French fort provided effective protection in case of conflict (Jennings, 1984: 109). The Iroquois also appreciated the proximity of trade goods, which the French brought in themselves, and the possibility of getting their firearms repaired. The presence of the French afforded the Onondaga additional opportunities to increase their influence within the League, more particularly with their closest neighbors, who from then on could better avoid the whims of the Mohawk (Beaulieu, 1992: 204, 221-222). However, the four superior nations – the Oneida, the Onondaga, the Cayuga and the Seneca – always remained divided as to the concrete advantages of an alliance with the French (JR, 42: 202), and even more so about the presence of the latter at the very heart of their country, where Huron captives were a constant reminder of all the wrongs they had done to them (JR, 43: 290); (Richter, 1985: 1-4).

In New France as well, the French settlements in Onondaga territory did not have unanimous approval. Many believed the undertaking to be foolhardy, complaining that public monies were being invested in a missionary project rather than in the colony, which could no longer assume even the costs of its administration and defense following the dramatic decline in the fur trade (Beaulieu, 1992: 175 and 225).[10] Certain families that the new Governor Lauzon had excluded from trading complained as far away as France about the abusive authority of the Governor and the Jesuits; and even the latter group recognized the "excessive expenditures" and the risks of the undertaking and found themselves "in a most troublesome situation" (JR, 43: 126) when they set out for the first time towards Gannentaha, in 1656. But the Jesuits ultimately decided to heed providence and risk the adventure (Beaulieu, 1992: 223-224).

The French reached Lake Gannentaha in July 1656; they were well received and immediately erected a spacious, solidly-constructed fort (Campeau, 1983: 27 and Ra: 118, 130-131). Approximately one month later, in August 1656, or a year later than planned, Des Groseilliers and the other French trapper who had been mandated by Lauson returned to Montréal at the head of some 250 Ottawa and Petun carrying a large quantity of furs (Campeau, 1996: 891). The arrival of this important convoy demonstrated that trade with the western nations could recommence and be as lucrative as before. And yet, the attack launched by the Iroquois against the expedition

---

10. Governor Lauzon advanced 8 000 pounds drawn from public funds to the Jesuits so they could execute their project (Campeau, 1983: 25).

hastily organized by the Jesuits to accompany these native allies to the Great Lakes, fatally wounding Father Garreau and forcing the other Frenchmen to turn back, proved that the peace concluded at great cost with the Iroquois in no way guaranteed the safety of the colony or of trade with the Great Lakes nations (Beaulieu, 1992: 251, 258-259). As of that point, the partisans of the alliance with the Huron and Algonquin nations of the Great Lakes seem to have taken the upper hand in New France.

Governor Lauson left New-France in the fall of 1656 and Ragueneau, the Jesuit Superior, resigned from the Council of Québec shortly thereafter (Campeau, 1983: 25). By summer 1657, even the Jesuits were losing patience owing to the arrogance of the Iroquois who sacked a number of French establishments in the colony.[11] Finally, in August 1657, shortly after the departure of the expedition to Gannentaha in which Radisson participated, Lauson's son, who had taken over temporarily from his father, ceded the position to Louis d'Ailleboust, himself a former Governor and partisan of the hard line against the Iroquois (DBC, Lauson of Charny). When d'Ailleboust learned of the murder of the Huron warriors witnessed by Radisson and by Father Ragueneau, he at once convoked an assembly of the colony's most influential habitants, which ruled that the alliance with the Huron and the Algonquins had priority and that henceforth the French could reply in kind to Iroquois "insults" (JR, 44: 192). D'Ailleboust then convoked the Huron and the Algonquins present at Québec to give them the good news and to tell them that they too could attack the Iroquois, although only at a healthy distance from the French establishments (Beaulieu, 1992: 250). Following the murder of three other Frenchmen in Montréal by yet other Iroquois, in November 1657 (Beaulieu, 1992: 239), d'Ailleboust threatened the Iroquois emissaries dispatched three months later to meet with him to discuss the issue: "There is but one word – make war or peace – and no longer be traitors; the Frenchman fears nothing when he chooses war" (JR, 44: 86-88).

The real stakes in the diplomatic waltz of the years 1654-1658 hinged on the need of the Great Lakes nations to procure European goods from the French, the only European nation still directly accessible to them, while the Iroquois did everything in their power to come between them and the French so as to better subjugate them, one and all (Richter, 1983: 539). The French

---

11. "These savages, in full view of our people in their territory, committed many insults, pillaging houses and killing the livestock of French farmers" (JR, 44: 192).

seem not to have understood this vital aspect of Amerindian geopolitics until the return of Des Groseilliers and the other Frenchman from the Great Lakes. In light of the number and strength of the nations the two French travellers encountered at Lakes Michigan and Superior, the Jesuits' attempt to induce the natives, be they friends or foes, to serve above all else the interests of the French seems somewhat naive. The Jesuits and their partisans wanted to continue profiting from the fur trade and to pursue their apostolic work by merely changing intermediaires. They believed they could disregard the mighty lines of force that united or divided the Amerindian nations. The group of Frenchmen opposed to the alliance with the Iroquois, especially after 1656, deemed, for their part, that the Great Lakes nations held the key to the fur trade and that it was essential to ally with them in the war they were waging against the Iroquois – by reviving the old Huron-Algonquin trade network and by developing it to serve the interests of all the partners. We shall see in the next two chapters how Des Groseilliers set about doing this, in the company of a few Huron, Petun, Saulteaux and Ottawa, the ever anonymous Frenchman and, of course, Radisson.

A societal debate and a social transformation

It is worth noting here that the *social dynamic* opposing these two interest groups – the partisans of the alliance with the Iroquois versus those who supported an alliance with the Algonquin nations – most certainly played a constructive role in the maintenance and development of New France during this difficult period.

At a time when the Iroquois had virtually annihilated several nations, allies of the French, and the colony was being savagely attacked while experiencing shrinking financial resources, it was probably imperative to accept the Iroquois offers of peace. Moreover, the repeated attempts of the Jesuits to include their Huron allies and the Algonquins in the peace process facilitated the return of the first Ottawa and Petun to Montréal, in 1654, followed by the departure of Des Groseilliers for the Great Lakes that same year, and ultimately his return in 1656, just when the French were settling at Gannentaha and relations with the Iroquois were at their best (Heidenreich, 1997: 104). Indirectly therefore, the reconciliation of the French and the Iroquois facilitated the rehabilitation of the alliance between the French and the enemies of the Iroquois, namely, the Great Lakes Algonquin Nations, while at the same time imperilling that reconciliation.

For if Des Groseilliers and the anonymous Frenchman had not accompanied the Algonquin nations back to the Great Lakes in 1654, then revived the alliance and managed to supply these nations with articles made of iron, in order to reinforce their position against the Iroquois, it is likely that these refugee nations would soon have found themselves in a tight corner facing their Iroquois enemies, who at that point could have exercised a quasi-monopoly over the provisions of European goods in the American East. The uncertain period during which the French coveted an alliance with one, then another faction – although such indecision proved costly to the life and liberty of many Huron who had taken refuge near Québec – seems in any case to have served the interests both of the French colony and of the Great Lakes Algonquin nations who were allies of the French.

The Jesuit clan could be reproached for having misunderstood the risks and the advantages of a mission in Onondaga territory since there seems to have been no increase in the fur trade in New France after its installation, and yet the Jesuits continued to demand funds in France to bolster this costly project. Moreover, it is clear that the Gannentaha mission was never profitable either commercially or spiritually (Campeau, 1996: 725); (Campeau, 1983: 43); (Beaulieu, 1992: 248). Nonetheless, the French did realize major political and diplomatic dividends from this adventure, in that the good relations they subsequently achieved with the Onondaga were to prove of lasting duration.

Radisson, an "Indianized" Frenchman

Radisson was among the French traders who frequented and also warred and traded with the natives while assisting the missionairies in their endeavors. His experience of life among the Iroquois, his knowledge of the bush, his endurance, his hunting skills, his mastery of native tongues, in particular that of the Iroquois, thus far rarely seen among the French, made him a prime candidate to accompany the Jesuits to Onondaga territory.

Radisson states that he volunteered for that expedition since he admired the Iroquois and wanted to see them again (Ra: 87). As we have seen, he spent six weeks alone with a few Iroquois without experiencing any major difficulties other than youthful squabbles and one brief moment of terror. He even seemed to have relative confidence in the Amerindians (Ra: 91, 96, 105)[12] and two passages in his narrative confirm that he shared certain native values and took pleasure in living with them. After some forty days travelling, when he and his four Iroquois companions finally overtook the main expedition, at the mouth of the Oswego River close to Onondaga territory, Radisson talks about the beauty of the surroundings and about his Amerindian acquaintances, rather than about feeling relief on meeting up with the French:

> we placed our cottages by a most pleasant delicat river, where for delighfullnesse was what man's heart could wish. There weare woods, forests, meddows. (…) One night I layd neare a fair comely lasse that was with us. There they take no notice, for they live in so great liberty that they are never jealous one of another. I admired of a sudaine to heare new musick. She was in travelle and immediately delivered. I awakened all astonished to see her drying her child by the fire side. Having done, laped the child in her bosome and went to bed as if that had been nothing, without moan or cry, as doe our Europian women. (…) some hours before, shee and I roasted some Indian Corn in the fire: being ready, shee pulled out the grains one by one with a stick, and as shee was so doing, shee made a horrid outcry, shewing me a toad, (…) wich was in the midle of the redd ashes striving to gett out. We wondered, for the like was never seen before. After he gott out of the fire we threwed stoanes and staves att him till it was killed. That toad lived 2 dayes in or under the fire (Ra: 117, 122).

I have quoted in full the evocation of this amorous encounter with an engaging Iroquois woman because this is the single sentimental interlude that Radisson relates in his entire narrative. It is evident that he shares his companion's apprehension for what this mysterious toad's appearance might portend and together they kill it to ward off any ill omen. Radisson's sense of wonder upon gazing at the beauty of his surroundings reveals the particular sensitivity he had developed for the American environment and its abundant resources, the veritable leitmotif of his first four narratives. At this point, before evoking the joy all the Frenchmen felt upon seeing one another again and in recounting their adventures, Radisson relates that the Jesuits blamed him for neglecting to baptize the newborn he mentions, fearing that

---

12. "Now whether it was an unicorne, or a fibbe made by that wild man, that I cannot tell, but severall others tould me the same, who have seene severall times the same beast, so that I firmly believe it" (Ra: 107).

he might be accused of causing its death, infanticide being a not infrequent phenomenon (Ra: 117).

A few weeks later, a second French expedition left Montréal led by another group of Onondaga. When they too stopped at the Île du Massacre, a Jesuit discovered a Huron woman half dead of hunger who had taken cover to escape the Iroquois frenzy. This priest, who recognized the woman as he had evangelized her, took her under his wing as far as the mouth of the Oswego River where she again disappeared, fearing that an Iroquois she saw reloading his rifle intended to kill her. The Jesuit told the Frenchmen who had come to welcome him about the "miraculous" survival of the Huron woman, which he believed: "shewss us *apparently* that wee ought not to despaire, & that keeps those that lives in his feare" (Ra: 119-120). Several days later, this same Huron woman was found alive and well a second time and the Jesuit took her to the French fort to impress his compatriots: "that we might see her as a thing incredible but by the mercy of God" (Ra: 120). Albeit deeply Christian in his own way, Radisson never subscribed to the Jesuits' extreme conceptions and, even after spending many months in their company, he attributed as much to luck as to the Christian God their having cleared the Lachine rapids unscathed, on their return to Montréal (Ra: 133-134); in like manner, he ascribed as much to his own ingenuity as to divine providence his escaping the storm which nearly engulfed his canoe on Lake Ontario (Ra: 115-116). All this indicates that Radisson remained close to the Amerindians, even after his return to New France, and that the Jesuits would have devoted as much energy to consolidating the wavering faith of certain Frenchmen, like Radisson, as to converting the Iroquois.

Radisson's role during his stay at Gannentaha also demonstrates his complicity with the Amerindians. At first he seems to have shared the responsibility of keeping the fort supplied with food[13] and the Iroquois with

---

13. Radisson worried constantly about food supplies, a more immediate concern for him than for the missionaries and administrators who wrote about New France. In reality, food was of such great importance for Radisson that his comments about the natural beauty of America are often related to obtaining food supplies: "After we came to a most delightfull place *for the number of stagges that weare there*" (Ra: 75), "I am satisfied to assure you that it is a delightfull & beautifull country. We wanted nothing to the view passing those skirts, *killing staggs, auriniacks and fowles. As for the fish*, what a thing it is to see them in the bottom of the watter, & take it bitting the hooke" (Ra: 98). Radisson's constant concern for procuring food supplies obviously represents a major factor in his successful career as a coureur de bois.

company: "we sought to take advantage of the country, some of us hunted, others fished," "for us, this was not a savage land, but one that abounded in all things" (Ra: 118). He admires the richness and the beauty of the country as he moves about the region; among other activities, he accompanies a Jesuit priest to a neighboring village, probably as a bodyguard (Ra: 120-121, 127). Later, when tensions begin to grow between the French and Iroquois, Radisson seems to assume a more important role by participating in the elaboration and execution of a strategy which will enable all the Frenchmen to leave Gannentaha, thereby escaping the Iroquois menace.

Iroquois tensions and expansion

During his brief stay in an Onondaga village with a Jesuit priest in 1658, Radisson witnessed events which elucidate the various reactions of individuals not all of whom may be viewed as calm and level-headed during disquieting times. Individual natives, each in his own way, endured the major transformations that were disrupting their social structures and causing widespread distress. Moreover, these disturbances seem to have provoked certain aberrations of which Radisson gives more than a passing glimpse: "I was in the village with the father and with another frenchman, where we see the cruelest thing in nature acted," adding: "Having remained in that village 6 dayes, we have seen horrible cruelties committed" (Ra: 120 and 122). From a man who knows the Iroquois well, who has himself endured torture and in all likelihood has also inflicted torture on certain prisoners, the comments seem to describe an extreme situation. Radisson recounts how, on a certain day, the elders of that village came out to meet a man who, of his own volition, had taken two woman and two children as slaves. The elders reminded him of the custom requiring that all captives be distributed by order of the chiefs gathered in council:

> So said, (...) gave a signe to some soldiers (...) to knock those beasts (those slaves) in the head, who executed their office & murdered the women. One took the child, sett foot on his head, taking his leggs in his hands, wrought the head, by often turning from off the body. An other souldier took the other child from his mother's brest, that was not yett quite dead, by the feete and knocks his head against the trunck of a tree. This a daily exercise with them, nor can I tell the one half of their cruelties in like sortes. (...) 0 wicked and barbarious inhumanity! (Ra: 121).

Even if the events Radisson describes cannot be imputed to all the Iroquois nations, they do illustrate the extent to which the many thousands of captives who were often viscerally loathed by the Iroquois[14] could have upset their captors and the traditional power structures, enabling individuals who, either secretly or publicly so desired, to give vent to their darkest desires for vengeance and domination.[15] What Radisson's narrative reveals, about the winter of 1657-1658 is that the fifty or so Frenchman living at Gannentaha, in the midst of disturbed and warmongering Iroquois communities – "their minds completely turned towards the wars which they love about all else" (JR, 51: 122); (Ra: 123) – no longer believed they could reasonably trust their hosts when rumors of their impending massacre began to circulate. It is understandable that, being in the midst of a divided nation, the French feared that the views of the most hateful, the most vindictive, might win the day and that they would all be forced to flee to escape torture and death (Richter, 1985: 5-7). Radisson most certainly had a say in assessing such peril.

The Jesuit influence

Before taking up the engrossing episode of the departure from Gannentaha, it might be useful to describe the influence the Jesuits had on the young "Indianized" Frenchman – Radisson.

In the XVIth century, Protestantism disseminated throughout Europe the seminal notion that every man could amend or improve his ways by instruction and reading the Bible, by self-examination and by self-discipline.

---

14. On the subject of adoption, the Jesuits speak of some one thousand Huron converts who were Onondaga captives, in 1654 (Campeau, 1983: 22), as well as of eleven different nations living with the Seneca in 1657. There was also an upsurge in slavery: "We wanted not slaves from that place to carry our packs" (Ra: 117), "you must know that all slaves, as well men as women" (Ra: 121), "We brought above 100 women, hurron slaves and others, all loadened with corne" (Ra: 122).

15. Richter underscores the difficulty the Iroquois had in integrating on a single occasion so many captives of other nations (Richter, 1983: 542); (Richter, 1985: 9). He also stresses the degradation of ritual adoption practices: "ancient customs regarding the treatment of prisoners were decaying as rituals degenerated into chaotic violence, and sheer murderous rage displaced the orderly adoption of captives that the logic of the mourning-war demanded" (Richter, 1983: 543).

This weighty concept also inspired Ignatius of Loyola to found the Society of Jesus (the Jesuits) in 1540, in his effort to counter the spread of Protestantism in Europe.

Within a few decades the Jesuits developed what is today called a multinational, to wit, a large, efficient international organization which carefully selects its members, then trains them intensively over long years.[16] The order was based on a hierarchical quasi-military discipline, on blind obedience to superiors and above all on the giving of oneself to the conversion and reconversion to the Catholic faith of infidels and pagans. The Society of Jesus rapidly took root in Europe and in several missionary territories in many countries of Europe as well as in Asia and America. The Jesuits set up an effective communcations network among all their teaching colleges in Europe, among the various administrative provinces and their missions, and among all their members at every level of decision-making. The Jesuits differed from other missionaries in that they were trained as "soldiers of God," who were expected to combat heresy and paganism (Loyola, 1908 (1548): 20). The Society of Jesus looked for energetic individuals who were, at once, determined, optimistic and pragmatic, and who could face the most wide-ranging situations, in China, South America and among the Iroquois.[17]

Even though Radisson wrote his narratives in England where the Jesuits were detested, the judgment he renders as to their work and their conduct appears mostly favorable. Admittedly, he records with disfavor their participation in the fur trade, a competition he deems disloyal

---

16. "The ideal Jesuit was a member of a spiritual elite; on his spiritual foundation was laid solid learning, the ability to preach and to teach, and a knowledge of how to deal with men" (Martin, 1988: 31); "The religious order established by Ignatus Loyola was the climax of the progressive organization and centralization in the development of religious life in Europe" (Martin, 1988: 107). The Jesuit colleges played a central role in the evolution of French Society in the XVIth and XVIIth centuries, forming a substantial part of the elite and many men of power (Martin, 1988: 61 and 230, 231, 233).

17. "The curriculum provided humanists with the stimulus as well as the means for an active rather than a contemplative life and favored active service to the community. (...) Another modernizing element of reformed Catholicism was an emphasis on action. (...) A final illustration of Jesuit activism is their confidence and optimism; they believed that their apostolic labors would produce positive results" (Martin, 1988: 31, 231, 232). "Frequently, an initial attraction to the [Jesuit] missionaries [...] must have become a heartfelt conversion simply because of the Jesuits' ceaseless efforts, evident dedication, and willingness to share in the lives of their charges" (Richter, 1985: 8).

(Ra: 93-94); (Trigger, 1976: 803-804).[18] But apart from this criticism and the skepticism with which he received their apostolic message at Gannentaha, he reveals of a certain admiration for their work and accepts their leadership during his stay at Gannentaha[19] (Ra: 102, 118, 131).

The Jesuits believed in the intervention of divine or supernatural forces in daily life,[20] as did the Amerindians (Delage, 1985: 187); (Clermont, 1988: 61). But that which each of the two parties viewed as the essential dialogue between the natural and the supernatural, the real and the spiritual, seemed only to exacerbate the Jesuits' intransigence and accentuate their desire to abolish all native spiritual practices, which they associated in their entirety with diabolical manifestations. However, it would appear that the dual influence of the Amerindians and the Jesuits had a rather salutary effect on Radisson, who attached great importance to his inner nature and felt at ease as much with Catholics as with Protestants or heathens. The exclusive relationship with the one real Christian God and with Catholic dogma as advocated by the Jesuits, coupled with the Jesuit conviction that they were superior to the popular masses of Europe, who indulged in collective rituals as disorderly, noisy and sensual as those of the Amerindians,[21] created a real distance between them and their native flock. For reasons related to the prodigious mental conditioning which every Jesuit was obliged to undergo, it is normal that they rejected viscerally certain Amerindian practices.

---

18. Neither Lauson nor the Jesuits denied having participated in the fur trade: "In the first half of the XVIIth century, they (the Jesuits) had participated in the fur trade to finance a few of their missions in New France and it is probable that they pursued the same policy at the beginning of the 1650s, as may be read in this passage of the *Relation* of 1656-1657" (JR, 43: 170); (Beaulieu, 1992: 213).

19. "There was the good ffather comforting the poore innocent women" (Ra: 100), "The ffathers Jesuits and others voluntarily ventured their lives for the preservation of the common liberty" (Ra: 125).

20. "Despite their reliance on the doctrine of providence to explain events and the doctrine of prayers to control them, Jesuits advocated self-help and hard work (...), taking their cue from that statement attributed to Loyola: "(We should act as if everything depended on us, but pray as if everything depended on God)" (Martin, 1988: 139). See also Delage (1991: 57-58); Ritcher (1985: 6-8).

21. "Jesuits were on the side of Lent in its opposition to the spontaneity and disorder of the lower classes" (Martin, 1988: 79 and 232).

Jesuit precepts applied

A French historian noted that the teaching dispensed in the Jesuit colleges of France had imparted to generations of students a great sense of *order* and "a distrust of *feelings* and *propensities* at every level from the irreducible to the *rational* (De Dainville, 1979: 204; my italics). This Jesuit "passion" for order and its opposite, their aversion to disorder, may be found in the fundamental text that every Jesuit is expected to meditate upon: the *Spiritual Exercises* of the founder of their order, Ignatius of Loyola, who had written this book expressly "to free oneself from all disorderly attachments" (Loyola, 1908 (1548): 13). Loyola also taught that it was necessary "to conquer oneself, in other words, that the senses must obey reason and that all the inferior parts be fully subject to the superior ones" (Loyola: 60), and all of that "without any compromise with the flesh and the world" (Loyola: 97), that is to say with honors and wealth.

Does this mean that Loyola wanted his Jesuit Fathers to become automatons, insensitive and untouchable? Not at all. On the contrary, he was seeking to develop a rational being who could combat and resist passions, as well as the temptations of the senses and the sentiments; several passages of his *Spiritual Exercises* are devoted to the delicate question of *controlling* the senses and the emotions. Loyola wanted a total channelling of the senses in God, in the person of Jesus Christ or in that of the Saints, and so he recommends "conversation with God or the Saints through the *affect*." Seeking to habituate the Jesuit to scorn himself and to learn obedience, he calls to a great extent upon the ability to see: "To *look* upon the corruption and wretchedness of my body (…). To *see* with the eyes of the imagination (…) Christ on the Cross (…)." (Loyola: 47, 49, 53). Loyola wanted to conquer the entire being and direct the Jesuit towards the only worthy objective: the conversion of as many souls as possible to the Catholic pantheon: "To ask what one *feels within*, so as to better follow and imitate Our Lord (…). That I may *realize* the disorder of my activity, so as to (…) reform and order my being (…). Through the *five senses*, to touch, to see and to feel the fire and torments of hell" (Loyola: 51, 53). Through the senses of *smell* and *taste*, to smell and taste the infinite suavity and sweetness of the Divinity…" (Loyola: 72, 73, 74, 76, 77).

To consolidate this channelling of the sentient being towards serving God and the Church, Loyola recommended that the Jesuit entirely cast aside his person: "To look upon myself as a wound or an abscess from whence

springs all my sins" (Loyola: 33, 45). On the delicate questions of power and material goods, Loyola held an ambiguous position. Whereas the Jesuit must always renounce the things that are personal, he must nevertheless remain vigilant
and "realize" when the divine will commands using a position of influence or a
substantial income to better serve God and the Church. In this way, Loyola left
the door open to the development and prosperity of the Society of Jesus.[22] Lastly,
he insisted on the strict surbordination of every Jesuit to hierarchical authority: "To achieve excellence in all things, it is necessary ever to be ready, in view
of that which I, myself, see to be white, to believe that same is black, if the hierarchical Church so decides" (Loyola: 187).

Given these precepts, constantly repeated to the Jesuits during their
lengthy training, one can understand why they participated in the fur trade
and why they were unable to accept the gluttony of the Amerindians, their
sexual liberty and their unconstrained and apparently disorganized society,
while they imposed upon themselves a strict personal discipline which aimed
at dispelling, diminishing and combatting sensual pleasure and the freedom
of spirit so splendidly incarnated by the unbaptized Amerindians. Radisson
and Des Groseilliers inherited through the knowledge they acquired from
the Jesuits, and from the Jesuits' concerted efforts to transform the native
cultures and communities, a certain capacity to intervene directly in Indian
affairs, so as to promote their own point of view and to moderate the behavior of their Amerindian partners.

A hasty depature from Gannentaha

It was in the middle of a strained and chaotic situation that the French
heard rumors of their impending massacre (Ra: 123). Radisson and, no
doubt, the others took the matter very seriously: "such news upset us greatly
as we well know how faithless this savage nation can be" (Ra: 123). The
French immediately imposed security measures and attempted to rally a
number of informers among the members of the Iroquois band councils,
by distributing presents. Thanks to this they heard several other, equally

---

22. "His (the Jesuit's) sole assertion is to want to keep a thing or not, according to that which
God our Lord places within his will and according to that which seems best to him, for him, so
as to serve and praise his divine Majesty. Non obstante, he will view himself as one who aban-
dons all in his heart, and he strives to refrain from wanting this or any other property, unless
such desire be dictated solely by the need to serve God our Lord (Loyola: 87).

disturbing rumors such as of the approach of an army of 500 Mohawk who wanted to annihilate them, or hints at the comparison the Iroquois were said to make between the French and the pigs they had brought into Iroquois territory, intimating in mocking fashion that they were fattening them before their slaughter.[23]

The French decided to build the two flat-bottomed boats they needed to reach Montréal carrying only the strict necessities. But an incident nearly compromised their project and illustrated the extreme, somewhat bizarre agitation that reigned owing to the influx of native captives and the presence of some fifty Frenchmen in Iroquois territory. A Christianized Huron, named Jaluck, whom the Jesuits had put to work at the Gannentaha fort, remembering the biblical story of Noah and the Ark, believed that the French were building a new ark and preparing to flood the land:[24] "Overcome by fear, (Jaluck) raced back to his village. His return terrorized one and all. Everybody spoke of it. The elders assembled to discuss what should be done" (Ra: 125). Thanks to the Jesuit who had remained in that village, the French were warned in advance of the next Iroquois visit and they fabricated a double floor to hide the boats under construction. The Iroquois saw nothing unusual in French dwellings having raised floors (Ra: 125). But "once bitten, twice shy" according to Radisson (Ra: 244), and the French remained on their guard all that winter, posting sentinels continually around the fort (Ra: 126). Radisson recounts several specific details about the plan which led to the departure from Gannentaha. Since he knew the Iroquois well, he

---

23. "Hearing such news, we make friends by store of guifts, yea such gifts that weare able to betray their country. What is that, that interest will not do? (...) Their dayly exercise is feasting of warrs, songs, throwing of hattchets, breaking kettles. What can we do? We are in their hands. (...) Yea, as much as a ship in full sea without pilot, as passengers without skill. We must resolve to be uppon our guard, being in the midle of our Ennemy" (Ra: 123-124). "What could fifty-three Frenchmen purport to do, realizing that enemies surrounded them on all sides, and that every day divers bands and troups were heading towards the French, to massacre them, along with our Savages?" (JR, 44: 214).

24. The flood is also a capital event in the cosmology of the Iroquois nations. It was in the wake of a flood that a rodent managed to dive down and bring back a small quantity of earth that permitted recreating the world on and in which lived the Amerindians of the XVIIth century. It is only normal that a Huron would attach importance to this biblical episode, interpreting it in his own way, then transposing it in his own material and spiritual universe, with all the shifts in meaning and intention that certain similarities between their two systems of belief might favor, to two spiritual, albeit distinct, worlds. However, the Jesuits saw these two worlds as antagonistic.

was no doubt consulted early on about this by the Jesuits and by the head of the fort, one Zacharie Dupuys, who was also a newcomer to the colony.

Radisson and a few other Frenchmen thus decided on a two-tiered strategy to escape the clutches of those who were menacing them (Ra: 126).

They invited the Iroquois to attend a first banquet at the fort, in April 1658. After the meal, while returning to the village where he resided, a Jesuit Father pretended to have broken his arm. The Iroquois brought him back to the fort where he was put to bed: "The French who were unaware of the ruse wept for the priest, which confirmed what the savages believed" (Ra: 127). Certain Frenchmen had no knowledge of the strategy whereas others fidgeted with impatience: "Many hoped to see the sun blaze with ardor, so fervently did they wish to be gone" (Ra: 127). As soon as everything was ready for the departure and spring sufficiently advanced, the Iroquois were invited to a second banquet, this one gargantuan, to celebrate the Jesuit Father's recovery, but in reality, to facilitate their departure. The French intended to stuff the Onondaga to the eyeballs, then, while they slept soundly, to take to their heels. I quote here a long passage from the narrative Radisson has left us about this banquet:

> The elders are invited. They weare sure not to faile, but to be first. Being come, there are speeches made to incourage them to sing and eat. It's folly to induce them to that, for they goe about it more bould then welcome. (...) In the meantime we weare not idle, the impatient father exercising himselfe as the rest. (...) Every one makes his bundle of provisions & marchandises & household stuff, gunns, &c. (...). (Then, the Iroquois get down to quite serious eating) there is nothing but outcryes, clapping of hands, & capering, that they may have better stomach to their meate. There comes a dozen of great kettles full of Indian corne dressed with mince meat. The wisest begins his speech, giving heaven thanks to have brought such generous ffrench to honnor them so. They eate as many wolves, having eyes bigger then bellies (...). Heare comes 2 great kettles full of bustards broyled and salted before the winter, with as many kettles full of ducks. (...) The best is that we are sure none will forsake his place, nor man nor woman. (...) there comes the thickened flower, the oyle of bears, venison. To this the knife is not enough; the spunes also are used. Wee see allready severall postures: the one beats his belly, the other shakes his head, others stopp their mouthes to keepe in what they have eaten. They weare in such an admiration, making strange kind of faces, that turned their eyes up and down. We bid them cheare up (...). In the end nothing spared that can be invented to the greater confusion. There is a strife between the french who will make the greatest

noise. But there is an end to all things; the houre is come, ffor all is embarked. The wildman can hold out no longer; they must sleepe. They cry out *Skenon*, enough, we can beare no more. "Lett them cry *Skenon*; we will cry *hunnay*, we are a going," sayes we (Ra: 127-129).[25]

Once the Iroquois were fast asleep, certain Frenchmen proposed slaughtering all those who had come to the banquet and even to take advantage of the hunters' absence to repair to their village and there massacre all the women and children out of vengeance and to weaken this "perverse and disloyal" nation (Ra: 130). The Jesuits refused. Others suggested instead to hold the fort strong and well stocked while a group of fifteen or so went to seek reinforcements at Montréal (Ra: 130-131 and 118). The Jesuits refused all these bellicose solutions, replying that: "they had been sent to instruct the people in the faith of Jesus Christ, not to destroy;" they elected therefore to abandon Gannentaha and attempt to bring back all the French colonists alive and well to Montréal (Ra: 131).[26]

Because the season was early, the return trip proved difficult. At times the French had to break the ice blocking their boats or shoot rapids swollen with rushing water; the melting snow and inundated banks virtually prevented them from halting. They endured bad weather, fear, danger, great haste and a boatwreck in which three men perished. After a voyage of six weeks (Ra: 132-133), the absconders finally reached Montréal on the last day of March. "We put an end to our great pains and our incredible dangers (...). We thank God for our deliverance" (Ra: 134).[27]

---

25. "He who presided at the ceremony, played his role with such skill and pleasure that each person wanted to contribute to the general rejoicing: who would utter the most piercing shrieks, at times, of war, at times, out of elation: the Savages out of complacency sang and danced in the French manner, and the French, like the Savage" (JR, 44: 176).

26. The great difference in viewpoint that exists between the Jesuits and Radisson may be noted in their respective comments on the country they are about to leave; the Jesuits speak, wrongly it seems, of a "poor and miserable country," likely reflecting on the failure they had suffered (JR, 44: 216), whereas Radisson regrets leaving this "marvellous land:" "How sad it is to leave such a place surrounded by these great lakes which form what may be called the largest part of the discovered world" (Ra: 124).

27. The Jesuits record that the expedition reached Montréal on April 3rd, in the evening: "On April 3rd, we disembarked at Montréal at nightfall" (JR, 44: 182).

Oddly enough, the "flight" of the French from Gannentaha contributed in a way to strengthening their image with the Onondaga, who believed them incapable of returning alone to Montréal at that time of year. Moreover, as a fresh snowfall had covered any trace of their departure, the Iroquois long wondered if these white "devils" had not sprouted wings as if by magic to fly home.[28]

---

28. "They open the door, the leaders enter on all sides; they go up to the attic; they go down to the cellars & no Frenchman, be he alive or dead, appears (...) fear seizes them; they believe that they are viewing the work of demons. (...) They become convinced that the demon French walked on the waters, or flew through the air, or even, and this seemed more plausible to them, that they were hiding in the bush. They seek them everywhere but nothing appears. They are almost certain that they have become invisible & since they disappeared abruptly, they will return suddenly to raze their villages" (JR, 44: 312).

CHAPTER 4

The Third Voyage: Médard Chouart, Called Des Groseilliers, Mentor of Radisson

D ES GROSEILLIERS HAD a determining influence on his young brother-in-law Radisson, who was some twenty years his junior (HBRS, 5: 232). He taught him ambition, the will to achieve social status and how to lead a fur-trade expedition in Amerindian territory.

Des Groseilliers was a man of experience. He served the Jesuits, who were active in Huron territory in the mid-1640s (JR, 28: 228), and thereafter remained their ally. That is why he was chosen by Governor Lauson to go to the Great Lakes in 1654. Upon his first return from Huron country, Des Groseilliers married one of the daughters of Abraham Martin, a rich and influential Québec tradesman. After the death of his wife, he wed in 1653 Marguerite Hayet, (Radisson's half-sister) in the presence of Governor Lauson and of the Jesuit Provincial, Paul Ragueneau.[1] The revenues, unknown but evidently substantial, from the trading voyage of 1654-1656 confirm the situation and status of Des Groseilliers at Trois-Rivières, which various other indications also clearly reveal, such as his holding the office of Burgomaster of Trois-Rivières in the early 1660s (Trudel, 1983: 575); (Ra: 175).[2]

---

1. (ANQ, series G3, vol. 2049, f. 13v).

2. As early as 1646, Des Groseilliers was already one of a minority of well-known "habitants" who were allowed to participate in the fur trade. He was therefore in the company of such well-situated persons as Jean Bourdon, Guillaume Couillard, Guillaume Couture, Robert Giffard, as well as the Godefroy, Juchereau and Legardeur de Repentigny families (Trudel, 1979: 176). Charles Aubert de la Chesnaye estimates at several thousand pounds per

Without being either very rich or very powerful, Des Groseilliers appears to have been an interpreter-tradesman with whom one had to reckon in New-France, particularly since he stubbornly insisted on remaining autonomous, using both his status and his power to preserve that autonomy, and was neither gentle nor docile of character. In a word, Des Groseilliers was not a tolerant man and even after his return from England in 1676, all continued to respect him, to the degree that he was invited, along with Radisson and some fifteen other notables from the colony, to give his opinion on the fur trade.[3] During that period, no one seems to have reproached him or opposed him publicly.[4] The Des Groseilliers with whom Radisson had close contact in his family, during the 1650s, was therefore a strong and respected leader, a man of experience. And so, Radisson had to demonstrate his own capabilities before being able to travel with him.

In 1659, these two men began to develop a very strong and complementary relationship that would last sixteen consecutive years. Together they formed a redoubtable team. In 1659, Radisson consented to follow his brother-in-law unconditionally; in 1668, Des Groseilliers agreed to share with his junior the total fruits of his audacious trading project at Hudson's Bay, and then in 1684, Des Groseilliers declared that the actions and discoveries of either of them at Hudson's Bay meant one and the same

---

coureur de bois the profits from the trading venture of 1654-1656: "two private individuals, who returned in 1656 with 14 or 15 thousands pounds each, also brought back with them a contingent of Savages with 100 thousand crowns" (*Memoire de Canada*, Aubert de la Chesnaye, 1697, ANQ, series F3, collection Moreau de Saint-Méry, folio 7). Des Groseilliers, who employed eight persons, also figures among the leading individual employers at Trois-Rivières before 1663; moreover, his wife was often asked to be a godmother, another mark of notoriety (Trudel, 1983: 278 and 558).

3.   (ANQ, Series F3, coll. Moreau-Saint-Méry, vol. 2, folio 32)

4.   Another indication that Des Groseilliers was in some way "untouchable" appears in one of the registers of the Ursulines: "The daughter of monsieur des groiselliers is registered for the second time in the boarding school, the 11th of October 1676. Monsieur her father must pay her fees in the amount of 120 pounds" (Archives of the Ursulines of Québec, *Registre des entrées et sorties des petites filles Françaises et Sauvages de 1641 à 1720*, folio 60v) (Register of the entrances and departures of French and Amerindian young girls from 1641 to 1720). The respect accorded him by the Ursuline Sisters is all the more significant since Des Groseilliers had recently had an illegitimate daughter with a married woman of Trois-Rivières, Marie-Thérèse Viel; in fact, this child was recognized by the legitimate husband of Marie-Thérèse Viel who did not wish openly to pick a quarrel with Des Groseilliers about this extremely sensitive question (Jetté, 1983: Chouart, Viel and Boyer).

thing.[5] Moreover, Radisson took the place of the other Frenchman in the voyage of 1654-1656 and also accompanied Des Groseilliers to Lakes Michigan and Superior, as he relates in his third narrative.[6] The two men were indeed very close to one another. Even though he did not himself make the third voyage, Radisson's narrative of it provides a means to understand the objectives Des Groseilliers was pursuing, the climate in which this voyage progressed and the approximate itinerary that Des Groseilliers and the other Frenchman followed in the Great Lakes region.

The voyage of 1654-1656

Radisson begins his third narrative with a collage. He first recounts his own departure for the west in 1656, with Jesuit expedition which had to turn back under Iroquois attacks. The precision and vivacity of this lengthy opening passage confers credibility on the entire third narrative, despite the subsequent imprecisions and incoherencies. There are two versions of the preparations and course of the aborted expedition of 1656: Radisson's narrative and that of the Jesuits, both of which concur. However, the subtle distortions of each version reveal how the authors managed to present their actions in a light flattering to all, with hardly any factual alterations.

The Ottawa who had just procured their first firearms in Montréal were returning home to the Great Lakes in disorderly fashion and without heeding the signs of potential danger.[7] One of the Iroquois sacrificed his life to warn them that they had to be more attentive, for they were taking great risks (Ra: 138-139);

---

5. In a deposition made by Des Groseilliers before the Royal Council of France in 1684, about the events that occurred on the Nelson River in 1682-83, Des Groseilliers reiterates the strong alliance that unites the two men: "I am obliged to tell the truth in regard to my conquest and that of my brother (Radisson) which is the same thing, taking as we did the same risks in the Amerindian territories" (published in Nute, 1943: 322-324).

6. I analyzed this question in detail in my first book about Radisson (Fournier, 1996: 69-78 and 100-101). If the beginning of the collaboration of the two brothers-in-law is attributed the proper date, based on all available documents, namely the year 1659, Radisson himself confirms that he did not participate in Des Groseilliers' voyage of 1654-1656, and that their collaboration began after his return from Gannentaha, in 1658: "my brother who the yeare before came back from the lake of the Hurrons *with other french*", and "*seeing me back from those 2 dangerous voyages* (…) thought I was fitter & more faithfull for the discovery that he (Des Groseilliers) was to make" (Ra: 134). For an analysis of this passage in detail, see Fournier (1996: 72).

7. "Those poor people, although warned to be on their guard, made much noise everywhere (…) those young scatterbrains relying on their courage and their number, heard only their own noise, very often stopping to fire at the game they encountered" (Campeau,

(Campeau, 1996: 895); then, the following day, the Iroquois attacked the convoy, forcing the French to retreat in the direction of Montréal.[8] Radisson maintains that among the French, only himself and Des Groseilliers were able to continue on their way with the Ottawa because they were more experienced and better acquainted with the Amerindians. The Jesuits have nothing to say about this and it is certain that Des Groseilliers, who had just arrived from a two-year voyage, did not participate in that expedition. But this is how Radisson emphasizes their mutual competence for the benefit of his English readers and, more importantly, so he can pursue the travel narrative feigning that he accompanied Des Groseiliers. For their part, the Jesuits claim that only the two Jesuit priests and two or three of their close associates continued for a time their voyage towards the Great Lakes, the other Frenchmen having abandoned them because they feared the worst (Campeau, 1996: 894 and 896). However Radisson indicates that all the French turned back at the same time (Ra: 141) and that "the best and most capable men for this sort of undertaking had been chosen" from the outset, at Trois-Rivières (Ra: 135), where Iroquois attacks were par for the course and courageous men did not go lacking.

To give even greater force and credibility to their mutual will to follow the Ottawa as far as the Great Lakes despite such difficult circumstances, Radisson at this juncture cunningly inserts the oath of mutual assistance and alliance that he and Des Groseilliers no doubt pledged to one another at some point during their common peregrinations: *"We encouraged one another, both willing to live & die with one another; & that the least we could doe, being brothers"* (Ra: 142).[9] Radisson thus manages to place his narrative on very solid foundations, while

---

1996: 895). *"No order being observed among them. (...) There was no need of such a silence among us. (...) Some 3 or 4 boats now & then to land to kill a wild beast, & so putt themselves into a danger of their lives, (...) We warned them to look to themselves. They laughed att us (...). That pride had such power that they thought themselves masters of the earth"* (Ra: 137-138).

8.   "Six canoes manned by Huron and a few other Algonquins preceding the larger contingent by some fifty or sixty paces (...) received a shower of lead, so sudden and so dreadful that many were killed (...). All at once the Iroquois (...) flung themselves on those who still lived and dragged them into their fort. (...) Our people (...) hastily erected a fort near enough to that of the Iroquois" (Campeau, 1996: 895). "Some twelve boats gott afore us. These weare saluted with guns & outcrys. (...) some men lands and runs away. We are all put to it (...). The first feare being over a little, they resolved to land and to make a fort with all speed, wich was done in less then two houres. (...) We mist 20 of our company, but some came safe to us, & lost 13 that weare killed & taken in that defeat" (Ra: 140-141).

9.   In reality, they were only brothers-in-law. But the alliance through women gave Amerindian men the status of brother, each toward the other. Radisson's abiding habit of calling Des Groseilliers his "brother", and vice-versa, clearly denotes an Amerindian influence (St-Arnaud, 1998: 146).

cementing his alliance with Des Groseilliers. As for the Jesuits, they succeed in transforming into an heroic mini-feat the involvement of a few of their priests and brothers in what proves in reality to be a failure: the death of Father Gareau and the abortion of their expedition.

Where was Des Groseilliers?

Historians have failed to agree on the places and the tribes that Des Groseilliers and the other Frenchman visited during their voyages; nonetheless, these debates have often overlooked Radisson's narrative, although, he relates therein the comments of a man he knows on intimate terms, while treating a subject he has mastered, namely, the reorganization of the fur trade in the Great Lakes region. Furthermore, Radisson encountered at Lake Superior in 1659-1660 several nations that Des Groseilliers had come to know during his earlier voyage and with whom he experienced quite similar situations and negotiations. I therefore propose a new hypothesis on the itinerary followed by Des Groseilliers and his ever anonymous companion based on Radisson's narrative and the location of the native populations Des Groseilliers encountered at that time.[10]

The nations which renew contact with the French

To thwart the Iroquois who were continuing their offensives on the Great Lakes and on the Saint Lawrence River, seven native emissaries renewed contact with the French in July 1653, to procure firearms and "make themselves redoubtable to the enemy" (JR, 40: 213-15); (Campeau, 1996: 961). The journal of the Jesuits describes in detail the project of the Great Lakes Amerindians (Campeau, 1996: 634-635) – "members of what remained of the Neutral and Petun nations and several allied Algonquin nations assembled at "A,otonatendïé, a three-day journey above the Sault Skia,é, somewhat towards the south" – to restore trade with the French. The Sault Skia,é is Sault Sainte-Marie, situated at the junction of Lakes Huron and Superior,

---

10. Also on a number of complementary documents: (Adams, 1961); (Delâge, 1985); (Harvard, 1992); (Nute, 1943); (Trigger, 1976); (Trudel, 1979); and the *Handbook of North American Indians* (H.N.A.I.), vol. 15. I was advised of another more recent interpretation of Radisson's third voyage after I had reached my own conclusions (Heidenreich, 1997: 106-107). However, Heidenreich's interpretation is in every way identical to mine, which proves that this third narrative is not as imprecise as has been maintained, when compared against knowledge of the Amerindians, refuged in – or natives of – the regions visited by the two Frenchmen.

2. Route of Radisson's Third Expedition

(Expedition of Des Groseilliers and an unknown companion to Lakes Michigan and Superior)

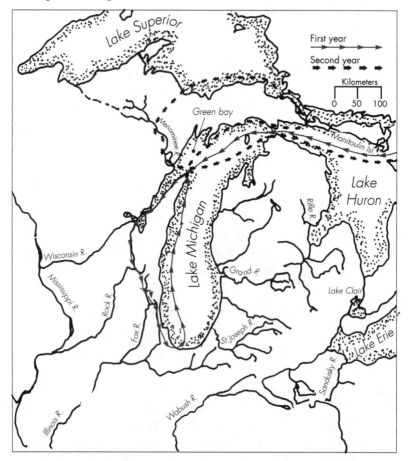

Between 1654 and 1656, Des Groseilliers and an unknown companion began their expedition taking the traditional route along the Ottawa River and Georgian Bay (north of Lake Huron) to the Great Lakes, where they stopped over on one of the islands separating Lake Michigan and the present day Green Bay. They then journeyed into Green Bay and, via an unknown route, reached the southern tip of Lake Michigan, but did not connect with the Mississippi River or any of its tributaries. During year two of the expedition, the two French voyageurs traveled into Lake Superior and wintered on its southeast shore. At spring, they returned by land to Green Bay and subsequently returned to Montréal via the route they took when they set out on their journey. The lighter line shows their route during year one of their expedition; the darker line shows year two of their expedition (according to HNAI, v.15: 610).

and the meeting place of the group was thus located in an area on the south shore of Lake Superior. Among the nations purportedly represented by the emissaries were included Huron, a number of Neutral and Petun and hundreds of Algonquins of many different nations who had been active in the fur trade prior to 1650, in the company of the Huron. Subsequent to the Huron rout, the mosaic of allied Algonquin bands who were living on the periphery of Lake Huron withdrew, heading, for the most part, towards Lake Michigan and the south shore of Lake Superior (Heidenreich, 1997: 102). These nations consolidated their former alliances and created new ones, eventually settling in a foreign environment and rapidly modifying their way of life (White, 1991: 46-47). With the ever increasing number of iron weapons and, particularly, firearms in circulation in the Great Lakes region, trade with the Europeans was becoming all the more vital. It was therefore a state of war, with all the attendant upheavals and climate of insecurity, that prompted the Algonquin nations to develop direct, regular relations with the French.

Traces and observations

The Jesuits provide a number of details about the some one hundred Amerindians who came for the first time to engage in the fur trade at Montréal, in June 1654. They were "part Tionnontatehronnons, whom we used to call the Petun nation, of the Huron tongue, and part Ondataouaouat, of the Algonquin tongue, whom we now call the 'Cheveux-Relevez' (...). All these peoples left their former land and headed towards the more distant nations, in the vicinity of the Great Lake that we call Lake of the Puants"[11] (Campeau, 1996: 683). It was thus towards the region of the Lake of the Puants – today, Lake Michigan – and in the area east of the southern shore of Lake Superior, where these nations had elected to assemble the preceding year, that the Amerindians, accompanying Des Groseilliers, returned to join their families and distribute the French goods. Hence, this was also the region Des Groseilliers and the other Frenchman must have reached.

The two Frenchmen first disembarked on an island where the Huron and the Ottawa, who had accompanied them thus far, wanted them to

---

11. The Algonquin nations were strong in number and had been allied together for some considerable time against the Iroquois, their age-old enemy (JR, 23: 208-224), (Savard, 1996: 102 and 178); (Ratelle, 1993: 32); (Blanchard, 1980: 448).

remain.[12] But Des Groseilliers had no intention of heeding the restrictions of his native partners and the decisive victory he soon won over a band of eleven Iroquois who were warring in the region – "We played the game so ferociously that no one escaped us," (Ra: 147) – gave him every latitude to insist that he accompany his native allies to the territory of the "Cheveux Relevés," where they intended to trade (Ra: 148). The nation of the "Cheveux Relevés" had only recently settled on the shores of another lake,[13] different from the first one: "it is another lake, but not so bigg as that we passed before. We calle it the lake of the Staring Hairs because those that live above it have their hair like a brush turned up" (Ra: 146). We call it the Lake of the "Cheveux relevés" (Ra: 146). This passage and others suggest that the "Lake of the Staring Hairs" was likely what is now known as Green Bay, a vast expanse of water cut off from Lake Michigan itself by a string of islands. As Lake Michigan was the only entranceway known to the French at the time, and it opened onto an unending expanse of water stretching towards the southwest called the *Lac des Puans* (Campeau, 1996: 39 and 45) when, in 1654, Des Groseilliers and the other Frenchman embarked on this body of water – today Lake Michigan – (Ra: 146 and 153), they quite naturally baptized it the *Lac des Puants*, or in English, "the great lake of the stinkings" (Ra: 149). When afterwards they entered on what appeared to them to be a second lake, in view of the great number and proximity of the islands that separated it from Lake Michigan, they gave it the name of the nation that Des Groseilliers was to encounter there, namely, the Lake of the "Staring Hairs," which became Green Bay only after the passage of Father Allouez

---

12. This was *Rock Island*, one of a number of islands that separated Lake Michigan from Green Bay, where the Huron tried to settle after having fled their ancestral territory (Heidenreich, 1997: 106).

13. The "Cheveux Relevés" could not have settled permanently at Green Bay before 1649, since Father Poncet had spent approximately three months among them in their former territory of Manitoulin Island in 1648, and it seems clear that they were forced to settle there (Marie de l'Incarnation, 1971: 379); (HNAI: 760). Moreover, a dramatic conflict nearly led to the disappearance of the Winnebago nation which inhabited the Green Bay region at that time: "Winnebago territory was overrun with Algonquian peoples and remnant Huron from the East fleeing the Iroquois" (JR, 41: 79). Perhaps this refers to the same conflict Radisson speaks of in that region (Ra: 147). The oral tradition of the Winnebagos reports the same events (HNAI: 692).

in the region in 1669.[14] Consequently, Des Groseilliers and that other, still unidentified, Frenchman were the first of their nation to explore Green Bay and Lake Michigan, since it is increasingly certain that Jean Nicolet never travelled in that region (Trudel, 1980).

The "Cheveux Relevés" wanted the two Frenchmen to help them destroy their neighboring enemies, the Potoueatamis, using the powerful weapons they could furnish them. But Des Groseilliers sought rather to negotiate peace between the adversaries, to the gratification of the Potoueatamis whom Des Groseilliers was able to visit that same winter. Through the intervention of the latter band, he made immediate contact with a nation called "Escotecke, meaning fire," also called Mascouten, among whom he spent three months (Ra: 148). The Mascouten mentioned to Des Groseilliers the name of certain neighbors, to wit, the Dakota, "who are very strong with those who war against them" and who live in the vast prairies situated to the west of Lakes Michigan and Superior; the Mascouten also spoke of the Crees, who were settled in the north and numbered among their allies in the conflict against the Dakota (Ra: 149); (HNAI: 725-726).

During the first year of his voyage, Des Groseilliers headed south. In the company of the Huron and the Ottawa, he travelled in summer 1655 as far as a country which would enchant him by its beauty and richness, most probably located to the extreme south of Lake Michigan, close to the Illinois River:

> We embarked ourselves on the delightfullest lake of the world. (...) We meet with several nations, all sedentary, amazed to see us, & weare very civil. The furthered we sejourned the delightfuller the land was to us. (...) those kingdoms are so delicious & under so temperat a climat, plentifull of all things, the earth bringing foorth its fruit twice a yeare (...). I can say that (in) my lifetime I never saw a more incomparable country (Ra: 150-151).

Des Groseilliers apparently encountered there nations living even further to the south, with whom the Huron and the Ottawa had been trading

---

14. "The mission of Saint-François-Xavier, at the Bay of the Puants, does not appear in this edition (of a geographical map). This would indicate that the general outline of our map was already determined in 1669, when *this new territory of the Bay of the Puants received its name*" (Campeau, 1992: 45). It is therefore in 1669, when Allouez notes that the Puants are settled on the shores of a bay distinct from a larger lake that he then calls Lake of the Illinois, that the Lake of the Stinkings becomes the Bay of the Stinkings, or Green Bay.

for many years along the Mississippi and its tributaries.[15] There he heard
speak of a great waterway which led as far as the southern sea:

> Being about that great sea (Lake Michigan), we conversed with people that
> dwelleth about the salt water (the Gulf of Mexico) who tould us that they saw
> some great white thing sometimes uppon the water, & came towards the shore,
> & men in the top of it, (...) I could not imagine what it could be, except the
> *Spaniard*; & the reason is that we found a barill broken as they use in Spaine
> (Ra: 151).

Des Groseilliers tried to convince his Huron partners to go in search of
a number of their people who had fled much farther to the west via the
Mississipi and the Missouri Rivers, to the very confines of the Dakota
(Delâge, 1985: 157). But they declined: "they refused to listen" (Ra: 152). And
so, in the second year, Des Groseilliers returned northwards, hugging the
shores of Lake Michigan where several nations had set up their summer fishing camps (Ra: 152); (Hickerson, 1960: 82-83).[16]

At Makinac, at the intersection of Lakes Michigan and Superior, Des
Groseilliers found himself with Amerindians of three different nations, all
bearing trade goods. The Mascouten wanted to take Des Groseilliers back
south but he refused because he was intent on overtaking the Saulteaux,
more to the west in the vicinity of Lake Superior, where he also hoped to
meet with the Crees (Ra: 154). The Mascouten turned back; Des Groseilliers
promised the Huron that he would rejoin them the following summer at the
island where they had first escorted him; then he convinced the Ottawa to
respect their promise and take him to the Saulteaux territory.[17]

Radisson next introduces a parenthesis to explain the conflict which had
been opposing the Saulteaux and the Dakota for several years. This conflict
between Amerindian nations, and many similar conflicts to which Radisson
was witness in the areas around Lake Superior and Hudson's Bay, reveal the

---

15. "The Hurrons & the Octanacks (...) comes to the furthest part of the lake of the
Stinkings (Lake Michigan), there to have light earthen pots, and girdles made of goat's hair,
& small shells that grow att the sea side" (Ra: 149-150). "In light of various relics found in
several pits, it may be deducted that they (the Huron) used to trade with distant tribes living
south of the Gulf of Mexico" (Vincent, 1984: 56).

16. The route followed by Des Groseilliers is similar to that taken by Joliet and Marquette
from Michillimakinac to Green Bay, to the Mississippi River, then to Lake Michigan, except
that Des Groseilliers did not learn the whereabouts of the Mississippi nor how to reach it
(Campeau, 1994: 44); (Campeau, 1992: 48 and 65).

17. "We contented the hurrons to our advantage with promises & others (the
Mascouten) with hope, and persuaded the Octanack to keepe his resolution" (Ra: 153-154).

connection between the commercial successes that the two brothers-in-law enjoyed and the many conflicts which divided the Amerindians at that time. Although based on rivalries that existed prior to the arrival of the Europeans, these hostilities were stirred up and exacerbated by the introduction of firearms, the establishment of European settlements on American soil and the relentless drive to conduct trade.

Des Groseillers spent the winter 1655-1656 on the south shore of Lake Superior, a little to the west of the meeting place determined in 1653, seeking to evade the Iroquois, who were on the warpath as far as the shores of Lake Superior (Campeau, 1996: 634-635), in the Keewanaw cove and at Ontonagon (Heidenreich; 1997: 107). He was accompanied by a few Saulteaux, Ottawa and Crees, along with a handful of Frenchmen who were already on the scene, apparently associated with another group of Amerindians (Ra: 155). It was at this point that Des Groseilliers obtained directly from the Crees much precious information about Hudson's Bay (Ra: 155) and that he noted their exceptional abilities as hunters (Ra: 155). In spring 1656, before leaving the Crees, he promised to make them a return visit and to join with them against their enemies.[18]

Leaving the south shore of Lake Superior, Des Groseilliers and his Amerindian allies then covered some fifty leagues by land, heading south, to reach a river where they could fish and build canoes. They went down this river as far as the land of the Potoueatamis, at Green Bay, where they stocked up with corn (Ra: 157-158).[19] The group would have thus reached by land one of the rivers that flows into Green Bay or Lake Winnebago, namely, the Menominee or a tributary of the Wisconsin River, before meeting up with the Huron on an island located between Green Bay and Lake Michigan, as had been agreed (Ra: 158); (Heidenreich, 1997: 107). Once there, the two Frenchmen had trouble convincing their Huron and Ottawa allies – who had

---

18. "We arrived then where the nation of the Sault was, where we found same French men that came up with us, who thanked us kindly to come & visit them"; "We weare long there before we gott acquaintance with those that we desired so much, and they in like maner had a fervent desire to know us"; the Crees finally joined up with the Saulteaux "by reason they might trade with those of the Sault & have the Conveniency to kill more beasts", "encouraging those of the North that we are their brethren, & that we would come back & force their enemy to peace or that we would help against them" (Ra: 155, 157).

19. The Saulteaux and the Potoueatami were officially allied as early as 1642, since the time of a Feast of the Dead which Father Allouez attended (Delâge, 1985: 153). At the same place, Des Groseilliers would also have encountered a nation called "Matonenock," which I have been unable to identify.

come in great numbers to trade their pelts – to accompany them as far as Montréal in order to procure firearms, as the Iroquois were blocking the corridor (Ra: 158-159).

The negotiations that took place immediately prior to the departure, as Radisson recounts them, provide a good idea of the organization needed for the Amerindians to launch the great fur trade of 1656, considering the time required to trap fur-bearing animals and to get from one site to another, as well as to establish communications between nomadic bands, constantly on the move, and the vital need to devise a plan for political organization between the nations involved (Hickerson, 1960: 86-87). Des Groseilliers realized that in such times of dirth, the corn flour which he had obtained from the Potoueatamis would be more than welcome to the Amerindians who had come to trade their furs in order to acquire European goods, stock up with corn and eventually reach New France, where they could procure firearms and even more foreign products (Ra: 159). Since Des Groseilliers was anxious to encourage the Ottawa to accompany him, he reserved for them a separate quantity of corn flour, fearing that those also known as the "Staring Hairs" might decide against the difficult and perilous voyage as far as Montréal for lack of food.[20]

However, shortly before the departure, alarming news reached them that the Iroquois had just won a great victory against the Huron. The elders thus felt it prudent to postpone the voyage until the following year, but Des Groseilliers and the other Frenchman refused to abide by their decision. They had no more flour or European goods to trade, "scarcely a knife between the two of us" (Ra: 159) and they feared for their lives, in the midst of Huron and other Amerindians who had exchanged all their possessions, arms and food, against furs, in preparation for this major trading expedition to Montréal. Des Groseilliers and the other Frenchman therefore intervened forcefully during a special council they, themselves, convened (Ra: 159-161). Neither of the two harangues Radisson recounts tells us who spoke exactly, Des Groseilliers, Radisson, or the other Frenchman, but they do reveal a specific approach, a particular situation about which we have little information. The main argument that Des Groseilliers invoked was that the Huron (and perhaps other groups) had exchanged all their

---

20. "My brother (...) putt up a great deale of Indian corne that was given him. He intented to furnish the wildmen that weare to goe downe to the ffrench if they had not enough. The wild men did not perceive this; ffor if they wanted any, we could hardly kept it for our use" (Ra: 158). The context allows for distinguishing two groups of "wild men" the "Cheveux Relevés", in transit, and the Huron and Petun who had recently settled on the island.

French goods against furs and now found themselves defenseless facing the dangerous Iroquois:

> if you have more witt then we, why did not you use it by preserving your knives, your hatchetts, & your gunns, that you had from the ffrench? You will see if the ennemy will sett upon you that you will be attraped like castors in a trape; how will you defend yourselves like men that is not courageous to lett yourselves be catched like beasts? (...), with castors' skins? how will you defend your wives & children?" (Ra: 160).

The two Frenchmen insisted on the vital need to procure firearms and metal articles, while emphasizing their own courageous commitment to defending the Amerindian cause: "I have risked my life to venture this far with you (...). Have you not seen me sacrifice my life with you? Who has given you life if not the French?" (Ra: 160-161). Then, at the end of Radisson's supposed intervention, in a more dramatic tone, the two Frenchmen threatened to abandon their allies and return alone to Montréal: "*doe what you will. For myne owne part, I will venture choosing to die like a man then live like a beggar. (...) Take all my castors. I shall live without you.*" (Ra: 161). According to Des Groseilliers, or Radisson, the aggressive stance adopted by the two Fenchmen in this situation finally rallied everyone to their cause and they were thus able to take command of the expedition towards Montréal (Ra: 162). Perhaps because the displaced native populations lived in constant fear and insecurity, perhaps because they were at war and weakened, or because the whitemen appeared to them spontaneously as exceptional beings – "*They imputing so much power to us*" (Ra: 125) – it seems that a well-armed man, strong and determined as was Des Groseilliers, could in a short space of time acquire considerable authority over populations who were seeking rapid solutions to glaring problems.

Radisson provides a few more precious details about those who were on the trading route in 1656. The group headed by Des Groseilliers was composed of Huron, Algonquins, Ottawa, Saulteaux, Ticacon and Amickoues – all Algonquins nations, longtime allies of the Huron, whom the French soon called globally the Ottawa[21] (Ratelle, 1994: 34). Des

---

21. "We had foure & 20 gunns ready, and gave them to the Hurrons, who knewed how to handle them better then the others. (...) the Algonquins att the other side, the Ottanak, the Panoestigons, the Amickoick, the Dakota, the Ticacon, and we both encouraging them all" (Ra: 64). He adds further on: "We had about 200 men that weare gallant souldiers. The most weare

Groseilliers led this group with audacity and determination against the ambushes laid by the Iroquois on the Ottawa River. More specifically, he had them charge in serried ranks advancing behind bales of beaver pelts that acted as shields against the onslaught of arrows and musket shots; this more European technique proved swift and less costly in human lives and, most importantly, led them to victory (Ra: 63-67). Des Groseilliers' status as native war chief was now beyond question.[22] Finally, they all reached Montréal at the end of August 1656, to the great joy of all the citizens of Montréal who were under siege and famished (Ra: 168).

In brief, it is certain that Des Groseilliers and the other Frenchman reached Green Bay in 1654. Radisson's testimony indicates that the two Frenchmen also accompanied Huron and Ottawa to the far south of Lake Michigan where they met and exchanged with nations who had journeyed up the Mississippi River; these Amerindians showed them objects which Des Groseilliers identified as being Spanish and that came from their land, a place were "it never snows and never freezes." But Des Groseilliers was unable to discover or even identify the waterways which led to the Mississippi River. It is also clear that in 1655 Des Groseilliers and at least two or three other Frenchmen explored the region southeast of Lake Superior, not far from the territory of the Dakota.

Resurgence of the Franco-Huron-Algonquin network

The groups most active in reorganizing the fur trade were therefore the confederated Algonquin nations of Lake Huron who were already experienced traders: the Algonquins, the Saulteaux, the "Cheveux Relevés" and the Amikoues;

Hurrons, Pasnoestigons, & Amickkoick frequented the ffrench for a time" (Ra: 166). These are all Algonquin nations from Lake Huron who were associated with the Huron in the fur trade. The nation of the beaver (Amikouès) belonged to a much larger Algonquin contingent called "Ottawa", who, at the time, occupied the (Manitoulin) archipelago: "people who have come from the nation of the "cheveux relevés" (RJ, 18: 230). The "Ticacon" are also a group of Ottawa close to the French (White, 1991: 66). See also HNAI (769).

22. Following one of those victorious charges, the native allies of the two Frenchmen praised them on their initiative: "Then was it that we weare called devils, with great thanks & incouragements that they gave us, attributing to us the masters of warre and the only Captaynes" (Ra: 164-165). This status of war chief is all the more plausible when the Jesuits describe the lack of determination shown by the Algonquin traders who transported their furs as far as Montréal in 1663: "the Algonquins of that nation are more tradesmen than soldiers, (…) although their number exceeded three hundred, they pretended to attack them (the Iroquois) & remained for several days hard upon that fort, preventing the Iroquois from leaving, yet not daring to launch an attack" (JR, 49: 244).

except that they were to replace the Huron as purveyors of furs as far as Montréal and learn to trade directly with the French. These different nations of the Algonquin tongue had the advantage of belonging to a single confederation that covered a vast territory. In their forced displacements towards the west, these "Ottawa" seemed to have encountered more allies and found more assistance than the Huron. More particularly, they struck better agreements with the horticulturist nations living at Green Bay, near whom – by force or by negotiation – they were able to settle permanently and take advantage of a regular supply of corn and wild oats, to replace the Huron crops.

For the Huron who had virtually monopolized relations between the French and the nations of the Great Lakes prior to 1648, the collapse was brutal. Over ten years, they lost their status of great trading nation, their territory, their wealth, and a goodly part of their power. Now that they were mingled with the Iroquois, or disseminated hither and thither in small, more or less prosperous groups within the Algonquin confederation, their survival as an autonomous nation was threatened, even if several Huron chiefs continued to play a diplomatic role at the highest levels.

A few details about Des Groseilliers

A few traces of Des Groseilliers have been discovered in the judicial archives of Trois-Rivières in regard to violent incidents (Nute, 1943: 20); (Trudel, 1983a: 583). The reader will also have seen that when travelling, Des Groseilliers refused to let his Amerindians partners direct him and, was usually able to convince them to take him where he wanted to go. He practiced the same behavior with the authorities of New France: Des Groseilliers refused to obey Governor Argenson when the latter forbade him to quit the colony in 1659, and he went to France to contest the fines which that same Governor had levied on his fur trade after his return in 1660. The portrait that Father Ragueneau traces of Des Groseilliers, whom he had known well, both on Huron ground and in New France, concurs with Radisson's narrative: "Here is a man capable of anything," he writes, in 1664, "audacious, resilient, opinionated in his undertakings, who knows the country well and who has been everywhere, even to the Huron and to the Outaoüak territories."[23] The assurance of Des Groseilliers is also shown by the title of "General

---

23. Paris, 7 November 1664, BN, Mélanges à Colbert, no. 125, f. 181). Marie de l'Incarnation, who also knew Des Groseilliers well, underscores his great independence on two occasions: "His was a spirit of contradiction and ill-humor", "instead of taking the route that

of the Ottawa Contingent" which he attributes to himself when he goes to recruit hirelings in France, in 1661 (Debien, 1952: 390), a title that he likely chose by analogy with that of "général de la flotte de la Communauté des Habitants" (General of the Company of the Community of Habitants) which Louis d'Ailleboust de Coulonge held before being appointed Governor of the colony (Trudel, 1979: 178).

The strong personality and great independence of Des Groseilliers cast a different light on the personnel with whom the Jesuits surrounded themselves in their Huron missions. Next to the God-fearing yoemen without reproach who were devoted to them and whom the Jesuits praise in their *Relations*, there certainly existed a group of fearless men who assured the safety of the Jesuits and could assist them in their non-religious tasks. Des Groseilliers was probably a redoubtable man, whom the Jesuits had recruited more for his resourcefulness than for his apostolic zeal. Like him there were Radisson and Eustache Lambert, who (the latter) evolved from being a servant to the Jesuits to become commander of a "mobile camp" charged with fighting the Iroquois (Campeau, 1996: 633), or Charles Lemoyne, Guillaume Couture and Pierre Boucher, all of whom possessed most particularly the ability to live, even to shine, in an Amerindian society, as well as to resist cold, fatigue and fear and to hold their own during altercations or when undertaking negotiations essential to positioning the French on the Amerindian geopolitical map. Des Groseilliers had acquired much sagacity under the Jesuits and he put to good use – first for New France, then for England, but always above all else for himself – the methods of effective intervention that he had helped to develop in the Jesuit missions in Huron territory.

Although Des Groseilliers had been a pupil of the Jesuits and long remained one of their closest collaborators, their relations began to deteriorate as of 1656, when Des Groseilliers chose not to reveal all about his voyage to Lake Michigan; then, the situation took a turn for the worse when he

---

the others were accustomed to taking, and where they had worked in vain, he went in the opposite direction, and searched so well that he found the great Northern Bay" (Marie de l'Incarnation: 742 and 874). Des Groseilliers reputation as an audacious individual reached Jean Talon, the notorious Intendant, who, in November 1670, when he learned that two European ships had wintered at Hudson's Bay the previous year, wrote: "Having carefully considered all the nations which could have reached a destination located so far to the North, I am forced to settle upon that of the English which, led by a man called Des Groseilliers, formerly an habitant of Canada, could have resolved to undertake such a perilous navigation of highly uncertain outcome" (Talon, Jean, in RAPQ, 1930-1931: 124).

returned from his second voyage to Lake Superior, where he had become much better acquainted with the interior of the continent than were the Jesuits.[24] Their relations soon reached a point of crass competition. The Jesuits, and others, made every effort to reach Hudson's Bay before Des Groseilliers and Radisson (Wien, 1998),[25] whose small team was in direct competition with the Governor of the colony, the Jesuits and the powerful families who fought over the scant trading revenues during those difficult years. The voyage to Lake Superior demonstrated the courage and exceptional sense of organization that were typical of Des Groseilliers, who knew how to use all he had learned about the values, customs and needs of the Amerindians to bring back to the colony, over a single year, a record quantity of furs. In due course, Radisson would prove a formidable complement to his irascible and independent brother-in-law, both by his talents as a negotiator and by his penchant for the peace-saving approach.

And so, it was a strong-headed individual whom Radisson unconditionally followed over the next sixteen years of his life, from Lake Superior to Hudson's Bay, with sojourns at the Royal Courts of France and England. Certain elements of Radisson's testimony allow us to distinguish between the extreme independence evidenced by Des Groseilliers and his obvious penchant for durable relations with those he sincerely loved and supported. If Des Groseilliers did encourage Radisson to choose the path of radical independence, it appears nonetheless that his brother-in-law followed him more out of fidelity than any strong desire for personal autonomy.

---

24. "My brother and I considered wether we should discover (reveal) what we have seen or no; and because we had not a full and whole discovery, (...) we would make no mention of it" (Ra: 172).

25. "the ffather Jesuits weare desirous to find out a way how they might gett downe the castors from the bay of the north by the Sacgnes (Saguenay), and so make themselves masters of that trade. (...) they weare very earnest with me to ingage myselfe in that voyage, to the end that my brother (Des Groseilliers) would give over his" (Ra: 173). Radisson speaks here of the second Jesuit attempt. Already in 1657, they had tried to reach Hudson's Bay by the North Atlantic (JR, 44: 188), a project quite similar to that which Des Groseilliers carried out in 1668, but which the Jesuits abandoned after the aborted attempt of 1657.

CHAPTER 5

Fourth Voyage: Radisson Accompanies Des Groseilliers to Lake Superior

From 1658 on, the increasingly hostile attitude of the authorities in New France regarding the Iroquois provoked fresh confrontations between them and the French. On his arrival, in summer 1658, the new Governor d'Argenson had to lead several expeditions against the Iroquois who were threatening Québec and Trois-Rivières (Trudel, 1979: 251 and 258). D'Argenson also hastened to reform the Council charged with controlling the fur trade, just as Louis XIV had ordered (Trudel, 1979: 247). These transformations aroused fear and dissatisfaction among several tradesmen of New France. The animosity was so great among members of the Communauté des Habitants (Community of Habitants) and those of the Compagnie des Cent-Associés (Company of the One-Hundred Associates) of France – who were also accusing the Trading Council of collusion and fraud – that the home of the representative of the Company of the One-Hundred Associates in Québec was burned to the ground in 1657 and the son of Péronne du Mesnil, the special investigator sent from France, was assassinated in 1662, in broad daylight on a street of Québec (Trudel, 1979: 243 and 254). This problematic administrative reform marked the beginning of a period of instability and strong rivalry within the fur trade in New France (Horguelin, 1997: 45-90), a situation that prevailed until the mid-1660s, when definitive legislative and administrative structures were instituted in the colony, under the authority of Tracy and Talon.

From 1657 to 1659, Des Groseilliers had to adapt to the new rules, which he and many others had difficulty accepting. No doubt without Governor d'Argenson's knowledge, but perhaps with the assent of the preceding Governor d'Ailleboust – who was pro-Montréal and supported Charles Lemoyne, with whom Des Groseilliers would share the profits of his trading voyage to Lake Superior – Des Groseilliers had succceeded in circumventing the reforms which in fact sought to restrict, indeed to eliminate, the fiscal evasions of the right to the quarter part. He reached an agreement with the Trading Council whereby he would pay only one tenth of his trade pelts as a tax because they were moose, not beaver. (Trudel, 1979: 284). This clever maneuver perhaps compensated for the extraordinary risks Des Groseilliers and Radisson would take in going to the Great Lakes, that same year. In fact, the Iroquois had resumed their forays "with even greater cruelty than before" fomenting fear and disorder throughout the entire colony (Trudel, 1979: 258). That same summer, even the Saulteaux had decided to take the northern route to reach Trois-Rivières and so great was their fear of the Iroquois that they asked "for a French escort when making the return voyage" (RJ, 45: 104).

Autonomous, irascible and determined

Des Groseilliers had first wanted to accompany two Huron to Green Bay, where they were to rejoin their families (Ra: 174). It was on this basis that he had begun discussions with Governor d'Argenson to obtain a leave of absence. But his project met with fierce opposition on the part of several Montrealers and Des Groseilliers had to abandon it.[1] It is true that Des Groseilliers had recently decided to change travel companions and take Radisson with him rather than the anonymous Frenchman of the earlier voyage.[2] This change of partner appears to have created difficulties for Des Groseilliers who not only had to find other Amerindian guides but also sign upon his return from Lake Superior, in 1660, a contract whereby he agreed to share half of his profits with Charles Lemoyne of Montréal. It is therefore clear that by the end of the 1650s, Des Groseilliers was limited in his initiatives and in his profits by a few powerful Montrealers, probably in the orbit of Charles Lemoyne (Nute, 1943: 69).[3]

---

1. "For more assurance, my brother went to Mont royall to bring those two men along (the two Huron). He came back, being in danger" (Ra: 174).

2. "*Both* (Des Groseilliers and the other Frenchman) weare upon the point of resolution to make a journey a purpose for to discover the great lakes that they heard the wild men speak off; yea, have seene before, (…) *he thought I was fitter & more faithfull for the discovery that he was to make*" (Ra: 134).

3. Wien opines that Charles Lemoyne and Des Groseilliers were angling "to become the exclusive supplier of the intermediaries coming from the northern locations" (Wien, 1998: 173). But this alliance of interests seems artificial to me and, in any case, will prove short-lived. "they had left Lake Superior, 100 canoes strong. 40 turned back & 60 arrived here charged with pelts weighing 2 000 000 pounds; they left fully 50 000 pounds in Montreal and

Another conflict opposed Des Groseilliers and the new Governor d'Argenson. It related to the autonomy and the margin of profit which Des Groseilliers could expect to enjoy. D'Argenson agreed to let him leave on condition that he take with him two of his servants and that he share half of his profits with them: "We made the Governor a short reply, and told him that as for us, we knew what we were, the Discoverers (who had arrived) before the Governors" (Ra: 174). Although Radisson faithfully reports their conversation with the Governor, the scathing tone must have angered the young d'Argenson who was already having difficulty in imposing his authority in New France and he forbade them to leave the colony without his permission (Trudel, 1979: 250-251); (Ra: 174).

Little is known about what Des Groseilliers did between his first return from the west, in August 1656, and his next departure, in 1659. Radisson even tries to skirt this period of three years, which has meant that the exact circumstances preceding Des Groseilliers' new expedition remain veiled.[4] It appears that he spent the entire three years in the colony gathering information and preparing for a new expedition to the west. The anticipated departure with the two Huron having been aborted, Des Groseilliers, who seemed determined to reach the Great Lakes that year, took advantage of the arrival of six Saulteaux canoes at Trois-Rivières, via the Saint-Maurice, to immediately communicate the news to Québec and try once more to obtain a leave of absence (Ra: 175). But d'Argenson again imposed conditions that seemed impracticable: he wanted everyone to await the return of the Jesuit Fathers from the Saguenay; "An insane response," Radisson comments, "for once their dealings are concluded, they leave" (Ra: 175).[5] The two brothers-in-law and another Frenchman thus left Trois-Rivières without

---

brought the rest to Three Rivers." (JR, 45: 160). By that contract, the profits resulting from the trade, no matter where on the Saint Lawrence River, were divided in two parts but only a quarter of the furs were to remain in Montréal, a measure that advantaged the intermediaries, merchants and associates of Trois-Rivières. The apportioning was therefore not quite 50/50 (contract published in Nute, 1943: 68). See also Trudel (1984: 298-306).

4. It is imperative to correct the error that locates Des Groseilliers at La Rochelle in the months of May and June 1659, whereas he in fact signed contracts of engagement there *in May and June 1661*. I am indebted to Gervais Carpin for this information; Mr Carpin is examining the immigration networks in New France under the "Cent-Associés" (doctoral thesis, Université Laval, 1999). The article of Debien (1952: 3900-391) is at the origin of this error.

5. The *Journal* of the Jesuits which reports the arrival of the Ottawa who were escorting Des Groseilliers, in 1660, confirms the fact: "arrived the 19th, left the (…) 22nd & arrived in 3. riv. the 24th. left there the 27th" (JR, 45: 160). Hence, the Ottawa stayed three days in Montréal and three days in Trois-Rivières before again setting out.

authorization, by night, to rejoin the Saulteaux guides who awaited them further on along the Saint-Lawrence.[6]

In that month of August 1659, Radisson and Des Groseilliers were thus quite ready to follow the Saulteaux; they were well armed, well supplied and equipped with a well-constructed canoe; they were moreover so determined to leave that they disobeyed the order of both the Governor of New France and the Governor of Trois-Rivières. For what reason?

It is not known if the Saulteaux informed Des Groseilliers that they intended to host that winter the great Algonquin Feast of the Dead or if he already knew this. But it is certain that he saw there a singular opportunity to promote close relations with a great many Algonquin nations already active in the fur trade and to maximize the fruits of his voyage. The Algonquin Feast of the Dead had served over many decades as a way to strengthen existing alliances and to contract new affiliations between the nations who participated in the Great Lakes fur trade (Hickerson, 1960: 81). Father Allouez, who attended one of these celebrations, in 1641, had immediately grasped their political ramifications: "I believed that I had to sieze the opportunity (…) to forge closer ties to these Savages, so as to find, in the future, greater means of promoting the Glory of God" (JR, 23: 208). Des Groseilliers understood therefore the importance and the meaning of this great celebration which, in 1660, looked as though it would prove to have decisive consequences. After the upheavals of recent years, the Saulteaux now wanted to make peace with the Dakota, on the territory to which they had recently migrated. In exchange, they planned to offer them regular supplies of European goods and, to give even greater weight and credibility to their promise, wanted to bring back a number of Frenchmen with them: "We presented gifts to the Savages, who dearly wanted us to accompany them" (Ra: 175).

Why did Des Groseilliers decide to replace his former travelling companion by Radisson? No doubt because he was as strong and resilient as himself and capable of supporting such a long voyage, made under hazardous and difficult conditions. In addition, Radisson already appeared to be an excellent orator, honed in Amerindian customs, as shown by the clever "trick" he had just played on the Iroquois of Gannentaha, a nation he knew intimately; his

---

6. "We went, 3 of us, about midnight. Being come opposit to the fort, they ask who is there. My brother tells his name. Every one knows what good services we had done to the country, and loved us, the inhabitants as well as the souldiers. The sentrey answers him, "God give you a good voyage." "We went on the rest of that night"; "We were well armed, & had a good boat"; "We had a great store of booty" (Ra: 175-176 and 221).

knowledge of the Iroquois would obiously have represented a considerable advantage at a time of Iroquois terror. Radisson had also proved to be a hardened warrior, and was fully acquainted with all the native techniques and military strategies, in short, and was his own master, a prudent yet courageous man. Finally, the young Radisson was a man of conciliation, one able to forge and maintain with ease good contacts and relations; he also readily agreed to play "second fiddle" and leave the initiative to Des Groseilliers whom he respected.[7] As well, the fact that Des Groseilliers and Radisson were brothers-in-law, in a context of confrontations among rival networks competing for influence, helped Des Groseilliers to develop even greater autonomy.

The voyage to Lake Superior

Having left Trois-Rivières at the end of August 1659, Radisson and Des Groseilliers reached Chekamegon Bay, at the extreme southwest of Lake Superior, at the end of October. They wintered with a number of Saulteaux, Wild Oat (or Menominee) and Dakota, on the territory of the latter band (Ra: 194 and RJ, 45: 160). Then, over the winter 1659-1660, they participated in that grand assembly of Algonquin nations during which peace was concluded between the Sioux and the Crees. The two Frenchmen then met individually with the Crees to trade and make separate agreements with them. Finally, at the beginning of summer 1660, Radisson and Des Groseilliers rallied many hundred Amerindians of various nations and conducted them all the way to Montréal, where they arrived on August 19th, (JR, 45: 160); (Nute, 1943: 57-74); (Trudel, 1983: 234-237); (Warkentin, 1996: 43-70).[8] Radisson's narrative about this

---

7. Radisson agreed to play backup roles: "He (Des Groseilliers) desired me to encourage them, which I performed with all earnestnesse"; "as soone as we are lodged we went to fish for more whilst the other kept the house. I was the fitest to goe out, being youngest"; "We overloaded our slide (...) seing my brother so strained, I tooke the slide, wich was heavier than mine, and he mine" (Ra: 181, 195 and 221). It is noteworthy that the young Radisson (24 years old) is still full of enthusiasm and curiosity for travelling, having a passion for exploration, nature and people. The voyage of discovery that Des Groseilliers is proposing to him thus gives Radisson feelings of great satisfaction: "We passed a sault that falls from a vast height. Some of our wildmen went underneath it, (...) & I myselfe had the curiosity (...). The watter runs over the heads with such impetuosity & violence that it's incredible" (Ra: 186); "what a wounderfull thing to see the industrie of that animal (the beaver)" (Ra: 192); "They have a very handsome shoose laced very thick all over, (...) swords and knives of a foot and a halfe long, and hattchetts very ingeniously done, (...) some made of a round head that I admired it," etc. (Ra: 212).

8. The voyage of 1659-1660 lasted twelve months and progressed without incident. This was a time of many lengthy peregrinations, a number of important negotiations, many fresh contacts with new nations and abundant trading. Radisson and Des Groseilliers proved to

3. Route taken by Radisson and Des Groseilliers to Lake Superior

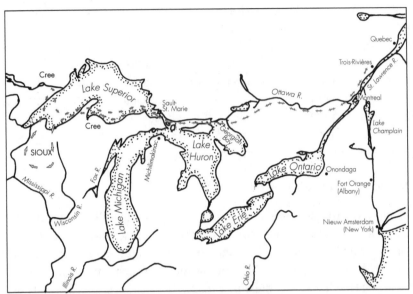

The 1659-1660 expedition went well. The two French explorers and their native allies took the most direct route for their return journey from Montréal to Chekamegon Bay, on the extreme southwest shore of Lake Superior. Again, they learned nothing specific about the Mississippi, despite the fact that they had camped near this great waterway, the whereabouts of which the natives chose not to divulge. It is difficult to determine exactly where Radisson and Des Groseilliers crossed Lake Superior to its north shore or just how far inland they traveled into Sioux territory. What we do know, however, is that their ability to travel more extensively was cut short by their return time schedule. There is consequently little doubt that they would have been unable to reach Hudson Bay that year, as Radisson recounted (according to Harvard's map, 1992).

be dynamic and enterprising voyagers. The descriptive elements of Radisson's narrative confirm the indication found in the archival documents about the length of the voyage: a single year, not two. All the events preceding the final negotiations and the preparations for the departure occur against a background of endless snow, with no temperate season in sight. Radisson's narrative also clearly indicates that the voyage took one year, a fact not found in his indications about lengths of time, which are doctored and incoherent in order to artificially extend the duration of the voyage to two years, but rather in the circumstantial descriptions of places, scenery and climatic conditions, which do not appear to have been altered. The Feast of the Dead, in particular, took place in wintertime, and not in the spring: "shelter to keepe us *from the snow.* (...) *The snow* was taken away," etc. (Ra: 210, 218, 220, 221, 222, 223 and 224). Recall that Radisson and Des Groseilliers were unable to make the detour by James Bay, for lack of time. As recounted by Radisson from the information given them by the Crees.

voyage is a model of precision. The numerous details he reports reveal the evolution of the Amerindian societies in that era of transition, as well as the objectives of the two Frenchmen, and, above all, the way in which they established alliances with several of the Great Lakes nations who had never before encountered Whitemen. Of further note are the coherence of Des Groseilliers' undertakings and the exceptional sagacity with which he employed the extensive though limited knowledge he had acquired about America and her inhabitants to develop the fur trade with the autochthons, to the fullest extent.

Partnership and collaboration

Although the Jesuits were able to take advantage of their status of "sorcerer" to impose their will in certain native communities, despite their meagre secular contribution to community life (Delâge, 1991: 59 and 61); (Vecsey, 1983: 167), the "ordinary" Frenchmen who wanted to acquire power had to integrate much more intimately in those communities. I will thus briefly revisit the integration of Radisson and Des Groseilliers in the Amerindian culture.

On the Ottawa River, between 1654 and 1660, Des Groseilliers was a warrior chief appreciated by the Amerindians for his ironclad confidence, irresistible drive and numerous successes. At times, he decided on direct assault to break through the Iroquois ambushes, for example, when he and his men concealed behind bales of pelts, thereby sacrificing very few of their number (Ra: 181-182). But Des Groseilliers also knew how to make use of the ruse, when, for instance, he thwarted another Iroquois ambush on the Ottawa River (Ra: 184-185); above all, he always remained vigilant despite his impetuosity (Ra: 165). Radisson's arrival crystallized these qualities (Ra: 179-180); henceforth, their team was that much stronger and more resourceful.

The narrative of the fourth voyage offers fresh information about Radisson's intensive efforts to integrate in the Amerindian communities and to espouse their mentality. It is fascinating to hear his assessment of a battle that he, Des Groseilliers, and his Saulteaux allies have just won over the Iroquois:

> They (the Saulteaux) filled their bellyes with the flesh of their ennemyes. We broiled some of it and kettles full of the rest. We bourned our comrades (...). It is an honnour to give them such a buriall. (...) The greatest marke of our victory was that we had 10 heads & foure prisoners, whom we embarques in hopes to bring them into our countrey, and there to burne them att our owne leasures for the more satisfaction of our wives. We left that place of masacre with horrid cryes (Ra: 183-184).

What European would have the stomach to remain like Radisson indifferent to human flesh being plunged into the communal cooking pot or
measure the scale of his victory by counting the number of "heads?" What
European would think to please his dear spouse by bringing her back a few
prisoners for her to braise nonchalantly over the open fire? As for the fero-
cious shrieks uttered by the groups of warriors at the moment of departure, Radisson had become inured to this practice while warring with the
Iroquois; furthermore, it was to his advantage to persevere in this behavior
in order to gain the trust of the Saulteaux band whom he wanted to lead
and upon whose will hung his very survival. Radisson confirms in another
comment the extent to which he felt close to certain Amerindians: "I was
so curious that I asked my dearest friends the name of that stream" (Ra:
188). Radisson's writings also hint at Amerindian influences on such crucial questions as war and hunting.

In war, Radisson affirms that one must risk his life in the company of
Amerindians to earn their confidence and assure a certain fidelity on their
part: "I volunteered my assistance, so they might see how much I wanted to
defend them; this is the only way to gain the trust of these savages" (Ra:
179).[9] In hunting, the passage where he evokes the "reflections" of the geese
that he is trying to bag reveals that he perceives these birds more like thinking creatures, like close relatives of human beings, a conception held by all
the Amerindians but increasingly discredited in Europe:

> the poore creatures, seeing me flatt uppon the ground, *thought* I was a beast as
> well as they, so they come neare me, whisling like gosslings, *thinking* to frighten
> me. The whistling that I made them heare was another musick then theirs.
> There I killed 3 and the rest scared, wich neverthelesse came to that place againe
> *to see what sudaine sicknesse befeled their comrads.* I shott againe; two payed for
> their *curiosity* (Ra: 195-196).

In the eyes of the Amerindians, a good hunter is in fact he who knows
how to detect the *presence* of the animal, he who can discover the game
animal by communicating with its *spirit*. Because of the vital need for food

---

9. Nicolas Perrot, a French interpreter and trader in the Great Lakes territory over the
years 1670-1690, concurs with this: "The nature of the Savages has them leaning more towards those who give them the most and who flatter them without restraint" (Perrot, 1973:
78). Engaging in military action alongside the Amerindians represented the consummate test
of an alliance which could thereafter only gain in strength and endurance.

and the superior capability certain individuals possessed to enter into contact with the guardian spirit of animals, to find them, mollify them, then kill them, hunting became for Amerindians a powerful manifestation of spiritual strength.[10] The vision of Nature that Radisson seems to have developed, that of an entity both tangible and spiritual rooted in a natural territory inhabited by a multitude of supernatural beings, appears to derive from the Amerindian influence (Ra: 189). It is now time to elucidate this Amerindian concept of power, a power in free movement among beings and one which Des Groseilliers and Radisson are keen to seize.

From Trois-Rivières to Chekamegon Bay

After having escaped the Iroquois ambushes, then travelling up the Ottawa River at full speed as far as Lake Nipissing, where they could rest and stock up with supplies, the voyagers progressed without mishap. The group of Saulteaux and Ottawa ("Octanaks") that accompanied the two Frenchmen hugged the northern shore of Lake Huron, stopping at Sault-Sainte-Marie to eat and rest, then continuing along the south shore of Lake Superior towards the west. The group encountered a first allied band "astonished to see us safe and sound once again, admiring the rich merchandise that their confederate brothers were bringing back from the French territory" (Ra: 189-190). A few days later, past the Keeweenaw headland, Des Groseilliers met up with a band of Crees that he knew, who were settled in their winter quarters: "They were overcome with joy at seeing us again. They took great pains with us and called us men so many times, not just once, for having fulfilled our pledge to return to them. We gave them many presents" (Ra: 193). The group finally reached Chekamegon Bay, where the few bands they had met in Lake Superior and who had followed them thus far separated (Campeau, 1992: 43-45 and 65). Des Groseilliers and Radisson

---

10. "Where other hunters failed to find him, I, myself, found the animal. (...) my eyes were as a spy glass beforehand. No animal could hide from me, this is why I was a good hunter" (Proulx, 1988: 58). "The Ojibwas believed that without the aid of the Owners of game animals (the guardian spirits of each species of game animal), individual animals would never be caught (...). If the Owner of a species was insulted or alienated, the hunter would not be permitted to kill, or even find, any member of that species. If the Owner of a species favored a hunter, the Indian would have success" (Vecsey, 1983: 76); "The souls of humans and animals were the continuity, the essential, lasting parts of the person which could transcend the body" (Vecsey, 1983: 62-63).

remained with the Saulteaux who feared they would not be able to find their families, since the Sioux had perhaps scattered or massacred them in their absence. The two Frenchmen decided to build a small fort on site as the Saulteaux, once they knew what to expect, might return to them, in order to transport all the goods to their country, if everything went well, or to assemble a great army and revenge the death of the Saulteaux families, if it proved necessary (Ra: 194-195).

During the twelve-odd days they waited, several Amerindians of the region came to inspect the fort and bring food to the two Frenchmen; they were astounded by the ingenuity of the small fort that the two had erected. Cautious, Des Groseilliers and Radisson allowed only one Amerindian at a time to enter their abode, fearing their covetousness and their considerable number (Ra: 197).[11] On the twelfth day, a few Saulteaux reappeared in the company of some fifty young men of the Menominee nation, come to transport the European goods to their village.

Acquiring power

The conduct of Des Groseilliers and Radisson and the commercial success they achieved during this voyage indicate that they applied with assurance a highly effective strategy that had three objectives hinging on the superior powers which the Amerindians conceded straightaway to the Europeans, once they had appreciated the force of iron and firearms, as well as the selective impact of the epidemics that killed many more Amerindians than whitemen (Delâge, 1991: 61, 65 and 78); (Delâge, 1992: 110); (Havard, 1992: 35-36).

First objective: the two Frenchmen were anxious to remain as long as possible on native territory. Since the Iroquois were more aggressive than ever on the Ottawa, it was to be expected that the Great Lakes Amerindians might hesitate to undertake a trading voyage as far as the colony or be satisfied with only the merchandise that the two Frenchmen and their Algonquin allies had brought them (Ra: 190, 199-200, 208, 213 and 217); (Delâge, 1985: 184). Des Groseilliers and Radisson were well aware that it would take very

---

11. "There is no ignominious act or insult that they are unwilling to forget, if those who insulted them make compensation by offering them substantial tributes. They will sell the life of their closest relatives and even agree to their friends being assassinated. (…) they will engage in wrongful wars and break without cause the peace treaties between nations" (Perrot, 1973: 77).

little – a rumor, a dream, a premonitory sign – to convince the Amerindians to defer their voyage. They also knew that any delay carried risks, because of Amerindian rivalries between those for or against the French – a phenomenon that Radisson had recently noted at Gannentaha – or the incipient envy between rival clans and nations who might fight over the advantageous presence of Europeans in their midst,[12] or because their trade goods and munitions were running low, or again, in anticipation of the conflicts that could break out at any moment among Amerindians, or, indeed, on account of any other unforeseeable event...

Second objective: they wanted to bring back in a single voyage the greatest number of pelts that could be obtained in New France. But to accomplish this, they needed to swiftly make their presence known, take advantage of all the opportunities to trade and, above all, induce the courage of the warriors so that a great many of their number would agree to make the voyage to Montréal. Failing this, the two Frenchmen risked being plundered, taken prisoner, or massacred by the Iroquois positioned along the Ottawa River.

Third objective: they were anxious to establish lasting alliances with the greatest number of Amerindian nations possible. This might well offend certain intermediaries who were jealous of their privileges or favor for others chosen by them, thereby perturbing native relations. The stakes were high, for by entering into direct contact with the beaver-hunting nations, the French could better control the fur trade, maximize their profits and seek to weaken those intermediaries whom they least favored.

Since none of these objectives appeared easy to achieve, Radisson and Des Groseilliers devised an audacious strategy, to ensure their every chance at success.

First of all, impress the Menominee

Radisson and Des Groseilliers had already acquired considerable prestige by reaching Lake Superior safe and sound with their trade goods, thereby providing tangible proof of their commitment to their partners (Boussin, 1997: 78-79). The Menominee also admired the fort they had erected, "call-

---

12. A phenomenon that Richter was able to note in the welcome that certain Iroquois reserved for the early Jesuit missionaries: "Iroquois leaders' initial responses to Jesuits can partly be understood against this background: any material or spiritual benefits, and hence any prestige, which priests might impart rebounded to leaders who developed close ties to them" (Richter, 1985: 4).

ing us devils at every step for having made such a machine" (Ra: 197) but they were even more impressed by the hearty feast with plentiful game birds which Radisson and Des Groseilliers were able to offer them thanks to their own hunt and to the gifts of neighboring Amerindians: "They brought us provisions, thinking we would be half-starved, but they were greatly mistaken, for we had more to offer them than they were capable of eating" (Ra: 197). It remained to consolidate the strong impression they had made on the Menominee, who might have feared or mistrusted them, rather than depend on them and seek their alliance.

The Saulteaux remarked that some of the trade goods had disappeared. Radisson and Des Groseilliers had buried them in a cache, not far from the fort, but, by evoking the support of a particularly powerful spirit in the Algonquin pantheon, they made the Amerindians believe that they had hidden the goods under water, out in the middle of the bay, where the *Underwater Manito*, their guardian spirit, had promised to protect them from rust and thieves (Ra: 197-198). In this way, Des Groseilliers and Radisson spoke not simply in terms immediately understandable to their guests but, more importantly, in a code essential to acquiring social influence among the Algonquins: "No matter the weight of power held by the chiefs, they never forgot that their capacities and skills depended on their relationship with the spirits. The community associated their chiefs with the spirits, as interpreters of the communal will and as instruments of their powers" (Vecsey, 1983: 164). To be recognized as chiefs by the Menominee, Des Groseilliers and Radisson had first to appear to be powerful spiritual intermediaries.[13] This is why they had chosen the Underwater Manito which numbered among the mightiest and most feared of all the spirits: "Each of these spirits had a direct influence on success in hunting and could determine whether or not an individual would survive" (Vecsey, 1983: 73).[14]

---

13. "The Scioux, who had no knowledge of firearms nor of the other instruments they beheld (in the hands of the Ottawa, who had retreated to the region), (…) believed they were spirits, since they knew how to use this iron which had no relationship to anything they possessed, such as stones and other objects" (Perrot, 1973: 85).

14. "As a composite, the Underwater Manito influenced the abundance and availability of land and sea animals. With its numerous underwater allies it controlled all game, witholding animals and fish from its enemies. (…) The Underwater Manito possessed great and dangerous powers. (…) It gave copper to the Indians (…). It was a creature to inspire terror and awe, as well as reverence" (Vecsey, 1983: 74-75). "The fundamental relationships that existed between the Menominee (Wild Oat) and the supernatural can only be understood in terms of power and power gaining. The emphasis was upon securing a guardian spirit to obtain power" (HNAI: 714).

Des Groseilliers and Radisson could well pretend to be the intermediaries of a powerful spirit, in view of the unusual nature of the merchandise they possessed and the exclusive control they had over their firearms,[15] but they nonetheless ran a risk by pretending to hold such great power, since the Amerindians also believed that "a person must never lie as concerns the power of the spirits (...) (nor must he) abuse such power (...) because it might harm him in return" (Vecsey, 1983: 124). They also ran the risk of *deluding* the Amerindians who would be observing them at close range over several months. But the game was worth the candle, or so they believed... In any event, Des Groseilliers and Radisson accorded greater importance to the needs, mentality and values of the Amerindians than did the Jesuits (Delâge, 1985: 208-209). They tried to *fasten* on to the Amerindian culture, to rapidly establish solid commercial and diplomatic alliances with their hosts who had all heard speak of the terrible catastrophe that the Whiteman's religion had triggered on the Huron territory. In consequence, the two Frenchmen apparently said little about the Christian God during their stay at Lake Superior, seeking on the contrary to respect the Amerindian cultural references and customs.[16]

Prior to their departure for the Menominee village, Radisson and Des Groseilliers set fire to the fort in a spectacular way, starting with the lighting system they had prepared to offset any attack after nightfall, made of many bark torches that ignited violently. Once the fort was reduced to ashes, all set out towards the Menominee village located inland, at a distance of five days on foot, without the two Frenchmen having to carry a single thing: "We were Caesars, no one to contradict us" (Ra: 198). Once on site, to create a strong impact on these people who had never before encountered Whitemen and to make sure they would be spoken of "one hundred years later" (Ra: 199), they gave their hosts, who were now quite overwhelmed, three series of presents, while espousing the customary Amerindian metaphoric figures.

---

15. "The fur traders became leaders in their own right because of their guns, wealth, and control over the lives of the Ojibwas. Traditionally Ojibwa leaders showed their power by their wealth; fur traders were wealthier than any of the Ojibwas" (Vecsey, 1983: 165).

16. The initial contacts of Father Menard with the Amerindians who had fled to Chekamegon Bay, in 1660, were unusually cold: "Besides these 'Eleuz' (two elders), Father Menard found the rest of those Barbarians opposed to the Faith (...). The slight hope of converting these people who indulged in all kinds of vices, made him resolve to undertake a new voyage" (JR, 48: 126). "The Ottawa, like most of the allied nations of the Great Lakes, refused henceforth to convert (for fear of drawing upon themselves the misfortunes that the Huron had suffered)" (Charlevoix, quoted in Delâge, 1991: 79).

The first present, a cauldron, was intended for the men, to encourage their inviting all the friendly nations to come and meet with them at the great Feast of the Dead that would be held at the end of winter; then two hatchets were given, to encourage the warriors to fight valiantly; followed by six knives, to stress the greatness and power of the French and their allies, and finally, a sword blade, to emphasize that Des Groseilliers and Radisson were the masters both of peace and of war, in other words, they could assist their Amerindian allies in their daily tasks and also help them vanquish their enemies. The second present was destined for the women; it comprised needles, scrapers, combs, red paint and pewter mirrors, to encourage them to accompany their husbands on trading voyages, when in season, and help them to sew many beaver-skin garments "because the French appreciate them," and last, but not least, so that they might make themselves beautiful and objects of admiration. The third present was for the children, whom Radisson and Des Groseilliers asked to gather in their presence just as an Ojibwais elder prepared to give them a lesson about how to live.[17] After having taken the children under their protection, they flung over their heads a handful of copper rings, tiny bells and glass beads: "You would have admired how they skirmished, each striving to grab the best" (Ra: 200), all this so that they might presently be happy and long remember the generosity of the French, once they reached adulthood.

Then there followed, over a period three days, several Amerindian ceremonies which were intended to ratify the alliance and seal the ties of friendship between the two Frenchmen and their Saulteaux and Menominee allies. Des Groseilliers and Radisson even offered four small presents in acknowledgment of these ceremonies, a manner of indicating that they fully accepted the Amerindian ways of conduct; this conferred upon them a great measure of authority among the Amerindians and pre-eminent standing on their council, in Radisson's words. The two Frenchmen thus found themselves in a position of power, just as they wanted (Ra: 200). In fact, so sure were they of their authority that, shortly thereafter, they abandoned the Saulteaux chief who had conducted them thither, but whom they little appreciated, to take, of their own volition, as adoptive parents, an old man of

---

17. "All the children would be gathered about some respected elder who would tell them how to live, illustrating his points with stories. A consistent theme in these stories was constraint and self-control" (HNAI: 718).

the Menominee nation and his wife – an audacious gesture that no one contested, considering their status of demigod (Ra: 201).

This event illustrates that despite the efforts of Radisson and Des Groseilliers to integrate in the Amerindian culture, by adopting native customs, they had no desire to conform strictly to the Amerindian tradition. They elected for example to excite the children instead of inviting them to practice self-control; they ignored the rule which accorded the "property" of a stranger and his network of contacts to the one who brought him for the first time into a community; they were also relying on the support of two somewhat antagonistic spirits: the Underwater and the Thunderbird Manitos. In all likelihood, these numerous infringements of Amerindian customs were not indiscretions: Radisson and Des Groseilliers were aware that deviant conduct such as that which had been practiced by the Jesuits, who opposed native rites and native spirits, proved at the same time the superior force of those who dared in such a way to transgress the rules with impunity and even to defy the traditional spirits.

Des Groseilliers and Radisson were therefore communicating a very clear message to the Amerindians, a cry for change, for an evolution away from a tradition they were prepared to respect but which they also believed should be *transformed*, albeit in less radical fashion than the Jesuits. By means of their actions and their words, they were affirming that they had something else to ask of the Amerindians, something *more* to offer them: *more* power, *more* furs, *greater* well-being and *greater* cohesion between the nations who might wish to participate in the great pacific project that they were proposing to them, namely the large-scale commerce of furs (Hickerson, 1960: 93). It is therefore in a rather restrictive sense that one should view the constant concern of Radisson and Des Groseilliers to conform to the Amerindian culture, which they adopted above all else, in order to be accepted, to *communicate* with their native partners and to establish good relations with them. They nonetheless told them unqualifiedly that America was changing and that now they had to appeal to the powerful spirits coming from Europe if they were to procure iron and so many of the other useful and efficient objects that could help them achieve a better life.

Radisson and Des Groseilliers manifested exceptional skill in negotiating a sphere of agreement which benefitted them, while at the same time satisfying native partners with whom they hoped to develop long-standing relations, such as the Saulteaux and the Crees.

Braving winter

At the beginning of winter, the many hundred Saulteaux and Menominee in the village scattered in small groups to better cope with the difficulty of obtaining sufficient food supplies for the winter months. The two French-men stayed behind in the company of some sixty Amerindians from a na-tion that Radisson does not identify and, very soon, the overabundant snows rendered hunting impossible, provoking a grave famine. Radisson evalu-ates at five hundred the number of Amerindians who died of hunger in the region that particular winter, while they themselves just barely avoided the same fate (Ra: 203-206). This dramatic event must have sown doubts in the mind of the Amerindians who were probably wondering if the extraordi-nary powers that the two Frenchmen seemed to hold were not, in the end, directed against them.[18] And, in fact, there was a real danger that the Saulteaux, the Menominee and the other Algonquin nations affected by the famine might view these two Frenchmen as being the evil instigators of their misfortune. It can be said overall that the force with which Des Groseilliers and Radisson intervened throughout the entire voyage was aimed precisely at avoiding such a reversal of situation. To everywhere flaunt and give proof of their power ensured that their hosts would not decide to take reprisals against them before having given it considerable thought, since the Amerindians had no wish to incur the wrath and vengeance of their powerful guardian spirits (Vecsey, 1983: 148). The status of the two French-men – good or bad, powerful or not? – appeared to remain ambiguous in the eyes of the Amerindians.[19] The fact that they had survived the famine

---

18. "Ideally, a shaman used his skills for the benefit of individuals and the community (...) and thereby increased the spiritual power and the physical well-being of his people. But a sha-man could also use his talents in harmful ways (...) thus the line was fine between a revered re-ligious figure and a detested sorcerer. (...) Community attitudes depended on the uses to which he put the forces at his command (Richter, 1985: 5). "certain individuals, endowed with an uncommon power, used it in an evil way by provoking imbalances (...). This harmful use of talents was considered to be one of the greatest crimes, and the identifiction of the instigators could lead to their being executed" (Clermont, 1988: 63).

19. Des Groseilliers did not appear to be affected by the famine because of the beard which hid the scrawniness of his face; seeing him thusly, the Indians:"said that some Devill brought him wherewithall to eate." Radisson, though, seemed to suffer like them, "For me that had no beard, they said I loved them" (Ra: 206). In the mind of the Amerindians, it was normal that the elder have more power than the younger: "One's power increases as he or she grows older" (HNAI: 715); despite the famine, the duo Des Groseilliers/Radisson continued to enjoy many advantages for having maintained credibility and a lofty status among the Algonquin nations in their entourage.

likely contributed to regilding their "image," yet their allies now had excellent reasons to mistrust them, since they had been unable or unwilling to save them from the horrors of that severe famine.

The Feast of the Dead

At the beginning of winter, the French and the Saulteaux had dispatched a number of emissaries to invite as many nations as possible to the Feast of the Dead, to be held a few moons later and on which occasion the Saulteaux and the two Frenchmen were to appear in a body to explain everything the "devils" – to wit, the spirits – might command them to say, "at which point (they) would offer them presents of peace and of union" (Ra: 201-202). Shortly after the famine ended, most likely in February 1660, eight Sioux emissaries came to meet with the Saulteaux to agree officially that the Algonquin feast be held on their territory and to lay the foundations for an alliance with the French.

In accordance with their custom, the Sioux emissaries offered the two fabulous whitemen, whom they were seeing for the first time, food and clothing. They massaged and greased their legs, then smoked with them the calumet reserved for important occasions, before throwing an abundant quantity of tobacco on the fire, in sacrifice to the spirits. The following day, Des Groseilliers and Radisson responded to their presents. To appear worthy of their reputation, they had a platform built for their purposes (Ra: 208). Then they replaced the feathers that decorated the calumet of the Sioux emissaries with twelve metal blades which they placed in like manner. Next, they placed the calumet against a steel hatchet that had been thrust into the ground alongside all their firearms, which were bolstered by wooden supports and lined up in order, to wit "5 guns, two musquetons, 3 fowling-peeces, 3 paire of great pistoletts and two paire of pockett ons"[20] (Ra: 196). By means of an interpreter (the Sioux tongue was of a different linguistic family than that of the Algonquin or the Iroquois), Radisson and Des Groseilliers accepted the presents of the Sioux, whom they solemnly took under their protection, assuring them that they would defend them as brothers, killing all their enemies. Finally, they substantiated their words with a very special sacrifice of tobacco by flinging an entire handful of gunpowder

---

20. According to Radisson, these firearms represented "the Gods of the earth among those people" (Ra: 195).

on the fire! The explosion was stronger than anticipated, projecting fire-brands in every direction; the Sioux took to their heels: "one ran in one direction, the other in another, for they had never seen so violent a sacrifice of tobacco" (Ra: 209). Radisson and Des Groseilliers had to fetch them from the huts where they had taken refuge to reassure them as to how they would use their power, in positive ways only to assist them.

This "aggressive" strategy conferred on the French a great ascendancy over the Sioux, who immediately sought to negotiate an alliance with them, "believing (...) that we were the Devils on earth. Then followed banquets during 8 days" (Ra: 209). As extravagant as may appear the strategy employed by Radisson and Des Groseilliers, it seems that it was fair game among native sorcerers who sought to manifest their power by resorting to this type of artifice.[21] The Jesuits report the instance of an Iroquois sorcerer who,

> to show that his remedies not only cured the sick, but could also revive the dead, he took from his pouch a tiny dead squirrel which he held secretly attached by the end of the tail (...) each one seeing it dead, he applies upon it his medicines, then pulling the cord as subtly as he can, he makes it enter his pouch and it appears resuscitated to the eyes of the spectators. (...) all this is done to cast out from young warriors the fear of being wounded in war, since they will find so sovereign a remedy. (Campeau, 1996: 878)

Even the Huron, at the Feast of the Dead of 1641, seem to have put to good use the contacts they had developed with the French to show that they had thus become *extraordinary*, beyond the pale. During a skill-testing competition where the men had to reach the summit of a smooth pole coated with grease, to win a prize – and no one succeeded – a Huron cheated by notching the pole with his metal knife and thereby easily hauling himself up right to the top before taking the prize, then departing the feast in cavalier fashion to the hoots of the crowd: "This disorder incited the Algonquin Captains to make a public complaint, (...) the Huron taxed themselves in the form of a present of porcelain, in reparation for this injustice" (JR, 23: 214). There is no doubt however that in this little game of who can impress

---

21. "Rival leaders attended one another's performances in order to learn each other's tricks and perhaps to expose a rival as fraudulent. (...) the Ojibwa specialists had to develop their procedures and tricks and constantly add to their repertoire, in order to show increased powers" (Vecsey, 1983: 163).

whom, the Europeans turned out to be the big winners, thanks to their cannons, guns, iron and huge ships, without counting other smaller marvels such as clocks, realistic images, mirrors, spectacles, and even writing... which magically carried afar words and thoughts.

Two or three weeks later, eighteen different nations gathered around the Saulteaux and the French to celebrate the peace and the common alliance, old as well as new, among all the nations present[22] (Hickerson, 1960: 92). Radisson describes the arrival of the Sioux delegation, the costumes, the dancing and the ceremonies in great detail and with great intensity, further proof of his keen sense of observation and talent as a storyteller and narrator (Ra: 211-212). But I shall concentrate more on the negotiations and the portentous issues at stake over the course of this feast, which Radisson has recorded and explained with great lucidity.

Stakes and negotiations

After the lengthy discourse of welcome given by the chief of the Saulteaux, Des Groseilliers and Radisson were called in the usual way of their being offered four presents, each one bearing a message, to the council to hear what the Sioux chiefs had to tell them.

First present: the Sioux have come to offer their sacrifice to the French, who are masters of all things, they have come to place themselves under the protection of the French, inviting them to come to their country, where all has been readied to receive them.

Second present: they are prepared to die for their new Algonquin allies and will keep the peace with them. They bid them welcome to their country and say they are pleased to celebrate their Feast of the Dead in the land of their allies.

Third present: the entrance to the Fort must be kept open so that they may go out to defend their women and their lands against the Crees, for since time remembered "they have been recognized as true and hardened warriors, (...) who would show by their actions that they were as courageous as their ancestors" (Ra: 214). They are affirming their capacity and their will to combat the Crees.

---

22. Heidenreich believes that the Feast was held in the Thousand-Lakes region, in Minnesota, in the spring (Heidenreich, 1997: 111).

Fourth present: they nonetheless ask for the advice and assistance of the French in order to choose between peace and war, even if they reaffirm their greater readiness to go to war and their will to procure firearms since in their view, "the only way to achieve victory was to have a thunderbolt, by which they meant a shotgun"[23] (Ra: 214).

The two Frenchmen did not reply until the following day, after having participated in a great feast organized by the Sioux, where they arrived with great pomp preceded by four men bearing their shotguns (which they had loaded only with gun powder to avoid any accident). By way of a crown, they wore "a role of porkepick" and they again took their place on a raised platform, covered with bearskins brought there by four comely young women. One of the elders who came to smoke the calumet with them declared that never in all his life had he known such a happy day, to at last be able to meet "these men whose words make the earth tremble," he then offered them his unconditional submission: "You are our masters; dead or alive you have full power over us, and may dispose of us as you will" (Ra: 215). In the harangue that followed, Radisson and Des Groseilliers declared once again that they were taking the Sioux as brothers and that they were going to protect them. Following this, to prove their mighty power, they fired their twenty rifles, in immediate succession; then they unsheathed their sword and their long knife to show the entire assembly that they were prepared to defend themselves, against all odds, "where struck the men with such terror that knew not if they were better to flee or to remain." Finally, they flung another handful of gun powder into the fire "to make more smoke and louder noise" (Ra: 215). What a demonstration of power for those who had never before seen whitemen nor heard firearms!

The next day, Radisson and Des Groseilliers responded officially to the Sioux proposal by offering five presents. The first of these confirmed that they agreed to ally with the Sioux, not only as brothers, but more particularly as fathers, in other words, they promised to act as arbiters and advisers in their conflicts, as well as to supply them with European goods to enhance

---

23. There existed a "natural" association between the guns and the *Thunderbird Manitos*, "who manifested themselves through thunder and lightening (...). Thunderbirds influenced the game of the air, all birds. The Ojibwas made offerings to the Thunderbirds to obtain success in hunting fowl of all kinds" (Vecsey, 1983: 75). Since firearms were also excellent tools for hunting game birds, the connections between the shotguns and the spirit of the Thunderbird appeared to be multiple and thus very powerful.

their well-being, reminding them that they had come from afar not to kill them but rather to help them live. The second present expressed their desire to see universal peace reigning in the Great Lakes territory, and even their *will* to establish that peace: "we shall settle all affairs so that we may see universal peace reign over the entire earth; (...) he who first shatters the peace we (...) shall grind to powder with our heaven-sent fire" (Ra: 216). And, in fact, the third present sought to *compel* both the Sioux and the Crees to accept that peace. More graciously, they offered a fourth present to thank the Sioux for allowing them to freely move about their territory. And finally, the fifth and last present was intended to encourage the women to receive them in their dwellings and give them food. Last of all, the two Frenchmen distributed a few additional gifts to the chiefs, in particular to the one who had spoken in their favor with the greatest enthusiasm; that chief received a hatchet rather than a sword. The Sioux accepted these presents and therewithal the messages they inferred, so that Radisson was able to leave without further delay at the head of some fifty native ambassadors to meet up with the Crees and advise them that the two Frenchmen had just established peace between them and the Sioux, which meant they could now join in the Feast of the Dead. In all, the ceremonies would have spanned fourteen days and assembled close to two thousand persons, with Radisson and Des Groseilliers continuing to play a central role in the proceedings.[24]

The duration, pomp and scale of the ceremonies on that occasion, as described by Father Allouez (1641), Radisson (1660) and Nicolas Perrot (1670-80), seem a good indication of the transformations these communities were undergoing; they had to learn throughout the XVIIth century how to better communicate amongst themselves and better coordinate their actions, to master and share new and coveted hunting territories, to assure their defense against rival nations, at times, better armed, and to constantly negotiate their part in a yet unstable and changing fur trade. The alliance and the peace were therefore the two major themes exploited by Radisson and Des Groseilliers during the Feast of the Dead of 1660 as a foundation for the exchanges of furs and European merchandise between the French

---

24. This is indeed possible in view of the commercial significance of this feast and the privileged treatment that Father Allouez had received there, in 1641: "The second Assembly was that of the Huron Nations, where the Nipissiriniens hosted the first Session, giving us the supreme honorary titles, & marks of affection, and these greater than to all their confederated bretheren" (JR, 23: 220).

and the allied nations present, for these themes bridged their preoccupations and served the interests of the two parties.[25]

But, what exactly is hidden by the digressions of the native chiefs who, in Radisson's words, qualify the brothers-in-law as "terrible men whose words make the earth tremble" or as "masters of peace and war?" What is the real status of these two Frenchmen in the eyes of the many thousands of Amerdindians surrounding them?

An understandable reaction on the part of the Amerindians

The Amerindian interpretation of the whiteman's great power seems coherent. The voyageurs and lay tradesmen they encountered, even the missionaries, employed a language that was relatively familiar to them and they discovered in their own cultural traditions all the baggage they needed for a plausible and correct reading of the transformations they saw occurring around them. Moreover, in their mentality and traditions, they even disposed of the usual prescriptions as to the most expedient conduct to adopt in such circumstances in order to mitigate and take advantage of the transformations under way. The firearms, whose spectacular effects they well knew, persuaded the Amerindians of the Great Lakes to attribute to the Europeans a power superior to their own, since apparently they could control such mighty spirits as the "Thunderbirds" whose manifestations took the form of thunder and lightening.[26] When Des Groseilliers and Radisson told the nations gathered together at the Feast of the Dead that they had come afar to help them *live,* they were referring to a more bountiful hunt, thanks to hatchets, knives and guns, and to a more expedient domestic existence by means of the scrapers, needles and iron knives that they brought to the women, and finally to greater success at war thanks to iron weaponry

---

25. The alliance: "acknowledging you for our brethren and children," "lead them to the dance of Union." The peace: "see an universall peace all over the earth," "If they should continue the warrs, that was not the meanes to see us againe in their Countrey" (Ra: 216-217). By this means, Radisson and Des Groseilliers inaugurated the official policy of the French in the region for the next one hundred years: "western Indians regarded Onontio and the Frenchmen who followed him as their allies, protectors, suppliers, and as the mediators of their disputes. Or, in Algonquian terms, Onontio was their father" (White, 1991: 36).

26. Perrot confirms these associations: "The Ottawa fired the few rifles they possessed, and the noise these made so confounded them that they believed it was lightening or thunder which they now controlled to exterminate anyone they wished to" (Perrot, 1973: 86).

and firearms. These many reasons explain why the nations in attendance accorded a superior status to the two Frenchmen, "because we were keeping them alive with our goods" (Ra: 213).

In my view, the globally coherent perception of the Amerindians seems to go even further. For the ability to make such a powerful spirit as the Thunderbird enter into a metal tube and then tell him exactly when and where to explode obviously meant possessing a mighty power, in particular, that of knowing how to *fabricate* this extraordinary object. The Amerindians very quickly realized at the sight of their rusty hatchets and their broken rifles, or when they lacked ammunition, that the whitemen had infinitely more *control* than they over these new and fascinating implements. Moreover, since no arms nor munitions factory existed in America, such merchandise arrived by sea from faraway lands, on ships that the Amerindians could never have built... These European goods were therefore imbued with an aura of the "beyond," a mysterious "elsewhere" which might well encompass many new or different spirits and engender a host of fantastic speculations.[27]

In any event, that winter, in a territory southwest of Lake Superior, the Sioux and Algonquin nations were responding one and all to Des Groseilliers and Radisson as if they were powerful spiritual intermediaries, or even spirits of a new order. The priority for these Amerindians was certainly to meet these Europeans, to speak with them and to observe them, in order to better comprehend the legends surrounding them. Consistent with their usual behavioral patterns, based on the giving and receiving of presents, the barter and the ritual commerce when negotiating alliances, the Amerindians who encountered Radisson and Des Groseilliers had first of all to respect them to avoid their wrath, then seek to ally with them by offering them

---

27. The case of iron is more disputatious. The Amerindians who saw on site the work and the techniques of transformation might have sought to appropriate this "advanced technology"; but only a few bands did in fact attempt to do this. It is therefore possible that the traditional spiritual interpretation, that of a powerful spirit whose alliance must be sought by the multiplication of exchanges, would have largely supplanted a purely technological interpretation which may well have represented a conceptual audacity for the Amerindians of that era. Despite the few cases mentioned by Delâge (1985: 168-169) and Calloway (1997: 168-169), who also believe that the whiteman was better off discouraging such technological transfers, it would appear that a sizable number of Amerindian nations invested much more energy in acquiring these objects themselves, by means of commerce and trade, than in seeking the techniques and knowledge needed to fabricate them.

presents, in the hope that the Frenchmen would in return offer them a present, such as favorable consideration. Since the ritual exchange was reciprocal, or else based over a long period of time on a more concrete exchange, such as the barter of meat and food grains between nomadic and horticulturist nations, the Amerindians, who were exhorted by Des Groseilliers to devote all their energies to the fur trade, could quite easily incorporate this activity among their habits and their customs, provided that the French respond to their most pressing expectations (Jennings, 1984: 84).

Even if the two cultural orbits did meet and to some extent overlap, they functioned nonetheless in different ways, each wed to divergent conceptual systems: an imperfect arrangement that led to major distortions which Radisson illustrates with a rather amusing example. The two Frenchmen were working the fur trade with an Amerindian of an unidentified nation when Des Groseilliers gave that man a holy picture of a kind much admired by the Amerindians; the picture represented a donkey upon whose back Mary and Jesus were seated, with Joseph guiding them on foot. Des Groseilliers pointed his finger at the donkey saying "*tatanga*," which means buffalo, to offer his interlocutor a familiar frame of reference since that individual had no knowledge of donkeys. All at once the Amerindian burst into tears and tore at his hair, gesticulating like a condemned man "until he was covered in sweat, and (he) drenched the other savages present with his tears." The two Frechmen were perplexed until at last the man came to his senses telling them they must be devils to know in detail not just the present but also the past. He then indicated that the picture given him by Des Groseilliers represented his own wife and son, who had been captured four years earlier by the nation of the Ox, "he took the donkey for the nation of the Ox, the Virgin Mary, for his wife, Jesus was his son, and Joseph, himself, all the while saying 'Here I am wearing my long robe, searching for my wife and my child'" (Ra: 228). This misunderstanding worked in favor of the two Frenchmen, and yet with communications being so confused and finding themselves in such extraordinary situations and times, the pair had to count on ever *wider powers* to avoid any faux pas that might be seen to provoke a famine, an epidemic, a military defeat or quite simply the dream of some eminent individual. In making a show of vast powers, Des Groseilliers and Radisson were taking care that no one could call for their captivity or execution with impunity. At this other end of the world, they believed that their best defense remained the offensive.

In short, during the early weeks of their stay in the territory southwest of Lake Superior, it is quite probable that the two brothers-in-law enjoyed the almost godly status that Radisson evokes: "We were Caesars." For, in fact, they held a greater technological power than their hosts and they were well and truly the first Europeans to directly supply the Amerindians of that region with European goods; everything contributed therefore to making them appear to be figures of great prestige in the eyes of the Great Lakes Aboriginals. Moreover, the alliance that certain nations such as the Saulteaux, the Octanaks and, more particularly, the Iroquois, had already established with the whitemen *actually* procured for them more power and prosperity. The strategy of the Amerindians whom Radisson and Des Groseilliers had come to know was therefore quite simple: they recognized the power of the Frenchmen, they agreed to bend to their will, at least for a time, and they hoped soon to glean concrete advantages from that association, be they metal articles, hopefully firearms, and, at the very least, the "tactical" support of the French against their enemies.

Living with is knowing... or the demanding life of a superman

The Algonquin nations believed that no one individual enjoyed privileged relations with all the spirits, all the forces that determined the survival and prosperity of their communities. This meant that no chief could alone represent all the power which the community needed, nor could he exercise or monopolize all the power in a given community. A man endowed with such power would have been a superman. And clearly, the nations that Des Groseilliers and Radisson frequented over the winter 1659-1660 quickly realized that these two Frenchmen were men not unlike themselves, in any case, that they were certainly not supermen. They soon ignored the opinion of the two Frenchmen as to certain questions and tended to settle issues in their own way. The peace imposed on the Sioux and the Crees, for example, dissatisfied one and all. Then too, the Octanaks, who were trading in their own right in the region, detested the habit the two Frenchmen had acquired of freely visiting all those with whom they wished to meet or all those who sought to meet with them: "They reproached us for it, saying that we should trust no one with whom we were unacquainted" (Ra: 227).

At this stage of the voyage, as the two Frenchmen had achieved almost all their objectives, they had less need of the *additional power* that their demonstrations of force had procured. They had negotiated several alliances and traded with some twenty Algonquin nations and with the Sioux; they had even kept their promise to come back and help the Crees. In such ways, they were re-embellishing the image of the French in the Great Lakes after their bitter defeat on Huron territory, first by speaking of peace and trade but, above all, by bringing with them the iron-made articles desperately needed by their allies to wage war against the Iroquois. In all likelihood, Radisson and Des Groseilliers no longer had much interest in "pressuring" their partners nor in offending their susceptibilities; and so, they became more docile, more discreet, in preparation for the return voyage.[28]

As to the dispute between the Sioux and the Crees, it was so rancorous that the two brothers-in-law changed their plans and ceased wanting to impose peace, now that they had profited from a few months of reprieve to ally and trade with both of these nations. Moreover, when they decided to return to the Crees on the north shore of Lake Superior, in spring 1660, they felt it preferable to say nothing to either the Sioux or the Saulteaux: "We resolved to better cover our tracks, and to hide our intention as if we were heading out to hunt" (Ra: 224). It may be supposed that the French presence in the region only served to inflame the conflicts between rival nations, since the dispute between the Sioux and the Crees involved hunting territories rich in beaver which both wanted to appropriate, without however remaining there all year long (Hickerson, 1960: 86). In summertime, the Sioux spent several months in the prairies southwest of Lake Superior, where they hunted bison, while the Crees fished and hunted at James Bay. But in winter, they crossed one another increasingly often in the same forests surrounding Lake Superior, where they hunted the finest beaver in the world, according to Radisson (Ra: 220); (Perrot, 1973: 92); (Havard, 1992: 25). The stakes were therefore considerable and the desire to make peace that Radisson and Des Groseilleirs had expressed carried little weight; as soon as the two Frenchmen left the region, war broke out once again between these two nations.[29]

---

28. "We said yea, (...) if we came to that sea (James Bay) we should warre against them, becaus they weare bad nation" (Ra: 227; see also Ra: 225).

29. This conflict between Amerindian nations and many others in the Great Lakes region, would continue over many more decades (White, 1991: 15-20).

Radisson would encounter this type of competition, this hatred and envy among nations and rival clans everywhere he went in America and in Europe, as much in "civilized" countries as in "savage" lands, in the bush and at Court: "You can see by this that envy and more envy reigns everywhere among these poor nations who are as savage and barbarous as courtiers" (Ra: 225). Very harsh rules structured the social spaces that Radisson occupied, both in America and in Europe; quite often, the law of the jungle prevailed.

Despite the political disagreements that arose and the many incidents that occurred between the two Frenchmen and their native partners, the alliance held firm. Radisson and Des Groseilliers both possessed almost untouchable leadership qualities. They remained negotiators for peace and victorious warriors, as well as agents for circulating wealth, who were viewed as a vital source of prosperity; in short, theirs were the qualities necessary to preserve a commanding status in a native community.[30] The nations of Lake Superior therefore must have continued to accord a place in their councils to the two Frenchmen, where the latter could try to convince their native audience of the validity of their proposals and their opinions, indeed in the same way as anyone else who might aspire to lead those communities.

It was thus in the capacity of chiefs of war and of commerce that Radisson and Des Groseilliers spoke out at the end of the voyage when the time came to encourage their allies to return with them in strong number to Montreal:

> All men of courage and vallour, lett them fetch commodities, and not stand lazing and be a beggar in the cabbane. It is the way to be beloved of women, to goe and bring them wherewithall to be joyfull. We present guifts to one and to another for to warne them to that end that we should make the earth quake, and give terror to the Iroquoits if they weare so bold as to shew themselves. (Ra: 228-229)

---

30. In the words of Jean-Marie Therrien, the overriding functions of the chiefs are: "to declare war, to negotiate peace, to act as an agent for circulating wealth, to protect customs, to direct feasts and ceremonies, to repair the natural and social order"; more particularly, the chiefs exercised their power by dint of persuasion, by the spoken word (Delâge, 1988: 160). Among the Saulteaux and their Great Lakes allies, "The leaders (...) were fiercely proud and individualistic persons who proved their closed relation with the manitos by their successes in hunting, curing, and warring. Each one (...) considered himself (...) superior to other humans and competed with other leaders for community status" (Vecsey, 1983: 163). According to these many criteria, Radisson and Des Groseilliers seemed to be excellent candidates for the office of chief, albeit in a highly competitive social environment.

In due course, they were able to assemble seven hundred persons; and so, a veritable fleet numbering some one hundred canoes of many different nations got under way in mid-summer 1660 (Ra: 229). Unfortunately, that which Des Groseilliers and Radisson feared soon came to pass when the hundreds of Amerindians they were accompanying met with a canoe manned by seven Iroquois on the prowl in Lake Superior. They chased them without success but this encounter, coupled with the rumor abroad as to the rallying of a huge Iroquois army, once more persuaded the Amerindians gathered in council that it was prudent to defer the voyage. Des Groseilliers and Radisson, frustrated "to see such a fleet and such an opportunity go up in smoke," tried to convince the chiefs that at all costs they had to proceed. To no avail. They no longer had the power to impose their will; and their intervention was even called into question, "saying that we were worse than the enemies by persuading them to court massacre" (Ra: 231).

Twelve days later, once the terror provoked by the Iroquois encounter had somewhat dissipated, just before the various groups were to go their separate ways, the two Frenchmen again attempted to convince their partners during a special council they had convoked. This time, they did not seek to impress their partners, nor to impose their will, rather they tried to reason with them. They offered them straightforward, concrete arguments to convince them that the Iroquois menace paralyzing the expedition was groundless. To begin with, they opined that since these Iroquois had attempted to carry away all their belongings with them in their flight – cooking pots, hatchets and guns – they did so because it was impossible for them to replace these articles by recourse to the moot army which, in any case, must have disappeared if, indeed, it existed – unless of course the Iroquois had renounced attacking them, in view of their great number. In either case, they concluded, the Iroquois menace was nothing but blather, the passage was clear as far as New France and they absolutely had to take advantage of the conjuncture since they were strong in number, powerful and carrying great quantities of furs... "Our arguments were heard and put to execution. The following day we embarked" (Ra: 231). Without any abuse of power or recourse to trickery, the two traders had managed to convince their allies that it was in *their own* interest to make the voyage that year, except for the Crees, since a new and unfavorable omen had convinced them, once and for all, to turn back.[31]

---

31. On account of the Iroquois, Nicolas Perrot was also constrained to authoritatively encourage the Ottawa to continue the trading voyage as far as Montréal: "That immense

Fortunately, the Iroquois army, indeed massed on the Ottawa River in May 1660, had encountered the small contingent led by Dollar des Ormeaux and lost a number of warriors; this they interpreted as their own ill omen and they scattered. The Amerindian fleet that the two brothers-in-law were conducting was thus able to reach Montréal August 19, 1660, without mishap, as promised, bringing back to the colony an impressive quantity of furs. The merchants who were getting ready to return home to France empty-handed and bankrupt were delighted:

> God has sent the Merchants for more than one hundred and forty thousand pounds of beaver, by the arrival of the Outaouak, who had sixty canoes full. This blessing from Heaven arrived just when these gentlemen wanted to leave this country, believing that there was nothing more to be done for the trade. Had they left, we would have had to leave with them; for without the correspondences that are maintained to promote the trade, it would not be possible to subsist here. (Marie de l'Incarnation, 1971: 637)

"Home Sweet Home" is not French

It is easy to assess the effectiveness of Radisson and Des Groseilliers by comparing the results they obtained with those of the eight Frenchmen who accompanied the same group of Amerindians in the west. The seven French traders (minus Father Ménard and a Jesuit yeoman who perished during the voyage) only returned three years later to Montréal, at the head of a scant thirty-five canoes (Campeau, 1994: 39). Per person/year, the yield of these traders is twenty times less than that of Radisson and Des Groseilliers.[32] It is equally easy to assess the impact of a trading venture such as that of 1660 on the economy of New France by comparing the annual balance sheets for that period. In 1659, the revenues from the fur trade proved insufficient to balance the colony's budget, despite a successful venture in the upper Saint-Maurice; then in 1661, the tax on beavers returned not more than three-fifths of the sum for the preceding year, which generated a surplus of 5 000 pounds on the current budget, thanks to the voyage of Radisson and

---

contingent of Ottawa already appeared shaken on seeing them (the Iroquois) and when the French told them that many other Iroquois bands were hunting to the South, they wanted to abandon (the project) at once. At that point, I had to reproach them their cowardice and having reassured them, they continued the journey" (Perrot, 1993: 120).

32. Half the quantity of furs, in a thrice greater time, by three times more persons.

Des Groseilliers. And so, as Marie de l'Incarnation indicates, that trading venture represented a godsend in the commercial desert that New France was then crossing (Trudel, 1979: 269-270, 279 and 284-286).

How then can it be explained that Radisson and Des Groseilliers were so badly received by Governor d'Argenson, who could surely appreciate the validity of their initiative even if they had disobeyed his orders at the outset? Radisson declares that the considerable sum this venture gave them aroused the envy of the Governor, who took advantage of the situation to unjustly levy on them a fine of 4 000 pounds to erect a fort at Trois-Rivières, and another 6 000 pounds "for the country," an amount that d'Argenson would appropriate for his own use (according to Radisson): "But the Blighter licked his chops with it" (Ra: 241). They also had to pay the right of the quarter and not of the tenth on their beavers, as Des Groseilliers had concluded before his departure. The total deductions thus reached 24 000 pounds, leaving them but a meagre (?) 46 000 pounds in profit (Ra: 241)... In short, no matter how distasteful their welcome, the financial situation of Radisson and Des Groseilliers seemed frankly enviable. Why then so much rancor, why take umbrage at abuses of power in truth quite normal for the era on the part of a Governor: "Is he not a Tryant to deal with us in such fashion" (Ra: 241).

In the end, the spite and rancor evidenced by Radisson well served his interests in England when he was writing this narrative. That same year, 1667, the absolute monarchy of Louis XIV dominated France, and many Englishmen perceived spontaneously the representatives of the French monarchy or of the papacy, as despots, be they piddling or mighty, who imposed on subjects without voice or right an uncertain and capricious regime, whose power and influence were greatly feared by one and all. Radisson saw there an excellent opportunity to draw closer to the English. At the same time, he was establishing a certain standard for determining the limits that he believed acceptable in regard to the value of his services. To convince the English that he had no intention of continuing to work for employers as abject as the French, Radisson pursued this course,[33] by suggesting that d'Argenson had incarcerated Des Groseilliers (Ra: 240), which is untrue since no document confirms this and Des Groseilliers, who was

---

33. Radisson announced in advance on three occasions their disappointing reception, to give the event all possible importance (Ra: 198, 231 and 232). In reality, the situation was more complex and more nuanced than Radisson indicates, as I shall explain further on.

known and respected, had brought to a colony in crisis some small measure of relief and prosperity. Radisson lies again when he maintains that Des Groseilliers returned empty-handed from the voyage he made to France to recuperate the overpayment of taxes on the fruits of his trading venture (Ra: 241-242); (Trudel, 1979: 284). It is quite probable that Radisson would have received part of the amount which Des Groseilliers obtained in France, since his beavers were also involved in the transaction. Moreover, d'Argenson was not directly responsible for this tax "extortion" since the management of the venture had been leased out to a group of merchants immediately prior to the return of Radisson and Des Groseilliers to the colony.

In May 1660, rumors reached Québec that a great Iroquois army was preparing to deal a deathblow to the French. Panic broke out: "The habitants abandoned their dwellings to take refuge in the houses of the communities or in the fort (made of stone). Everyone, everywhere was barricaded in the lower town; (…) to protect the Ursulines, the Governor had posted guards and ordered that redoubts be erected" (Trudel, 1979: 258-260). Since this was the same army that Dollard des Ormeaux had encountered on the Ottawa River, the Iroquois never reached Québec, nor even Montréal, but the alert had greatly agitated everyone and convinced the Governor that the colony was extremely fragile (Trudel, 1979: 261-262). D'Argenson leapt into action once summer arrived, first leading a solid counter-attack against the Iroquois, then ordering all the habitants to fortify at least certain houses and a few bastions where they could gather and offer greater resistance. Then, the Governor and the Jesuits of Trois-Rivières took advantage of the arrival of Radisson and Des Groseilliers to finance various fortification efforts, on the pretext that they were on home ground and that Des Groseilliers was Burgomaster.[34]

The new Trading Council that d'Argenson had set up in 1658 had never suited him and in 1659 he replaced it by a system that had been employed in New France and in several other colonies, that of the monopoly enterprise which could alone, in his opinion, impose a tighter control over the fur trade. He therefore entrusted full management of the fur trade to a small

---

34. "Being wee were inhabitants and did intend to finish our days in the same country with our Relations and Friends" (Ra: 241). "1660 is perhaps the year from which date (…) Fort Sainte-Marie (…) in the Seigniory of Cap-de-la-Madeline, Fort Saint-François and the Fort called du *moulin à vent* (Windmill) in the same Seigniory" (Trudel, 1979: 263); (Campeau, 1995: 41).

group of merchants of Rouen, the "Compagnie de Normandie" (Company of Normandy), who contracted to furnish to New France over a four-year period the funds needed for her administration, to wit, 50 000 pounds per annum. It was with the representatives of this Company that Des Groseilliers had to negotiate the taxes payable on his trading venture, and not with the Governor. In the eyes of certain well-informed habitants who had spent the winter of 1659-1660 in France in order to bargain for an advantageous position in the reorganized fur trade, it was clear that Radisson and Des Groseilliers represented major competitors that had to be brought to heel (Trudel, 1979: 259-262).[35]

In the few short months between the departure and the return of the two brothers-in-law, management of the fur trade had thus considerably changed in New France (Trudel, 1979: 282-284). At the same time as the competition was becoming ever more active among the many fur traders in New France, the rules of the game and the conditions for attaining success became increasingly dependant on what was taking place across the Atlantic – the support that might be garnered in Paris and at the Court of France, where Louis XIV had just officially assumed power. This is why Des Groseilliers decided to return to France and plead his cause himself before the young King and his Royal Council, before returning to the colony, stronger and richer than ever, in summer 1661.

---

35. The year 1660 was very profitable for the Company of Normandy, which registered a good profit and could fulfil all its obligations. The situation was quite to the contrary the following year, when the new Governor d'Argenson broke the lease at the first opportunity, bringing closure at the end of November 1661 to the short-lived commercial enterprise (Trudel, 1979: 284-285).

CHAPTER 6

Radisson and Des Groseilliers
Leave New France

A FTER HE HAD WON HIS SUIT AT PARIS and recovered a great deal of money, Des Groseilliers spent two months at La Rochelle to ready his return to New France. For himself and for another resident of Trois-Rivières, he hired a female servant, four laborers and, in his capacity of "Admiral of the Autaois (Ottawa) Fleet," a blacksmith-harquebusier. He also purchased wine that he had loaded onto the ship "Le Taureau," bound for Québec.[1] With his female servant, his five workers and his store of wine, nothing indicates that Des Groseilliers was planning an early departure from New France. On the contrary, he seems to have elected to invest a considerable sum to develop his lands and his commerce, by offering to his Amerindian and French partners agricultural products and a repair service for iron objects and firearms.[2] However, the climate in New France was hardly propitious to the development of land or commercial ventures (Wien, 1998: 173); (Trudel, 1979: 264).

In September 1661, the new Governor d'Avaugour was amazed that his predecessor had been able to defend the colony with so few forces (Marie

---

1. Communal archives, Bibliothèque municipale de La Rochelle (Municipal Library of La Rochelle), Minutes of the Notary Moreau, manuscript of 1850, year 1661, f. 104v for Crespeau, 122 for Vallet, 135v-136 for Romieux, 137-136v for Daulney, Gaborit and Vergonneau. (Debien, 1952: 391) and Jean Fabertas in (Debien, 1952: 391).

2. In hiring these workers, Des Groseilliers contracted to pay 429 pounds per annum in wages over three years. Another document attests that Des Groseilliers did own an operative ironworks, in 1662 (Nute, 1943: 82).

de l'Incarnation, 1971: 673) and he demanded that reinforcements be dispatched to him without delay, or else he would resign his post, for the Iroquois that Dollard des Ormeaux had repulsed the preceding year were renewing their attacks with even greater vigor (Trudel, 1979: 264). Lambert Closse and several other Frenchmen of Montréal had been killed or captured, then the Iroquois attacked Trois-Rivières, the Île d'Orléans and Tadoussac and were on the prowl as far as the Mistassin territory north of Lake Saint-Jean. The Iroquois menace prevented Des Groseilliers from developing his land in the Cap-de-la-Madeleine district (Trudel, 1979: 267) and rendered more dangerous than ever any future voyage via the Ottawa River, which no Amerindian was to attempt either in 1661 or in 1662. The same situation prevailed on the Saguenay, where Fathers Dablon and Druillettes had barely escaped death, the preceding summer (JR, 46: 178-180),[3] as well as on the Saint-Maurice, blockaded since 1661 (Marie de l'Incarnation, 1971: 666).

The state of the colony

No doubt encouraged by the absolutist wave engulfing France, the Baron Dubois d'Avaugour, of undisputed nobility, wanted to govern the colony as he pleased, with a firm, militaristic hand. From the outset, he demanded that his remuneration be doubled, then he obliged the Superior of the Jesuits (Ragueneau) to again sit in Council, at the side of Bishop Laval who had just acceded to that body. He was thus able to break the lease of the Company of Normandy in 1661, then, in April 1662, in an absolutist surge that the French authorities disclaimed, he also suppressed the Council of Québec to create a new entity, more to his taste, that he imposed in consummate illegality (Trudel, 1979: 275-276, 286, 290, 326 and 336-338).

In the early 1660s, sectarian disputes, the non-respect of institutions, arrogance and covetousness fomented much disorder and uncertainty in New

---

3. The Iroquois had dismantled there the last trading network still intact. Pursuant to this, the Jesuits deplore an appreciable deterioration in the fur trade at Tadoussac, "the source of castor remains scanty owing to the losses of those who convey pelts to our habitants" (quoted in Trudel, 1979: 272). In 1662, the Iroquois again journeyed up the Saguenay fjord and pursued their offensive further to the north, towards Hudson Bay (Trudel, 1997: 564), while they were leading attacks in every direction: "in 1661-1662, they (the Iroquois) struck the Abenaki of the New England region, the Algonquians of the subarctic, the Siouans of the Upper Mississippi area, and various Indians near Virginia, while continuing the struggle with enemies closer to home" (Richter, 1983: 541).

France (Trudel, 1997: 150-151). The Iroquois continued to war while suing for peace, negotiating at Québec while they attacked Montréal (JR, 47: 276). The colony was unable to mount its forces and a climate of despondence as described by Marie de l'Incarnation prevailed:

> Since the departure of the vessels in 1660, signs have appeared in the Heavens to the great distress of many (...). A man in flames and shrouded in fire has been seen aloft. A flaming canoe and a great fiery crown have also been observed near Mont-Réal. On the Île d'Orléans, an unborn child has been heard wailing in its mother's womb (...). These many incidents have incited terror to the fullest extent imaginable (...). It has (also) been discovered that there are Sorcerers and Magicians in this land (...) (and) there is every reason to believe that these villains have poisoned the air. (Marie de l'Incarnation: 667-668, September 1661)

Are we among the French or with the Amerindians where blame for a deadly epidemic may be attributed to sorcerers or magicians holding sinister powers? In all reality, the similarities between the spirituality of the native and French cultures was considerable, as concerns *visions,* for example. For the aboriginals, the vision, the dream, represented a constant guide, a witness to the continued and multiple contacts between the visible world of living beings and the invisible world of spirits. For Catholics, the vision signified a highly exceptional event, a grace from God which could forever mark a person, such as Marie de l'Incarnation for whom a vision had revealed her missionary vocation in Canada. But a vision could also represent a sophistic or diabolical maneuver by the "forces of evil." It was therefore imperative to scrutinize dreams and visions with extreme care. For although the Catholic clergy did not seek to eliminate the *marvelous,* the *magical,* to which many Europeans, like Radisson, remained attuned, there was nonetheless a need to circumscribe this within certain prescribed or authorized forms, which the clerical hierarchy could *control.* The inhabitants of New France had therefore every liberty to conceive of a magical world peopled by supernatural spirits and so could also act in ways very similar to the Amerindians, provided that these spirits be saints and that the supreme Power presiding over the *incomprehensible* be the Christian God and the dogma as defined by the Catholic Church. On a question as fundamental as a dream or a vision, to wit, as concerns the direct and privileged communication with God or with the spirits, the Christian and Amerindian persuasions were irreconcilable in the eyes of the Jesuits, who remained ever intransigent on this question, despite or more likely because of the similarity between these two conceptions.

For his part, Des Groseilliers refused to be demoralized by the defeatist climate prevailing in New France. He had reached a firsthand agreement with a ship owner of La Rochelle, in spring 1661 (Ra: 242),[4] to circumvent the increasingly insoluble Iroquois problem and to try to reach Hudson Bay by the North Atlantic and the Hudson Strait, using the information given him by the Amerindians during his two earlier voyages (Heidenreich, 1997: 111). If Des Groseilliers succeeded in "rediscovering" the entryway to Hudson Bay, which certain English explorers had successfully navigated at the beginning of the XVIIth century,[5] he would be able to trade directly with the Crees of James Bay, at a healthy distance from the Iroquois and without any native intermediary. Finally, he would know peace of mind and be in a position to trade in all tranquillity just he had always wanted.[6]

"A man of contradiction"

In May 1662, without advising Governor d'Avaugour, who had just illegally abolished the Council of Québec, Des Groseilliers took pains to bypass Québec on his way towards the "North Sea."[7] No doubt he wished to avoid once again seeing his projects thwarted by the unstable temper of a Governor. The nine men with the expedition (Ra: 242) hastened to reach Percé where Des Groseilliers was to rendezvous with the ship from La Rochelle (Ra: 242). To the general dismay, it was a Jesuit Father who awaited them. He informed them that the expected ship would not be coming for the Jesuits had rectified that situation, at La Rochelle. He further warned them that it was "pernicious" to seek thusly to destroy a country and he exhorted

---

4. Des Groseilliers will conclude at least one high-risk contract with the merchant Ézechiel Dioré for trade goods, ANC, Departmental Archives, Charente-Maritime, Amirauté de La Rochelle (Admiralty of La Rochelle), Series B, vol. 203, p. 3.

5. At least three English expeditions had crossed the strait and explored Hudson Bay between 1610 and 1631, under the successive direction of Hudson, Button and James.

6. "Some time ago a Frenchman from our Touraine called Des Groseilliers married in that country; and failing thereat to make a great fortune, he took it in his mind to repair to New England, there to try to make a better one" (Marie de l'Incarnation, 1971: 874).

7. Father Jérôme Lalemant writes in the Journal of the Jesuits, May 1662: "I met en route Des Groseilliers *who was heading towards the North Sea*: he spent the night anchored offshore from Québec in the company of 10 men (including Radisson) and upon arriving at Cap Tourmente, he advised Sieur the Governor of his intent" (JR, 47: 278-280).

Radisson to leave his brother-in-law (Ra: 242). The reasons that may have prompted the Jesuits to pose such a radical gesture remain somewhat vague, or at least as Radisson presents them.[8] It seems that motives of a commercial and political nature encouraged the Jesuits to intervene in this way; for in all truth, the initiative of Des Groseilliers threatened the economic viability of the leadership in New France.[9] The Jesuits probably feared that the undeniable experience and talent possessed by these two explorers, who were determined to gain wealth, might well imperil all they had built in the colony, if the brothers-in-law managed to divert too large a quantity of furs towards Hudson Bay.

As of 1660, the French, thanks to the Amerindians, were aware of a least six waterways leading to Hudson Bay, from the Saint Lawrence and the Ottawa Rivers, as well as from Lakes Huron and Superior (JR, 44: 236-244). The race was thus under way between various influential groups who were anxious to appropriate the largest possible part of the northern fur trade. Des Groseilliers had chosen the most difficult but most promising route, to wit, the route via the Hudson Strait;[10] for their part, the Jesuits opted for the Saguenay, as did Governor d'Avaugour and the merchant Charles Aubert de La Chesnaye, and finally, several other associates, who also launched an expedition via the Saguenay, in 1663, but without success (Nute, 1943: 73-74).

---

8. There exists a "religious" interpretation of this forceful Jesuit takeover, one that accords considerable weight to the conflict between Protestants and Catholics, and more particularly to the harsh persecutions leveled at the Huguenots of La Rochelle in 1661-1662 (Bosher, 1993b: 299). This wave of persecutions ostensibly induced the Jesuits to sabotage Des Groseilliers' expedition as he was an acknowledged Huguenot (Bosher, 1993a: 71-75). Yet, nothing allows for linking Des Groseilliers or Radisson to the Huguenots of La Rochelle and, more importantly, nothing indicates that their religious allegiance inspired mistrust on the part of the Jesuits before their long sojourn in England; on the contrary, they had both been close collaborators of the Jesuits. This hypothesis therefore seems flimsy.

9. In any case, the Jesuits had a direct interest in assuring that the finances of the colony remain secure, in that the authorities of New France were paying them an annual subsidy of 5,000 pounds, when the monies coming in were sufficient. The subsidy in question represented a substantial part of the Jesuits' budget.

10. This decision is abundantly clear, in view of what he declared to Father Lalemant of Québec, about his subsequent efforts to reach Hudson Bay both from New England and England and based on what his wife declared at the court of Trois-Rivières, April 27, 1663: "saying that her husband had undertaken an extremely dangerous voyage upon the Bay of the North from which it is to be feared that he will not return" (quoted and translated by Nute, 1943: 81). Jean Bourdon had attempted a similar voyage in 1657 for the Jesuits, but he went no further than what is today Labrador.

New France was largely counting on the opening of new fur-trading networks north of the Saint Lawrence to compensate for the difficulties of trading in the west occasioned by the Iroquois blockade. In reality, the colony's survival depended on a regular supply of furs and thus on the uninterrupted to-ings and fro-ings of merchant ships which could bring the tiny colony on the shores of the Saint-Lawrence everything it lacked, just as Marie de l'Incarnation elegantly states: "although Canada can dispense with France as concerns basic necessities, (...) she depends on the mother country for clothing, tools, wine, brandy and indeed for an infinite number of small commodities, all of which are brought to us by the trade" (in Delâge, 1985: 281). Radisson describes this dependence more bluntly: "no beavers, no boats, so how will we obtain essential commodities?" (Ra: 240). The discovery and development of new trading networks north of the Saint Lawrence thus became trump cards for maintaining the colony.

The Jesuits rightly believed that it would be exceedingly difficult for the authorities of New France to collect the right of the quarter part on the furs that Des Groseilliers or others would bring back from Hudson Bay, furs that could be transited only via Percé, Acadia or New England, or else be brought directly to Europe...[11] The Jesuits therefore had every reason to worry about Des Groseilliers' likely success and they seem to have decided that it was in their interest to compromise his expedition. Was it the cavalier manner they adopted or the simple fact of opposing the single-minded Des Groseilliers? In any case, it would have been wiser not to thwart in such brutal fashion the projects of a man whom Marie de l'Incarnation and Paul Ragueneau later described as a "man of contradiction" "opinionated in his undertakings." New France paid dearly for the decision which Des Groseilliers took at that juncture to seek elsewhere than in the colony or even in France the conditions necessary to complete the Hudson Bay trading project that was so dear to his heart.

What to do? Where to go?

A most urgent problem now faced the tiny expedition: how to clear the trade goods that they had acquired in the colony without a vessel to get to Hudson Bay? The Iroquois were on the rampage everywhere to the west

---

11. The logistics of that aborted expedition very closely resemble those of the expedition that Radisson and Des Groseilliers will undertake in 1682-1683, with Percé as their point of departure and arrival, precisely to avoid collection of the right to the quarter part.

and to the north and so they headed towards the southwest, towards French Acadia, the only region still accessible. Des Groseilliers had helped one of the landowners in this contested territory, Nicolas Denys, to recuperate his lands on the Ile Miscou and on Cape Breton Island some ten years earlier; and Denys had managed to maintain there four small enterprises despite the constant pressure exerted by his competitors (Campeau, 1996: 379 and 633); (Baudry, 1995: 21-26). From Percé on, it was thus relatively easy for these seasoned voyagers to reach the habitation of Mister Denys on Cape Breton Island, "where we exchanged merchandise for moose hides" (Ra: 242). The nine or ten Frenchmen in the expedition then journeyed to Canseau, where Denys was trying to develop an on-site fishing enterprise. However, a rival group of Frenchmen blocked their initiative (Ra: 243); (Trudel, 1997: 612); (Baudry, 1955: 26).

Again at Canseau, probably discouraged by the disorganization and severe lack of resources paralyzing Acadia (Trudel, 1997: 594-595), Des Groseilliers must have confided to Radisson his project to reach New England (Ra: 243). And so, the expedition separated into two groups: those who wanted to remain in French territory and those who were ready to follow Radisson and Des Groseilliers to Massachusetts, where business opportunities appeared rosier: "this is why our lives were in great danger" (Ra: 243). They transited by Port-Royal, under English control since 1654, before reaching New England, where they were able to rapidly mount a maritime expedition and then reach the Hudson Strait the following summer (1663), "by the 61st latitude" of the Northern Hemisphere (Ra: 243), scarcely one year after leaving New France.[12]

The short account that Radisson gives of their stay in New England, which extends from 1663 to 1665, is plausible but incomplete. He mentions

---

12. Two documents of 1663 confirm that the two brothers-in-law concluded an agreement with the Bostonians and reached the Hudson Strait in 1663, as Radisson so relates (Ra: 243). The first document is the declaration of Marguerite Hayet of August 1663 that I already quoted in footnote 10 on the voyage that her husband would undertake to the "baie du nord" (North Bay) (Nute, 1943: 81). The second is a letter of Marie de l'Incarnation which relates the arrival at Québec, July 29, 1663, of a vessel from New England come to return five French prisoners. On that occasion, she learns that "Savages from a faraway land" had recently arrived at Boston, brought by people who "had discovered a thing long sought after, namely, *the entryway to the great sea of the North*" (Marie de l'Incarnation, 1971: 698-699) Radisson writes that during this voyage "Wee had knowledge and conversation with the people of those parts" (Ra: 243).

the preparation for a new expedition planned for 1664 and the wreck of one of their ships at Sable Island during a fishing trip; then he relates the controversy that followed between them and their Boston backers (Ra: 243-244). As there is no trace to be found in the Boston archives concerning the sojourn of Radisson and Des Groseilliers in that town, I have given more particular attention to one crucial query: how did the two brothers-in-law manage to arrive in the English colony of Massachusetts, without assistance of any consequence, then leave there some three years later with the promise of a private audience with the King of England?

Radisson describes in an extremely summary fashion the circumstances surrounding their departure towards Europe: "the representatives of the British King arrived at this place (Boston), and one of them asked us to accompany him to New Yorke (then New Amsterdam) and another invited us to come to England to offer our services to the King; this we did" (Ra: 244). Radisson omits the essential, to wit, under what circumstances were they recruited and why were they trusted? In December 1665, Colonel Cartwright insisted on this trust when he explained to the English Secretary of State Arlington why he was bringing Radisson and Des Groseilliers to London: "finding there sufficient proof of the accuracy of what they said about the beaver trade, esteeming highly probable the truth of that passage (…) and of a great beaver trade via this route (Hudson Strait or Bay) (…), I believed that they were the finest present I could offer to His Sacred Majesty" (quoted in Nute, 1943: 95, and translated by the author). Cartwright hereby implies that the King's representatives received early on tangible proof of what Radisson and Des Groseilliers were advancing. This proof ultimately convinced them to trust what the two brothers-in-law affirmed as to the Hudson Bay project. I have attempted to identify this undeniably tangible proof and the substantial services that Radisson and Des Groseilliers were able to render to the King's representatives, in that these paved the way to their eventual introduction to the highest levels of power in England.

Welcome to the land of the English

In 1662, a disorganized French Acadia was reduced to a state of dependency. A very close link now tied its main center of population, Port-Royal, to the powerful neighboring colony of Massachusetts, which had imposed its jurisdiction over the entire western area of what is now Nova Scotia, in

1653 (Bailyn, 1979: 115-116).[13] Once they had reached Boston, the commercial center of the English colonies in America (Bailyn, 1979: 95 and 98), it was easy for Radisson and Des Groseilliers to meet with potential investors at the *Townhouse*, "the actual center of commercial life in Boston (...) at the main intersection of the city (Bailyn, 1979: 97). The interest of Boston merchants for the fur trade was all the greater since that resource was in decline throughout New England (Bailyn, 1979:50-60) and because their priority at the time was market expansion; for if the merchants wanted to prosper, they were obliged "to always be on the lookout for new markets where new types of products could be sold" (Bailyn, 1979: 100). The merchants also held the political power (Delâge, 1985: 328), so that the commercial interest could iron out many difficulties, such as the French origin of the two brothers-in-law or the audacity of their project.

Radisson and Des Groseilliers were able to rapidly integrate the dominant economic forces of the English colony. But Radisson's narrative fails to reveal whether or not they associated with the older generation of puritan merchants, who had virtually founded the colony, or instead with the new generation of royalist traders coming out from England since the restoration of King Charles II, in 1660. These young Englishmen were dynamic and ambitious, both royalists and imperialists; they were also well-connected to circles of power in London, and they came out to America to make their fortune in the colonial trade, then in full expansion (Bailyn, 1979: 111).[14] Major transformations were thus rippling through Massachusetts when the two brothers-in-law were there. The restoration of King Charles II, after four years of a Commonwealth, revived tensions between the republican puritans and the royalists of New England. Radisson and Des Groseilliers had therefore to learn another language, become familiar with a different mentality and customs, and learn to maneuver among the factions confronting one

---

13. "Nova Scotia was virtually the northeastern extension of Massachusetts" (Rawlyk, 1973: 30) Towards 1660, Acadia numbered about 500 persons, including the population of Port-Royal, in addition to more than 30 000 persons in New England (Rawlyk, 1973: xiii).

14. The biographer of one of these businessmen, Richard Wharton, typifies the men who came over to make their fortune in New England: "He (Wharton) enjoyed "playing the game" (...). His imagination, power of organization, courage in taking risks, ability to inspire confidence in prospective investors, driving force, tireless energy, optimism, are all characteristic of the successful captain of industry" (quoted in Bailyn, 1979: 111).

another when the Royal Commission arrived at Boston, in 1664. The aban-
donment of the initial Boston supporters after the wreck of a ship off Sable
Island suggests that the participation of Radisson and Des Groseilliers in the
activities of the Royal Commission represented a handy way out.

Charles II set up this Commission because certain royalists residing in
Massachusetts had made numerous complaints to the Court about the ap-
propriations of puritan (republican) merchants and politicians in New
England. The royalists denounced the desire for independence on the part
of the group's leaders, their lack of loyalty to the Crown of England and their
many abuses of power (Bailyn, 1979: 98-99 and 114-116). The Commission's
mandate was to tour the English colonies of the north in order to carefully
assess the situation and to make sure that the King's authority was respected
by all. The Commission was also expected to "report on Indian affairs," in
other words, to ensure that Indian conversion to Christianity was progressing satisfactorily and that the converts were being well treated. However, the
Commission's greatest priority was to eventually take possession of New
Holland (Reid, 1977: 63 and 65 and Reid, 1981: 149).

It was widely believed in London that the conquest of New Holland
would enhance relations between the Commission and the colonies but the
English Crown, perhaps ill-informed, mistook the impact of that conquest
since the merchants of Maryland and Massachusetts had in fact been arming and supporting the Amerindians in their territories against the Iroquois
for many years, in the hope of conquering New Holland in their own right
and taking over the most flourishing fur trade of the entire region (Jennings,
1984: 126-129). Thus the Commission had difficulty recruiting on site the
guides and intermediaries needed to neutralize the native allies of the Dutch
and to renegotiate trade agreements with them, after the conquest. In this
context, Radisson and Des Groseilliers had every reason and every opportunity to acquaint the commissioners of their ability to negotiate both with
the Iroquois, who were the principal allies of the Dutch, and with the
Amerindians of the English colonies with whose language and customs they
were also familiar. Since Charles II had promised exclusive jurisdiction of
the territory of New Netherlands to the Duke of York, his brother and heir
to the throne of England, if the operation succeeded, the rapid conquest of
New Netherlands under the authority of the Royal Commissioner dashed
the hopes of many in New England and increased the widespread hostility
towards the Commission.

Under the prevailing circumstances, Radisson and Des Groseilliers had many opportunities to prove to Colonels Nicholls and Cartwright – who took charge, respectively, of the conquest of New Amsterdam and Fort Orange (New York and Albany) – that they had, multi-faceted experience in Amerindian affairs and the fur trade in the region.[15] One such opportunity arose when three members of the Commission (including Cartwright) journeyed north in 1665, to the colony of Maine, where they received a better welcome and took possession of a territory uncontested by Massachusetts, between the Kennebec and Sainte-Croix Rivers. In this sparsely populated region, the fur trade with the Algonquin nation of the Abenakis, allied with the French, continued to flourish (Campeau, 1996: 633-634); (Rawlyk, 1973: 36-37). It is possible that Radisson and Des Groseilliers acted as advisers or negotiators in this acquisition of a territory rich in furs, in that several weeks later, Colonel Cartwright embarked for England, where he was to report to the King on the activities of the Commission; and he took Radisson and Des Groseilliers with him. The chances for the two brothers-in-law to realize their trading project at Hudson Bay now seemed better than ever.

---

15. "A Habitant from here (Des Groseilliers) (…) repaired to the English side some two years ago, and gave them, as far as we know, the knowledge of many things about the Iroquois country, and about the great profit they could make from the trade, if they were the Masters of same. It is believed that this may be the reason which led them to attack New Holland" (Marie de l'Incarnation, 1971: 742). In this, Marie de l'Incarnation shares the opinion of the Jesuits. But the decision to conquer New Holland had been taken in England, before the departure of the Commission. It was thus more at the level of *how* that Radisson and Des Groseilliers were able to play a role. Radisson, in particular, was at ease with the Iroquois language and knew personally several Mohawk (his adoptive family), it was no doubt easy for him to make good use of his acquaintances. Father Ragueneau also feared that Des Groseilliers might ally with the Iroquois and the English to crush New France (Ragueneau to the Count d'Estrades, 7 November, 1664, B.N., Mélanges à Colbert no. 125, f. 181), a fear that proved groundless since the English gave little support to the Iroquois, in particular at the time of the French attacks of 1666. It was only after 1675 that the English again armed the Iroquois so that they might participate in the English war effort against French territorial expansion south of the Great Lakes (Jennings, 1984: 130, 134-135 and 142).

4. Radisson's and Des Groseilliers' Expedition from Québec to Boston

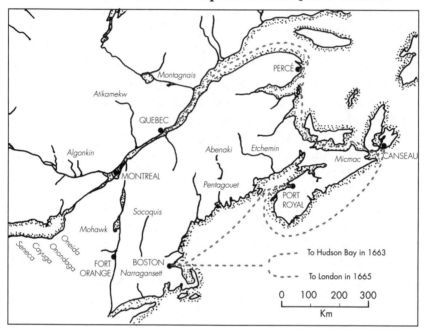

Natives from the Maritimes were French allies and reputed to be great travelers. Some were known at times to travel in large birchbark canoes from what is today New Brunswick or the Gaspé Peninsula to Québec. Given the experience of the French voyageurs on this expedition, they were readily able to travel the distance between Québec and Percé in birchbark canoes and make their way to Cape Breton in 1662. Des Groseilliers and Radisson continued on to Port Royal and Boston in 1663 and left for London in 1665.

Crossing the Atlantic

European power

Before turning to the eventful times that Radisson and Des Groseilliers experienced in England and at Hudson's Bay, I would like to revisit for a moment the "superior powers" with which the Amerindians vested the French.

For centuries the Europeans had been developing and mastering metallurgy. They knew how to make powerful cannons and intricate clockworks, how to cast huge bronze sculptures and to weave delicate coats of mail; they knew which alloys gave springs their elasticity and tools their resistance. They knew how to melt glass, blow it to form vases and employ it to make lenses as well as stained glass, spectacles and telescopes. They had knowledge of the magnetic pole and navigated using the compass and the sextant on increasingly larger-scale ships that were much easier to maneuver. The Europeans also had the ability to cut stone, to build vaults, towers, fortresses, cathedrals and sumptuous palaces. They knew mathematics and were learning to apply it to architecture and engineering, to astronomy and commerce; they instituted banks, set up chartered and capital stock companies, created scientific and technical associations, kingdoms and codes of law. They were skilled at crafts and at inventing machines which sawed, hammered, packed, husked, milled, spun and churned; they had refined the art of pumps and pulleys, hoists and coaches; they were also acquainted with glass mirrors, chimes, silk, silver and gold plate, cannon powder and fireworks... Long is the list of the technical and institutional capabilities that Europeans had mastered by the middle of the XVIIth century.

The pooling of specialized knowledge and skills, the quasi-uninter-
rupted safeguarding, revitalization and development of certain traditions
among apprentices, in schools, monasteries, libraries and universities, among
Princes and Kings, all this illustrates that the Europeans of that era possessed
a far greater *power to intervene in the area of the real* than did the aboriginals
of America. To imagine that in two or three generations the Amerindians
might be able to assimilate that much knowledge, develop that many pre-
requisite techniques, both mental and cultural, in short, that they might be
capable of acquiring, over a very brief time span, a *power equivalent* to that
of the Europeans, seems unrealistic. The Amerindians were rich in an entirely different tradition and could not have "telescoped" over a few short
decades so many centuries of Mediterranean scientific and technical history,
especially in the context of the demographic and cultural upheavals that
marked the early contacts.

The interpretation that large numbers of aboriginals seem to have privileged appears pertinent. If they wanted to rapidly acquire such powers, they
had to lean on their own tradition and ally with the Europeans by *bartering
and* by *commerce*, exactly as the Europeans desired that they do. The interests of the two parties seemed for a time to be complementary. For the
Amerindians, the paradox of the period of contact was perhaps that they
could not acquire the whiteman's power without preserving the basic structure of their own culture, their way of understanding the world and of entering into contact with it so as to remain good hunters, thereby taking advantage of the fur trade, trying in such fashion to better adjust to the changes
that the Europeans were introducing.[1]

The trump card of Radisson and Des Groseilliers

During their voyage to Lake Superior, in 1660, Radisson and Des Groseilliers
had remarked that the Crees believed they were being wronged by their
Algonquin partners and felt themselves "treated as slaves among the other
nations, even though they supplied them with beavers" (Ra: 229). The Crees

---

1. The oral accounts of the initial contacts between Amerindians and Europeans as analyzed by Denys Delâge leads him to conclude: "the Chippewa chronicle marks the difference
of these new types of men less by what they are than by what they possess: sailing ships, pearls,
firearms, fabrics, alcohol but above all else metals and their greater efficacy. With the arrival
of this merchandise, unknown until then, began a new period (Delâge, 1992: 114).

therefore appeared enchanted to learn that Radisson and Des Groseilliers wanted to come and deal with them directly via the North Sea.[2] Despite its harsh climate, Hudson's Bay offered a good many geographic advantages: it was far from the Iroquois, far from the bustle and keen competition of the Great Lakes[3] and at a healthy distance from competitors in New France. Moreover, the Crees were excellent hunters, they inhabited a vast territory rich in beaver and they wanted fervently to trade directly with the whitemen. From every angle, such a project looked promising; this is why Radisson and Des Groseilliers seemed determined to risk the adventure with any partner at all. Their encounters with the Crees, the information that they obtained from them about James Bay and even the map the Crees had drawn for them[4] gave them a considerable lead over all their competitors.

What a story!

It is quite difficult to get at a clear idea of another era, or of a material, social and cultural environment that can be imagined only to some degree. And yet, by closely scrutinizing another time and another person's life, by trying to define little by little an existence different from our own, by dint of examining the traces this, person and, indeed, his era have left, in the end we can get a better idea of it, one that is more exact and more complete, just as we come to know our contemporaries, or indeed ourselves, as time passes.

---

2. "Those poore Christinos (...) weare *overjoyed that we promised them to come with such shipps as we invented*" (my italics), "They weare overjoyed when we sayd we should bring them commodities" (Ra: 224-225 and 227).

3. On several occasions, Radisson mentions the extremely strong and all-consuming desire of the Amerindians to obtain European commodities: "we met with some in that lake (Superior) that joined with us (...) in hopes to get knives from us, *wich they love better than we serve God*", or "those poore miserable thought themselves happy to carry our Equipage, for the hope (...) we should give them a brasse ring, or an awle, or an needle" (Ra: 193 and 198). Radisson even speaks of an often uncontrollable fascination: "Hearing that they have had knives and hattchets, *the victualls of their poore children is taken away from them*" (Ra: 203) (See also, Ra: 148, 155, 159-161, 184, 199-200, 208-219, 221-222 and 224.) It is this intense *Amerindian desire* that Radisson and Des Groseilliers were able to exploit with great success, but the density of the populations and the intensity of relations among them rendered the Great Lakes region much more unstable and dangerous then the Hudson's Bay region, which itself was not free from conflicts.

4. "They made us a mapp of what we could not see" (Ra: 225).

The phenomenon of coming into contact with the past brings it back to life, transforms it. History is a virtually inexhaustible source of possibilities and of human diversities, an arena of accomplishment, a well of reality, indeed, a prolific turning point. For that which is most important in history is the link it creates between today and yesterday, it is the living relationship history cultivates among the three poles of a single journey through past, present and future. Hence, imbibing history always means courting adventure, by setting out towards the unknown... I would like to share my fascination for this singular journey with the reader.

CHAPTER 7

Radisson Embraces England

I WAGERED THAT IT WOULD BE EASIER to understand Radisson having a better knowledge of the social and cultural realities that surrounded him, by discovering who had influenced him–who had unearthed his talents, then brought them to the fore to put them to profitable use. In brief, which individuals, what opportunities, did Radisson use to his own advantage?

When Radisson arrived in England, he still had much to learn about his new host country, although he did notice certain similarities with New England. But he needed to become intimately familiar with life in a major European capital, while learning to adapt to new ways, and new values; in short, he had to find his place within a new social network. Since Radisson wrote very little about his life in England, I would ask that the reader try to understand him by assuming a stance similiar to Radisson's when he was trying to understand and adapt to English customs and values, between 1665 and 1675, a time rich in momentous events.[1]

---

1. The notoriety of the first shareholders in the Hudson's Bay Company and the care with which they from the outset filed administrative documents, quite apart from the luck which placed the celebrated English diarist Samuel Pepys in close contact with several persons frequented by the two Frenchmen, enabled me, with reference to such firsthand documentation, to investigate the causes, attitudes and tendencies that in all likelihood directed the action and influenced the behavior of Radisson and Des Groseilliers while they were in England.

Two difficult years

Radisson and Des Groseilliers arrived at London in December 1665, at the end of the terrible plague that decimated more than a quarter of London's population and literally paralyzed affairs of State. Terrified by the plague, the King, his Court and many influential people took refuge in the cities surrounding the capital (Pepys, 1972: 93 and 166). This is why the two Frenchmen met with George Carteret – Treasurer of the Navy and one of the most powerful persons in the Kingdom – at Oxford. Although it seems that they were unable to meet the King there, they were provided bed and board at his expense over a period of three months (Ra: 244). Then the King sent them to his cousin Prince Rupert, at Windsor (Ra: 245), where they met James Hayes, Secretary to the Prince, who would support their project and actively participate in the development of the Hudson's Bay Company. In the spring of 1666, at London, the two Frenchmen met another very influential individual, Peter Colleton, who was to give them a ship and all the equipment needed to launch a pilot expedition towards Hudson Bay (Ra: 245). However, the ship was readied too late and the Dutch and English fleets that clashed in early summer 1666, off the coast of England, effectively compromised the expedition planned for that year (Ra: 245). Radisson does not indicate who looked after them the following year, nor how they subsisted between June 1666 and December 1667, when the first capital stock of the Hudson's Bay Company was issued, serving among other purposes to pay each of them wages of at least 2 pounds sterling per week (HRBS-5: 203).[2]

What exactly did Radisson and Des Groseilliers do over this period of nearly two years that enabled them to set up a capital-stock company grouping a number of wealthy, experienced and competent colonizers? Answering such a knotty question will take us to the very heart of English society over the years 1665-1670.

---

2. Or 100 pounds each yearly; this represents a healthy emolument since an income of 50 pounds sterling per annum was considered comfortable by London standards at that time: "an income of about £50 constituted a lower boundary for the middle station of London society; and £50 was from three to five times the annual income of a labourer" (Shapin, 1994: 49).

Many plagues

Between the years 1660 and 1669, an influential employee of the British
Royal Navy, one Samuel Pepys, kept a very detailed and confidential diary
(he spoke of it to no one) about his personal life, his work and the overall
situation of the English State. Pepys resided in London for a considerable
period of time during the plague and on several occasions was witness to
the havoc the disease wreaked on the realm at every personal, political and
economic level. Pepys noted for example that as the months passed, the
gaping rifts which the plague created in the social fabric of London were
generating a wave of cynicism among its inhabitants: "Lord, how the re-
gards and words of everyone in the street concern death and nothing else,
only a very few come and go, the city has the look of a miserable place –
and forgotten as well," "the epidemic makes us cruel like dogs one towards
the other" (Pepys, 1972: [30 August 1665], and 212 [4 September 1665]).

The state of disorganization in the Kingdom could not however be attributed solely to the epidemic, which was only aggravating a growing dissatisfaction with Charles II, who had been returned to the throne after the
execution of his father Charles I, in 1649, and the some fifteen years of republican rule that followed the regicide. The enthusiasm aroused by the
establishment of Charles II on the English throne in 1660-1661, following
the death of the dictator Cromwell, quickly faded. The business sectors
deplored the laxness evidenced by the King and his closest collaborators and
if Parliament refused to grant the budgets Charles II needed to support
sectors as vital to the country as the Royal Navy, again it was because of waste
and laxness. The population at large and several members of the elite also
reproached the Court and even the King himself for the dissolute and cor-
rupt life they were leading, following the many years of moralizing auster-
ity under the Puritan Republic of Cromwell.[3]

---

3. According to the biographer of Samuel Pepys, the fact that this jovial fellow given
to fleshly pleasures himself denounces the dissolute practices of the Court, indicates the extent to which the Court had a bad reputation (Ponsonby, 1972: 103-104).

In autumn 1665, as the plague waned and just before the arrival of Radisson and Des Groseilliers, the state of disorganization in the Kingdom had attained epic proportions according to persons in Pepys' orbit: "as things are going right now, the whole State will end in ruin,"[4] (Pepys, 1972: 218). Even if Radisson and Des Groseilliers could count on the support of a few influential courtiers after their arrival, the overriding circumstances, namely, the war against Holland, the lack of financial resources, the hostility of Parliament and the disorganization of the Kingdom, placed the early realization of their project in serious peril, unless they were able to arouse strong interest in it and thereby enlist the close association of a few redoubtably enterprising individuals.

During their first stay at Oxford, Radisson and Des Groseilliers were able to make their representations to the Duke of York, calling his attention to the role they very likely played in the conquest of New Holland and most certainly did in the reorganization of the fur trade in that territory. In reality, York seems to have represented the most valuable source of assistance that Radisson and Des Groseilliers had as of their arrival at the Court of England and over many subsequent years. The two Frenchmen also made use of this stay to convince George Carteret of the worth of their project, thereby garnering his financial assistance as early as 1667. Radisson and Des Groseilliers therefore tried immediately to gather as much support as they could from the influential persons that they encountered: Carteret, Hayes, Rupert, Colleton, all of them certainly less powerful than the King himself but surely more accessible and probably of greater assistance.

Nonetheless, any endeavor to curry favors carried risks in the highly volatile ambiance of Royal power. Charles II was surrounded by clans and factions whose infighting could significantly affect the fortunes of lesser courtiers like Radisson and Des Groseilliers. The case of Samuel Pepys illustrates the importance of the phenomenon; Pepys had obtained his first lucrative assignments in the Royal administration thanks to the lightning ascent of a distant relative, to whom he had rendered various services before the restoration of Charles II. When the King gave this relative, Edward Montagu, the title Lord Sandwich, then promoted him to the rank of Admiral for his services in support of his restora-

---

4. "Talking of the ill-government of our Kingdom, nobody setting to heart the business of the Kingdom, but everybody minding their particular profit or pleasures, the King himself minding nothing but his ease – and so we let things go to wrack" (Pepys, 1972: 210).

tion to the throne, Pepys was able to commence his career as an administrator in the Royal Navy. He knew however that he could not count in any permanent way on the favor of such a high-placed individual, constantly threatened by disgrace; and so Pepys tried to make himself indispensable by his diligence at work, by a thorough knowledge of his dossiers and by an honesty that far surpassed what was usual for the era (Pepys, 1972: 285). Very often, Pepys recounts how he was obliged to indulge his many social relations to avoid angering or turning any of them against him, by seeming to favor a given individual or clan to the detriment of another (Pepys, 1972: 285).[5] At one point, this comedy became so ludicrous that Pepys decided to broach the subject directly to his patron Sandwich-Montagu, so as to convince the latter of his entire neutrality in the conflict which pitted him against his other immediate superior, Sir Coventry (Pepys, 1985: 584 and 586). Pepys knew he was taking a huge gamble by risking not only the displeasure of his mentor and relative but more significantly the permanent withdrawal of his support. However, Sandwich accepted his neutrality and Pepys was thus able to retain his post when Sandwich was dismissed a few months later.

Radisson's situation is in some way similar to that of Pepys; neither of them could count on a family fortune or a title and both sought to take their place by dint of hard work. The two men were about the same age; they were both successful arrivistes and left behind narratives about a part of their everyday life, similar in the vivacity of the style and its great variety, and in the highly detailed content of the respective texts. Radisson's acceptance into the upper echelons of English society did of course pose problems much more delicate than those Pepys was to encounter; but the diarist's testimony remains ever pertinent to understanding the milieux which the two Frenchmen were trying to penetrate and the problems they likely encountered.

Mutual assistance and commercial networks: the clienteles

Understanding the mutual assistance and alliance networks, the indispensable ties of friendship and affinity that had to be developed to succeed in business and in English society, as well as the rivalries between such networks, is crucial to grasping the England of that era and the events that

---

5. "Lord to see in what difficulty I stand that I dare not walk with Sir William Coventry for fear my Lord [Sandwich] or Sir G. Carteret should see me; nor with either of them for fear Sir W. Coventry should" (quoted in Ponsonby: 106).

marked both the highs and lows of the life of Radisson and Des Groseilliers in that country.

In London then, it was normal for those involved in big business to include a virtually secret yet negotiable personal commission that they imposed on each of their transactions. This additional profit, more or less hidden, more or less costly, was dictated by the cunning and voracity of the individual and represented both the "spice" of commerce and the "cement" binding the ties of alliance and commerce between economic and social partners. In the England that Radisson came to know, if an individual was unable to participate in this type of commercial-exchange network, he was quite likely to remain at the bottom of the social ladder. However, if the same individual took an active part in a network of dynamic exchanges, it was possible for him to multiply his assets and his influence by negotiating supplementary margins of profit and by engaging in the discreet trading of favors to obtain positions or contracts.

Pepys, who established more rigorous administrative and accounting practices for Navy affairs, nonetheless often took advantage of this widespread practice. When Lady Sandwich asked him about the character of an individual named Creed who had a bad reputation, Pepys told her that all the Englishmen he knew were scoundrels: "I believed him to be a man as deceitful and shrewd as anyone in England but he whom I would most fear must needs be even more clever than myself in all matters – with which she fully concurred," he further notes (Pepys, 1972: 15 [18-01-1665]). This sort of "arrangement" even seemed *moral* to Pepys who thanked God for the many "marginal benefits" he obtained from his strategic duties as supplier, treasurer and accountant: "may the almighty God of heaven and earth be praised for these blessings (…) I am now worth £1, 900" (Pepys, 1972: 180). Pepys gives a number of examples of negligible or extravagant commissions, as well as of bribes to obtain princely contracts from the Navy, even including the systemactic theft of the royal bedclothes by his servants, to the extent that Charles II was no longer able to procure adequate supplies of bedsheets (Pepys, 1985: 595 and 826).[6]

---

6. The Secretary of the Duke of York applied two basic principles in matters of business; one of these was: "suspecting every man that proposes anything to [me] to be a knave (scoundrel); or at least to have some ends of his own in it" (Pepys, quoted in Ponsonby: 106).

Pepys' ethics in the matter of favors or special commissions seem to lie more particularly in the "manner" one adopts, in the level-headedness one displays or in the efforts one expends to obtain a "well deserved" gratuity, keeping in mind the prudence and vigilence required if one hopes to prosper while preserving his good repute (Pepys, 1972: 204). It would appear that the English of that era believed that such practices should remain reasonable and discreet. However, they seem to have gone well beyond that boundary by 1665, and indeed the prevailing corruption was beginning to attract severe criticism and specific measures of redress (Pepys, 1972: 75, 83, 95 and 119).[7] While the obtainment of a lucrative office in the Royal administration was reserved for those Englishmen who supported the King and his courtiers, Court favors could be granted to foreigners like Radisson, Des Groseilliers, and others. The case of the Dutch Captain Van Heemskerk illustrates certain aspects of this "recruiting by favor" as practiced by the Court of Charles II.

Vade mecum for courtiers

Having left the Dutch Navy and operated for a time as a spy for France, Captain Van Heemskerk, on one occasion, led some ten English warships to a spectacular victory against 150 merchant vessels coming from Holland (Codignola, 1990: 515). Assured of the appreciation of Prince Rupert and the Duke of Albemarle who had assisted his exploit, Heemskerk also won the favor of the King and Prince Rupert, who entrusted him with major responsibilities during the war against Holland. Heemskerk then sought to take full advantage of the King's support, assuring him that he could have a ship built that would be swifter than any other in the English Navy. Charles II backed his efforts until the launching of the experimental ship, which proved to be as rapid as other English ships... but not more so. Heemskerk

---

7. Nor do examples of embezzlement in high places go lacking, such as the Paymaster to the Navy Treasurer, John Fenn (for a time shareholder in the Hudson's Bay Company), of whom it was said that he exacted the sum of £12, 000 per annum in "secret" commissions, not counting the gratuities he realized from the provisioning service that Pepys "supervised" Pepys (Surveyor-General of the Victualling) – a situation that enabled the latter to double his net income in 1665 (Pepys, 1972: 341); (Pepys, 1972: 40). The treasurer, George Carteret, in his own right, appropriated a personal commission of a little better than 1% on all the transactions of the Royal Navy, a colossal sum! (Pepys, 1972: 117 note 1, and 191, note 4).

was subsequently discharged from his functions and left without any source of income. A final royal gift was not sufficient to cover the debts he had contracted and his family was evicted from their dwelling place: "only the generosity of Prince Rupert saved them" (Codignola, 1990: 517). Heemskerk thus left England in 1670 and at once offered his services to the French, initially to build the same ultra-rapid ship, then to lead an expedition to Hudson Bay, for he alleged having accompanied Radisson the year before, which was untrue.[8] When Heemskerk returned empty-handed from this voyage towards the Bay, Colbert also abandoned him.

The difficulties Captain Van Heemskerk had with the Courts of France and England give a fairly clear picture of the rules that governed recruiting by favor. These may be summarized in four salient points which applied to Radisson and to Des Groseilliers, both in France and in England. Rule number one: the courtier must first *give* something of note to the personages whose assistance he is seeking, or convince them that he can procure for them something of great worth (a gesture that brings to mind the Amerindian logic behind the exchange of gifts); second rule: to keep the favor of important persons, one must always be a *contributor*, never a *burden*, if only in the manner of presenting the promise or the project; third rule: a courtier's fall from favor may occur abruptly if he is incapable of fulfilling his promises or if the humor of those in power turns against him; fourth rule: at times, the ties of grace and favor may be based on real esteem and complicity between a "patron" and his "creature," in that such ties may represent a pledge of greater fidelity between partners; a fall from favor may not always be definitive and a courtier may in time regain at least some of the benefits he has lost.

A maiden circle of supporters

The difficult circumstances prevailing in England during the 1660s provoked many falls from favor and losses of responsibility among the King's closest collaborators. Since the persons who welcomed and supported the two Frenchmen were almost to a man part of this effervescent milieu, Radisson and Des Groseilliers had to maneuver with the greatest precau-

---

8. "Heemskerk's quarrel with his landlord at least proves that he could not have been at the same time voyaging in the Artic on board of the Wivenhoe (accompanied by Radisson) as he later claimed to have done" (Codignola, 1990: 517).

tion amidst the preferences and the political and religious convictions of each and every one, to keep as much support as possible during their early years in England.

In September 1666, another catastrophe struck the city of London. Over a few short days, a conflagration ravaged close to a third of the metropolis; almost immediately, a rumor of comparable intensity began to spread to the effect that the French had set this great fire by intent. On September 6, Pepys wrote that "it is becoming dangerous for foreigners to be seen in the streets" and that riots threatened to break out at any moment on account of this so-called French plot (Pepys, 1987: 309-310). The sheer scale of the destruction had many other consequences. The losses suffered by the population, the merchants, and even the King – who the following year had to launch a mammoth and costly reconstruction program despite a sizable drop in property taxes – involved colossal sums of money. The commercial affairs of a weakened State were seriously impaired and widespread acrimony was soon the order of the day (Pepys, 1985: 669).

A Frenchman, accused of having ignited the great fire, was hanged in October 1666. On the 15th day of the same month, Pepys noted that Charles II for the first time was wearing a particular cloak as a sign of opposition to France, as did "several other personages of the House of Lords, the Commons and many illustrious courtiers" (Pepys, 1985: 682). The anti-French sentiment grew apace while all the businessmen whom Pepys encountered seemed pessimistic as to the future of the country: "Upon the Change (…), I find all people mightily at loss what to expect, but confusion and fears in every man's head and heart"[9] (Pepys, 1985: 689 [9 November 1666]). In June 1666, the Royal Navy suffered a crushing defeat at the hands of the Dutch (Fraser, 1993: 145); in September, the conflagration struck London and that autumn, the quasi-permanent financial crisis was paralyzing the country. All things considered, few Englishmen had much hope of conquering the Dutch.[10]

---

9. "Myself to the Popeshead (a Coffee-House), where all the Houblons (prominent merchants) were (…), and I do find that they, and all merchants else, do give over trade and the nation for lost – nothing being done with care or foresight – no convoys granted, nor anything done to satisfaction. But do think that the Dutch and French will master us the next year" (Pepys, 1985: 692-693 [14 November 1666]).

10. Holland was England's major commercial rival: "The increasing importance of the mercantile element, both in England and Holland, and their desire to encroach on the trade of one another in all parts of the world (…) was responsible for the war (the second Anglo-Dutch war of 1665-1667)" (Zook, 1919: 63).

In such circumstances, it seems clear that Radisson and Des Groseilliers had to make a very good impression on the individuals they met if they wanted to convince them to invest in their project. Such personages may well have appreciated their audacity and determination, their dynamism and evident competence, for men with these talents could help England develop her control over America, while at the same time weakening the French; thus, various influential Englishman gradually began to back the two brothers-in-law. And yet, in that winter of 1666-1667, the position of Radisson and Des Groseilliers appeared less than solid, despite the illustrious names in orbit around the nascent company. Several business opportunities, more promising and less risky, were offered to early partners, like Carteret and Colleton, persons very active in the colonies of the south; but these men were also involved in attempts to settle such serious and urgent domestic problems as revamping the fleet of battleships, rebuilding London, resuming current affairs and resolving the never-ending conflicts pitting the King against Parliament, and crippling the country. Other factors nonethless worked in favor of the two Frenchmen. Carteret, Ashley, Colleton and others of their stripe were members of the imperialist elite who wanted to develop additional colonies and increase trade between these and the metropolis: London. The project of Radisson and Des Groseilliers thus met the primary objectives of such individuals.[11]

In November 1666, Colleton-senior sent word to the Secretary of State, Arlington, to advise him that "Captain Goosberry" (Des Groseilliers) would call on him that same afternoon, with witnesses, to speak to him about a certain Tourette who was suspected of seeking to divert the two Frenchmen from service to England. This same Tourette, whom Des Groseilliers had

---

11. "The Restoration policy in imperial trade was a close-knit and purposeful policy, (...) it accepted the integration of domestic and colonial trade into one over-all balance, and it aimed at supplementing the economy of Britain by that of her colonies, who would provide markets for her manufactures, raw materials for her industries, and a transport system which would give a reserve of ships and seamen for wars. So integrated, the imperial economy would become increasingly independent of alien supplies or markets and stronger because, as an imperial unit, it would achieve a balance of exports over imports" (Rich, 1958: 21-22). "Such a challenge as Groseilliers and Radisson embodied was almost certain of support in London. Courtiers, financiers, administrators and scientists, equally anxious to make their own fortunes, to strike a blow at French trade and to probe the mysteries of the Arctic, were all bound to be interested. So it proved" (Rich, 1958: 25).

himself denounced, was subsequently forced to explain his suspected dealings with France and Holland. At the end of the confrontation, confidence in Des Groseilliers and Radisson was renewed and Tourette imprisoned (Nute, 1943: 106-107). The situation of the two brothers-in-law seemed to be back on firm ground after they over came the initial anti-French frenzy and this aborted attempt to undermine their reputation. The same cannot be said about England, which ultimately suffered the humiliation that all feared. Between June 10 and 13, 1667, or just before the aborted departure of Radisson and Des Groseilliers towards Hudson Bay, several Dutch warships sailed up the Thames as far as Chatham, port of registry of the Royal Navy, where they shattered the line of protection, set fire to the docks and burned or captured several great English warships (Pepys, 1985: 790). The news spread panic throughout London; Pepys, for example, immediately dispatched his father and his wife to the country, "with close to 1300£ in gold in their travelling case (…) my heart filled with trepidation" (Pepys, 1985: 788); (Fraser, 1993: 149). The expedition was therefore cancelled once again. The Dutch journeyed up the Thames a second time, several days later, to show who had the advantage in this war and Charles II was forced to sign a hasty and ignominious peace at Breda, in July 1667 (Codignola, 1990: 515). Then commenced the search for culprits, the fall of illustrious authorities and the power struggles in high places to fill the positions left open. Over the ensuing months, it became obvious that this Dutch raid had triggered a major redistribution of roles and responsibilities at the Court of Charles II.[12]

At the turn of the years 1667 and 1668, when Radisson and Des Groseilliers received their first wages from the nascent Hudson's Bay Company, the situation in the country at large was far from rosy. In March 1668, the riots known as the "Bawdy Houses" broke out in London, implicating some twenty to thirty thousand persons who sacked several brothels and threatened to attack the "worst brothel of them all," namely, Whitehall Palace where King Charles II and his entire Court resided. As the rioters rallied in a way that recalled the mustering of republican armies during the civil war (Harris, 1987: 82), the King and his entourage were seized by fear and

---

12. This quarrel lasted for several months, weakening the monarchy since at bottom it opposed King Charles II and the legitimate heir to the throne, the Duke of York (Pepys, 1985: 813); (Fraser, 1993: 156).

quelled the riots with force. However, in the end it turned out that the regime was not really under threat (Harris, 1987: 91). At the same time, the project of Radisson and Des Groseilliers was progressing full tilt, in part thanks to the peace concluded at Breda[13] and also because they could count on a new team of collaborators (Ra: 245). And so this time, they got underway as planned towards Hudson Bay, June 3, 1668, on board two small vessels 40 and 36 feet long, the *Eaglet* and the *Nonsuch* (Johnson, 1946: 10).

It is difficult to appreciate the progress of Radisson's career in England without knowledge of the events that led to the creation of another trading company, the Royal Company of Africa, which would have a determining influence on the formation, shareholding, evolution and situation of Radisson and Des Groseilliers in the Hudson's Bay Company, which they founded.

The Company of the Royal Adventurers Trading into Africa

The father of Charles II, Charles I, was incapable of imposing absolute monarchy in England when, at the same time, Louis XIII and Richelieu had done so in France. The English were determined to preserve their numerous elective and representative institutions, such as Parliament, the Mayorality of London, and the Craftsmen's Corporations; and so, in 1645, for religious and other imperatives, they overthrew King Charles I, then beheaded him in 1649. At that point, Cromwell instituted the first republic of Europe, a Commonwealth, which underwent a series of phases and crises until the restoration of the monarchy, in 1660-1661.

The conflicts that opposed over several years the partisans of the monarchy and Cromwell's armies forced Prince Rupert to flee as far away as Africa, in 1652. Once there, Rupert came to believe that deposits of gold had been discovered in a region near the Gambia River and, when Charles II was restored to the throne, Rupert hastened to spread the "good news." In a few short months, he managed to gather together several prestigious investors from the Court, such as the King, the Duke of York, Count Craven, George Carteret and other future shareholders of the Hudson's Bay Company, for

---

13. For the English as well as for the Amerindians, the peace went hand in hand with trade. One month before the official declaration of war against Holland, in 1665, "Sir G. Ascu (...) chiefly spoke that *the warr and trade could not be supported together* – and therefore, that trade must stand still to give way to (war)" (Pepys, 1972: 11).

the purpose of forming a huge new trading company: The Company of the Royal Adventurers Trading into Africa (Zook, 1919: 8 and 12). Even before any official charter was issued, the King promised to lend five ships to the future company (Zook, 1919: 10). Getting the enterprise under way thus took very little time. A maiden expedition reached Africa in March 1661, but the hot and humid climate was so grueling that efforts to find tolerable environs, indeed merely to survive, took precedence over trade. This first expedition, albeit largely in deficit, did confirm the feasibility of the venture and the possibility of building a number of forts on the islands in the region (Zook, 1919: 11).

In 1662, some ten ships were sent to Africa and shares worth several thousand pounds sterling were sold, even if the investment remained fruitless. Certain shareholders of the City soon suggested that the Company be reorganized and managed in a much tighter way (Zook, 1919: 12); hence, in January 1663, the Company obtained a new charter and from that point on concentrated its activities on the slave trade instead of on gold and ivory. Encouraged by the most important official of the State, who supported without reservation the young company: "a Model which will help promote English commercial ventures more successfully than any other company, even that of East India (then the most powerful)" (Clarendon, quoted in Zook, 1919: 16). A second fund-raising effort proved successful and better than doubled the capital stock. In 1663-1664, some fifty shareholders invested the colossal sum of £102 000 and sent out close to sixty ships to Gambia. Unfortunately, all these efforts and the money involved yielded almost nothing "and the company was once again facing a critical financial situation" (Zook, 1919: 18-19). The Achilles' heel of the enterprise was the armed opposition of the Dutch West India Company whose members were fighting with the English for control of the commercial interests and territory in the Gambia River basin. The support of King Charles II, the minting of gold coins called "Guineas" and the personal promotion of the Duke of York, along with a few military victories in Gambia, allowed for increasing to some extent the Company's capital stock (Zook, 1919: 19). The great aristocrats backing the enterprise continued to express unbounded optimism, predicting "within reason a return on the investment in the region of £200 000 to £300 000 *per annum*," a staggering amount! (Zook, 1919: 20). At the same time, the Dutch Admiral, De Ruyter, reduced English commercial perspectives in Africa to virtually nothing, by seizing almost all their establishments. As of 1665, the now bankrupt Company authorized a few individual expeditions over its remaining territories but it could no longer act in its own name. After only five years of activity and four years living from hand to mouth, by 1669, "the company was no longer of any importance" (Zook, 1919: 21-22).

This adventure provided a patent example in the business field of the muddle-headed inconsequence of an aristocracy already judged incompetent and irresponsible in a great many other areas. Despite the real commercial potential of the slave trade between Africa and America, this Royal company had disbursed in vain close to a hundred thousand pounds sterling in less than a decade, without adequately evaluating the possible risks, while continuing to make full use of the Court's support and backing to amass its capital stock. Neither Rupert, nor York, nor even the more respected Carteret could impress anyone with this undertaking and the financiers and merchants of the City found themselves so heavily in deficit that they were obliged to relaunch the enterprise under their own name to try and recuperate some part of their investment. In January 1672, they jump-started the Company under a new guise; the Duke of York was again elected Governor but an experienced businessman was appointed to the position of Deputy Governor (Zook, 1919: 23 and 26). The bitter lesson all the big businessmen drew from the Royal African adventure revealed that it was better to keep the management of ordinary affairs out of the hands of courtiers and to mistrust their impulsive enthusiasm for poorly assessed projects.

Indeed, it was no longer enough for Radisson and Des Groseilliers to merely announce that they enjoyed the support of Prince Rupert and a number of lesser courtiers to convince certain financiers of the City to invest in their project, and ensure that it was on firm ground and had promising perspectives. No doubt on the advice of their strongest ally in England, James Hayes, Radisson and Des Groseilliers now sought to gain the support of influential merchants.[14]

---

14. "In October 1667, Françis Millington, a Customs Commissionner of London, connected by blood and interest with the banking circles of the City, began to advance small sums (...). So did his wife's uncle, the greatest banker of the London of that day, Sir Robert Vyner; and John Fenn, Paymaster of the Admiralty, always on the look-out for a shrewd investment for the funds which passed through his hands, began to advance cash for working expenses in December 1667. Here was the beginning of support from the financiers (...) the great private banking interests were also represented at this time by John Portman" (Rich, 1958: 32).

James Hayes, an ambitious secretary

James Hayes, Prince Rupert's secretary, soon became the main "accomplice" of the two Frenchmen in designing, then setting up, the Hudson's Bay Company. It is certain that he was a reliable and steadfast ally of the two brothers-in-law, particularly of Radisson, with whom he is said to have developed a more intimate relationship (Mood, 1945: 49). Three inserts in the Company Archives reveal the direct links that exist between Hayes and Radisson's narratives. The best known passage has him noting that he spent £5 for the translation of a "book of Radisons" (HBRS-5: 171). According to the minutes of a Company meeting in 1687, Sir James Hayes apparently relayed to the Company's representative "the narrative of Mr Radisson and the Diary of Captain Benjamin Gillam" which he kept among his belongings (HBRS-9: 325). Finally, a third document confirms that Radisson's last two narratives were written in French and that Hayes possessed a copy of same, in 1685 (HBRS-9: 324). Hayes also took the initiative of offering a gold chain and medal to Radisson, in December 1673, in recognition of his good services and to confirm that the Frenchman could continue to count on his support in the Company (HBRS-5: 69).

Radisson, for his part, speaks with affection and confidence about the two persons who welcomed him on his return to England, in 1684, namely, James Hayes and William Yonge; Radisson qualifies them as "special friends" (Raw: 101).[15] The valuable, even irreplaceable contribution that Hayes could bring to the project of the two Frenchmen was his knowledge of English business practices and of the milieux of both the Court and the City; he knew who could support, fund or manage such a project. In this way, Hayes could save them from wasting time, making mistakes or being duped. He most certainly would have recommended that they establish their project on a solid administrative and financial structure, one protected by a Royal Charter with

---

15. The *w* of Raw indicates that this extract is taken from the *Manuscrit de* **Windsor** (Windsor Manuscript), a copy of which, recently discovered in the archives of Windsor Castle by Mr Jean Radisson, contains the fifth and sixth travel narratives and a message to the King, hitherto unpublished and dated 1685. This copy, after having been authenticated and correctly dated (Warkentin 1996b), was translated by Mary Ricard (translator of this biography in its entirety). I have used this new translation from the still unpublished Windsor Manuscript for every reference to Radisson's last two travel narratives, since the two published English translations of these final narratives, that of Skull (published in 1885) and that of Bymner in 1896, do not meet contemporary standards.

the guarantee of a commercial monopoly, which was the winning formula for such enterprises in that era.[16] Only Hayes, in collaboration with Radisson and Des Groseilliers, could tie all the strings of the project, secretly, on Rupert's behalf, as well as that of a few illustrious courtiers and bankers who were showing a keen interest, while enabling the two Fenchmen to keep control of the enterprise.

Aged thirty-odd in 1664, Hayes belonged to the same generation as Radisson and Samuel Pepys. The latter met Hayes on two occasions; at first, he described him as a lively and enterprising individual, albeit too optimistic in money matters. Their second encounter made a better impression on Pepys who believed he could make a friend of such an "incredibly ingenious man" (HBRS-5: xx). It is significant that Pepys would have used the term *ingenious* to speak of Hayes, since they were both members of the Royal Society and that epithet was particularly appropriate to describing their fellow members. Hayes was one of the founders of this restricted group of persons who were interested in inventions and their applications, as well as in technical and scientific matters, and he had himself elected to the Board of Directors of the Society in 1667 (Mood, 1945: 49). At about the same time as Radisson was writing his narratives, Hayes was just as active in the Royal Society as in the Hudson's Bay Company, raising funds for both organizations in the same milieu, at times by approaching the same persons.

To assist the nascent Hudson's Bay Company, Hayes put people in contact; he also gathered, assembled, advised and prepared; in addition, he attended to details and minor expenditures (Clapham, HBRS-5: XLVI-XLVII); (Rich, 1958: 52). The numerous entries in his book of accounts indicate that among the initial shareholders, he is the one who profited the earliest from the Company's activities: "the practices now in vogue convince us that a fraction of each entry in the accounts book remained in his hands" (HBRS-5: XLIX). His business acumen drew him closer to the City milieux where he successfully recruited a number of experienced administrator-shareholders to support and manage the enterprise he was setting up, towards the end of 1667 (Rich, 1958: 39); (MacFarlane, 1945: 20); (HBRS-5: XIX, XIV and XLVI).

---

16. "For the seventeenth century the chartered company was appropriate both in its ability to raise finances and in its ability to win the support of government; (...) it was accepted that the forts and factories needed for 'Traffique with infidels and Barbarous nations' could only be established and maintained by companies. There was very little criticism which was based on a genuine belief in free trade in colonial produce" (Rich, 1958: 11-12).

The path Hayes chose betrays his ambition to obtain great wealth and to climb the rungs of the social ladder. To begin with, he married the widow of a wealthy aristocrat, then he sat on the Board of Directors of the Royal Society and became a shareholder in the Hudson's Bay Company. Finally, the King knighted him, a mark of prestige which enabled him to become Executive Director of the Hudson's Bay Company, from 1676 to 1685. After his departure from the Company, in 1688, he retired to the country to a residence that he had had built in the county of Kent, where he died in 1693. James Hayes was able to seize every opportunity that came his way; he had fashioned his destiny and earned his privileges, by dint of hard work, shrewdness and opportunism. Everything indicates that he was a model for Radisson in England.

Radisson and the Royal Society

There is little doubt that Radisson wrote his first travel narratives largely for James Hayes. The only indication that Radisson's text provides is this phrase: "If one were to dwell on the dangers involved in important undertakings, you, ingenious men, would rather become cooks" (Ra: 82). Radisson addresses these "ingenious persons" on many occasions in his narratives, thereby indicating that such men were his familiars; he speaks to them as a trusted equal in a tone of jocular spontaneity and with an honesty that has him admitting to certain personal weaknesses (Fournier, 1997: 20-26). To make the most of this indication individuals Radisson of the wanted to convince of his competence, I tried to decipher the exact meaning of the term ingenious in London circles, towards 1660.[17]

Who is "ingenious?"

It is not enough to be intelligent or competent to be qualified as ingenious, although it is necessary to show great wit, clear thinking and an ability to act as the situation dictates; an *ingenious* person is above all one who can

---

17. On the basis of about twenty incidences of this term, in five authors of the XVIIth century: Samuel Pepys, John Evelyn, Robert Hooke, Henry Howard and Radisson, along with two contemporary historians who specialize in this period: (Pepys, 1972: 18, 22, 23, 63, 66, 70, 79, 93, 125 and 200); (Pepys, 1985: 149, 313 and 825); (Pepys, quoted in Ponsonby: 21); (Pepys, quoted in HBRS-9: 321); (Hooke, quoted in Biagioli, 1995: 1425); (Evelyn, quoted in Ponsonby, 1972: 23); (Howard, in Birch, 1968, v. 3: 22) and (Ra: 82 and 212). The historians are Ponsonby (1972: 12 and 41) and Mood (1945: 49).

put his knowledge to practical use, who *accomplishes* feats or who masters a subject *in practical ways*[18] (Ra: 212). At that time, two areas of activity were particularly suited to this qualifier, first of all, the milieu of inventors, scientists and scholars, members of the Royal Society, then, the business milieu. In business, shrewdness, skill, and success are the capacities that set the ingenious businessman apart from his peers (Pepys, 1972: 66, 70 and 79). But it is with reference to the newer sciences that the term ingenious seems to have found its most spontaneous and most frequent application. For example, in their respective diaries, Pepys and Evelyn, two contemporaries of Radisson, were in the habit of qualifying themselves and all their Royal Society colleagues as *ingenious*; and today's historians still closely associate this qualifier with the great English scholars of the XVIIth century (Ponsonby, 1972: 12); (Mood, 1945: 49).

To inform the reader about this medley of scientific knowledge, the curiosity, enthusiasm and common sense that characterized the regular activities of the Royal Society, towards 1665-1670, Pepys' passion for the microscopic universe, one that he had discovered thanks to his renowned colleague, Mr Hooke, is an excellent example:[19]

> After dinner, to the business of my microscope [which Pepys has just purchased], (...) that objects appear in a most striking way, quite beyond all imagination. This was our work throughout the entire afternoon, trying out different lenses and different objects; among these, one of my dishes, where the lines could be viewed so clearly, that it is impossible to believe such could really be the case... (Pepys, 1985: 647 [29 July 1666]).

Alongside the activities of a few great scholars, much of the research under way at the Society was resolutely turned towards practical applications, such as the repeated experiments on blood transfusion, improvements in the lighting provided by coastline beacons, the fabrication of hemp cables and

---

18. Pepys, for example, believes that a certain Mr Slingsby is "very ingenious" because he can explain to him the basics of economic theory which indicate to him the amount of money he must put in circulation, as officer responsible for the Royal Mint, to keep the economy of the country running smoothly (Pepys, 1972: 22-23). It is this mix of pertinent considerations and their fruitful application which distinguishes the ingenious person from those who are merely scholarly, cultured, or intelligent.

19. "Reading Mr. Hookes' Microscopicall Observations, the most *ingenious* book that ever I read in my life" (Pepys, 1972: 18).

perfecting suspension-spring carriages (Birch, 1968, T.2: 30-65); (Pepys, 1942: 3, 35, 94 and 213). The "technical do-it-yourself" dimension inherent in the development of experimental research (if only because of the need to perfect devices for measuring and experimenting), the penchant for invention, for improving the ability to spin, observe and navigate by machines and instruments, could but attract the merchants and businessmen of the City who saw in this precocious "scientific" lather real promise for technical development and profits.[20] This is why the Royal Society membership included many businessmen.

James Hayes, in any case, believed sufficiently in the new spirit embodied by the Royal Society to actively promote it while working to assure its extension and development; as soon as he was on the Board, he launched a subscription campaign to build a college where the Experimental Philosophy advocated by the Royal Society would be taught.[21] It is therefore certain that through Hayes, Radisson not only came into contact with certain members of the Society, but was also influenced by the style, the way of perceiving and the preoccupations of this early scientific academy, where, over the years 1660 to 1670, men like Newton, Boyle and Hooke presented highly constructive hypotheses on celestial mechanics, terrestrial gravitation and the nature of light. In writing his first narratives, Radisson likely went through

---

20. "It is not surprising, as Paolo Rossi (1668) has said, 'that the Puritan bourgeoisie should have referred to Bacon as their master, for they were a class of technicians and merchants who despised the 'abstract', 'useless', 'aristocratic' educations and ideals of the early English humanists." (Spiller, 1980: 40). "A respect for trade and consideration of its interests is noticeable in pro-Royal Society literature" (Spiller, 1980: 43). "Natural knowledge was not just a matter of *belief*, it was also a resource in a range of practical activities" (Shapin, 1998 [1996]: 14).

21. January 2, 1668, at the assembly where Hayes was sworn in as member of the Board (Birch, 1968, v. 2: 234). Two meetings later, on January 30, 1668, the President of the Society contributed the amount of £100 to the campaign, and James Hayes, that of £40 (Birch, 1968, v. 2: 244). Although it had been decided that each member would be free to contribute or not ("the business of voluntary contributions for building a college"), the fact that Pepys feels he is under constraint to contribute indicates that the campaign was off to a good, even an aggressive, start: "there I was forced to subscribe to the building of a College, (...) but several I saw hang off, and I doubt it will spoil the Society – for it breeds faction and ill will, and becomes burdensome to some that cannot or would not do it" (Pepys, 1985: 900). Mood writes of James Hayes that he enjoyed: "the companionship of learned and ingenious men. Robert Hooke, the great experimenter, a leading member of the Royal Society, and the familiar of Robert Boyle, more than once refers to him in his diary" (Mood, 1945: 49).

Hayes to address other members of the Royal Society, in all probability those among the commercial and colonizing fringe groups who were particularly interested in geography and discovery.[22] The five or six other individuals who had supported and financed Radisson and Des Groseilliers since their arrival in England, those who prepared the expedition and signed the orders for the captains of the ships, in 1668 – hence, those most involved in the project – were all either members of the Royal Society or closely associated with the Society – James Hayes, Prince Rupert (who had his own laboratory), the Duke of Albemarle, George Carteret's son, Philip, and Peter Colleton (who did not become a member until 1677, but who was already consulted because of his great knowledge), and Count Craven[23] (Stearns, 1945: 8-12); (Nute, 1935).

These persons had also launched or supported a number of trading or colonial companies. And so, it was they Radisson was addressing when he describes in detail what happened to the Royal Company of Africa: "I say it because the Europeans are fighting one another for a rock in the sea, or for a sterile land and a loathsome country, where people who are sent hither and thither die because of the change of air that provokes diseases" (Ra: 150-151). And again for them, and more particularly for such men as Carteret, Craven, Ashley and Colleton – who were among the eight proprietors of the new colony of Carolina, neighbor to Spanish Florida with whom they traded, as well as being among the first shareholders of the Hudson's Bay Company – Radisson further declared that within America, "There are still more countries to conquer as beautiful and fertile as those of the Spaniards; this may be accomplished without hindrance, and prove as plenteous, if not more so, for bread and wine, and all other things in as great a quantity as any other

---

22. One consideration that clearly supports the idea that the narratives targeted businessmen rather than aristocrats is the virtual total exclusion of allusions to sexuality. The businessmen and financiers, more sympathetic to Puritanism, condemned the sexual license prevailing at Court. If Radisson had addressed only influential courtiers, it would have been shrewd of him to include at least a few spicy episodes for their amusement and to interest them in Amerindian sexual mores that would prove novel and titillating.

23. It is noted in the Company's Archives that Craven was a member of the Royal Society, but his name does not appear on the Society's official list. His frequentations most likely prompted this omission.

place in Europe. I have seen all this, and I am certain that the Spaniards do not possess as much" (Ra: 196).[24]

Radisson probably wrote his narratives at the beginning of his stay in England, at a time when the confidence of the few individuals closest to him firmed and there was talk of establishing a major trading company around the two Frenchmen, in late 1666, early 1667.

The failed expeditions of the first two years left Radisson ample time to plan and compose this long and dense narrative.[25] It is probable that Radisson wanted to take advantage of the immediate interest manifested by certain members of the Royal Society, upon their arrival in England, and that Hayes, who was closely associated with that body, guided the actual writing to make sure that Radisson met to the fullest extent the criteria of appreciation common to the scholars and businessmen in orbit around that select group.

Since Radisson wanted to profit from the interest these influential persons manifested, he would try to prove Des Groseilliers' and his own abilities. His narratives could also constitute a solid basis for inviting shareholders to support the project; in addition, they furnished Hayes a tool for promotion, probably making it easier for him to attract City managers, who could see in the existence of such a document the draft procedure for sound business practices founded on transparency and rigor, both in the keeping of accounts and in the archival storage of reports, thereby allowing for a follow-up on the many decisions and processes deemed increasingly indispensable to the development of solid and prosperous enterprises. Finally, Radisson's rich and detailed narratives provided Hayes with proof of his own integrity; if the adventure went sour, anyone at all could consult Radisson's testimony and discern the basis upon which Hayes had solicited them; a testimony that

---

24. As in this other passage where he praises the climate and the agricultural potential of the American midwest: "Contrarywise those kingdoms (around Lake Michigan) are so delicious & under so temperat a climat, plentifull of all things, the earth bringing foorth its fruit twice a yeare, the people live long & lusty & wise in their way. What conquest would that bee att little or no cost (?)" (Ra: 150-151).

25. Given the rules governing the life of courtiers, it would have been unwise for Radisson to accumulate delays and failures without having some work to do: writing this long narrative offered a way to satisfy his supporters and maintain their confidence, by giving them further proof of his competence along with a new promotional tool.

he seemed to conserve for the moment in his possession, no doubt as a precious source of personal information.

It is certain that for Radisson the long and painstaking process of writing in which he was then involved allowed him to enjoy even greater recognition on the part of the gentlemen, businessmen and courtiers who had met with him and indicated their interest in his knowledge and his adventures. By producing such a long and detailed document, Radisson was posing as a competent and credible informant, on a level with his interlocutors, or almost. And yet, the credibility of the witness and the veracity of his testimony involved power games. It was allowed that gentlemen and indeed all those who were under no obligation to work for a living and who had cultivated their mind and their manners, while refining their powers of judgment, were imbued with a natural aptitude for lucidity and honesty. For Radisson to pose as a qualified and honest informant meant signifying to his interlocutors that he wanted to become a gentleman himself and that he believed he had all the necessary makings to that end.[26]

Experimental science, trade and Radisson

For two foreigners who possessed exclusive geographical knowledge of great commercial potential, the micro-milieu of the Royal Society – which numbered 191 members in 1667 (Purver, 1967: 38) – represented a particularly welcoming "niche." In theory, the Society was open to all nationalities, to all religious persuasions and to all types of knowledge, hence to all brilliant thinkers and inventors of whatever origin: aristrocratic, commercial or artisan class (Purver, 1967: 138); (Biagioli, 1995: 1423).[27] The experiments

---

26. "If the relations of a man of honour were to be believed, then such a man might unconditionally colonize other's minds, *constituting their sense of what was the case. An honor culture molded truth to the contours of power.* (...) all gentlemen not categorized as pertinently handicapped or defective were competent sensory agents. That which was available to be experienced, and thus reported upon, in the natural and social worlds was in fact registered by their senses and experienced in a manner deemed normal within the relevant community. The asumption of perceptual competence (...) was *not* one which gentlemanly culture extended without qualification to all sorts of human beings whatsoever" (Shapin, 1994: 73 and 75).

27. "It is to be noted than they (the members of the Society) have freely admitted Men of different Religions, Countries, and Professions of Life. (...) For they openly profess, not to lay the Foundation of an English, Scotch, Irish, Popish, or Protestant Philosophy; but a Philosophy of Mankind" (Purver, 1967: 151); (Spiller, 1980: 122).

and discussions which animated the Royal Society, during that era, most certainly laid the foundations of modern experimental science (Purver, 1967: 28, 66, 75 and 239); however, several members were more interested in the geographic and ethnographic discoveries that were being accumulated on faraway countries, where as certain members or persons in their entourage wanted to set up trading posts and found colonies. The archives of the Society contain four or five of these early, rigorous surveys on specific questions that were put to voyagers worthy of confidence. These surveys had two main objectives: to accumulate information useful to those who would travel to far-off countries and to lay the foundations of a new "natural philosophy" that would be both irrefutable and operational. A pamphlet published in 1670 by an anonymous member of the Royal Society provides a summary of the entire program of modern experimental science.[28] The spirit in which the members of the Society expected voyagers to answer their questions was thus quite different from that which continued to animate the courtiers and the French voyagers of the same era, a time when the English who needed to directly address King Charles II had first to boast their successes and flatter the great personages who were supporting them.

Two exhaustive lists of questions and answers dating from 1671 indicate the specific interests Society members had about foreign countries. A series of sixteen questions were addressed to Captain Gillam and Governor Bailey upon their return from Hudson Bay, in 1670 (Birch, 1968 v. 3: 43-47), and another of thirty questions to a certain Henry Howard about Morocco, that same year (Birch, 1968, v. 3: 22-28). The travelers were queried about the climate, the health of native populations, the diseases and the medicines utilized, about the fauna and flora, the quality of the soil and the type of agriculture practiced; a few questions concerned the peaceful or bellicose temperament of the populations, or the exact number of inhabitants, their

---

28. "They (the members of the Society) have esteemed it a laudable and useful Undertaking to endeavour, that all industrious and sagacious Inquirers of Nature every where may conjoyn their Researches, studies, and labours, (...) in order to the composing a faithful History of Nature and Art, that may contain a competent stock of Observations and Experiments, frequently and carefully made by Intelligent and Cautious men, which may serve for a Magazeen of Materials, of which hereafter, by duly considering the whole, and comparing all the parts together, may be raised (if possible) such a Systeme of natural Philosophy, as may give a rational Accompt of the Appearances and Effects of Nature, (...) as may conduct to the greater benefit and ampler accomodations of Humane life" (quoted in Purver, 1967: 97).

stature, etc., or addressed more specialized subjects such as metallurgy, child education, the political order and religion. The Moroccan list, more complete, also included four questions about that country's mines, minerals, lakes and rivers.[29]

In their entirety, Radisson's four narratives answer *all these questions* in munificent detail. On a great many occasions, Radisson interrupts the course of his story to provide very specific information about how the Indians behave and what they eat, about their history and their perception of the world, about the colonial customs of New France, about the American climate, geography, fauna, flora, hydrography, warring and hunting practices, the health and temperament of several Indian nations; and finally, he relates a great many intimate facts about his state of mind, opinions, weaknesses and small pleasures as a voyager-narrator. In brief, the dominant characteristic of Radisson's first four travel narratives is the extent to which the content offers the reader *informative details* with the greatest precision,[30] in full accord with the fundamental principles of the Royal Society which took inspiration from the reflections and guidance of Francis Bacon: "a vague and approximate observation produces erroneous or ambiguous information. (...) (One must) start out directly from the simple sensual perception"[31] (quoted in Shapin, 1998 [1996]: 87); (Purver, 1967: 57).

One can also discern the influence of the Society's new scientific spirit in the tone and the form of Radisson's narratives, in their simple, direct and highly descriptive style, which meets the expectations of the Society.[32] Since at least a few persons in Radisson's entourage were prepared to accord him the status of "intelligent and careful" observer, all the information he could furnish was valu-

---

29. Sixteen questions were put to Howard to verify already known but uncertain information about Morocco, to wit, about epidemics, the astonishing behavior of certain animals, or the effect of a substance called *Ihashish* which rendered one "half drunk" (Birch, 1968, v. 3: 22-28). Captain Gillam was asked six questions about navigation between England and Hudson Bay, one about the habits of the beaver and a final question about organizing for the winter months at the Bay.

30. The replies of Gillam and Bailey seem meagre alongside the documentary plenitude of Radisson's narratives about Hudson Bay (Birch, 1968, v. 3: 43-47); (Raw).

31. "Nothing duly investigated, nothing verified, nothing counted, weighed or measured, is to be found in natural history; and what in observation is loose and vague, is in information descriptive and treacherous" (quoted in Shapin 1998 [1996]: 87).

32. "Bacon recommended to the new scholar (...) that he employ a simple, direct, even austere, language" (Purver, 1967: 54). The problem was as follows: since the direct information sought could often be acquired only through an intermediary (Shapin, 1998 [1996]: 69 and 87), many worked to develop a method of observation, reliable in itself, virtually inde-

able in and of itself, at least for those persons, insofar as he could communicate it in a clear and precise fashion. Radisson was expected to provide the tangible information needed about America and the Amerindians in order to exploit the commercial potential that he and Des Groseilliers had identified at Hudson Bay. If he spoke the truth, his assets, his credibility and his influence would all of a sudden expand; this is surely why Radisson was careful to report faithfully everything he had seen and experienced.[33]

Radisson had fully understood this new craze among members of the Society for as *neutral* and exact an observation of reality as possible, and for recording raw facts. Pepys recommended that his nephew do just that to make the most of a voyage he was about to undertake; Pepys encouraged him to note exactly what he had seen without judging or deforming a single thing (Ponsonby, 1972: 28); (Biagioli, 1995: 1448). This approach seemed appropriate to the candor and sincerity which characterized Radisson's portrayal of his "inner reality," for he no longer had to continually pose as the hero of his own adventures and could on occasion adopt the position of a neutral observer who notes the facts and faithfully reports them: for example, when he discribes his leg wounds, how he was seized at times by feelings of terror, his admission of having eaten human flesh[34] or his inconsistencies as to his French or Iroquois identity, at Fort Orange, all this without tarnishing his reputation as a capable and responsible explorer-trader (Biagioli, 1995:

---

pendent from the observer, as well as a more "objective" type of written report about the phenomena observed. Radisson would never apply the method that the scholars of his era were slowly perfecting, but he clearly understood how he had to *formulate* his narrative to please such curious, meticulous and enterprising people: "Experience might be extended (...) by *writing* scientific narratives in a way that offered distant readers who had not directly witnessed the phenomena (...) such a vivid account of experimental performances that they might be made into *virtual witnesses*" (Shapin, 1998 [1996]: 108).

33. "In 1660, the *Gentleman's Companion* picked out the practical advantages of scrupulous truth-telling: 'Keep thy word and promise punctually, though but in slight and small matters; so shall thou be believed in greater'. A Restoration jurist noted that (...) the habitual liar is cut off from that trust and confidence which is necessary in interdependant social undertakings" (Shapin, 1994: 80).

34. Some 20 years later, rumors were still circulating in France concerning this act which was repugnant to European eyes, even though the correspondent, or in this instance, the rumor, confuses Radisson with Des Groseilliers: "you (Father Renaudot) are more lenient towards these discoverers than you realize, indeed, you pardonned des Groseilliers (...) for having eaten human flesh" (French Ambassador to Rome to Renaudot, 11-11-1684, BN, Fonds Renaudot (Renaudot papers) f. 171).

1425).[35] Radisson had discovered a small group curious to hear and read everything that he believed useful to recount about his life and his voyages in America and he seems to have taken his role as a narrator very seriously, since he devoted considerable time and energy to his writings. He partially restructured his adventures to his greatest advantage, but he had to prove his sincerity, his lucidity and his honesty if he wanted to eventually integrate in the circles he frequented, or at the very least retain the concrete support he had mustered.[36]

In the end, this partial autobiography probably crystallized the deep-rooted transformation that Radisson was undergoing in England, owing to the successes he had known among the Amerindians. He now sought to succeed in a radically different sociocultural environment, in wealthier, more powerful and more impressive milieux than those of America. Now that he had concluded writing about this period in his life, he was likely able to appreciate with greater insight the transition he was undergoing and the resources he had at his disposal to find his place in the sun in England (Barros, 1992: 1). By producing a text longer and more detailed than anyone expected of him, Radisson did not however leave his mark on the history of the sciences nor on enthography, and apparently very few shareholders in the Hudson's Bay Company or even members of the Royal Society examined the quasi-"privileged" information to be found in his narratives. But he did thereby prove his competence and his commitment towards those who actively supported him and Des Groseilliers in England. These narratives gave more substance, more credibility, to the trading project for they placed Radisson well above the rank of mere adventurer or coureur de bois by demonstrating to a number of his supporters that he too could be part

---

35. "Experiments were to be detailed in great numbers, *and failures were to be reported as well as successes.* (...) *A circumstantial and a sincere way of writing might transform readers into witnesses.* Experience could be extended and the *factual grounds* of natural philosophical *practice* could be made more secure. Once the factual foundations of natural knowledge had been guaranteed by these means, the philosophical search for causes could safely proceed" (Shapin, 1998 [1996]: 108-109).

36. The narrative on the fourth voyage to Lake Superior, in particular, leaves the impression of uninterrupted activity, of great efficacy, of considerable cunning and exceptional productivity. Such qualities corresponded to those which Radisson's English counterparts expected of a prosperous businessman: determination, pride, industriousness and self-control (Pepys, 1985: 759); (Ponsonby, 1972: 106); (Pepys, 1985: 879).

of the lettered elite and take his place among the movers and shakers, those who could assume responsibilities and inspire confidence.

Shareholders true to the image of English society

Among the first investors and the ten or so shareholders who joined the Company when Radisson returned to England with a full cargo of furs were found representatives of the movements then shaking up English society.

Since the support of Charles II was indispensable, a prestigious "patron" had first to be found to present the dossier to the King; and so, the King's cousin Prince Rupert was chosen. The support of this member of the Royal family accorded greater force and credibility to the project, the investors now having every possibility of seeing their exclusive trading rights protected by a Royal charter;[37] but the fact that it is Prince Rupert and not the Duke of York, or for that matter the King himself, who sponsors the enterprise, explains its rather modest launching, since Rupert had no reputation as being a front-rank organizer or even as a leader, nor was he considered a shrewd businessman (MacFarlane, 1945: 20-21); moreover, he had little influence at Court.[38] However, as Rupert did indicate a real interest in this project of exploration and trade, he made several useful moves, for example, as initiator of the project and then as the Company's first Governor.[39]

Radisson and Des Groseilliers could also count on the support of a few aristocrats and influential intendants of the State such as the likes of George Carteret, Treasurer of the Royal Navy, the Duke of Albemarle, and Count

---

37. "The companies (...) required some sort of a charter to give them their claims to lands and trade, to promise them support against foreign rivals and to grant them monopoly against rivals of their own nation. Without such a charter and promise of support they could not get the financial backing necessary for such speculative ventures as overseas settlements" (Rich: 1958: 11).

38. As Pepys points out: "The Prince is by no means well esteemed by anybody" (Pepys, 1985: 82). His relations with the Duke of York were particularly bad (Pepys, 1972: 134-135); (Nute, 1935: 419).

39. He supported the proposals made to the King to have the Crown loan a small ship to the Company, in February 1668. He signed the orders given to Captains Gillam and Stannard, in June 1668. He was elected Governor of the Company in 1670, attended four general assemblies in 1671 and 1672 and held four others at his place of residence, Whitehall Palace, in 1673 and 1674. He remained Governor until his death, in 1682 (HBRS-5) (Nute, 1935: 419 and 423).

Craven (HBRS-5: 216-217); (Mood, 1945: 52); (HBRS-5: 223); (Pepys, 1985: 669). All three had served under Charles I and fought against the Republican troops during the Commonwealth of Cromwell. Following the restoration of Charles II, they were able to rely on their fidelity to the Crown to recuperate lands, fortune and power. The majority of them took little interest in the Company's regular affairs and they certainly had scant contact with Radisson and Des Groseilliers, except for Carteret and perhaps Prince Rupert, under whose roof they spent several months.[40]

The Company shareholders also included a few royalists who, like Peter Colleton, were not as committed. In 1666, Colleton inherited the Barony that the King had given to his father, for services rendered to the Crown. He also inherited property rights in Barbados and one eighth of the new colony of Carolina, of which his father had been one of the most fervent promoters (HBRS-5: xxi). In 1667, he allied with four of his regular partners, Carteret, Craven, Albemarle, and Ashley, who had invested with him in Carolina and Hudson Bay, to purchase the rights to lands and trading in the Bahamas (Rich, 1938: 31). Colleton was one of the first to back financially the project of Radisson and Des Groseilliers and he kept up this support until the Company's first official fund-raising effort (HBRS-5: 161 and 203). He was at the core of the preparations for the expeditions of 1667 and 1668 and was a member of the first steering committee, from 1670 to 1672 (HBRS-5: 218-219). Afterwards, his interests in the south diverted him entirely from the fur trade, more particularly after 1673, when he became Governor of Barbados (Mood, 1945: 53); (HBRS-5: 218-219).

At the center of the political arena stood Sir John Robinson, the Company's first Executive Director. He too had actively promoted the restoration of Charles II and had profited from that loyalty by securing both the title of Baron and the key appointment of Lieutenant of the Tower of London; in the latter capacity he was charged with assuring safety in the City of London (a position he kept from 1660 to 1678). However, Robinson led concurrently an important public career: between 1661 and 1679, he was elected without interruption to the House of Commons and sat several times

---

40. Carteret represented without doubt a "natural" ally for the two Frenchmen on their arrival in England, in that he had himself lived and worked in France, that he remained in touch with the people of Saint-Malo and that he was fascinated by the shipping trade (HBRS-5: 216); (Pepys, 1985: 619). "He (Carteret) stood firmly behind Groseilliers and Radisson for many years" (Rich, 1958: 25).

as alderman on the Municipal Council of London, also becoming Lord Mayor of the City in 1662-1663. In addition, he was a member of the steering committee of the East India Company, the most important trading company in England (HBRS-5: xvii and 57). Even if he was a monarchist, it is clear that Robinson drew a great deal of his political power from the corporative, commercial and financial interests of the City, from members of the same elites who had elected him to Parliament and the Mayorality.

Robinson boasted, quite justifiably, of having successfully bridged the Court and business milieux, but with a self-importance that Pepys at first found insufferable. In time though, as his diary progressed, Pepys developed a more favorable impression of Robinson whom he met on several occasions, and he comes to describe him as a man who is enterprising, sanguine and easy to approach.[41] Robinson played a key role in the Company's early years. He would choose the first Governor sent out to Hudson Bay, Charles Bailey; he would establish the first administrative practices; moreover, he adjusted the initial project to conform to the actual situation prevailing at Hudson Bay, in 1671, after the return of Bailey, Radisson and Des Groseilliers (HBRS-5: xvi and 3-58). Robinson had confidence in Radisson and Des Groseilliers (HBRS-5: 205); (Nute, 1935: 423). During the years he was Executive Director of the Company, the two Frenchmen were well treated and consulted frequently on subjects they knew intimately, such as the choice of trade merchandise and the selection of furs. Robinson also paid them several substantial sums of money in his capacity as Treasurer. In short, he was a strong ally of Radisson and Des Groseilliers and one of the Company's prime movers.[42]

---

41. "Lord, the simplistic conversation we had en route, him glorifying his great undertakings and the care he has taken over the past two years (as mayor of London), and how he has managed the city to the satisfaction of all parties, all this from a quarreler who knows almost nothing of any import" (Pepys, 1985: 342). "It was a furious dark and rainy and windy stormy night; and which was best, I with drinking small beer, made them all drunk drinking wine, at which *Sir Jo Robinson* made great sport" (Pepys, 1985: 554); (Pepys, 1985: 358, 581 and 766). Others found Robinson conscientious and level-headed: "he hath been most industrious in the civill government of the cittie, watchful to prevent anything that might reflect any prejudice or dishonour upon the King's government, happy in dispatch of businesse, to the great contentment of the people" (report on the Aldermen of London, 1672, in HBRS-5: 250).

42. Robinson's role has been considerably discredited by the official historians of the Company (Rich and Clapham), yet the documents provide irrefutable evidence of his dominant role. I do not know why they have tended to marginalize him (Rich, 1958: 31).

The Company also included an important – albeit somewhat disenchanted – royalist, in the person of the wealthiest banker of London, Robert Vyner (HBRS-5: 250-254). He was the principal financer of Charles II but became increasingly reticent to advance him the monies he needed to defend and develop his realm, in view of the administrative incompetence all too often rife in high places, along with the impending financial deadlock.[43] Between 1667 and 1672, Vyner devoted much energy to getting the Company off to a good start. He seems to have decided upon the definitive financial structure of the Company, of which he was the first official shareholder.[44]

Other merchants of the City, men of a more republican stripe, were present from the outset and they would gain an increasingly greater hold over the Company, at the same time and pace as political events split public opinion into two major factions. On the one hand, the partisans of a sort of absolute monarchy in England – the royalists; and on the other, the republicans who sought to retain a certain control over the King's purse and the affairs of State, thanks to Parliament, whose members were elected by a few groups of some ten thousand property owners overall. The leader of the republican wing within the Company and to no mean extent within the country at large was Lord Ashley, a regular business partner of Craven, Albemarle, Carteret and Colleton, and an opponent of Radisson and Des Groseilliers.[45]

---

43. The King was no longer able to borrow, even for the Royal Navy: "By and by comes Alderman Maynell and *Mr. Viner,* and there my Lord Treasurer (Carteret) did intreat them to furnish me with money upon my tallies (...). They did at present declare they could not part with money at present. My Lord did press them very hard" (Pepys, 1972: 121 [8 June 1665]). "I find our Tallys will not be money in less then sixteen months; which is a sad thing" (Pepys, 1972: 133 [21 June 1665]). "We are endeavouring to raise money by borrowing it on the City; but I do not think the City will lend a farthing" (Pepys, 1985: 630 [10 June 1660).

44. Vyner participated in all the earlier projects of incorporation and his name figures on the first official charter of 1670. Subsequently, he attended seven of the earliest meetings of which the minutes were preserved and the first of these, a general assembly, took place at his residence, October 24, 1671, as did two other meetings, held November 14 and 28, 1671 (HBRS-5: 7 and 11). Together with the first Director, John Robinson, and the other members of the steering committee: Colleton, Kirke, Portman, Millington and John Forth, Vyner would establish rigorous business practices (HBRS-5: 3-6).

45. The progressive takeover by the business milieux of trading companies founded by Restoration aristocrats represented a significant trend during the 1670s, a movement which would assure solid foundations for the developing English commercial and territorial empire, while concurrently directing a substantial part of the revenues towards the bourgeois milieux of commerce and finance, who in turn would increase their own political power until the end of the XVIIth century.

Finally, Sir John Kirke, an up-and-coming royalist businessman, played a key role in consolidating the Hudson's Bay Company and in Radisson's personal life. He was the agent for a number of important trading companies and was a member of the Kirke family who had participated in bringing about the fall of Québec in 1629 (HBRS-5: 237). He had therefore been trading for many years with the Amerindians of Newfoundland and the Gulf of the Saint-Lawrence; hence he was able to extend to the Company his precious experience in the North Atlantic and Amerindian fur trades (Rich, 1958: 17). Kirke was also a member of the steering committee from 1670 to 1676 and he participated assiduously in the decisions and ongoing activities.[46] The Company logs reveal his personal involvement in the enterprise, as for example, when he offered on the docks a barrel of brandy to the crews bound for Hudson Bay; on the same occasion, he gave sums of money to the Captains, to Radisson, Des Groseilliers and several other seamen just before their departure (HBRS-5: 175).

John Kirke also purchased trade goods together with Radisson and Des Groseilliers and with them he often graded and assembled furs before they were sold (HBRS-16 and 19); in addition, he gave them money and, on several occasions, settled their accounts on behalf of the Company (HBRS-5: 203-205).

John Kirke was part of the limited group whose members financed the solo expedition that Radisson undertook, in 1669, and, of particular note, he agreed to allow him to marry his daughter Mary, in 1672. This gesture confirms the good opinion Kirke had of his son-in-law's competence in matters relating to the fur trade and also indicates Radisson's personal success in England, since the Kirkes were a respectable family.[47] For Radisson, this marriage represented a major advantage by permitting him to enjoy an even greater integration within the English social fabric.

---

46. It is he who attended the greatest number of meetings during the period for which minutes were preserved (October 1671 to July 1674), *ex-aequo* with James Hayes.

47. John Kirke was knighted by the King, in June 1674. This title confirms the respectability of Radisson's in-laws, Radisson had at least two children by Mary Kirke, Hannah and Mary (the documents concerning the children were recently discovered in the British Archives by Mr. Jean Radisson); (HBRS-5: 238).

CHAPTER 8

Radisson and Des Groseilliers in England and at Hudson Bay, 1668-1675

The orders given to the Captains in 1668[1]

The orders given to Captains Gillam and Stannard on their departure from Gravesend, the port of London, June 3, 1668, reveal the indispensable assistance that Radisson and Des Groseilliers were able to provide to the nascent company. They alone knew where to go in the immense Hudson Bay territory to engage in fruitful trade: "you are going to journey as far as the place where 'Mr Gooseberry and Mr Raddison' will conduct you in the Bay." They alone knew how to establish then maintain good relations with the Amerindians and how to deal profitably with them; thus, they supervised the fur trade "in accordance with the specific instructions we have received from 'Mr Gooseberry and Mr Raddison.'" They had sold procelain necklets (wampum) to the Company that could be used in exchanges with the Amerindians, but more importantly they would also determine which river offered a passage towards the Great Lakes and the sea of the South: "where the opportunity may arise according to the notice and the instructions of 'Mr Gooseberry and Mr Raddison' or either of the two." They also knew how to survive in the northern environment, among the Amerindians; and so the Company was relying on them to assure the safety of those members

---

1. The persons who signed these orders – in all likelihood those most involved in the project, as I have noted – were Albemarle, Carteret, Colleton, Craven, Hayes and Rupert (HBRS-5: 156-181).

of the expedition who were to remain at the Bay for a lengthier stay. Finally, Radisson and Des Groseilliers were able to convince their partners of the need to exercise extreme caution in Amerindian territory; "You will always pay extraordinary attention to your vessels so as to avoid any surprise"[2] (published in Nute, 1935: 419-421).

It is clear that Radisson and Des Groseilliers had no intention of exploring the regions located to the west of Hudson Bay, as they preferred to concentrate on those more to the south. The exploration projects are very carefully delimited in the documents of 1668 and 1669 and although less than ambitious, they are certainly realistic; Radisson and Des Groseilliers wanted to journey up one of the three or four large rivers that flowed into Hudson Bay and, hopefully, reach Lake Huron or Lake Superior. They had told the English that by heading south from these Great Lakes, it was possible to reach a vast waterway which led to the southern sea. I believe that the orders of 1668 offer Des Groseilliers' version because they are sketchy:[3] "they [Radisson and Des Groseilliers] told us it took seven days by canoe or by sailing vessel to get to the river where they intended to trade (...) as far as the Lake of the Stinkings (perhaps Green Bay?), and not more than another seven days to reach the strait that leads to the sea they call the southern sea (possibly Lake Michigan?), then from there, less than forty or fifty leagues to the sea itself (most certainly the Gulf of Mexico)" (published in Nute, 1935: 421). The version that appears in the charter of the smaller group who financed Radisson's solo expedition, in 1669, in all likelihood his own version, is much more explicit: "according to the information provided by persons of experience (Radisson and Des Groseilliers), a few of the Great Lakes of North America offer an outlet via navigable waterways that lead to Hudson's Bay (...) a great boon to us (...) in discovering a passage by way of these Lakes as far as the southern sea (via the Mississippi)" (in Nute, 1935: 423).

The close collaborators of the two Frenchmen surely entertained no illusions as to the discovery of a "Northwest Passage" towards Asia. Moreover, Des Groseilliers and Radisson made them no such promise, either in 1668

---

2. Same recommendation for caution during the exchanges with the Amerindians: "deliver unto them the goods you carry by small parcells with this Caution that there be no more than fifty Pounds worth at a time (in Nute 1935: 419).

3. This confusion brings to mind the one which muddles Radisson's third travel narrative, which is most likely the voyage Des Groseilliers made in 1654-1656, and that Radisson relates only as told to him by Des Groseilliers.

or in 1669. Their objective was to find the Cree bands with whom they had already slated a rendez-vous in 1660, or other nations, and to trade with them; guided by the Amerindians, they would be able to discover the waterways leading to the Great Lakes. Then, if the opportunity arose, either Des Groseilliers or Radisson could look for a passage leading from Lake Michigan to the Mississippi and the Gulf of Mexico; although at most, this was but a future possibility. And so, when it came time to decide on the actual preparations for the expeditions, Radisson and Des Groseilliers were forthright with their collaborators as to what they really knew about the interior of the North American continent. They stopped pretending to have already reached Hudson Bay, as Radisson recounts in his fourth narrative, since the Captains' orders make no stipulation about returning to a particular location or even to following a well-known route, but rather refer to *explorations*. No doubt when they first arrived in England, the two Frenchmen couched in glowing terms all the information they had obtained from the Amerindians about the immense network of lakes criss-crossing America. But in 1668, after two aborted departures, the objective had to be both viable and lucrative: Radisson and Des Groseilliers were to reach Hudson Bay and trade there, explore to some extent, then return to London as swiftly as possible to prove the feasibility of the undertaking, and, most importantly, to take possession officially of the rights and privileges over the territories they had discovered.

These same orders were proof positive of the vital role that Radisson and Des Groseilliers had been able to sustain in a very English association, whose members were influential men of the world: "It is our wish that you kindly use the said 'Mr Gooseberry and Mr Radisson' with all possible civility and courtesy, and that you take great pains so that your people show them a particular respect, since they are the persons thanks to whose efforts we have undertaken this expedition."[4] Everything indicates that Radisson and Des Groseilliers were able to communicate their conviction and their enthusiasm to the Englishmen who were supporting their project, and that their assurance and powers of persuasion would guarantee the proper organization and success of the entire undertaking.

---

4. The hierarchy allows for correctly determining the "weight" of the two Frenchmen in the expedition. The orders stipulate that members who are to remain with the expedition will be under the orders of 1) Captain Gillam, 2) Radisson, 3) Thomas Gorst, and the *mate* Mr Sheppard (who will later become Captain in the service of the Company) (in Nute, 1935: 420).

The expedition was to progress as follows. Upon reaching the Bay, all were to proceed speedily to ensure that one of the ships could return to London within the year, bringing back furs and information about the geography of the area, the endemic minerals, etc... Des Groseilliers would be on the return voyage. The other ship was to remain at the Bay until the following year; Captain Gillam and Radisson would continue to trade with the natives while increasing their store of information concerning the terrain. If no Company ship joined them before the end of the following summer, it was up to Gillam and Radisson to decide what should be done to assure the general safety and interests of the Company: leave or stay. However, it had already been determined that, should the two Frenchmen be unable to locate the Amerindians or the rivers in question, Gillam was to return his ship without a cargo to England, while Stannard would take the other vessel to Newfoundland; once there, he would sell his trade goods to the Kirkes, before travelling to New York or New Jersey where the Governor, Philip Carteret, cousin to George Carteret, could provide him assistance (in Nute, 1935: 420-422). One final item of some importance: all were permitted to trade in their own right, in other words to engage in what the Company called "private trade," albeit on a small scale, everyone fetching the same amount, but *only under the aegis of Radisson and Des Groseilliers* who were to control all exchanges with the Amerindians.[5] In the end, however, everything went awry.

Radisson and Des Groseilliers at James Bay

A storm at sea nearly sank the *Eaglet* with Radisson aboard, and the ship had to return to Plymouth for major repairs, whereas the *Nonsuch* entered Hudson Bay, in mid-August, and piloted by natives of the region, reached the Rupert River by the end of September 1669. The vast experience of the Company's shareholders in setting up colonies, the sizable amounts of money they had invested and Des Groseilliers' fur-trading expertise, all represented powerful guarantees for a successful expedition, thereby confirm-

---

5. "Wee conceive that some small private adventurers may be also carryed by you and your men (…) but doe absolutely restraine all persons from tradeing themselves with the Indians because thereby our Trade may be distroyed and the said Mr Gooseberry and Mr Raddison loose their credit" (in Nute, 1935: 422).

ing that the entire project was well buttressed materially and organized shrewdly. The crew built a dwelling place out of wood, using rushes for the roof. A cellar was excavated to store beer and all manner of provisions: hops to brew the new beer, meat, cereals, seeds for sowing, and, of course, fish and game, both of which were plentiful in the region. From the very beginning, relations with the Amerindians were amicable and trading, straightforward. Over the entire winter of 1668-1669, no one took sick, nor developed scurvy, as Des Groseilliers had agreed to share his knowledge about that disease with the English[6] (Rich, 1958: 62). The some three hundred Amerindians who came to trade their pelts in the spring were probably not the Crees to whom Radisson and Des Groseilliers had promised a rendezvous in 1660, as these were to be found more in areas along the Moose and Albany Rivers, west of the Bay. In fact, several Cree bands, more or less allies, more or less rivals, were settled around the entire James Bay periphery (Oldmixon, 1708: 382), and the competition between them seems to have influenced the institution of the first trading posts in that region.

In summer 1669, the *Nonsuch* departed for England, reaching London without incident October 9, 1669. The furs were sold over the following weeks, bringing in sufficient monies to effect the official incorporation of the Company of Royal Adventurers Trading into Hudson's Bay and the issue of its definitive charter in April 1670 (Rich, 1958: 42). Radisson participated with Des Groseilliers in preparing for the ambitious expedition of 1670, without there appearing the slightest sign of animosity between them, even though Radisson had made the solo expedition a few months earlier. Following his unavoidable return to London, at the end of 1668, Radisson had been able to raise enough money to launch a new expedition even before it was known whether or not Des Groseilliers' trek had been successful. Only six of the fifteen initial investors supported Radisson on this occasion, and it may be presumed that the six included his closest allies in the Company; and indeed, the six investors were James Hayes, John Robinson, John

---

6. The expedition of Captain Thomas James as far the Bay that today bears his name experienced major problems with scurvy and with obtaining supplies of fresh meat by hunting. Des Groseilliers brought to the expedition of 1668-1669 a wide knowledge of traditional native remedies against scurvy and a lengthy experience in forging trade relations with the Amerindians, who at that point were more actively contributing to enhancing the welfare of their European allies ("Adventures...," 1944: 136-137).

Kirke, Peter Colleton, Robert Vyner and Edward Hungerford.[7] This tiny group, dominated by commercial elements from the City, obtained a trading monopoly quite distinct from that which the King had accorded the group of fifteen the previous year.[8] But several days after the charter was issued, Des Groseilliers arrived at London with his furs and the group had to rewrite the charter to stipulate that their monopoly applied only to the territories "that are not at the present time held by one of Our Subjects" (Nute, 1935: 246). Radisson returned empty-handed from that expedition and the definitive charter was granted to the larger group of investors. Radisson's effort and the good relations between the two brothers-in-law clearly indicate that they were not in competition with one another at Hudson Bay. On the contrary, their project and its outcome appeared to be attributable as much to one as to the other; indeed, either of the duo could have made profitable such a high-risk enterprise. It would seem therefore that the two brothers-in-law shared a singularly *Amerindian* concept regarding the ownership and sharing of the resources they would be exploiting at Hudson Bay.[9]

At this same juncture – early 1670 – the Director of the Company, John Robinson, had a Quaker fanatic, Charles Bailey, released from the Tower of London so that he could appoint him first Governor of the Company, in situ

---

7. Edward Hungerford is the brother-in-law of Hayes; he thought he could count on the notoriety of his in-laws to obtain a new charter and dispense with Rupert. Subsequently, Hungerford played a low-key role in the Company (HBRS-5: 237).

8. "[1669] a royal grant gave the sole trade of the northern parts of America to a group of men who were in fact the City element, as distinct from the courtiers and scientists (…). There is no record of any kind of rift between these City men (…) and the rest of the members of the group. (…) The grant therefore cannot be taken as evidence of a rift among the supporters" (Rich, 1958: 41). Rich ties here to simplify the history of the Company for it is well known that internal factions were indeed created and power struggles nourished between the republican and royalist groups, between short-term commercial returns and long-term colonial investments.

9. The relationship "patron-dependent" which could also characterize the relationship Radisson had with his elder, a man richer and more powerful than he, smacked of a hierarchy. It was normal that the patron obtain more than his dependents from the total of any exchanges, whereas the division of the Hudson Bay resources seems never to have been restrictive nor subject to a cut-and-dried distribution between Radisson and Des Groseilliers. All the available facts and documents indicate a continuously harmonious situation, characterized by a ready give and take between the two brothers-in-law, who always tried, either alone or together, to make the very most of their presence at the Bay.

at Hudson Bay. And so, Bailey had to jump on the bandwagon and rapidly take the reins. This was an individual who knew nothing of the rules for trading with the Amerindians; nor did he know how to detect the quality of a beaver pelt or assess the difficulties of navigating in the north seas. However, the Company was anxious to have an *Englishman* directing operations at the Bay, even though they had every confidence in the two Frenchmen and were paying them a stipend equal to that accorded to Bailey (£50/ year); yet, since the Company was always loathe to leave the full responsibility for operations to the two Frenchmen, particularly in an environment that they knew better than anyone at that stage, they were careful to appoint an Englishman as their superior – first Gillam, then Bailey, and over time, others. To clearly indicate the hierarchical difference that existed between a Governor and the other Company retainers, Bailey was offered shares in the Company valued at £300, just a few days prior to his first departure to the Bay (Johnson, 1945: 24).

One again, two vessels got under way: the *Prince Rupert* (Captain Gillam at the helm), with Thomas Gorst and Des Groseilliers aboard – the latter again mandated to trade with the Amerindians[10] – and the *Wivenhoe* (Captain Newland), with Radisson and Governor Bailey aboard (Rich, 1958: 66). The expedition had two ambitions – as soon as feasible, Radisson would try to set up a second trading post on the Nelson River, far to the northwest of the Rupert River, where the Amerindians insisted that a great number of fur-purveying nations would come to trade. Bailey's presence at Radisson's side vouches for the fact that the Nelson River was to become the center for Company operations at the Bay. In addition, "the shipping of bricks and construction materials, munitions and 'large canons to be left at the Bay'" clearly indicates that the shareholders intended to consolidate and secure their positions (Rich, 1958: 67).

After clearing the Hudson Strait, the two ships separated. Gillam reached the Rupert River September 8 and Newland arrived at the Nelson River on the 12th of the same month, after having confronted all manner of hurdles.

---

10. Having been taken on as supercargo aboard the *Nonsuch*, Gorst had spent the winter 1668-1669 at the Bay, in the company of Gillam and Des Groseilliers. In 1670, he was assigned to assist the new Governor Bailey and he faithfully kept a diary or log concerning the voyage. The information we have about the second expedition of 1670-1671 and the third expedition of 1672-1675 derives in great measure from Gorst's diary, reproduced in part in Tyrrell ([Oldmixon], 1931: 383-396) and Nute (1943: 286-292).

At Nelson, they found several signs of recent Amerindian occupation, sufficient resources and an environment propitious to setting up a post. But
fog and head winds prevented Captain Newland from navigating the river
harbor and he nearly lost his vessel in the maneuver. Soon after, the bitter
weather coupled with discouragement and sickness – two men died and the
Captain became seriously ill – prompted their retreat to the Rupert River
to avoid an impending catastrophe (Gorst, in Nute, 1943: 292). However,
when Newland died on October 18, Gillam was obliged to convey the ship
to her winter quarters, there to dry-dock her on the shore alongside the
Prince Rupert, so as to avoid the vessels being crushed by the winter ice or
washed away by the spring breakup (Rich, 1958: 62).

As it was too late in the season to build a third log dwelling, the crew of
the *Wivenhoe* were obliged to spend the winter under tents they had fabricated out of the sails of their vessel.[11] However, the installations proved to
be adequate and the provisions sufficient to ensuring the crew's basic needs:
"We had a large brick hearth and we did not spare the wood, this country
providing enough of it to keep us ever in summer inside, while outside there
was naught but snow and ice. We also built a good oven and enjoyed game
pies at our pleasure" (published in Nute, 1943: 289). It is clear that both crews
were well nourished over that winter, a vital consideration according to
Pepys, who emphasizes that a proper diet is the sovereign remedy against
mutiny, for sailors "love their stomach above all else" (in Ponsonby, 1972:
8-9). As concerns food supplies, the expedition of 1670 seems to have been
impeccable, probably under the influence of Radisson and Des Groseilliers
who attached great importance to that concern.[12]

The first aboriginals whom Gillam and Des Groseilliers encountered on
their return to the Rupert River, in 1670, had been Christianized, and they
compared the two adventurers to Noah and his brother (Gorst, in Nute,

---

11. Well out-fitted and adequately heated, such tents could provide sufficient shelter
against the rigorous winter at the Bay, especially if the permanent installations of the other
crew could be used on occasion, as seems to have been the case, at least for food supplies.
The Amerindians were used to spending the winter months in similar tents (Gorst, published
in Nute, 1943: 287-288).

12. It was even possible to properly celebrate Christmas: "Christmas day wee made merry
remembering our Friends in England, having for Liquor Brandy & strong beer & for Food
plenty of Partridges & Venson besides what the shipps provisions afforded" (Gorst, in Nute
1943: 290).

1943: 286). It was clear that the natives knew the French and wanted to trade with them, or with other Europeans. Three weeks later, a large number of Amerindians came to encamp alongside the English establishment, before scattering in the bush for the winter months (Gorst, in Nute, 1943: 286-288). The neighboring aboriginals soon took to exchanging game for dry peas, an acceptable replacement for the grains they habitually exchanged with the horticulturist nations to the south.[13] From January 29 to March 14, 1671, Radisson journeyed to the Moose River, one hundred kilometers west of Rupert, to make contact with the Crees in that area to encourage them to trade with his group, the following spring. The passage in Gorst relating that event indicates the rivalry that rapidly developed between the two French-men and Governor Bailey. Indeed, in spring 1671, when the Crees that Radisson had encountered at Moose River came to trade at Rupert, Gorst tried to minimize Radisson's role, writing that the Indians would have brought their pelts to the Rupert River even if no one had gone out to fetch them (in Nute, 1943: 290). But, when one appreciates the importance of the initial contacts between the whitemen and the Amerindians – the equiva-lent of a pledge of alliance between two persons or two groups – it becomes abundantly clear how significant it was that Radisson be the very first Eu-ropean to encounter those Cree tribes. Another substantial trade took place at Moose River in mid-summer, after which Bailey explored the James Bay islands with Gorst. Then, all set sail for London on July 24, 1671.

Competition and instability

The arrival in England of the two fur-laden vessels, ten weeks later, was the subject of the first written reports of the Hudson's Bay Company (24-11-1671 and following). At a general assembly, held at the home of Robert Vyner, the shareholders in attendance decided to offer the pelts for sale as quickly as possible and to acclaim the return of the two Frenchmen with full regard by paying them a bonus of £5 each (HBRS-5: 2). Since the return of the two ships and Governor Bailey had not been anticipated, Robinson, Kirke and Portman, as of the next meeting, decided upon a whole series of measures to adjust the initial project to the prevailing situation, by adopting

---

13. "[23 December 1670] The Indians brought us a young Deere (…) & they used af-terwards to bring us fresh Venson & truck it for our peas which they love extremely" (Gorst, in Nute, 1943: 290).

a clearer definition of the current operations and by imposing a stricter control over private trading (HBRS-5: 5). The responsibilities appeared to be equally divided among the principals: Bailey, Radisson, Des Groseilliers and Gillam were asked to present their opinion, in writing, as to the organization and needs for the next expedition (HBRS-5: 6, 15-16, 27, 33-34). Most likely on Bailey's recommendations, the steering committee resolved to establish their center of operation at Moose River rather than at Nelson River, with Radisson and Des Groseilliers as the key promoters. Then were settled several instances of private trading, among same those of Bailey, Radisson, Des Groseilliers and Gillam.[14] It is also important to consider another decision taken by the steering committee that winter to offer the Duke of York shares in the Company worth £300, after having consulted the most influential shareholders (HBRS-5: 28 and 35). This highly political gesture had few immediate consequences but it would soon divide and weaken the Company, confound its operations and inhibit its growth.

Although private trading in beaver pelts was permitted on the first voyage, the Company decided to prohibit the members of the 1672 expedition from engaging in private trade (HBRS-5: 38). Yet, at the same committee meeting directed by Robinson, the trade in *beavers* undertaken by Radisson and Des Groseilliers the previous year – when such practice was prohibited – was nonetheless authorized and the Company paid them the £162 "which we owe them for beaver" (HBRS-5: 40). This seems a somewhat less than auspicious way to ensure that the rules ordained in 1672 be respected by Company retainers… The problem was all the more dicey in that this practice was the widespread order of the day for "secret commissions"; moreover, persons employed at the Bay seemed to view the right to private trading as a legitimate premium for working in a risky environment very far from home. It is of note that the £162 that Radisson and Des Groseilliers received represented a bonus of 150% over and above their annual stipend of £50; and although the two brothers-in-law were the uncontested champions at this game, their fellow retainers must have been sorely tempted to engage in at least a few direct exchanges with the Amerindians.[15] Finally, it is impor-

---

14. "In 1670 the two Frenchmen and Gillam were definitively of the opinion that they might conduct their own trade as well as that of the Company, and so must Bailey have been. Captain Newland, too" (Rich, 1958: 70). See also (HBERS-5: 20) for confirmation of Bailey's personal trading ventures.

tant to emphasize that the two Frenchmen participated actively in the preparations for this third expedition and that Des Groseilliers seemed to have gained in authority, since he was now qualified as "Capt. [Captain] Gooseberry" (HBRS-5: 205).[16] Hence, it would appear that at London, in the winter of 1672-1673, Radisson and Des Groseilliers had reinforced their position in the Company and were now actively participating, along with some ten others, in the decisions affecting the direction and activities of that body.

The young company was now in excellent shape (Rich, 1958: 68), except for a small problem of capital reserves that Hayes solved by requiring that each shareholder contribute an additional £50 for every £300 in shares, this to assure the financing of the Rupert River post and the instituting of new posts at the Moose and Nelson Rivers (Rich, 1958: 77). Little is known about events at Hudson Bay over the following three years (1672 to 1675). The single document to shed light on that period is the diary of Thomas Gorst and the partial transcription of same as presented by the first historian of the Hudson's Bay Company, Oldmixon, in 1708. As Gorst was a faithful supporter of Bailey, who, in turn, was opposed to Radisson and Des Groseilliers, and Oldmixon, markedly in favor of the English, to the detriment of the French,[17] this document, although invaluable, must be consulted with a degree of skepticism.

Des Groseilliers "takes up residence" at the Bay

The trade was excellent at Rupert in 1672-1673. Everyone spent the winter on site and, once the ice melted, the two large vessels were able to set sail for England laden with pelts (Rich, 1958: 71). And so, Radisson returned posthaste to London, but Bailey, Gorst and Des Groseilliers remained at

---

15. Ten years later, in 1682, Governor Nixon believed that almost all the sailors and their superiors participated in the trading networks then solidly implanted at the Bay: "indeed most or all of them have got privat trade more, or less, which I can not possibly come to the knowledge of, they being so great with the maisters and the ships company, that I am no more looked upon at that time then a cipher especially when they are in their drink, (...) these things hath not only fall'n out in my time but were in Mr. Bailys also (Nixon, in HBRS-8: 244).

16. The first historian of the Hudson's Bay Company, Oldmixon, also refers to Des Groseilliers as "Capt." on several occasions, based upon what he has read in Gorst's diary (Oldmixon, 1708: 387, 393 and 394).

17. "The Indians having sent their best to *Canada*," "the French having perswaded them to come to *Canada*," "By which we may perceive the French ran away with the best of the Trade" (Oldmixon, 1708: 386, 388, 390). And yet, French sources speak of a major decline in

Hudson Bay. In July 1673, Governor Bailey sent Des Groseilliers and a certain Cole to the Nelson River, by water, to make contact with the Amerindians in the region. It seems that Des Groseilliers took command of both the ship and the expedition since Oldmixon speaks of "Captain Gooselier" and "Mr Cole"; but their mission failed. Just as before, they found signs of recent occupation, but sighted no Amerindians in the area. On the return journey, Des Groseilliers would not even be able to locate the New Severn River, albeit indicated on a map he had with him (Oldmixon, 1708: 384). We also learn that the following year, in April 1674, "was held a council of the most important persons at the Fort; Mr Bailey, (...) Captain Groseilliers and Captain Cole were present" (Oldmixon, 1708: 387). The three men had to decide on a course of action to protect themselves against the Amerindians who were threatening to attack the fort; Bailey wanted to leave Rupert at once and repair to Moose River; Cole preferred staying put, whereas Des Groseilliers wanted to go to Moose River once all the Amerindians, friends or foes, had left the region to hunt. Des Groseilliers' option won the day, but it was only at the end of May that the three men headed out towards Moose River to trade.

According to Oldmixon, on that occasion they procured only 250 beaver pelts, the Amerindians blaming Des Groseilliers for dealing with the Rupert River tribes and exhorting other Company representatives to come and settle permanently at Moose River. Gorst, for his part, contends that Des Groseilliers was such a hardheaded entrepreneur that the Amerindians refused to trade with him.[18] About one month later, Bailey also went to the Moose River where apparently he traded some 1 500 beaver pelts with a nation come from the Albany River (one hundred kilometers further to the north) for the express purpose of meeting with him (Oldmixon, 1708: 391). According to Gorst and Oldmixon, Des Groseilliers' activities at Hudson Bay between 1672 and 1675 may be summarized as follows: a) Des Groseilliers fails in his attempt to make contact with the Amerindians of the Nelson River;

---

the fur trade following the establishment of the English at Hudson Bay; the Jesuit Father Nouvel writes in 1673 that "the English have already diverted large numbers of Savages from the lands in the region of Lake Superior" (JR, 57: 20-22, quoted in HBRS-8: xlii). French military action against the English trading posts of Hudson Bay also confirms the negative impact of these posts on the fur trade in New France.

18. "The reason they got no more Peltry now, was because the Indians thought Gooselier was too hard for them, and few would come down to deal with him" (Oldmixon, 1708: 390).

b) he fails in his attempt to renew contact with the Amerindians of the New Severn River; c) he decides as to the procedure to follow in order to protect the English from the hostile Amerindians at Rupert, but is unable to fetch more than 250 beaver pelts from Moose River, whereas Bailey brought back 1500; and finally, d) it is discovered that before the departure of the expedition towards England, in summer 1675, Des Groseilliers had been in the habit of visiting the Jesuit Father Albanel, who had reached Rupert in August 1674[19] in an effort to convince Des Groseilliers to return to the service of France and whom the English had subsequently taken prisoner (Oldmixon, 1708: 394). All this is scarcely believable of an active and experienced man like Des Groseilliers who could just as easily navigate James Bay or Hudson Bay, or indeed travel up any boatable river in a small craft, a rowing boat or a bark canoe, as he was able to cover ground inland by shank's mare or wearing snowshoes… Des Groseilliers' activities during those years are most certainly under-documented and it may be readily inferred that he achieved a somewhat greater success than indicated by Gorst who, ostensibly, was unable to fraternize with him in any permanent fashion.

A tense atmosphere at James Bay

In early winter 1673-1674, some of the Amerindians who had come to trade at Rupert advised the English that they had seen a number of dead Indians at Moose River (Oldmixon 1708: 385). Then when spring arrived, the Cuscididahs, allies of the English, settled at very close proximity to the fort, fearing an attack from enemy tribes, allies of the French; these last had just recently encamped at a distance of eight days by canoe from Fort Rupert, so that they could commandeer as many pelts as possible (Oldmixon, 1708: 387). That same spring, a dispute between two Amerindians occurred right inside Fort Rupert and Bailey decided to forbid all future entry to Amerindians, with the exception of a few chiefs. Some weeks later, a shaman pitched his wobbly tent close by the English fort and announced to his

---

19. Father Albanel had first reached the mouth of the Rupert River in June 1672, with Simon Denys, and had left for Québec on July 6, without encountering Radisson, Des Groseilliers or any of the Englishmen who had all returned to England the previous year. Albanel found two dwellings (that of 1668 and the other of 1670); he took possession of the locality in the name of France. Three of the Company's ships returned to the Rupert River in August 1672, shortly after Albanel's departure.

fellows that their enemies the "Nodways" would soon arrive and that they should "be on their guard and also [be wary of the] 'Mistigooses,'" meaning the English" (Oldmixon, 1708: 389). This Cree shaman was in fact advising his people to be chary of their English allies, no doubt because of the reciprocity with the Moose River bands that Bailey wanted to effect. All indicates that the situation was troubled and tense at James Bay, in 1674.[20] The English attacked the "Nodways" on at least two occasions, without Des Groseilliers, who seems to have been elsewhere. Then, Bailey returned to Moose River to trade advantageously a great number of pelts with the Amerindians of the Albany River region, this time accompanying them to their settlement. Helped by other guides from the New Severn River, he attempted to reach the Nelson River but one of his guides was frightened by the ship's compass and the Amerindians were able to convince Bailey that there were no beaver further afield, only more ice. The Governor gave in to their intimidation tactics – common to all the Amerindians – in the hope of conserving as long as possible their certain knowledge of the region's geography, while keeping them involved as intermediaries in the fur trade (Oldmixon, 1708: 391-392).

The competition that developed almost from the beginning between Radisson and Des Groseilliers and Governor Bailey,[21] coupled with the pressures brought to bear by the French of the Saint Lawrence region almost as far as James Bay and the long-standing rivalries between the Amerindian nations, created a conflictual climate in all the peripheral regions of Hudson Bay (Oldmixon, 1708: 393). To compensate for his "deficiencies" when compared with the veteran Des Groseilliers, who spoke fluently the Algonquin tongues and had also continued to maintain a close contact with the Amerindians over a great many years, Governor Bailey saw his advantage in receiving the complaints of the natives he encountered to the effect that

---

20. "Their coming [the arrival of the Hudson's Bay Company associates] freed the Indian trappers from the economic domination of the tribes which had acted as middlemen between them and the Europeans, and the English understood this advantage. Their coming disturbed the whole balance of native affairs" (HBRS-8: xli-xlii).

21. This conflict appears in the information reported by Oldmixon and in the data issued by the steering committee as of 1673. Captain Gillam was also in competition with the two Frenchmen, but as he spent a shorter length of time at the Bay and had little autonomy on land, Captains having to attend to their vessel, it is likely that his role in the dynamic of exchanges between the Amerindians and the English was of lesser importance.

the French were selling their goods more cheaply than the English.[22] However, Des Groseilliers, who knew the price of French goods and the additional cost of their transport as far as Hudson's Bay, was quite aware that his prices were the lowest; so he stood his ground.[23] Bailey agreed to cheaper rates than those which the Company recommended, on the advice and counsel of Radisson and Des Groseilliers, so as to stabilize a situation which thus far had benefited those with much more experience than himself. It came as no surprise that the Moose River Tobittee refused to deal with Des Groseilliers and that the Albany River Shechittawams preferred trading with Bailey, of whom they kept excellent memories long after his departure from the Bay, in 1679 (Rich, 1958: 80). In the end, the Company administrators reproached Bailey for having "misused the Company's property" to the tune of £828 15s. 6d. during the nine years of his mandate, or approximately £100 per annum. It will be seen that there were definite limits to Governor Bailey's price-slashing policy (Rich, 1958: 77). His immediate successor, Governor Nixon, believed that Bailey did not possess the audacity needed to impose his authority on the retainers working at the Bay, who tended to view physical strength and force of character as the only guarantees for gaining respect.[24]

---

22. "They [the French] oblig'd Mr. Baily to lower the Prices of his, to oblige the Indians, who dwelt about Moose River" (Oldmixon, 1708: 387).

23. Oldmixon maintains therefore that French goods were cheaper. A scarcely credible opinion for, if it is true that the French employed "many Artifices to hinder the Natives trading with the English" for example, by offering lavish gifts to conclude a first agreement or good prices for less valuable furs (Rich, 1958: 75), the price of French goods was always higher at the Bay: "the difficult land routes made their expenses (the English) so much less that they could afford to give the Indians better terms than the French offered" (HBRS-8: xli-xlii); (White, 1991: 119). Radisson and Des Groseilliers were counting on this advantage to secure a better margin of profit but Bailey, who seems not to have immediately understood the Amerindian negotiating practices – that the French spent decades mastering – agreed to accord them preferential exchange rates. The Amerindians appreciated this treatment and allied more readily with him (Johnson, 1945: 24-25).

24. "Baily came on-board, (...) there was then alongst with him, Capt. Powers, and doctor Rainer, both of them so drunk as beasts, who abused him after such a gross maner, that it was ashamed to see their cariage towards their ould governor (...). I wrote to yor. Honors, and informed you fully what trouble and vexation a governor was in, at such a drunkne tyme, when all things are doon in haste and confusion" (letter from Nixon to the steering committee, HBRS-8: 244-245 [1682]).

Owing to a critical shortage of food and munitions at Rupert, at the end of summer 1674 (Oldmixon: 391 and 394), Bailey had decided on a general departure for England no later than September 22; then on the 18th and 22nd of that same month, two Company vessels finally arrived. Since these ships were not intended to winter on site, they carried very few supplies. Moreover, the crossing had been much longer than anticipated and it was now too late in the season to weigh anchor; hence all were obliged to resign themselves to wintering at the Bay and enduring the inevitable privations.[25] That same year, at London, several changes had occurred within the Company. Most important of these was the recall of Governor Bailey whom apparently Radisson had attacked severely, upon his return to London. The individual designated to replace him, Governor Lydall, personally gave him the news on his arrival. Lydall subsequently refused to follow the advice of Gorst who wanted to ration the supplies immediately; and so, all were suffering cruelly from hunger when spring finally came (Oldmixon, 1708: 396). Lydall detested his experience at the Bay and decided to return to England with his entire staff, at the breakup. In view of the state of widespread disorganization at the Bay, Bailey and three of his men obtained authorization to stay put despite the orders of the administration, so as to guarantee the permanence of the English occupation and maintain trade relations with the Amerindians. However, Father Albanel and Des Groseilliers were on the return voyage, reaching London September 25, 1675.

Radisson's English journey 1670-1675

In contrast to the role of Hudson's Bay pioneer that he had to assume at the outset, Radisson spent much more time at London than at the Bay; rather, it was his brother-in-law Des Groseilliers who actually carried out their trading project in the James Bay region. From the start, Radisson also appeared to be considered as the second in command or assistant to Des Groseilliers (at the time of the Tourette affair, notably) until such time as he attracted the attention of his entourage by writing his first travel narratives, then by

---

25. The steering committee had decided that henceforth the return trip London/the Bay/London had to be made the same year, to avoid the long and costly winters on site. Unfortunately, that measure had been adopted without forethought, as though such a long voyage could be controlled by the steering committee or the Captains. This initial attempt in 1674 was nothing less than foolhardy.

proving, in 1669, that he too could rally investors on the strength of his own capacities, mounting a solo expedition that reached the Hudson Strait. His marriage with Mary Kirke, in 1672, confirms that he was able to integrate the English milieu he had come to know and wherein he had sufficiently distinguished himself to be welcomed within an honorable family. Thus, Radisson's journey differs considerably from that which the initial orders announced in 1668. Radisson's first two stays at the Bay were of brief duration (winter 1670-1671 and winter 1672-1673);[26] he did not return there until 1682. The evolution of his career in England indicates that he swiftly made use of his many talents in the capital, particularly in the business coterie that he came to know; he was also able to assist the Company other than as a coureur de bois or expert in Amerindian relations. Between the years 1665 and 1675, Radisson gradually phased out his adventures in the bush to become a curious mix of gentleman and adventurer; he was always able to share the life of the Amerindians that he knew so well, but could also hold his own in literary circles and participate in the economic expansion of the English realm on the strength of his many talents as explorer and businessman. His values, objectives and attitudes underwent a sea change during this period.

Transformations taking place within the Company

Ever anxious to control private trade and in the interest of obtaining detailed information about the progress of the latest expedition, the steering committee asked Radisson to come to London on his return from the Bay, in September 1673. Since England was again hard at war with Holland which, in turn, meant that the coastal waters were unsafe, the furs had to be conveyed overland from Plymouth to London. Everything seemed to be proceeding smoothly up until the election of the new steering committee on November 24, 1773. That day, the general assembly designated Lord Ashley, Earl of Shaftesbury, as the new Executive Director, probably because he had a lengthy experience with trading companies and colonization, had

---

26. Unfortunately, no document exists to indicate what Radisson did at Hudson's Bay that year. Everyone would have spent the winter at Rupert and the Company historians believe that a first permanent trading post (a dwelling) was established at Moose River; in such case, Radisson probably participated in setting it up, since he had known success at Moose River the previous year.

manifested a growing interest in the Company since the previous summer and, most significantly, had just resigned as Lord Chancellor, the loftiest post in the entire Royal administration, one that he had occupied over the previous twelve months (HBRS-5: 220). This quite significant nomination can be explained by the general political and economic situation in which Radisson had to maneuver, both at London and in the Company, to maintain his own and Des Groseilliers' position in the midst of their powerful and influential English partners.

A meeting had been held at the home of John Kirke a few days before Shaftesbury's appointment, the last meeting that Robinson chaired as Executive Director. On that occasion, the committee gave Radisson part of his stipend and, as was their wont, asked him to prepare a list of articles that he deemed useful for the next expedition (HBRS-5: 53). But with Shaftesbury as Director, things were to change rapidly; this "workaholic" (Haley: 404-405) apparently needed to exhaust his energy, or better yet, to aim his spleen at something or somebody, after having been dismissed by Charles II who had preferred his rival, Danby, for the post of Lord Chancellor. In short order, Lord Ashley imposed a series of transformations that pushed the Company in a direction that it had never taken before, fomenting a crisis which it nearly failed to overcome. To appreciate exactly what was at stake in having the Company's current administrative affairs taken in hand by the Earl of Shaftesbury and to understand the quarrel that ensued among the shareholders for control of the Company's direction and development, between 1673 and 1679, it is useful to know something about this powerful personage.

Lord Ashley, Earl of Shaftesbury

A biography of Lord Ashley speaks of this astonishing individual's political career as follows:

> From Royalist to Republican during the civil war, from member of Parliament under Cromwell (…) to the faction in opposition to the Protectorate [of Cromwell] (…) from service to Charles II to the camp opposing him. (…) [His opponents suggested] that these changes of direction were proof of Shaftesbury's essential dishonesty, one in whom no rational person should place his confidence. (…) [Many] called him the Eel of Dorsetshire because he was always able to slither away from anyone's hold (Haley, 1968: 742).

Shaftesbury therefore spent his entire very brilliant political career switching from one side to the other. Because he was prone to defending his personal convictions with great determination, he was ever seeking out the best and most powerful ways to impose same: "He was never ashamed of recognizing his many changes of allegiance; indeed, he was proud to have recognized the most expedient moment and the cleverest way to take such action" (Burnet, quoted in Haley, 1968: 742). His unusual cunning and underhanded behavior gave rise to much distrust and Pepys wrote that he was "detested by all" (Pepys, 1985: 914). He also had a reputation for being ruthless in business (Pepys, 1972: 218); (Haley, 1968: 363).

Under Charles II, who named him Chancellor of the Exchequer (Haley, 1968: 158) shortly after his return to the throne, Shaftesbury proceeded to impose a number of reforms for the purpose of limiting corruption in the King's affairs and curbing the negligence in accounting that was then facilitating embezzlement.[27] He thus acquired the reputation of being a superior public administrator and, slowly but surely, he gained the confidence of the King, who appointed him to key posts (Haley, 193, 286-287 and 334). Shaftesbury was one of the most constant defenders of freedom of religion in England, except as concerned Catholicism. However, in the mid-1670s, he actively supported the *Test Act* which Parliament imposed on the King to halt the movement towards religious tolerance promoted by Charles II (Haley, 1968: 323-325). The defection was radical for Shaftesbury, but his intention was to attack directly the Duke of York and the Catholics in his entourage; under the *Test Act*, all public officials were obliged to swear allegiance to the Anglican Church, the official denomination of the English State, independent of Rome. Very soon, the Duke of York was obliged to relinquish all his charges and responsibilities. However, this brilliant success would occasion Shaftesbury's fall from the position of Lord Chancellor (HBRS-5: 221).

For a long time, many had suspected York of being a Catholic and a partisan of absolute monarchy. Then in 1673, he married a declared Catholic, thereby publicly confirming his religious allegiance. York's provocative

---

27. And yet, he took advantage of his position as Lord Chancellor, as others did of theirs, to advance his own interests: "Shaftesbury made no bones about using his patronage in the customary manner of the period, for the benefit of his own dependants" (Haley, 1968: 311).

– or honorable? – behavior had the immediate consequence of undermining the entire English Monarchy and the position of his brother King Charles
II, who subsequently distanced himself from the Duke of York. This episode
also marked the beginning of a fight to the finish between the Duke of York
and the Earl of Shaftesbury, who obstinately refused to let an absolutist
Catholic accede to the throne of England. At the opening of the Parliamentary session of January 1674, Shaftesbury (who was sitting) "began to pro-
claim his anti-papist message as loudly as he could," insisting that within the
City there were 16 000 Catholics ready to take such desperate action as
slaughtering all the citizens of London... (Haley, 1968: 355). From then on,
Shaftesbury's life would revolve around this sole objective: because the Duke
of York was Catholic and absolutist, he must, at all costs, be deprived of his
legitimate right of succession (Haley, 1968: 347). At that same juncture,
Shaftesbury took over the administration of the Hudson's Bay Company,
whose steering committee, the preceding year, had graciously offered shares
in the Company worth £300 to that selfsame Duke of York...

Shaftesbury's genius, determination and cunning were such that as of
his first speeches in Parliament decrying the Catholics, the French and absolute monarchy (Haley, 1968: 338-3399), until the time of the great popular manifestations that he inspired or organized, at the end of the 1670s, the
Whig opposition that he formed and, to a large degree, led, very nearly overthrew Charles II and deprived York of his right of succession. And although
to a slighter degree, Shaftesbury revealed the same strength and determination when he took the reins of the Hudson's Bay Company. Three days after
his appointment as Director, it was decided that Radisson and Millington
would choose together the hatchets needed for the next trading venture and
Kirke would see to their purchase in France (HBRS-5: 58-59). But a week
later, this decision was overturned because, as may be read in the minutes,
there were equally good hatchets to be found in London and, as a priority,
the Company should procure supplies from English merchants; this time,
Millington *alone* was responsible for the purchase (HBRS-5: 61). For a merchant like Kirke who had French ancestors, or for Radisson and Des
Groseilliers, the French hatchets regularly employed by the Amerindians
were quite acceptable; however, this was not the case for a great imperialist
colonizer like Shaftesbury for whom the purchase of French hatchets or any
other French goods was an aberration (HBRS-5: 173 and 175). Shortly thereafter, Radisson and Gillam successfully avoided the earlier interdiction on

private trade (HBRS-5: 60); and finally, Shaftesbury proposed that the next general assembly rule on the feasibility of sending an expedition to Buss Island, located somewhere in the North Atlantic, to set up a fishing colony.

On January 22, 1673, the general assembly ordained that henceforth all the Company retainers and indeed all its suppliers would be obliged to pledge an oath of allegiance. At a special meeting held the same day, Rupert, Arlington and Carteret were charged with obtaining the charter for Buss Island. Again on that occasion, a committee including Hayes and Kirke asked Captain Shepard, the man who only recently had "rediscovered" Buss Island, to prepare an estimate for all that would be required to set up the colony as planned (HBRS-5: 69). One week later, on January first, Shaftesbury called another meeting on the prickly subject of private trading, after having received a letter denouncing transactions that had occurred at Plymouth; his reaction was immediate, with Captains Morris and Gillam being promptly called to account. Their representations were deemed inadequate and, two weeks later, legal proceedings were instituted against "Captain Gillam and Captain Morris, the remaining crewmembers and other company retainers on this last voyage," in short, against those who had participated in the most recent expedition to engage in private trading (HBRS-5: 71).

With Shaftesbury at the helm, ten meetings were held in less than two months; they stirred up a veritable "witch-hunt" against private trading, as well as modifyed the supplying of trade merchandise and redistributed a measure of the responsibilities among the Company's retainers. But most important was the decision to launch a risky colonization project at Buss Island, even though the Company had yet to consolidate its few Hudson's Bay trading posts. Did Hayes and Kirke, who attended those ten meetings, support Shaftesbury's initiatives or were they simply attempting to minimize the potential commercial losses? A difficult question to answer. The harassing of Captains Gillam and Morris could increase the authority and margin of maneuver for individuals like Radisson, Kirke and Hayes; but Gillam's experience was indispensable to the Company and it was risky to harass such a valuable retainer, even worse to dismiss him, as Shaftesbury would do later on. Moreover, the two Frenchmen were far from being without reproach and sooner or later, if private trading persisted, they risked suffering the consequences. Thus, it seems likely that the Hayes, Kirke and Radisson cohort tried to "follow" Shaftesbury, the driving force behind so many abrupt changes, being astounded perhaps by such a rapid evolution in the situation. But the pace imposed by Shaftesbury was excessive and, rather than improving the overall state of affairs, quite soon there was a sudden deterioration in the Company's management practices and its profitability.[28]

Interdiction on private trading

In any case, Shaftesbury's handling of the private-trade issue came to naught. In January 1674, a number of retainers – including Radisson – received their full stipend despite many vexations (HBRS-5: 72-75). Then in February, Radisson and his associate Palmer (second in command) were again harassed and forced to swear allegiance, a means the steering committee now employed to encourage denunciation in an effort to make more thorough enquiries about certain retainers. Captains Gillam and Morris were soon dismissed and replaced by Captains Draper and Shepard. The assembly then decided to recall Governor Bailey,[29] without appointing his successor, yet stipulating that that person was expected to suppress systematically "private trading under any guise whatsoever" (HBRS-5: 81).

However, all these good intentions delayed the preparations for the coming expedition and Shaftesbury was obliged, at last, to capitulate. At mid-March, he ordered the dismissed Captains to meet with him again, reinstating them a few days later, with no penalty; in fact, Captain Morris was accorded "fifty pounds in compensation for his beaver pelts that had been confiscated by the Company at Plymouth" (HBRS-5: 86). The cases of Radisson and Palmer were also settled that same day and they too obtained their due, without any penalty. On that same occasion, the steering committee even went so far as to relax its policy to some extent, but it very quickly returned to prohibiting all private trading (HBRS-5: 88 and 110).

---

28. The most telling indication of change is the frequency of meetings, which increased from a small number – 15 in 1671-1672 and 9 in 1672-1673 – to a veritable explosion of 45 meetings in the first eight months of 1673-1674. Then as of July 1674, minutes are no longer kept.

29. The Company's historians believe that Radisson was responsible for Bailey's recall and it is quite probable that he spoke against him to the steering committee but Bailey was also Robison's creature, thus a partisan of York, abeit an ex-prisoner and an untitled and inexperienced man, whose mentor had "extricated" him from the Tower of London to designate him Governor. Of course, such a dizzying ascendancy was scarcely in tune with Shaftesbury's understanding of the social hierarchy (Haley, 1968: 307). Consequently, the general assembly and Shaftesbury had many reasons to order Bailey's recall.

That same year, Radisson was consulted only about the purchase of glass beads, a staple much appreciated by the Amerindians and that he knew better than anyone (HBRS-5: 100). But his position within the Company was now uncertain. His decision (or that of the Company?) not to return to the Bay in 1674 is easily explained; either the Company no longer wanted him there, or else Radisson preferred to remain at London to see to his and Des Groseilliers' affairs, before losing too much authority or quite simply being ousted from the Company. It is clear that Radisson tried to inform Des Groseilliers about the changes under way at the London headquarters and about the uncertain state of their affairs, especially since they had continued to engage in private trading. It is also quite probable that Des Groseilliers took a long and serious look at his future in England while listening to Father Albanel's proposals that he return to France (Rousseau and Roy, 1950).

An internal dispute

Three elements emerge from the minutes of the meetings held during 1674. The first of these is clearly the importance of Hayes, who will assume a number of responsibilities, despite Shaftesbury's manifest antipathy to his presence in the Company (HBRS-5: 92, 104, 112 and 116).[30] Of further note is the fact that Radisson was able to keep the trust of a majority of shareholders and succeed in having his annual stipend doubled (to £100 per annum), even though he was subjected to constant pressure tactics. This would indicate that a considerably smaller group of shareholders, Shaftesbury presiding, recognized that Radisson was then playing a useful role in the Company, even at London, since they agreed to increase his stipend in the amount representing the top end of the wage scale in force within the Company.[31] The steering committee's intransigence in regard to private trading may

---

30. "Shaftesbury's papers (…) reveal a malevolent mistrust of Hayes, whom he accused of being a secret Papist, a vice-sodden profligate who had killed his first wife with desease and had run through the fortune of his second wife, a pander who for a mere five shillings would supply 'pretty women to chance acquaintances'– a mean and dishonnest rogue" (Rich, 1968: 87). Such serious accusations are taken from the notes that Shaftesbury was preparing to defend himself against Hayes, were the latter individual to be summoned to testify against him in the proceedings that Charles II instituted against Shaftesbury at the turn of the 1680s.

31. "That there bee allowed to Mr. Raddison one hundred poundes p. annum from the time of his Last arivall at London, in consideration of services done by him;" Shaftesbury, Hayes, Forth, Millington, Hawkins, Griffith, Walker and Baynes ratify this raise (HBRS-5: 120-

well have made such an increase necessary, to avoid seeing the incomes of the two Frenchmen drop abruptly, thereby triggering the departure of these two men of uncontested experience.

Be that as it may, an ever-widening division was separating two groups within the Company, each with a particular conception of this enterprise. For his part, Shaftesbury was forced to accept that colonizing Hudson's Bay seemed impossible; then, no doubt in an effort to jumpstart the charter project that had been shelved, he and two of the earliest investors, Craven and Carteret, launched a new colonization venture at Buss Island. This Island had been situated approximately at the 55th parallel of the northern latitude where fishing was purported to be exceedingly abundant (HBRS-5: 103). As the Island was never located, this costly and futile project collapsed, delaying the consolidation of the James Bay posts and the establishment of a new post at the Nelson River. There was also a political conflict between the Company's two strongmen, Hayes and Shaftesbury: "For Shaftesbury, Hayes represented the triumph of the despicable Roman Catholic Church and the adulation of James, Duke of York" (Rich, 1968: 87); this conflict is continually evident in the Company reports, as indicated by the auditors and the witnesses for each faction.

Both men spied upon one another, each employing his particular knowledge and experience in orienting company activities to assure the promotion of his own advantage; still and all, this infighting might well have profited the shareholders if the conflict had not intensified to the point of undermining even current affairs (HBRS-5: XLI). After seven months of administrative upheaval, at mid-1674, all written reports on Company activities were abandoned for a period of five years. At the turn of 1674-1675, Company sales, purchases and classifying of shares indicated important maneuvers on the part of the two main shareholders, Hayes and Shaftesbury, each seeking to obtain a majority of votes at the assemblies. In addition, the Company was unable to strike any agreement with the two Frenchmen, who left England in December 1675. Shaftesbury's presence was certainly not the only cause of their departure, but he did represent the principal factor of change in the immediate environs of Radisson and Des Groseilliers. The personal conflict between Hayes and Shaftesbury, the lat-

---

121). That same year, several retainers were earning £20 or £30 per annum; the surgeon and the second captains were paid £48 per annum and Governor Lydell received the same stipend as Radisson, to wit, £100 per annum (HBRS-5: 100 and 108-109).

ter individual's ardor in defending his opposition to York, absolutism, the papacy and the French, in conjunction with a tense socioeconomic situation at London, in 1675, all seemed to weaken the position of the two brothers-in-law to the point of rupture... that is until Des Groseilliers returned from Hudson's Bay with Father Albanel and touched off a crisis.

Radisson and Des Groseilliers leave England

As early as 1661, Shaftesbury held the view that within the colonial empire, all trading and all ensuing profits had to remain, as far as possible, under English control: "The Scots were to be excluded from the colonial trade, along with all the other foreigners" (Haley, 1968: 236). Again in 1675, Shaftesbury stood up in Parliament to oppose the importation of Irish cattle, a gesture that created problems for the English gentry whom he represented (Haley, 1968: 190-191).

Shaftesbury's uncontested experience[32] automatically placed him in a position of authority within the steering committee of the Hudson's Bay Company; moreover, he had taken over as Company Director immediately after relinquishing the loftiest position in the Royal administration. Shaftesbury's overriding self-confidence (Haley, 1968: 308) allowed him to apply his regular methods and to pursue the same objectives that he had promoted in the southern colonies, without adapting them to the particular situation of the North Atlantic and Hudson's Bay. In the south, agricultural activities were essential to the prosperity of the companies in which Shaftesbury participated; however, in the north, agriculture was virtually impossible and rendered establishing a colony extremely risky – even on Buss Island, a location probably too far north to institute there, in any lasting fashion, the fishing colony so dear to his heart. But Shaftesbury had decided to emphasize the Company's colonizing vocation, to the detriment of the fur trade and of short-term gains.[33] He also elected to wage war on private

---

32. "He was more keenly interested in matters of trade and overseas expansion than any other important politician of his day" (Haley, 1968: 227).

33 "The terms of the Charter had implied settlement and Shaftesbury and the courtiers who went with him (there remained only Rupert, Carteret and Craven) stood for settlement" (Rich, 1958: 87). "He was attracted to the new, pioneering enterprises, to new companies, new trades, and new plantations further south. (...) reviewing all these overseas enterprises, we may resonably conclude that he was attracted by the challenge of planning the course of development at least as much as by greed of gain" (Haley, 1968: 234).

trading, prompting the departure of the two Frenchmen, to be followed by Captain Gillam, who would take his revenge at a later time by participating in an armed expedition against Carolina, a holding of several of his former employers (Rich, 1968: 85).

Shaftesbury enjoyed a good reputation among the traders, merchants and financiers of the City who had been his allies under Cromwell's Republic (Haley, 1968: 172). After 1670, he again fraternized with them, initially, *in* the King's interests, by amassing the funds needed to conduct a fresh war against Holland (Haley, 1968: 287), then, *against* his interests, by rallying a powerful parliamentary and popular opposition movement against the absolutism represented by the eventual accession of the Duke of York to the throne of England. Shaftesbury had thus enjoyed a lengthy aquaintance with the most influential businessmen who, in turn, founded the Whig party with him (Haley, 1968: 405); many of these men shared Shaftesbury's strong anti-French leanings and some would soon play an active role in the Hudson's Bay Company.[34]

Since the riots of 1668, the King's principal opponents had succeeded in concentrating the population's widespread dissatisfaction on three major themes which rallied the many and various grievances and enabled all the protesters to unite in a common front against the established order; these were the attachment to elected institutions, independent of the King,[35] a fierce opposition to Roman Catholicism and a more or less exacerbated antipathy towards foreigners, particularly the French, major promoters of political and religious absolutism (Harris, 1993: 29). The years 1673-1675 saw the merger of these three themes around the unifying slogan: "No popery." It seems obvious that under these circumstances, Radisson and Des

---

34. "The opinion of the merchant classes in the City of London, with which Ashley was well familiar, was steadily hardening against France" (Haley, 1968: 284). Since Colbert introduced new rates in 1674 on French products coming into England, at a time when the two countries were allied against Holland, the English traders were champing at the bit: "In the months before the French made peace with Holland, parliamentary and commercial opinion in England became so exasperated against them [the French] that England seemed on the verge of going back into the war on the other side [with the Dutch, against France]. As we have seen, parliament [...] prohibited imports from France" (HBRS-8: xlv).

35. "At least three-quarters of the City's 20 000 male householders were freemen who could vote in ward elections. (...) The proliferation of local offices which these institutions entailed meant that perhaps one in ten householders [at London] held annually some form of office" (Harris, 1993: 18-19).

Groseilliers, who were French, Catholic and probably absolutist – Radisson had consigned this leaning to the written page[36] and he was a friend to Hayes who was close to York, who, in turn, was an absolutist – could not have enjoyed an easy life in the London of that era.

A great many public demonstrations took place against the Pope and the French workers who "were stealing" English jobs.[37] King Charles II knew that Shaftesbury was one of the key leaders of this opposition and he forbade his consorting with London's political milieux. Charles II had to reiterate this interdiction when he learned that Shaftesbury was either chairing or simply participating at meetings of the Hudson's Bay Company in the Capital (Haley, 1968: 364-365). In the end, Shaftesbury retired to the country from where he continued to look after his various colonial, parliamentary and domestic affairs.[38] Certain colonial affairs appeared to irritate him more particularly at that time: "A letter dated June 1675 (...) reeks of exasperation at every line: he (Shaftesbury) therein reveals his apprehension on seeing that by spending some 9 to 10 000 pounds, we have purchased nothing more than the obligation of maintaining some 5 to 6 000 individuals who expect us to support them'" (Haley, 1968: 254-255). The Earl of Shaftesbury also wrote a scathing pamphlet which appeared in November 1675 and was

---

36. "That wild nation [the Iroquois], that have neither faith nor religion, neither law nor *absolut government*" (Ra: 123).

37. English tailors submitted a petition against French workers in 1670 (Harris, 1993: 26); in 1671, the cloth merchants and the weavers took to the streets to manifest against them (Harris: 200-201); in 1674, it was the carpenters' turn (Harris, 1993: 202); then in 1675, the protestations of the tailors, the felt makers, the hatters and the weavers came to a head at the time of the great riots called the "Weavers' Riots" which were directed more particularly against the looms – "the French inventions" and the French Harris (1993: 201-203). See also (Harris, 1993: 31 and 93) for the anti-papist and anti-French processions.

38. As a proper aristocrat, one who is convinced that society's elite deserves favors and privileges but also as a clever scientist, since Ashley was a member of the Royal Society, he ordered this strict ritual for serving meals: "Besides his own table, there was to be a Steward's Table for the eight most important members of the household, 'to be set with fresh victuals a little after my Lord's' (Shaftesbury). Fifteen more were to sit at the Gentlemen Waiter's table and seven at the Groom's Table together with the servants of the visitors; these had to wait until the Earl's diner (Shaftesbury) was over and to dine from the warmed-up victuals left over from his table. (...). It was a carefully regulated hierarchy, organized evidently in the most businesslike and economical fashion" (Haley, 1968: 386). It could be added that this service also reflects the strictly hierarchical conception of society that Shaftesbury continued to promote, an order that divided both the nature and the scope of each person's privileges.

distributed at little cost in the streets of London. In it, he directed a charge against the partisans of an absolutist and arbitrary government, those same men who accorded the monarchy and the clergy the prerogative to drape themselves in divine right "and not to be subject to any human law" (Haley, 1968: 390). When Parliament reconvened in autumn 1675, Shaftesbury gave a number of important speeches about the principles and political institutions that should prevail in England. Once published, these proposals would constitute the political foundation of the Whig movement, which, in turn, would lead to the great reforms of the Glorious Revolution, culminating in the institution of the system of Parliamentary Monarchy, England's since 1688-1689.

An irresistible sociopolitical movement

At London, several lobbies were positioned to exercise substantial pressure thanks to the intervention of a member of Parliament or a municipal representative or even by eliciting the support of well-organized popular pressure groups.[39] Shaftesbury's faction in fact included a parliamentary constituent and another well-integrated constituent for popular protest, which groups assured him the support of a part of the elite – persons capable of appreciating the rigor and decisiveness of his ideas – and a strong popular cohort within the clientele networks of members of parliament and wealthy businessmen, supporters of the "Whigs or Liberal Party who, in turn, were egged on by marches, pamphlets, caricatures, hearsay and compelling slogans. Shaftesbury's machinations therefore represented a real threat to the Government of Charles II whose members tried to check his influence by prosecuting him, then jailing him, as well as by organizing counter-demonstrations and attempting to outlaw the coffee-houses, where the King's opponents often congregated[40] (Haley, 1968: 403).

   If a compilation is made of the protests directed against the French craftsmen involved with the Hudson's Bay Company, such as the felt-makers and hatters, to which should be added the fight between pro and anti-

---

   39. "It was common practice to petition the lord mayor, court of aldermen and common council to put pressure on any central government which seemed to be threatening the rights and freedoms of Londoners" (Harris, 1993: 29-30).
   40. "Political debate was increasingly being conducted in the public arena. Political matters were discussed by societies meeting in ward-clubs and in taverns and coffee-houses, where gentry, shopkeepers and artisans mingled freely" (Harris, 1993: 27).

York factions in the Company and the popular quasi-paranoia against Catholics, it becomes clear that the attitude of the steering committee towards Radisson and Des Groseilliers, in 1675, went well beyond personal preferences to involve the Company's *public image*; at that juncture, the Company could see its contact and mutual assistance networks either hold together or completely disappear depending on the positions it adopted in regard to the two Frenchmen, the Duke of York, the *Test Act* and a number of other controversial issues. The margin of maneuver enjoyed by Radisson and Des Groseilliers became increasingly tenuous and, unfortunately for them, neither the diplomacy of the younger, nor the truculent manners of the elder, were able to prevent the collapse of this fragile equilibrium.

The straw that broke the camel's back

The worst scenario imaginable came to pass. Des Groseilliers returned from Hudson's Bay in the company of one Father Albanel, a French Jesuit, with whom he had fraternized over several months. This Jesuit, a man inspired by notions of religious and political absolutism, was nonetheless well received at the Court of Charles II, despite the order of expulsion to affect all Jesuits, indeed all Catholic priests, that the King had just signed (Fraser, 1993: 194). In Shaftesbury's view, the Court's attitude was dangerous and that of Des Groseilliers, who had associated with a French Jesuit on Company territories and in Company vessels, was no less than disgraceful. Radisson and Des Groseilliers also found themselves in a weak position to assert their point of view since the situation at the Bay remained tenuous; there priority still had to be given to investments, the French were threatening the existing trading posts and a new post had to be established at the Nelson River without delay. It is obvious that the two Frenchmen now found themselves in a vulnerable situation, especially as they were insisting that to counter the French threat they had to have the absolute trust of their associates, even though they frequented and much appreciated the French Jesuits.[41] For Shaftesbury, their proposal was simply unacceptable and to

---

41. Chapter 3 indicates that Radisson was rather favorable to the Jesuits; the following passage shows that he was very favorable to them: "their designe is to further the Christian faith to the greatest glory of God, and indeed are charitable to all those that are in distresse and needy, especially to those that are worthy or industrious in their way of honesty. This is the truth, lett who he will speak otherwise, ffor this realy I know meselfe by experience. I hope I offend non to tell the truth" (Ra: 175).

stave off any undesired consequences, he returned posthaste to sit on the steering committee immediately following Des Groseilliers' return to London.

Des Groseilliers, for his part, found just as unacceptable the Company's new policy governing private trading, which amounted to prohibition, pure and simple. Never had Des Groseilliers willingly paid the tax on the quarter part of his beaver trade in New France; in fact, he had reacted violently when d'Argenson imposed fines on him. Now that the Company prohibited all manner of personal trading, how was Des Groseilliers'– who had just spent three full years at the Bay – going to conclude the trade he had most certainly conducted during that period, if only on the smallest feasible scale? How would he possibly handle the inquiries, the pressure, the threats and the suits that Radisson and the other retainers had endured? A slight adaptation of Radisson's narrative written on their return from Lake Superior, in 1660, shows the extent to which the Company and Des Groseilliers were in disagreement: "very dissatisfied with our (his) reception, which was indeed poor considering the service that we (he) have (has) rendered to the country (the Company) (…), seeing a Governor (Shareholders) become wealthy thanks to the pains and the perils of others (…) who agree to risk their lives to further the interests of the country (the Company)" (Ra: 236).

Who could defend the viewpoint of the two Frenchmen before the steering committee? Only the Executive Director, George Carteret, and the advisers, Shaftesbury, Hayes and Kirke, had the actual facts about the key role that Radisson and Des Groseilliers had played at the outset; Kirke had a great deal to lose in that confrontation and he probably tried to help Radisson. Hayes may well have pleaded in their favor but he also had to fight to conserve and consolidate his own position in the Company, opposite a group of powerful enemies who were trying to reposition the Company's activities, thereby sapping his influence. Thus, it is uncertain whether or not Hayes did all he could to support the two brothers-in-law.[42] Carteret had returned to the Company at the same time as Shaftesbury, after a few years' absence, and it was he who piloted the Buss Island colonization project (Rich, 1968: 81). Moreover, his relations with the Duke of York were relatively bad

---

42. In 1675, "there is here the making of what might be called a Hayes party on the Court (on the steering committee) well before his election as Deputy (Executive Director, in November 1676)" (HBRS-5: xlvii).

(Pepys, 1985: 583, 584, 596 and 951). It is thus likely that Carteret sided with Shaftesbury, even if the conciliatory attitude that he had developed with age (he was then over 70) (Pepys, 1985: 594-595) and the good relationship he had maintained thus far with Radisson and Des Groseilliers might have encouraged neutrality on his part.

As for John Robinson, the Director who had supported and apparently retained unreservedly the services of the two Frenchmen, his name no longer even figures on the list of shareholders in 1675 (HBRS-5: 168); (Mood, 1936: 18). In any event, his decision to support them involved a highly public dimension. In August 1675, at the time of the major disturbances know as the "Weavers' Riots," Robinson refused to launch his police forces against the rioters, and even went so far as to sympathize with the four persons representing the often indigent craftsmen who had sought him out to ask for his help: "Go home, all of you" he is said to have replied, "and I shall do what I can for you" (Harris, 1993: 194). When a few of these rioters were set in the stocks, the Venetian Ambassador remarked that no one molested them; quite to the contrary, they aroused the sympathy of the crowds (quoted in Harris, 1993: 194).[43] How could a public figure like Robinson in such conditions openly support two highly paid Frenchmen? As for the likes of Lindsay, Carew, Bence and Munden, who were recent members of the steering committee, it would have been surprising if any of their number openly opposed a man as powerful as Shaftesbury. Finally, since Prince Rupert was a regular business partner of Shaftesbury and Carteret but no longer took an active interest in Company affairs, it is likely that he tended to support his longstanding English partners.

But whatever the reasons, there is no doubt that Radisson and Des Groseilliers left the Hudson's Bay Company and England in December 1675, to thenceforth serve France.

---

43. The importance of the 1675 riots and the hesitation of the City forces to suppress them indicate the extent to which the King's power was tenuous: "without fairly extensive support amongst the London populace, effective law-enforcement could be placed in jeopardy. The lesson of 1640-42 [the Civil War] was there to be learnt, when constables and militia refused to suppress the crowds that demonstrated in favour of the parliamentary cause, with the result that Charles I lost control of the streets of London." Shortly thereafter, Charles I also lost the throne (Harris, 1992: 22).

An ambivalent departure

Although Des Groseilliers' gesture is quite easily understood, it seems much more difficult to explain why Radisson elected to leave England as well, in such abrupt fashion. After all, not only was he leaving his wife and his children behind him, he was casting aside a successful social integration and the respect of several Company members who had recently granted him a substantial pay increase. Radisson perhaps believed that his situation would become intolerable were he to remain alone at London, or perhaps, he put his fidelity to Des Groseilliers above his own marriage vows... unless he thought he could negotiate an ulterior arrangement with his wife's family, just as long as he and Des Groseilliers were able to get away from an immediate situation that had become too contentious.[44] It is very difficult to elucidate Radisson's real motivations but certain possibilities can be eliminated, such as disloyalty towards the Company as some historians suggest (Rich, 1968: 33-34).[45] This interpretation says nothing about the real, quite ambiguous, situation in which Radisson then found himself. Because of his actions, he was losing so very much more in the adventure than could be justified by a vulgar question of self-interest or greed. John Kirke, for one, never forgave Radisson for having inflicted on him yet another "French defeat;" thereafter, he obstinately refused to let Radisson take his wife to France, even at Colbert's insistence.

Nowhere in Radisson's narrative, nor in the documents concerning the two brothers-in-law, is there even the slightest hint of any angry or rancorous feelings between the two in regard to their mutual actions and decisions,

---

44. The rumors that were circulating in France, ten years later, to explain his departure from England, reflect the fragility of his position in that country, and may also point to his overweening ambition and the problems that Des Groseilliers seems to have encountered with the Company's Direction as concerns private trading: "Indeed, I would like to know if by making so handsome a marriage (...) he (Radisson) might not have wasted his time both materially and spiritually. And for the good English merchant to bring opposition as he did in all justice" (French Ambassador at Rome to Renaudot, 8-05-1685, BN, Fonds Renaudot (Renaudot collection) f. 219).

45. In this passage, Rich says little of substance about a very complex situation which I believe is handled with greater subtlety by Shaftesbury's biographer: "Shaftesbury's times were far from being normal. In the general political instability only extreme supporters of Divine Right monarchy and extreme Republicans could adopt the attitude of undeviating loyalty to a party even if it entailed exile or martyrdom. For the great majority, political life was not a matter of attaching oneself to one or other of two clearly defined parties and devoting one's career to it; rather it was a question of constantly revising one's attitude in the confusion and rapidly changing circumstances and deciding what course of action and what affiliations were most likely to further one's general objectives, public and personal" (Haley, 1968: 742).

including the sudden departure from England. However, this team of two, who might well be described as "inseparable,"will prove unable to withstand the abrupt and difficult changes yet to come.[46]

Unfortunately for Radisson and Des Groseilliers, Father Albanel's promises concerning their eventual hiring failed to materialize under the auspices of the few individuals authorized to take such decisions in France; furthermore, Colbert reviewed the entire question somewhat negatively, stating that he did not need the services of the two coureurs de bois at that point. However, he did cover all their debts, granting them a cash stipend worth little more than 40 pounds sterling by way of thanking them for again seeking to serve the interests of France. Then, he suggested that the two return to New France to engage in the fur trade. And so, in 1676, the two brothers-in-law were to be found once more at Québec where they participated in a meeting of the fifteen most influential merchants and fur traders in the colony. The lengthy report on this meeting reveals the instability of New France's economy at that juncture and the difficulties experienced by the least powerful traders in earning even a minuscule profit.[47] Nonetheless, Des Groseilliers remained in New France; he may well have participated in fur smuggling – then a widespread, albeit illegal activity – since nothing further is heard about him for a number of years.[48] As for Radisson, he decided to throw in his lot with the French Navy, far from furs and the bitter cold.

---

46. Radisson and Des Groseilliers formed a tight-knit, dynamic and complementary team. It is clear that the "two Frenchmen" were perceived in the Company as an inseparable duo, strong and stable, as indicated by the entries concerning them in the Company's accounts book; therein are noted the amounts attributed to one or the other, or to both, indifferently. All the other accounts concern but one individual at a time (HBRS-5: 203-206).

47. (ANQ, series F3, coll. Moreau-Saint-Méry, vol. 2 f.32-48).

48. It is quite possible that Des Groseilliers and the merchant de la Chesnaye formed a partnership to engage in the contraband trade of furs on the south shore, at Rivière du Loup, where La Chesnay had a "seigneurie," since they were partners, in 1682, with Radisson and a few others during a contraband expedition to Hudson's Bay. The Intendant de Meulles pointed out that the post at Rivière du Loup created many problems for the holders of the monopoly because moose hides and beaver pelts could be shipped out of New France using small boats headed towards Gaspé, from whence they were conveyed to Acadia by the Saint-Jean River (ANC 1683c: 361); (Johnson, 1994: 33-34). "In 1681, an anonymous memoir (…) in fact informs us that the Intendant Duchesneau, Le Prévôt and La Chesnay "have other stores in several villages (…). They attract the savages and also trade with the coureurs de bois" (ANC 1683c: 359)" (Grabowski, 1994: 48).

5. Des Groseilliers' Expeditions to Hudson Bay

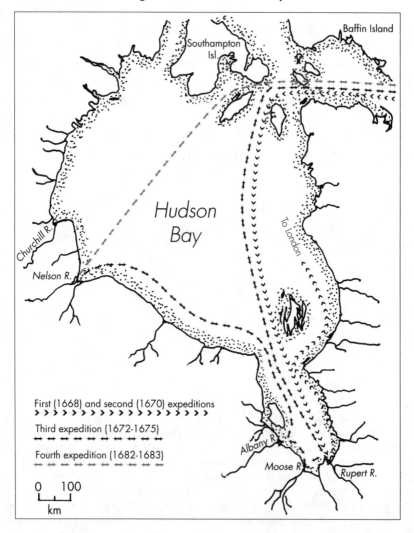

Des Groseilliers made four expeditions to Hudson Bay. The first two were brief: he arrived at the Rupert River in the fall of 1668 and fall of 1670. He spent the winter and spring trading, then returned to England for the summers of 1669 and 1671. His third expedition lasted three years: Des Groseilliers arrived at James Bay in the fall of 1672 and this time did not leave until the summer of 1675, after traveling as far as the Nelson River and trading between the Rupert, Moose and Albany Rivers. Des Grosseilliers' final expedition to the Nelson River took place between the spring of 1682 and the fall of 1683, in the company of Radisson, who was also on a return trip only. This journey required the necessary winter stopover in the Bay to reestablish contact and to trade with the natives (based on a map published by *The Beaver* magazine in 1936).

CHAPTER 9

Radisson, From South to North, Between France and New France

A halfhearted welcome in the motherland

When Radisson and Des Groseilliers arrived in France, at the end of 1675, the Canadian beaver, once a sure source of wealth, had become a problem that Colbert was unable to solve. Admittedly, New France could not do without the fur trade which assured the regular to-ings and fro-ings of merchant vessels between the metropolis and the colony and helped foster good relations with the Amerindians; nonetheless, in France, it had become impossible to dispose of the ever-increasing stocks of beaver pelts. A few individuals who were well aquainted with the Laurentian colony, such as Colbert and the Intendant Patoulet (he had been Jean Talon's Secretary in New France, from 1665 to 1672), were urging the "Canadians" to develop other economic sectors, particularly the fisheries.[1] It seems that Radisson and Des Groseilliers, in an early effort to comply with the wishes expressed by French authorities, submitted to the Court a project for launching fisheries in Canada, as stated in a short memorandum duly presented by the two brothers-in-law and which enabled them to obtain exclusive rights to fish for seal off Anticosti Island (Nute, 1943: 293-296); (ANQ, series B, vol. 7, f. 15v16v). However, Radisson makes no mention at all of this project in his narratives, rather he states that Colbert encouraged them to return

---

1.   "If the trade (in furs) were to fall flat, so much the better, the Minister (Colbert) went on to say, the people would soon turn to 'angling and other types of fishing, prospecting and manufacturing goods, all of which would offer them many more advantages'" (Colbert to Talon, June 1672, quoted in Trudel, 1997: 591). Patoulet also officially encouraged the development of the fishing grounds (Trudel, 1997: 471, 795 and 803).

to fur trading in New France (Raw: 6). Since the fisheries project never materialized, it is probable that the two brothers-in-law seized on this idea, then in
vogue, solely to oblige those in charge of colonial affairs, thereby gaining swifter
access to the circle of power.[2]

Radisson looks for a favorable environment

New France

For the first time in fifteen years, the two brothers-in-law went their separate ways: Des Groseilliers remained in New France, where no one openly
blamed him for his sojourn in England, while Radisson decided to invest in
the naval campaign that Vice-Admiral d'Estrées was preparing to launch
against the Dutch possessions in the South Seas (Raw: 7). This campaign
was to be a joint enterprise: the King of France furnishing the ships, with
the Vice-Admiral, Baron d'Estrées, arming them, in other words, supplying
them with crews and equipment, aided by partners like Radisson, who apparently contributed the sum of about 2 000 French pounds (£200 English)
to that expedition.[3] The profits would derive from Dutch spoils and cap-
tures which were to be divided among the partners (Sue, 1845: 184).

The expedition in which Radisson participated was the second headed by
Vice-Admiral d'Estrées in the South. He had conquered Cayenne the year before, but the Island of Tobago, hastily fortified by the Dutch, had successfully
resisted his efforts, and he even lost several vessels (Roncière, 1934: 659).
D'Estrées returned to France seeking reinforcements; and this campaign which
had at first amused Louis XIV now became a very important venture for the
Sun King (Sue, 1845: 230). Several hundred soldiers embarked on some twenty
vessels, which set sail towards Tobago at the end of September 1677. Radisson
had obtained a post as marine guard on one of these ships.[4] The expedition met
with unexpected success, reaching Tobago without mishap in December that
same year. A thousand soldiers landed; cannons and mortars were taken ashore,

---

2. It was all the more expedient to take an interest, or to feign taking an interest, in the
fisheries since, only a few short months before, Colbert had granted to Cavelier de la Salle
the permission to develop the fur trade towards Lake Ontario and in the Iroquois territory,
hence yet another source of furs, in an already saturated market (Campeau, 1994: 47).

3. Letter from Radisson to Colbert (c. 1681), B.N. Melanges à Colbert; notebook 125,
f. 61-62).

4. "I had asked Sieur de Chambly to request of Sieur the Baron d'Estrées to allow me to
undertake the voyage south as a volunteer, for at Brest he had so graciously spoken out on my
behalf, even more than I deserved, to the Intendant who accorded me the post and the stipend

then placed on a height overlooking the Dutch fort. With the explosion of a third bombshell, the French troops struck the fort's magazine provoking a huge detonation which literally blew the garrison to smithereens. The panic-stricken city was taken without a fight. Then, once troops were safely garrisoned at Tobago, the Vice-Admiral's squadron continued on their way west, putting into port for a few days at the Island of Grenada, whence Radisson wrote a lengthy letter, relating the capture of Tobago and the salient events of the voyage thus far; this he consigned to a small but pithy logbook.

France

Radisson enjoyed no real support in France, and certainly not in high places. Colbert let him cool his heels in the palace corridors before advising him that many found it peculiar his wife had remained in England and that he would not be considered trustworthy until she was at his side, in France (Raw: 6-7). The influential persons that Radisson had to convince, such as Colbert and his son de Seignelay, remained skeptical and from the outset preferred not to entrust him with any responsibility. In such circumstances, the expedition of the Baron d'Estrées offrered him an excellent opportunity to prove his worth and to carve out a place for himself in the French navy; under Colbert, France's navy had seen an immense expansion but there was never enough competent manpower (Roncière, 1934: 369 and 550).

That long letter written by Radisson at Grenada indicates his concern for gratifying the ruling circle of the kingdom and for gaining their confidence at any cost. Since he was an astute observer, he had understood what was expected of him, namely, that he adopt a flattering, submissive attitude;[5] and so, he made every effort to meet the expectations of Colbert and of all the other powerful men who controlled his destiny:

> The honor you have accorded me Sieur Commander in asking me to note the events of our voyage gives me leave to address these few lines to you with the

---

of marine guard (letter from Radisson, 1-01-1678, in Nute, 1943: 304). Radisson's status is not unique: Julien, Cossodon, Descloches, all were volunteers serving as marine guards (Saint-Yves, 1899: 219). He had probably obtained this post through the Intendant Patoulet, who seems to have been one of Radisson's earliest supporters in France (he was formerly Secretary to Talon) and who was chief purser on this expedition (Saint-Yves, 1899: 222-223 and 232).

5.   "Be ever persuaded," wrote Colbert to one of the Captains in his navy, "that you can do nothing more for your own glory and your own advantage than to contribute to the glory and the advantage of those who command you (…). There is nothing which the King, our Master, seeks more ardently to establish than the blind subordination of inferiors to their superiors" (quoted in Roncière, 1934: 352).

ardent hope that I shall be able to write an even more polished narrative in a yet
better style, failing this may your generosity pardon me... (Radisson, letter of
January 1, 1678, published in Nute, 1943: 303).

The political system instituted by Louis XIV functioned like a mechanism, a delicate timepiece that a single move could set in action, with all the
works flawlessly regulated as if by a master craftsman, in this instance, by
the King and his restricted team of ministers and advisers. They alone were
positioned to determine the place each should occupy so that the entire
mechanism would operate to best serve the interests of the kingdom: "The
main function of the monarch is to assure that each of his men occupies the
post where he may serve the public interest (...). We appreciate that we cannot do everything: but we must order that all be done properly"; Louis XIV
offered those words of advice to his Dauphin (quoted in Fox, 1960: 138).
Submission to the King's supremacy could be carried to extremes by his
"liege men" as shown by the plainly irresponsible comment of a navy squadron leader: "Sieur the Vice-Admiral (d'Estrées) acts against the will of all the
competent folk. But I am of the ilk who have faith in their generals and their
abilities, wherever it is so written and signed: Louis" (quoted in Roncière,
1934: 550). Even worse, the Vice-Admiral d'Estrées himself, during the campaign of 1677, believed he could impose the King's will and his own authority
as a powerful aristocrat, well beyond sober reality: "The Baron de Sourdis
(...) wanted to take a map and consult with others as to the course to follow: the Vice-Admiral folded it saying: 'We know that;' then he made this
other telling remark, directed at those who spoke to him of difficulties: 'None
must be mentioned; the King so orders it' (Saint-Yves, 1899: 245).

Guided by such principles, it was hardly a surprise that the naval expedition of 1676 was only moderately successful and that the 1677 expedition
suffered a crushing defeat after leaving Grenada. The Baron d'Estrées conducted the squadron just as he pleased; and the fleet now included French
buccaneers from Santo Domingo who were heading to Curaçao. However,
he refused to heed the warnings of his officers and paid no attention to the
advice of the pilots who were well acquainted with the region. On the night
of May 9, 1678, the squadron engaged in battle on the shoals of Aves where
they lost seven vessels, scores of sailors and much equipment, without counting several small pirate ships that were accompanying them (Roncière, 1934:
662-665; Sue, 1845: 238-247). As Louis XIV was greatly annoyed by this dis-
tressing outcome – "with a few more such campaigns, France would be in
grave danger of no longer having a fleet" (Saint-Yves, 1899: 246) – he ordered an inquiry to learn the circumstances and causes of this shipwreck as

well as the names of those ultimately responsible for the disaster. Thanks to that inquiry, today we can see that by virtue of the tenets of absolute monarchy, incompetence was allowed to reign supreme whenever an unfortunate appointment or a bad decision emanated from the top of a social pyramid which Louis XIV had sought to root exclusively in the nobility (Apostolides, 1981). Various accounts about the insufferable arrogance and manifest incompetence of the Baron d'Estrées were given at the time of the Royal inquiry (Sue, 1845: 187); here was a man one addressed with trembling "so great was the universal fear that he might unleash his wrath," declared his assistant, Maricourt (in Sue, 1845: 241).[6] Since the Baron d'Estrées belonged to the old aristocracy, he was never chastised for his errors; Colbert asked only that he remain quietly in the West Indies to keep watch on the comings and goings of France's enemies in that region (Sue, 1845: 248).[7]

The circumstances of this shipwreck indicate that the marks and symbols of nobility have greater importance for the high-ranking officials of France than the practical knowledge and experience of competent persons who were unable to rely on social status or a title, or on the insistent recommendations of some influential peer (Roncière, 1934: 664). Yet, this was precisely what Radisson had to offer the crown of France: great and well-tested knowledge of a practical nature, a clear mind, enthusiasm and considerable ambition, but he was not of noble extraction, nor had he the wherewithal to buy a title, or even a function like ship's captain that could lead to his obtaining a title. By sending to France a long letter in which he provides an unusually precise and exhaustive account of the early weeks of the expedition to the West Indies (according to Sue, 1845: 231-236; Saint-Yves, 1899: 235-242; Roncière, 1934: 659-662), Radisson hoped to prove his abilities as an informant, one who is submissive, yet no less devoted and clearheaded:

> [following the explosion of the powder magazine at Tobago] the smoke dispersed and the fort no longer to be discerned, the survivors of the shipwreck who were

---

6. "Let no one do me the honor of making me serve on the vessel of Sieur the Vice-Admiral, (…) methinks that purgatory cannot be so harsh," the same Maricourt had declared prior to actually serving under d'Estrées (Roncière, 1934: 551); all the statements made during that era by these Captains confirm the assertions of Sieur de Méricourt, (…) Sieur d'Estrées, so full of self-importance and utterly devoid of the knowledge needed to engage in a profession he had embraced rather late in life, always embarked obscure advisers whose advice he appropriated in order to bedazzle ordinary folk with his so-called abilities, as Sieur de Méricourt was wont to say" (Sue, 1845: 248).

7. This extract, taken from a memoir of Louis XIV, states a principle that was extended to all members of the high-ranking nobility who, in turn, enjoyed full immunity just as long as they did not antagonize the King: "It is imperative to agree always that no matter how bad a prince

able to walk fled this horrible sight along the shore, fearing the French fury once they reached the Cartier point as they had been told. But they soon saw that the victorious French are more clement than their similars in any other nation of the world and it is a mark of glory for these people to have the honor of becoming the subjects of the most compassionate, the most invincible and the happiest king of the world whom God shall bless with many thousand victories. Thus do I express my wishes for his immortal glory – and I trust that he shall continue to be my benefactor through the offices of yourselves, my noble patrons. I saw the bomb fall and had the honor of being the first to shout out long live the King (quoted in Nute, 1943: 307).[8]

A good informant, perhaps… but a lamentably bad writer, even if this letter was penned in haste. Radisson was quite aware of this failing: "your most humble servant writes begging you that if you find these words to be acceptable that you clarify same for those noble friends to read…" (quoted in Nute, 1943: 308). Radisson knows that the post of marine guard belonged to the rank of non-commissioned officer whose number were then being trained in the best schools, to relieve at the highest levels the aristocratic officers, whom quite often, though they usually had no experience, Colbert would appoint at the same time as the ships were launched. These guards received training that was just as important at the cultural and social levels as for the military and naval spheres, this in a country where the spoken and written word had also become an instrument of selection and power.[9] Indeed, since the mid-XVII century, the publication and frequent reprinting of Vaugelas' plea for a highly civilized, well protected French language had contributed to instituting a form of control of the language by the *Académie française* (French Academy), which, for its part, took

---

may be, the revolt of his subjects is infinitely more criminal. He who has given men Kings [God] wills that they be respected as his lieutenants, reserving for himself alone the right to examine their conduct. His will requires that whosoever is born a subject, shall obey without making any distinction" (Louis XIV, quoted in Fox, 1960: 139).

8. The spelling has been corrected somewhat to facilitate reading the text.

9. At times, the marine guards received a command even in the presence of officers, which indicates their superior status, a status that required advanced education (Saint-Yves, 1899: 237): "[the marine guards] receive professional training from masters of hydrography; from drawing masters, and masters of the dance and fencing; they receive everything that a man of breeding should know" (Roncière, 1934: 364). "Educating young men from the best families to assume positions in the Navy" was one of Colbert's constant preoccupations (Roncière, 1934: 363); this is why he instituted special colleges at Saint-Malo and at Bordeaux in 1669, at Montpellier in 1671 and at Paris in 1677. "Colbert entrusts the King's vessels only to members of the best families, to men of quality and property" (Roncière, 1934: 356).

inspiration from "the manner of speaking of the most enlightened element at Court."[10] To speak like Vaugelas signified, above all else, as Roland Barthes writes, "attaching oneself to the exercise of power" (quoted in Merlin 1994: 370). Radisson therefore had no other choice than to improve his linguistic skills if he intended to acquire a loftier standing in France.

When the letter – as awkward as it is informative – that Radisson wrote from Grenada is compared to the log that one Captain Jean Barbot, a native of La Rochelle, brought back, the following year, from a slave-trading expedition in the same region, Radisson cuts a sorry figure:

> The city of Cayanne [...] amounts to a collection of houses (100 to 120) that stand just below the cannon of the fortress. These houses are enclosed by a double row of trees and a ditch 12 feet wide, all of which makes for an excellent effect as we near land because the fortifications as an entity are adroitly situated thereupon. The attached diagram [...] you will be able to more easily peruse the entire assemblage (Barbot, 1978: 365).

Barbot's log was also abundantly illustrated by maps and coastal diagrams, fish and exotic objects (Barbot, 1978: 235). This comparison demonstrates the extent to which the competition was fierce in the milieux that Radisson was hoping to penetrate. The perceptible difference which exists between the Grenada letter and the fifth and sixth travel narratives, written some six and seven years later, indicates that during his time in France, as a marine guard or otherwise, Radisson made every effort to polish his manners and round off his education, in order to meet the very exacting requirements of the French Court.

England

On his return to Paris from the fruitless naval expedition to the Islands of the South, in early 1679, Radisson found himself in the worst position imaginable for a courtier: he had little to offer and something he needed to request, namely, compensation for the losses he had suffered owing to the wreck of his vessel. Thanks to the support of Vice-Admiral d'Estrées and an Intendant (probably Patoulet), he obtained the sum of 100 gold louis and another 100 louis to again try to bring his wife to France, "after which, I was

---

10. "The manner of speaking of the most enlightened element at Court conforms to the manner of writing of the most enlightened authors of the day. When I refer to the Court, I include women as well as men, and many individuals from the city where the Prince resides (Paris), who, thanks to their contacts with courtiers, participate in the great civility of the Court" (Vaugelas, quoted in Merlin, 1994: 381).

assured that I would most certainly have a suitable occupation" (Raw: 8).
And so, Radisson returned to England in summer 1679. He met with his
father-in-law, Kirke, who remained inflexible; he also made contact with
certain members of the Hudson's Bay Company "in an effort to take up
with them again, [but] my attempts were unavailing" (Raw: 9).

It must be said that this was a particularly difficult juncture for the Company and, quite obviously, the shareholders did not view Radisson's return as a
good way to restore prosperity to the enterprise, even with John Hayes occupying the position of Director.[11] The previous year (1678), the Company had lost
a ship and, of the two vessels sent out in 1679, the smallest had not even gone
beyond the English coasts because her captain was dead drunk. Almost all the
earliest shareholders had left the Company, which was now debt-ridden and had
as yet paid no dividends (HBRS-8: 307-308). The situation was so bad before
the return of a full cargo of furs in December 1679, that the steering committee felt it was imperative to reassure the new Governor whom they had just sent
out to Hudson's Bay:

> The truth is the interest of the Company lookd. wth. so ill an aspect untill the
> arrivall of the John & Alexander that those worthy persons and sevll. others
> [Shaftesbury, Colleton and others] were discouraged to continue longer in the
> bottome where they were. But the value of our Actions is now more consider-
> able in the opinion of the world though wee have had no great reason yet to
> boast (quoted in HBRS-8: xxi).

Radisson was unable to bring his wife back to France, or obtain a position in the revival of the Hudson's Bay Company. After several weeks in
London, he returned empty handed to Brest, at the end of 1679 (Raw: 9).

France, New France, England...

Back in France, Radisson found himself up against an impregnable for-
tress. Having noted that he had failed to fetch his wife, d'Estrées and Patoulet
sent him to explain the situation to the marquis de Seignelay, Colbert's son,
who at that time was responsible for the navy, a duty he shared with his
father (Roncière, 1934: 344). De Seignelay lost his temper: "he reproached
me for continuing to manifest English sentiments, all the while stating that

---

11. "Besides the financial position there were other reasons for gloom. There were ir-
regularities...," "The Company's management had been at fault in the elementary matter of
sending out their ships in time to get clear of the Bay while the navigation was still open"
(HBRS-8: xx and xxii).

I should not expect to gain anyone's trust nor to obtain any employment whatsoever" (Raw: 9-10). At that juncture, to count de Seignelay among one's adversaries was probably the worst thing that could happen to a French courtier; Radisson tried to submit the matter to Colbert senior, but in vain. Both father and son held their ground: there would be no employment for Radisson as long as Mary Kirke had not joined him in France (Raw: 10). Since Radisson seems not to have worked subsequently in his motherland, nor to have managed to fetch his wife from England, the Colberts, father and son, succeeded in curtailing Radisson's career in France.[12]

A few months later, the powerful minister concluded that Radisson might yet serve in New France and he so advised him. The situation had evolved in the colony since 1676 and a group of merchants were organizing around Charles Aubert de la Chesnaye to compete with Governor Frontenac and his associates, who had virtually monopolized the fur trade to the west and south of the colony. The new group wanted to favor the north, and since Radisson had already submitted a memoir along these lines to the Court, and as he was one of the undisputed specialists on questions relating to Hudson's Bay, Colbert believed that La Chesnaye and Radisson were born to get along. The two men soon met at Paris and indeed agreed on a project to establish a settlement at the Nelson River, the following year[13] (Borins, 1968: 22). But first of all, Radisson tried one last time to bring his wife to France; he also made inquiries as to the intentions of the Hudson's Bay

---

12. "Radisson even believed, a long time ago, that I had made a poor judgment for more than one reason, especially since I thought he was (not) steadfast in his religion and that I was obliged from time to time to exhort him to perseverence. However, I would very much like to know if by making so advantageous a marriage, he did not change sides – God forbid – for he would have ill-used his efforts both temporally and spiritually," "you have yet to ask me if he (Radisson) had become a Huguenot like his wife and his father-in-law," (French Ambassador in Rome to Renaudot, May 8, 1685 and June 1685, BN, Fonds Renaudot (Renaudot Collection, f. 219 and 229). Radisson was thus perceived as a Protestant sympathizer – or even worse a Protestant – and also as pro-English ("his good friends the English," letter of 11-11-1684). The comment as to Radisson's inordinately great eagerness is no doubt in reference to the consequences of his return to France, at which time his father-in-law Kirke virtually abandoned his daughter, Radisson's wife, whom he (Kirke) suspected of having converted to Catholicism (Radisson to Colbert, c. 1681, B.N. Mélanges à Colbert, 1.125, f. 61).

13. Hence in 1680, not 1681, as Nute suggests (Nute, 1943: 177). In an unpublished memoir (Borins, 1984, McGill University), Borins reaches the same conclusions as I do on the exact chronology of events: Nute omits a year and Radisson adds one. Borins relies on the interpretations of Nute and Rich, which are based largely on the British archives, but also on several French sources.

Company concerning himself and the possibility of a Nelson River settlement (Raw: 11). Kirk remained as obdurate as ever[14] and Radisson saw no indication of any opening for him on the Company's part: "I was considered as either a perfectly useless servant, *or a man quite unable to cause harm*; I was allowed to leave without being accorded the slightest mark of good will [...], *I decided to survive this disgrace*" (Raw: 12). At the time, England was plunged into the political maelstrom known as the Exclusion Crisis against the Duke of York; hence it is normal that Radisson did not get the warm welcome he wanted. Then too, the majority of the Company's new shareholders were from the business elements of the City; they were mostly Whigs and unacquainted with Radisson.[15] Consequently, they had no intentions of taking this Frenchman back into their service, in the midst of such widespread anti-papist and anti-French turmoil.[16]

And so, Radisson decided to establish a trading post at the Nelson River under the French flag.

But La Chesnaye had left for New France when Radisson returned to Paris. He spent the winter in the French Capital, renewing contact with Colbert, as well as with the Jesuits and a group from Saint-Malo who were interested in the fur trade at Hudson's Bay. Tenacious, Radisson again defended his projects before the Court, but without success (Nute, 1943: 315-317). Louis XIV and his courtiers had little confidence in Radisson and wanted to keep control over the strategic action that it would be expedient to take, later on, at Hudson's Bay.[17] The same problem prevailed at Québec, where La Chesnaye was uncertain of obtaining permission from Governor

---

14. "His Lordship [Colbert] had accorded me 1000 [French livres] to fetch my family to France [...] my wife's father opposed my will, intending to disinherit his daughter of a considerable fortune, if she followed me, nor did he allow me to see my child," (letter of Radisson to Colbert, c1681, BN, Mélanges à Colbert, book 125, f.61v).

15. "Two or three recruits from the aristocracy took the place of the two politicians who had gone; nearly all the other newcomers were business men" (HBRS-8: xxiii).

16. Louis XIV confirms this connection between the political and religious absolutisms of the French: "such law (obedience) so formal and so universal, [...] is salutary to the very people upon whom it is imposed, and who can never transgress it, without exposing themselves to even greater evils than those they purport to dispel. There is no better maxim established by Christianity than the one which dictates the humble submission of subjects to those who are sent to govern them" (Louis XIV, quoted in Fox, 1960: 139-140).

17. "Monsieur Radisson obtained nothing from the Court and I think this will always be the case. He would do well to go north if the Company [that of La Chesnaye] wanted to send out a ship – this was mentioned to them but I do not know if they will agree upon it. The group from Saint-Malo would have been pleased to undertake it if they had not been hindered, as this could have engendered problems for the company of Canada. I shall pay

Frontenac to send Radisson to Hudson's Bay, since this mission was clearly intended to weaken the Governor.

After a final brief sojourn in England (ASQ, letters-folder N. no. 60), Radisson finally joined La Chesnaye in Québec, at the end of September 1681; at which time, he reported to Frontenac for his approval to repair to Hudson's Bay. The Governor knew that Radisson and La Chesnaye were part of a group opposed to him; moreover, he had anticipated the quarrels that would arise between France and England over Hudson's Bay (letter of 2-11-1681, in Borins, 1968: 24), he therefore had no interest in backing this expedition and, in fact, he refused to do so. But La Chesnaye had an alternative; he proposed to Frontenac that Radisson return to France to ask for the Court's opinion as to this question. Frontenac accepted. But, in truth, this was a ruse so that Radisson could spend the winter in Acadia, before reaching Percé in spring 1682, in transit towards Hudson's Bay (Raw: 13); (Brins, 1968: 26).

Des Groseilliers soon joined in the venture; Radisson and their backers had no other choice than to resort to dissimulation and illegality if they wanted to reach Hudson's Bay that same year. La Chesnaye had to send a boat to meet Radisson at Percé, with all the equipment and supplies necessary for establishing a trading post at Nelson River. In return, the furs were to pass through Percé then be conveyed directly to Europe, without paying the quarter part in New France (Borins, 1968: 27); such amount represented the share reserved for Radisson and Des Groseilliers (Raw: 13-14). The expedition began on a precarious footing either in legality or illegality because the two brothers-in-law would be deprived of the official support they might need to dispel the competition at Hudson's Bay; furthermore, Frontenac already suspected them of plotting behind his back; or so Radisson believed (Raw: 14).[18]

---

200 livres to monsieur Radisson as I was asked to do [illegible]…(Dudouyt at Laval, March 9, 1681, ASQ, letters-folder N, no. 52). One might ask if Radisson really did prove to be an able strategist in France, when, for example, he recalls his attachments and his successes in England in a letter asking for Colbert's assistance: "my wife […] was forced to sell the portrait of the King of England that he, himself, gave to me as a gift, like the gold chain that he placed around my neck;" one might further ask if the latter present from the King was not, in truth, the gold chain that James Hayes had offered him, for services rendered to the King, which would be consistent with Radisson's art of lying (BN, Mélanges à Colbert, 1. 125, f.62).

18. Radisson had obtained Frontenac's permission to take with him Jean-Baptiste Des Groseilliers (son of Médard Chouart, both experienced coureurs de bois), Jean-Baptiste Godefroy (another seasoned coureur de bois) and Pierre Allemend (pilot in the colony); he thus believed that Frontenac realized they were actually heading towards Hudson's Bay and not France.

It could be asked why Radisson and Des Groseilliers were in so great a hurry to reach the Nelson River that year, on dilapidated sloops procured for them by La Chesnaye and with so little backing at their disposal. However, the tide was turning at the Court of France where Frontenac was falling into ever greater disfavor; and so, it was likely that in the immediate future, such an expedition could proceed in all legality, supported by the Governor of the colony and perhaps even by the Court of France.[19] But the situation had been festering for a long time; then too, Radisson had probably learned in London that the English Company now intended to found a settlement at the Nelson River. And so, Radisson and Des Groseilliers seemed determined to get to the Bay and once there to oust any and all rivals, with or without an official commission.

Fifth travel narrative at the Nelson River, 1682-1683

Radisson wrote his fifth and sixth travel narratives with a quite different perspective than that of the first four. After his "forceful takeover" on the Nelson River, Radisson found himself at the heart of a very serious dispute between France and England, as well as in England alone, where his enemies seized on the opportunity to malign him. In his fifth narrative, Radisson sought to present his version of the events and to prove that under the circumstances, he had acted in a responsible and honorable fashion. Yet, he knew that his point of view would be scrutinized by many intermediaries (Nute, 1943: 350), who, in turn, would compare his version with that of other actors; in consequence, he had but a slight margin of maneuver for disguising the facts if he wanted to preserve his credibility. In the end, the best he might do would be to try to justify himself by presenting his actions in as favorable a light as possible.[20] Given the few other documents available, Radisson's narrative is far and away the best source of information about what actually transpired at Nelson River in 1682-1683.

The events

In May 1682, La Chesnaye formed a partnership with four other Québec merchants to mount an expedition for Hudson's Bay; this alliance failed to

---

19. In fact, Frontenac was recalled that same summer, in July 1682 (Borins, 1968: 27); (Nute, 1943: 179).

20. I refer in the main to Radisson's most detailed narrative to present the events which occurred at the Bay. However, the versions of Company representatives, of all the sailors on board the *Bachelor's Delight* and of Radisson do concur. Exchanges of memoirs and diplomatic discussions about these events continued over more than fifteen years (HBRS-11: 103-104).

offer Radisson all the guarantees of authority and cooperation that he wanted. He saw arrive at Percé "an old sloop of approximately 50 tons [...] [bringing] enough merchandise for the trade, but few provisions" (Raw: 15). Fortunately, Des Groseilliers joined him a few days later at the command of a second smaller sloop, carrying a few more men. The two brothers-in-law reached an agreement: they had to undertake the expedition, whatever the cost, but they had "great difficulty in convincing [their] followers who were petrified at the thought of exposing themselves to a voyage of 900 leagues in such tiny vessels, facing seas so turbulent" (Raw: 15).[21] The expedition left Percé bound for Nelson River on July 11, 1682 (Raw: 16).

After thwarting two attempts at mutiny and avoiding a few narrow brushes with danger, the fears of the crews resurfaced at the sight of the ice floes and desolate coastlands they sailed alongside. Finally, the two sloops reached the Hayes River – very near to the Nelson River – the first, on August 26 and the second, on September 2, 1682 (Raw: 16 and 18).[22] Once reunited, the two French sloops sailed upriver some fifteen miles to a spot where most of the men set about erecting a fort while Radisson, his nephew, Jean-Baptiste Des Groseilliers, and another Frenchmen continued on upriver by canoe. It was only after eight days of navigation that they finally came upon an Amerindian, who was hunting (Raw: 19). Their communication was easy and immediate, despite the Amerindian's astonishment, since the three Frenchmen were quite at ease in the native language. The hunter ran to fetch the other members of his band and, the following day, nine canoes carrying twenty-six Amerindians came to meet with the three Frenchmen (Raw: 19-20). Radisson immediately offered them his alliance; then, the Band Chief indicated that this pleased him immensely: "young people" said he to his partisans, "you have nothing to fear, the Sun shines upon us once again; now our enemies shall fear us, for here is the man we have been praying for since the birth of our fathers" (Raw: 21). Radisson very easily struck an alliance with this band, a connection which promised to be strong and advantageous for both parties, then Radisson conducted several of their number to the French fort where he wanted to present them their "father," Des Groseilliers (Raw: 22).

The next day, they heard distant cannon fire: Radisson at once asserted to his Amerindian guests that this was the ship from France he had been awaiting; and they believed him. This innocuous pretension is the first in a lengthy

---

21. Radisson's sloop had a crew of twelve, that of Des Groseilliers, fifteen, for a total of twenty-nine men, including the two brothers-in-law.

22. These dates were obviously subject to controversy since each of the three expeditions claimed to be the first to arrive at the Nelson River.

succession of crafty tactics that Radisson will deploy over that entire winter, to control and offset his rivals without having to fight them. On this question, his narrative is transparent: "It is true that I made use of all the wiles that I could invent to achieve my purposes" (Raw: 4). Radisson explains in detail the nature and effects of his innumerable ploys, which demonstrate his immense power of persuasion, and, more importantly, his exceptional mastery of the northern environment, among the Aboriginals. This gave him a clear advantage over any rivals from England and New England that he chanced to confront there, those for whom the rigors of life at the Bay and the problems in communicating with the Aboriginals represented permanent obstacles.

A few days later, the Frenchmen discovered the source of the cannon fire. They came upon some fifteen men busy erecting a fort near where they had berthed their sloop, on the Nelson River (the French had dropped anchor on the Hayes River) (Raw: 24-25). Radisson and his men waited for a time in ambush hoping to capture a prisoner who would tell them who they were (Raw: 16 and 18); but as no one left the site, the Frenchmen decided to come forward, dressed as they were like savages or coureurs de bois; at first the boat people thought they were Indians: "they began to cry out to us, as if inviting us to approach them, speaking a few words in an Amerindian tongue that they took from a book" (Raw: 25). To begin with, Radisson answered them in Cree; then he switched to French, and finally, to English, asking them to identify themselves. He learned that they numbered fifteen "very resolute Fellows," up from New England to trade, with neither licenses nor commissions of any sort (Borins, 1968: 61). Radisson urged them to decamp: "I told them that I had located in the country before them, on behalf of the French company" (Raw: 26); he went on to say that he had a fort, nearby, and enough manpower to prevent their trading at his expense. He further indicated to them that he was waiting for another ship from France, strongly advising them against "staying here any longer" (Raw: 26). Howerver, when Radisson learned that the young Benjamin Gillam, whom he knew personally (the son of Captain Gillam of the Hudson's Bay Company), was commanding the expedition, a less aggressive negotiation took place on board ship where Gillam received Radisson at dinner... all this while his companions, at some distance, held at bay two hostages from New England, as a measure of prudence (Raw: 26-27).

Gillam had the cannon fired again, a demonstration of might; and he impressed on Radisson that it was to their mutual advantage for them to come to an understanding since the season was too far gone for him to weigh anchor. Radisson agreed to let them winter on site provided they abstain from fortifying their dwelling, a precaution he deemed needless, since, as he maintained, "I had absolute power" over the Amerindians in the region (Raw: 27-28). The two men promised to remain in contact and to take neither aggressive nor harassing action one against the other: "after which we parted company, each quite pleased with the other, he, with full knowledge that I indeed had the forces to back up my resolve and me, determined that he retain this excellent opinion" (Raw: 28).

Immediately upon leaving Gillam, Radisson and his men sighted another ship heading up the Nelson River. They at once sent up "a heavy smoke signal" to warn the vessel of their presence and bring it to a halt. The shipped dropped anchor opposite them; then the following day, Governor Bridgar of the Hudson's Bay Company and six of his men rowed to shore to encounter those who had sent up the smoke signals. Radisson posted three men at the edge of the woods and headed alone towards the shore, feigning Amerindian shrieks, to see if they knew the native tongues. No reaction. Radisson then forbade their coming ashore before identifying themselves; this time, he loosed a real shriek, then "knowing full well because of the ship and the demeanor of the seamen that they were Englishmen" (Raw: 30), he spoke to them in English. They answered him at once "what business have we with you? We are Englishmen"; Radisson retorted that he was French, enjoining them to withdraw (Raw: 30-31). His companions had to come out of the woods for Bridgar to tell them that he was mandated by the Hudson's Bay Company to establish a settlement at Nelson. For a moment, both Radisson and Bridgar claimed to have full jurisdiction over the location; then, to ease the situation, the two men, who, in fact, knew one another, decided to deal with questions in a more personal fashion aboard the Company ship commanded by the senior Gillam, even though Radisson distrusted him, "who at London declared himself my enemy, being, as he was, a creature of those who forced me to abandon service to England" (Raw: 32). He took this risk despite the warnings of his followers, who of course held several English hostages, pending his return.

During this repast, Radisson declared to Bridgar and Captain Gillam that he had two ships at his disposal, (in reality, two sloops) "a large number of Frenchmen in the woods" (he would soon send out two of them), that he was awaiting a third ship (false) and that his men were building a fort (true); "happily, [Bridgar] [...] believed me, for had he taken the trouble that I did to venture 40 leagues through the bush, and to sleep on the hard ground, in order to make discoveries, he would have been swift to recognize my weakness" (Raw: 32). Despite his pretentions, Radisson knew that he could not get rid of his competitors "by show of force"; and so, he elected to count on his familiarity with the surroundings, the climate and the Amerindians, to catch his rivals off-guard by recourse to subterfuge, at the most opportune moment.[23] Even though they were fewer in number than all their competitors in one body, the French had among them men of considerable experience, like Des Groseilliers, his son, Jean-Baptiste, Élie Grimard and Jean-Baptiste Godefroy, so that together they had a much greater margin of maneuver at the Bay than did their opponents. It was enough for the Frenchmen to carefully prepare their interventions and to profit from the foibles of their adversaries if they wanted to control the situation handily. At least that is what Radisson believed (Raw: 36).

But Radisson was not a man to count his chickens before they were hatched; hence, he spent a great deal of time, that same winter, spying on his rivals' behavior in the bush, going from one fort to the other so as to repeat his prevarications, as well as making sure of the state of his adversaries' forces and of their intentions, all the while consolidating the alliance he had forged with the first native band and reinforcing the guard of the French fort, to avoid any surprise. As Des Groseilliers was in charge of the rear guard, Radisson could concentrate his efforts on offensive tactics, while Jean-Baptiste Des Groseilliers and another Frenchman accompanied the Amerindians into the bush to meet with new bands whom they encouraged to come trade with them (Raw: 33-34). Because he was sure that he had nothing to fear from Bridgar or the Company, Radisson intervened at first with Benjamin Gillam's group, which he found to be rather audacious. Indeed, they had erected a stout, well-flanked fort that was easy to defend despite the orders given them by Radisson, whose authority they had begun to defy. Radisson resorted to further trickery to foil them.

Benjamin Gillam feared the representatives of the Hudson's Bay Company almost as much as did the French, because they could, in all legality, prohibit their trading and even expel them from the region. At first, Radisson concealed the arrival of the Company ship from the New Englanders, but he soon thought better of it and gave them this news along with a proposal of alliance against the Company (Raw: 38). Radisson also revealed to the young Gillam that his father captained this ship and that he was sick; if he wanted to see his father under cover, Radisson was ready to help him, by disguising him as a coureur de bois and passing him off as one of his men (Raw: 38-39). In this way, Radisson was able to reaffirm his authority over the group from New England, whom, in

---

23. "It is true that I had the great advantage of controlling the savages, which for me replaced any superior force" (Raw: 32).

Gillam's presence, he ordered to refrain from shooting the cannon, to remain ever discreet and to distrust anyone and everyone who approached their fort, including the French, unless they gave the password agreed upon by all. These precautions would prevent their being discovered by the Company men (Raw: 39). The encounter between the Captains Gillam, father and son, occurred at some point over the following days. Both men were moved at seeing one another, and they were able to exchange a few words in private, before Radisson and his men departed. Some days later, the Company ship was carried beyond the Nelson River by the ice floes and Captain Gillam, senior, went down with his ship (HBRS-9: XXVIII). This accident dealt a cruel blow to the ambitions of Mr Bridgar, who, all at once, found himself minus a ship, not to speak of several seamen, and facing a severe shortage of supplies (Raw: 47-48). The group that Radisson least feared now became even more vulnerable.

Radisson retired to the French fort waiting for the rivers to completely freeze over so that he could again navigate among the three forts. He learned from the two French hostages he had left with the New Englanders that the two English expeditions had made contact. Radisson felt that it was time to take action before the English could organize and league against his group of Frenchmen (Raw: 46-48). His first move was to meet with Bridgar to offer him assistance over the winter months – an attempt to seduce and intimidate him at the same time, which in no way altered the vindictive attitude that Governor Bridgar nourished towards Radisson: "he spoke ill of me in my absence, [...] he said openly to my people that he would ruin my trade, by giving six hatchets for each beaver to the savages and as much other merchandise in proportion; I have, in my possession, the attestation to this fact"[24] (Raw: 50).

Radisson thus presents the events of winter 1682-1683 as a struggle between three groups and three leaders for control of trading at Nelson River. These three groups were determined to trade with the Amerindians of the region to avoid the failure of their expedition; hence, whether or not they had the right to engage in the fur trade at Nelson River seems to have been relegated to the back burner by all the actors involved. The two brothers-in-law, having always believed in the potential of the Nelson, were certain that their "conquest" would be well received in New France, perhaps even in France, where the group that included La Chesnaye, Le Moyne, Le Ber and

---

24. This comment clearly indicates that Radisson was aware of the large number of depositions gathered concerning this affair and the many debates that occurred over the actual development of events and the behavior of participants.

6. Location of Forts along the Nelson and Hayes Rivers (Winter 1682-1683)

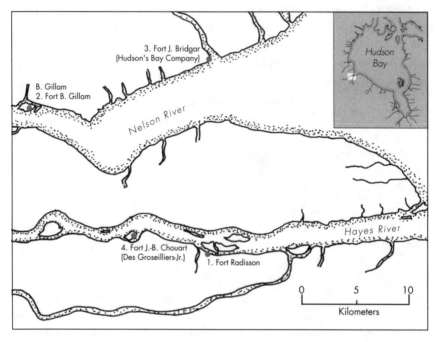

At around the same time, three different trade expeditions had reached the two neighboring rivers, Nelson and Hayes, on the west shore of Hudson Bay. The rivers were approximately 10 km from one another, which was the distance separating Forts Benjamin Gillam (New England), John Bridgar (Hudson's Bay Company) and Radisson (New France). This was an opportunity for Radisson to outwit and take a lead over his competitors (Jean Baptiste Des Grosseilliers and the seven French voyageurs who remained built a fourth fort, further upstream on the Hayes River, after Radisson's departure).

others continued to gain support. In any event, they too had accounts to settle with their merchant backers and they wanted to return from the north with something more substantial than dashed hopes. Benjamin Gillam and his men had similar designs; they had never resigned themselves to the situation, despite the illegality of their presence at Nelson, and no doubt convinced that having come to the far end of the world, it would be stupid to simply throw down their arms. As for Bridgar, who could rely on the King's influence, as well as on an official charter and precedents, he made it a personal affair and persisted to the bitter end in trying to impose his authority and vanquish Radisson, even at the cost of transgressing Company orders and betraying the interests of his men who were to find themselves in an unfortunate situation after the loss of their ship. Bridgar's determination would have been to his credit had his bravado and the overall inefficacy of his strategies not ultimately led to his being separated from his men and then expelled from Hudson's Bay by Radisson, in summer 1683. In view of what the Company expected of him, Bridgar's expedition was an unqualified failure.

Before taking action against the New Englanders, who were more hard-headed than the others, Radisson again resorted to cunning. He invited Benjamin Gillam to come visit his fort, convinced that the latter individual had long wanted to know its location and the extent of their force. Gillam accepted and even spent an entire month at the French fort – happy indeed and proud to note that in reality the Frenchmen had very little protection. Then one fine day, Radisson put his cards on the table, announcing to Gillam that until further notice he was his prisoner; moreover, that he intended to seize his fort and his ships (Raw: 52). Gillam flew into a rage and apparently replied that Radisson would never succeed, even with a hundred men. In a show of bravado, Radisson asked him to choose, himself, the eight men he (Radisson) would need to successfully conclude the operation; Gillam apparently did just that (Raw: 54).

However, the New Englanders' fort and ship were much easier to take than anticipated, as no one was exercising adequate surveillance. In no time at all, the nine Frenchmen took control of the situation. A Scotsman alone managed to escape and ran to inform Bridgar about what had transpired (Raw: 56-58). The Governor immediately organized a counterattack, which the French, on their guard, easily quelled, even capturing three Englishmen and the Scot who had escaped (Raw: 58). After the arrival of a reinforcement detail of four men up from Hayes River, Radisson decided that it was time to confront Bridgar. He reproached the Governor for having attacked him, stating that henceforth no other Frenchmen would ever come to his assistance, no matter his predicament: "I only wanted to intimidate him, thereby forcing him to deal with me honestly; and from time to time, I might give him the help he needed. But above all else, I wanted to make sure that he set aside all thoughts of trading and that he realized the need to depart in the spring" (Raw: 60). Concerning this, Radisson's partner, Des Groseilliers, wrote to him that he was worried about his strategy and wanted to discuss the matter with him; Des Groseilliers felt he was far too "lenient" with the English whom Radisson had hesitated to disarm as they would thus be unable to hunt (Raw: 61-62). However, what Radisson has to say about all this must be taken with a pinch of salt as it is abundantly clear that he was seeking to promote his own good conduct. Hence, it is altogether possible that his attitude towards the English was somewhat less exemplary than he claims; even though it is true that he never resorted to "brute force" against his adversaries, none of whom complained of cruelty or even the slightest ill-treatment before the episode surrounding the departure.

The forces of England and New England were now "under control" despite Bridgar's fluctuating moods; moreover, Radisson invited the Governor to the French fort, in his turn, but, in reality to keep an eye on him. While he was there, Jean-Baptiste Des Groseilliers returned from the bush accompanied by a fresh group of Amerindians who offered supplies and a military alliance with the French, promising them two hundred beaver pelts if they allowed them to destroy the Nelson-River fort of the Hudson's Bay Company. Radisson again refused, it is said, on the pretext that the English would have no other choice than to retreat when summer came, as they were in such a weakened state. Then he tried to dissuade Bridgar from having any contact with these Amerindians, for the safety of himself and of his men, maintained Radisson, whereas, if the truth were known, he wanted to keep the Amerindians ignorant of the preferential trading conditions that Bridgar was prepared to accord them (Raw: 64-65).

The spring breakup resulted in such extensive damage at the mouth of the Hayes River that the two French sloops were smashed outright, despite the care that had been taken to moor them as far ashore as possible (Raw: 67-68). They were able to construct a boat using what was left of the two wrecks; but the Frenchmen were more concerned about the *Bachelor's Delight*, the single ship in relatively good condition still in the region, and that was captained by Benjamin Gillam. Fortunately, the spring precautions had protected the vessel well enough which meant that the negligible damages it sustained were easily repaired.

Preparations for the departure were lengthy and laborious. Radisson continued making the rounds from one fort to the other in a bark canoe, making sure that the ships were being repaired while restraining Bridgar's impulses, in particular, but also those of the New Englanders who became increasingly recalcitrant as the trading season approached. The French became more cautious and also more suspicious (Raw: 75-77), especially after the chief of one Amerindian band, who was aware of the prices offered by the English traders at James Bay, openly reproached Radisson for his deceitful proposals: "you call yourselves our brothers, yet you refuse to give us what those who are not (our brothers) accord us; accept our presents (or the market values he was proposing to them) or we shall no longer attend you; we shall seek out the [English]" (Raw: 80). Radisson countered this more commercial attack with a frankly military riposte, presenting the Amerindian alliance with the French as a question of commitment, of "party," and not of "price"; he further retorted to the "insolent" chief that perhaps he would obtain more merchandise for his furs from the English, but only after confronting innumerable dangers in reaching them, and a thousand more should he decide to attack the powerful French and their allies. For that year, it can be said that trading was far from easy, especially since Bridgar succeeded in making contact with the Amerindians, offering them excellent rates of exchange. Radisson however managed to limit the damage by again playing the cards of power and authority, by offering the Indians many more gifts and by intervening directly in the family affairs of the first band with whom he had forged an alliance (Raw: 84-88). Once the preparations for departure were well under way, Jean-Baptiste Des Groseilliers was chosen to head the group of eight Frenchmen who would remain behind. The two English forts were then emptied of their contents and put to the torch.

The *Bachelor's Delight* and the cobbled-up French sloop departed the mouth of the Nelson River July 27, 1683 (Raw: 91); but the ship remained jammed in a mass of ice and the sloop, forced to draw alongside the ice floe to remain close to the ship, as had been agreed, split open: "we had at once to provide help, and to place the vessel's contents on the ice to better careen her; this we did with great care. We remained in this perilous position surrounded by ice floes until August 24" (Raw: 91). The some ten Englishmen from the Company were finally able to start out again aboard the patched-up French sloop heading for the James Bay posts, at about eight days of navigation towards the southeast, while the *Bachelor's Delight*, carrying all the Frenchmen, Mr Bridgar and the New Englanders, turned towards Percé; they reached that destination in October 1683 (Raw: 93-94; Borins, 1968: 62). Radisson and Des Groseilliers brought back only two thousand beaver pelts, a somewhat modest return for such an impressive investment of efforts and monies.

The final phase of the expedition was to turn even more sour since a representative of the Ferme générale de la Nouvelle-France (Farm General of New France) – more simply put, a tax collector – was waiting for Radisson and Des Groseilliers at Percé to halt the transfer of furs to France. Consequently, the *Bachelor's Delight* had to go to Québec with her furs and her "prisoners" from New England (Borins, 1968: 64-65), where the taxman seized her cargo. The new Governor, one La Barre, promptly sent the ship back to New England to avoid a diplomatic incident; and, he even gave Captain Gillam the sum of one thousand livres in compensation for damages incurred (Borins, 1968: 67). La Barre, who was financially involved in this trading venture, also contested the seizure of the beaver pelts; moreover he indicated that he favored a full exemption from the quarter part "in view of the fact that they (the investors) had run extreme risks, suffered severe losses and come from a greater distance (that which separated New France from Hudson's Bay) than the shores of France" (La Barre, 4-11-1683, in Borins, 1968: 66). Finally, a few days after their arrival on November 8, 1683, bills of exchange were issued for three quarters of the total cargo value, thus, minus the stipends of Radisson and Des Groseilliers, which monies were put aside pending the King's decision as to whether or not the exemption of the right to the quarter part on those pelts might stand (Borins, 1968: 66). The two brothers-in-law therefore saw their gains placed directly in the hands of the King, who, in turn, would decide where that sum should be accorded, either to Radisson and Des Groseilliers, mere pawns on the chess board, or to the powerful collaborators who collected and managed his taxes. No consideration was given at any time to the fact that Radisson had already experienced various difficulties at the Court of France. And so, to better defend their cause or, as Radisson writes, to comply with the wishes of Colbert who wanted firsthand information about the opportunity of establishing a post at Hudson's Bay, the two brothers-in-law set sail for France, scarcely three days after seeing their share of the profit "frozen" by the colonial administration (Raw: 96).[25]

A few months earlier, the Court of France had had occasion to note the "tetchiness" of the English when it came to the rights held by the Hudson's Bay

---

25. "The selfsame Sieur de la Barre [...] told me that I must needs leave without delay to comply with the desires of Mr. Colbert concerning this issue, and to leave my things in the care of Sieur de la Chesnaye, even though I was not satisfied with his behavior, he having been most dishonest with me" (Raw: 96).

Company over the Northern territories. At that juncture, the new Governor La Barre had encouraged the creation of the Company of the North, at Québec, having advised the King of his intent to oppose the policy of the Hudson's Bay Company, which now wanted to set up inland trading posts, uprivers, claiming that the entire hydrographic basin of Hudson's Bay was theirs in all legitimacy. France had warned England about La Barre's intent and the English at once took umbrage, replying that the Company's Royal Charter accorded them indisputable rights (Borins, 1968: 68). The highly immoderate conduct of Radisson and Des Groseilliers at Nelson River was going to provoke an even stronger backlash.

When news about the events at Nelson reached London in December 1683, the Company, represented by James Hayes, immediately demanded the diplomatic support of the Crown and its irrevocable condemnation of the action taken by the two Frenchmen. Straightaway, Lord Preston, the English emissary, took this short communiqué to Paris:

> I, the undersigned, Envoy Extraordinary of the King of Great Britain, have received order from His Majesty to give notice to your most Christian Majesty that it is the man called Radisson who was the instigator and the leader of the undertaking [...] that the said Radisson disembarked some time ago at La Rochelle, and must presently be at Paris. The said Envoy has also received order from the King [...] to very humbly beg [...] Your Majesty to give such orders as he deems appropriate, to assure that the author of such great violence shall not avoid the punishment he deserves (ANQ, C11A, vo. 125, f. 37).

Upon their arrival at La Rochelle, in December 1683, Radisson and Des Groseilliers discovered that Colbert, the one person upon whose consideration they counted, had died. Radisson reached Paris on January 15 "where I learned that serious complaints had been brought against me to the Council of France by milord the Viscount Preston" (Raw: 96-97). And so, another very bad reception seemed to be in store for the two adventurers. However, not only did the French Court hesitate to make a tragedy out of the affair, they even procrastinated for some months over the prickly question of the Hudson's Bay hydrographic basin[26] (Nute, 1943: 201-207). Louis XIV was trying to have his cake and eat it too; but above all, he wanted to improve

---

26. Radisson writes that he was fairly well received by the marquis de Seignelay and other influential courtiers: "far from such [Radisson's conduct] being blamed at the Court of France, I can say without flattering myself, that I was applauded for it, but I do not wish to say that

his relations with the Duke of York, who became Governor of the Hudson's Bay Company after Prince Rupert's death. Now that York had managed to preserve his right of succession, Louis XIV was counting on him to spread Catholicism in England. Pleasing the Duke was therefore a priority for Louis XIV, which was why he finally decided to return the Nelson River post to the English, in April 1684 (Borins, 1968: 72)... while continuing to listen to the opinions coming from New France as to the importance of Hudson's Bay. Confusion at the Court was so widespread concerning this issue that in 1684, Governor La Barre and the Intendant De Meules both had to ask the King whether or not their instructions supported the establishing of French posts along the rivers flowing into Hudson's Bay (Borins, 1968: 71).

With respect to the right to the quarter part, the Royal Council soon resolved the issue to the benefit of the King's financiers and, in the days immediately following this decision – which of course was poorly received by Radisson and Des Groseilliers, each of whom had risked his life during this voyage – Lord Preston and the Hudson's Bay Company changed their plans and tried to bring Radisson back on board.[27] As he appeared receptive to their advances and in that he had something to offer the Company, he and his former partners quickly reached an agreement. A few weeks later, at most, Radisson had already set sail for the Nelson River under the English flag; he had promised to assure their regaining absolute control of Nelson and to return to London before Christmas with a full cargo of furs.

Ready again to leap into the fray

Radisson was still in France when he wrote his fifth travel narrative in the French language (Raw: 100); but the sixth narrative, which had to have been written at London after his return from the Bay, in October 1684, was also in French, indicating that Radisson had not returned from France empty handed and that he attached importance to the social status and high *cultural* standards that he had sought and acquired, at least to some extent, on the continent. Radisson even presented a fine copy of them, written in good French, to the

---

I deserved praise" (Raw: 97). It is quite true: "you [Father Renaudot] are kinder than you think for those who make discoveries; you indeed pardoned Radisson for having fleeced his friends, the English" (Ambassador at Rome to Renaudot, 11-11-1684, BN, Fonds Renaudot, f.86).

27. On April 10, 1684, a Royal edict confirmed that the tax on the quarter part applied in full to the trading ventures of 1682-1683, as well as to all the furs that would come thenceforth from Hudson's Bay (Borins, 1968: 74-75). Radisson was surely weary of his reverses in France: "it was wrong to recall Radisson from England, then neglect him as was done" (French Ambassador at Rome to Father Renaudot, 24-04-1683, BN, Fonds Renaudot, f.216v).

Duke of York, now King James II.[28] It should come as no surprise that he promoted to the hilt the knowledge and experience he had gained in a France, them at the acme of her power and her glory, where this native son had succumbed, like so many others during that era, to the splendors of the Court, all the while admiring the immeasurable power that Louis XIV held over his Kingdom and hailing many of his achievements – like the very rapid development of the navy – even to the point of endorsing certain aspects, such as the French language and absolute monarchy, on his return to England.

In his fifth narrative, Radisson (Raw: 23, 26, 30, 32, 35, 38, 40, 43, 53, 62) appears to be a particularly *wily* individual, one who is able to extricate himself easily from a tight spot and seize the advantage during difficult negotiations. With respect to business dealings or commercial competition, he had proved that he could be as valuable as he was dangerous for the Hudson's Bay Company, all the while acting with a certain civility, according to a code of conduct not unlike that of the gentleman. The fifth narrative also reveals that Radisson did not depend solely on powerful allies in either Court to act; he was dangerous in all circumstances, confronting anyone at all, because of his keen sense of observation, his constant vigilance and attention and because he reacted rapidly to any situation, most of the time getting the better of his competitors.

As a specialist on questions relating to Amerindians, Radisson gave valuable advice and offered eloquent examples of his knowledgeability.[29] The alliance that he forged with the first Amerindians encountered on the Hayes

---

However, Radisson's final undertaking at Nelson, although pardoned, was perceived as a mistake by those who were thinking of supporting him or as a blunder by his enemies, who took advantage of the opportunity to reactivate the alliance of De Seignelay with Frontenac, who regained his position as Governor of New France, and with de la Salle as explorer (letter of February 1684, Fonds Renaudot, f.97v-98). In September 1684, or a few months after Radisson's departure from France (and before it was known that he was to return to Hudson's Bay in the employ of the English), another letter intended for Father Renaudot confirms that it had been decided to dispense with his presence: "Radisson and his brother [Des Groseilliers] did not deceive either myself or you, [I had recognized in the former person extravagant notions that discouraged one and that I forever renounce as do you" (letter of September 2, 1684, BN, Fonds Renaudot, f.194).

28. This is the "Windsor Manuscript" to which I have refered.

29. "Your Majesty shall see [...] the small considerations, the ways of acting that I practice with the savage peoples, and that I have established myself with them as a figure of authority and worth, so as to be able to take profitable advantage of the trade" (from the unpublished introduction to the copy of the fifth and sixth travel narratives, given to the King of England in 1684, and called the Windsor Manuscript because it was found in the Windsor Library by Jean Radisson, a descendant of Pierre Esprit). See Warkentin, 1996b).

River, in 1682, illustrates the exceptional mastery he had achieved over his many years of dealing with the native peoples:

> I gave each of the Savages tobacco and pipes, noticing that one of them used a tiny piece of flattened steel to chop up his tobacco; I requested that he give me that object and then I threw it on the fire which surprised them all, because at the same time, I pretended to weep and dry my tears, telling them that it pained me to see my brothers so destitute and deprived of all things; I assured them that they would no longer lack for anything as long as I remained among them, and then, I removed my dagger that I had at my side, and gave it to him from whom I had taken the piece of steel; I also had them bring from my canoe a few packets of small knives which I distributed among them; I encouraged them to smoke, then gave them food; and while they were eating, I spread before them the presents I had brought, including a rifle, gunpowder and lead, for their Chief. When I gave him these presents, I told him that I took him for my father; he then adopted me as his son, covering me with his garment (Raw: 22-23).

This *adopted* father[30] and his band soon became sure and faithful allies both to Radisson and the French, an alliance that Radisson carefully nourished to keep it alive.

The natural elegance with which Radisson explained to his Amerindian allies, the following year, why he had passed from the French camp to the English camp, from 1683 to 1684, is proof positive that he was quite capable, as he maintains, of settling various disputes among Amerindians and of turning any number of embarrassing situations to his advantage (Raw: 120, 125 and 146):

> I then told him [the Chief of a nation with whom Radisson was in the process of finalizing a treaty] that the French were poor seamen and that they dreaded the ice floes through which they had to pass to bring them (the Indians) merchandise; moreover that their vessels were unsafe and ill-fitted to resist the north seas; whereas the English were a robust, hardy and enterprising race; they had knowledge of all the seas, and possessed large and strong vessels equipped to bring them goods at all times and with no interruption; the savage chief came to dine with us, after indicating that he was satisfied with our palaver (Raw: 121).

---

30. On several occasions, Radisson uses the expression "adopted father" in his last two narratives. This is because the French now took as a matter of course the adoption initiative; their Amerindian fathers are thus no longer adoptive but rather adopted, just as he indicates.

Here, Radisson has stuck as far as possible to the facts; it was quite true that he had arrived the year before in tiny, ill-fitted, French-manned sloops and that those same Frenchmen had experienced many difficulties navigating, whereas the English, had been sending out well-rigged ships to the Bay since 1668, in the footsteps of the first English navigators who had explored that great inland sea some fifty years before.

Radisson, the mature man

In his fifth narrative, Radisson depicts himself as a man of wisdom, one who is strong enough to impose respect and authority not only on the Amerindians, but also on the Europeans, in the difficult environment of Hudson's Bay. He seems to be a skillful leader of men, sure of himself and meticulous in giving orders and exacting respect, a helmsman who, by his dynamism, commitment and sense of responsibility, appears to be equal to the status he covets, knowing instinctively how to avoid or, when necessary, settle the mutinies and dissensions that can compromise any expedition (Raw: 61, 83, 92). However, it is the extensive knowledge of Amerindian techniques and lifestyles that underpins the superior advantage and the abilities that Radisson claims he and a few other Frenchmen have ; this upper hand represents for him, the key to their success at Nelson River, since they know better than anyone else how to establish solid, durable and profitable relations with the Amerindians.[31]

Certain constant values guided Radisson's undertakings throughout the narratives and over the years. Towards 1667, he wrote "that it is proper to be just towards one's Enemy" (Ra: 101) and he affirms in 1685 that he wanted above all "to avoid bloodshed" (Raw: 29). Over long years, Radisson learned to use words and wiles rather than weapons and force to achieve his ends; moreover, he soon realized that in England the "mild-mannered approach" – or at least a particular version of same – constituted an essential element of the bourgeois, the worldly and aristocratic mix, developing at that time around the persona of the *gentleman*. That which increasingly

---

31. The French were able to find their bearings and get about the territory; they also knew how to hunt, shelter and clothe themselves and to survive in the bush, virtually unassisted. For example: Radisson and a few other Frenchmen slept out in the open during two cold subarctic autumn nights (Raw: 32). Radisson and his French companions travelled about in bark canoes (Raw: 43 and 70); they also hunted successfully, on a regular basis (Raw: 34-40, 42, 44, 48, 60, 78, 79).

characterized any gentleman of common (not noble) extraction, who was seeking, by dint of his wealth, his fine manners and his conduct, to ascend the English social hierarchy, were, first and foremost, financial independence, sound judgment and coolheadedness; these qualities were bolstered by self-discipline and much civility in direct relations with others, the whole being crowned by the virtues of honesty and rectitude, which placed such gentleman above and beyond any suspicion (Shapin, 1994: 65, 75, 79-80). Everything indicates that Radisson actively sought to acquire, then demonstrate these attributes which could make him not just an adventurer and a mere underling in the company he had helped to found, but rather a member of the elite, a decision-maker, a man to whom one could entrust responsibilities and accord privileges, despite his turbulent past.[32]

It is also abundantly clear that Radisson was able to show he was equal to achieving his ideal; and so his fifth travel narrative recounts events about which his English rivals could have no complaint, that is up until the time of the departure, when Radisson pillaged and torched the English forts, sent the twelve Company seamen back to the James Bay posts aboard a ramshackle sloop and took the others as prisoners all the way to Québec.[33] Before then, Radisson, who headed the French expedition, had apparently shown consideration to the individuals in his power, as any gentleman would do; on several occasions, he gave supplies of food to his rivals (Raw: 60, 61, 78 and 79); and, at the time of the encounter between the Gillams, father and son, he showed them great deference by leaving them alone (Raw: 60-

---

32. "The gentleman was (and was supposed to be) free of want and that he was under no mundane necessity to labor. The culture that testified to the gentleman's identity [...] laid particular stress upon the facts of his independence and integrity relative to individuals in other social categories. A Restoration courtesy text typically observed that a gentleman 'fears nothing, he' despiseth nothing, he 'admires nothing' [reason's empire over the senses and the emotions]. In English Christian conceptions of gentility 'a Gentleman is a Man of himself,' one "that is God's Servant, the World's Master, and his own man' [...] discipline was central to the identity of the early modern English gentleman; it was valued and legitimate only insofar as it was visible as self-imposed, not exacted by any other save God and the sovereign" (Shapin, 1994: 49). Concerning the privilege and the power to direct, see also Shapin (1994: 47).

33. "If they wanted to treat me fairly, they (Radisson's rivals) would acknowledge that they have more reason to praise than to disparage me in that I have always dealt with them most honesty [not harshly, but with rectitude], for as long as they wanted to remain with me" (Raw: 3-4). The complaints lodged in France against Radisson concerned solely the final episode in the events of 1682-1683, at the time when Radisson emptied and torched those English forts, and on that same occasion, dealt harshly with the English sailors who set out to sea at the same time as he did (HBERS-11: 105).

41). Finally, he refused to let his men open fire on the fugitives "my people wanted to shoot, but I stopped them; for this reason, they muttered against me" (Raw: 57).

Another vital point in the self-defense that Radisson delivers in his fifth narrative is his determination to impose rates of exchange on the Amerindians, a policy that the Company encouraged without reserve and which the two Frenchmen had themselves initiated, then sustained, since the very beginning. It is likely that Radisson's wish to establish a stable, advantageous rate on exchanging furs for merchandise represented a major asset for facilitating Radisson's eventual return to England.[34] The sense of responsibility he now boasted of possessing had to have some positive effect on the reactions of his interlocutors, by signifying efficiency, careful management and profitable operations at the Bay. Other considerations had but slight importance. Radisson had not lost the North, and now he was banking more than ever on the practical, directly exploitable aspects of his competencies... that he was offering to anyone ready to take advantage of them.[35]

Political evolution in England

England's political evolution had a growing influence on Radisson's career as he was of Royalist conviction and probably absolutist, in a business milieu and indeed a country that were increasingly Republican.[36]

Before May 1684, it is difficult to ascertain whether or not Radisson was a partisan of the Duke of York. The two Frenchmen had certainly tried earlier on to vaunt their role in the conquest and the exploitation of New Netherland, today, New York State; but it is not clear that they played that card to the hilt nor is it known exactly when York took notice of their

---

34. In date of May 16, 1684, the committee expressed in writing their discontent to Governor Nixon for having lowered unilaterally the rates of exchange with the Amerindians: "we injoyne you to use all the Art & Diligence you can to bring our Goods to the old Standard... and to fasilitate the business we have at this time sent you very good Goods... and therefore we hope you will advance those goods above the Standard" (HBRS-9: 237).

35. It should be said that Radisson probably found himself obliged to conclude an agreement, if he wanted to find an engagement after the disappointment of his most recent voyage to the Bay and in light of his earlier financial situation: "I had subsisted solely on what my wife sent to me up to the very last of her rings" (BN, Mélanges à Colbert, Tome 125, f.61v.).

36. The passage concerning the third voyage (written towards 1667) where Radisson speaks of the advantage of an absolutist government, and the passage about the fifth voyage where he overtly disapproves of New England's desires and pretentions for independence from England (Raw: 52) (written in 1684-1685), without mentioning the particular support that

representations. Since Hayes and Robinson were partisans of York, it could well be that Radisson united with his principal backers in support of York, before 1675. Howerver, by 1685, it had become manifest that Radisson touted himself as an ardent supporter of absolute monarchy for England, to the extent that his overattentive attitude towards Charles II and the Duke of York, upon his return from Hudson's Bay in 1684, immediately harmed him within the Company, where the Whigs had not forgotten the very nasty fights they had just lost against York and Charles II. The split between the Royalists and the Republicans remained gaping both in the Company and in society at large, even though a majority of Englishmen had eventually accepted the legitimacy of York's coming reign as part of a widespread effort to calm and stabilize an increasingly anarchical situation that reminded many of the social disorders and revolutionary exactions of the years 1640.

The population reacted no less vigorously when Charles II died prematurely and York became King much earlier than anyone had anticipated. James II imposed absolutism and Catholicism as many had feared and, in no time at all, England was engaged in a second revolution to remove the new King from power and replace him by a Royal couple of Protestant allegiance that they had "imported" from Holland: Mary Stuart (an Englishwoman) and William of Orange.[37] And so, the problems Radisson encountered because of his Royalist convictions commenced immediately after his return from the voyage of 1683-1684 to Hudson's Bay.[38]

The only man for the situation?

In 1682-1683, Radisson showed great *audacity*. He had decided to set out for Hudson's Bay on board two old ill-fitted sloops, boldfacedly professing that he was acting for the King of France, although this was far from the

---

he accorded to York/James II in 1684-1685, indicate that Radisson had a strong preference for absolute monarchy, highly effective in France, between 1660 and 1680, in contrast to the chaotic system of the English Restoration, which saw the King and parliament cohabiting with great difficulty, from 1660 to 1688.

37. provide certain details about this audacious political takeover by force in the next chapter.

38. Mr Squire Yong [...] did me the honour of presenting me to his Majesty [Charles II], and to his Royal Highness [the Duke of York], to whom I recounted what I had done; and as a gesture of satisfaction in respect of my zeal and my fidelity to their service, these great Princes ordered Squire Yonge's sister to ask the Company to look out for me, [...] a few

truth (HBRS-11: 103-104); he also refused to concede even the slightest advantage to his competitors, yet disdained resorting to force – in all, a display of considerable audacity. In his first four narratives, Radisson emphasized his undisputable courage and his almost limitless taste for adventure and discovery. However, as of 1685 this innate energy had turned into audacity because Radisson was now targeting clearly defined, ambitious goals that he would seek to achieve at any price, fully aware of the risks and hurdles he might encounter. It could even be said that he had taken over from Des Groseilliers whose strategy, during the voyage to Lake Superior in 1660, for example, was singularly audacious. Their shared intrepidity explains why these two men are to this day viewed as great adventurers, of historical importance for their exploits and their discoveries.

Nonetheless, Radisson's constant preoccupation, his ever-persistent way, indeed, the single factor which seems to have contributed most to his success remains his great prudence; this is evidenced by the priority he accords to food supplies, by the infinite number of tiny details he constantly regulates, such as leaving Benjamin Gillam's fort to head out in the opposite direction to where he actually intended to go (Raw: 43), or by having a Frenchman, knowledgeable in English, successfully spy upon the English prisoners, or again, by the fact that he and Des Groseilliers installed lighting systems around their fort, both at Lake Superior and at the Nelson River, thereby assuring adequate protection against attacks after nightfall (Raw: 53). With Radisson, prudence will always temper his bursts of audacity with a seemingly incongruous approach, but one that was to prove highly effective.

By the time he reached about age 50, Radisson had already absorbed all his experiences with the Iroquois and the other Amerindians of the Great Lakes and Hudson's Bay. He was familiar with them; he was well acquainted with their values, and with their customs; and he was able to make his way almost as easily as they did in the North American environment. And yet, it is quite clear that after his return to Europe, in 1665, Radisson became a full-fledged European in regard to the values and objectives that would count for him thenceforward. Natural affinities seemed to push him more towards the English camp where he enjoyed a better reception, where his knowledge and his experience were more readily appreciated. But, it is equally true that Radisson was quite captivated by the French culture during the most extravagant years of the Sun King's reign. Then too, although in the end he spent the largest part of his life in England, his last two narratives and the more than "sensational" measures that he took to gain the attention of Charles II, then of James II, leave the impression that he was returning from France to England with all the self-assurance and convictions of a man anxious to take a role in "civilizing" England. This he would seek to do by bringing her the blood, the language, the ideas and the fine manners of the French Court. Ultimately, this seems to suggest that the hierarchical social order to which Radisson was now subscribing placed France at the summit, with England second down and America bringing up the rear.

CHAPTER 10

Radisson Wins the Day at Nelson
and Remains in England

I N A PARTICULAR PASSAGE OF HIS FINAL NARRATIVE, Radisson relates in concise fashion exactly why he left England with Des Groseilliers in 1675, and why he returned, in 1684, shortly after encountering his nephew, Jean-Baptiste Des Groseilliers, at Nelson River, for the first time, when he also tried to convince the young man to work henceforth for the English. Apparently, it was in particular, the "refusal of certain ill-intentioned individuals with the Hudson's Bay Company to satisfy our requests" (Raw: 116) on two prickly questions that led to their eventual departure: the two brothers-in-law had been unable to secure a dominant role in organizing the fur trade at Hudson's Bay, and they failed to obtain permission to trade for their own profit. Radisson goes on to explain the return in these terms: "we [he and Des Groseilliers] preferred the benevolence of a clement and sanguine Monarch *following our inclination to serve as men of courage and honor*, to the offers the French King had instructed his Minister make to us in order to oblige our working indirectly for his glory" (Raw: 117).[1] Clearly, Radisson had had more than his fill of the French intrigues and procrastinations that had deprived him of many thousands of livres in income, left him for a considerable period of time without employment and brought

---

1. The italics are mine. Radisson even claims that at that juncture, Médard Chouart Des Groseilliers was quietly resting in England, "assured of his subsistence," whereas he had refused to work again for the Company and, in reality, was then in New France (Raw: 117). This is ample evidence that Radisson was prepared to do anything and everything to execute his project.

him only scant recognition for his talents and his efforts – to which misfortunes Radisson was indeed sensitive. In England, quite to the contrary, he had been well treated over a period of several years; he had established solid and lasting affiliations with several individuals and had even married a Kirke, a woman he claims to have loved most tenderly. In 1684, in an effort to encourage his return to England, Radisson was promised a personal audience with both the King and the Duke of York, as well as an opportunity to confirm his allegiance and, more importantly, to gain royal support.[2]

Secret negotiations had preceded Radisson's decision to return to England, during which each of the two parties had considered the offers and conditions of the other. Radisson maintained that he was now in a better position to help England and the Company than at an earlier time, especially if his merits and his social status were to receive proper recognition (Raw: 102). Thanks to the intervention of Lord Preston and a letter of recommendation from "Squire Yonge" (Raw: 102), the Monarchy and the Hudson's Bay Company guaranteed Radisson conditions that met with his full approval (Raw: 102), even though these remained vague. In the maneuver, Radisson gained a new wife, the daughter of one Gédéon Godet; he conducted the first negotiations in France, obtaining, for his efforts, the post of Permanent Secretary to the British Embassy in France (Nute, 1943: 212-221).

James Hayes, Executive Director of the Company and William Yonge, member of the Steering Committee and Radisson's personal friend, welcomed him on his return to London, May 10, 1684 (Raw: 104). And just as they had promised, they presented him to the King and to the Duke (Raw: 105). Shortly afterwards, Radisson submitted in glowing terms to the shareholders gathered "in an assembly and as private individuals" the details of the enticing offer he had made them from France, albeit after he had taken a public oath of allegiance to the Company (HBRS-9: 248):

> I advised them as to how they must act to establish advantageously the beaver trade in the country of the north; I thus described the best ways to make it

---

2. "I was again advised that since his Royal Highness (the Duke of York) honored the Hudson's Bay Company with his protection, he would most likely consider me" (Raw: 102). It is clear that Radisson was counting on the personal support of these two powerful men, the Duke of York and Charles II, and that he hoped to take advantage of a lull in the English social climate: "the psychological pressure exerted by the memories of 1642-60, shared by virtually all men of property in late Stuart England, had an important restraining effect on the embittered Whigs in 1681 and in 1685" (Arnold, 1981: 13).

thrive and how to ruin apace the trading ventures of foreigners. To achieve these purposes, I would commence by making them masters of the fort and of the French settlement; in addition, they would retain all the furs they had traded since my departure; the whole, on condition that my interests be protected, and that my nephew whom I had left to command the fort, and the other Frenchmen, be paid their lawful due; these gentlemen seemed satisfied with what I said to them, and they believed quite justifiably that they could trust me in all matters (Ra: 105-106).

Radisson promised to leave London without delay, to convince the French still at Nelson to give him their furs, and to work for the English; he also agreed to bring back several thousand beaver pelts to London before the year ended. The Company accorded Radisson a salary inferior to that of the Governors, to wit, £50 for the year, but he was further accorded a privilege to which he attached great import: that of holding shares in the Company (for a value of £200) just like the Governors and like some fifty wealthy and distinguished Londoners. Finally, he was given the amount of £25 to mark his timely return (HBRS-9: 240-241). Since the shareholders had accorded Radisson their confidence, he wanted to reply in kind; and so, he required no written document on their part to confirm the oral agreement they had concluded.[3] The sixth narrative thus appears to be a primordial document for Radisson, who explains therein to the Company members how he fulfilled the mandate they had entrusted to him, as well as indicating the rewards and the acclaim he expected from them, now that success was his.

A lightning voyage

Radisson left the port of London one week after having put in there on board the *Happy Return*. Reaching the Nelson River somewhat behind schedule, he immediately tried to make contact with his nephew, Jean-Baptiste Des Groseilliers; it so happened that that young man had left him a message at the agreed place, to the effect that the French had been forced to move

---

3. "All was done without my taking any precaution as concerns my interests, for I wanted no contention with these gentlemen; and I told them that since they had confidence in me, I, for my part, wished to repay them in kind, giving my every attention to the success of my voyage and my eventual return, in the hope which I entertained that they, in turn, would appreciate my honesty, and that after having given them evidence of my sincerity, [...] they would afford me all the justice that I might needs expect from men of honor and integrity" (Raw: 106-107).

their fort the preceding autumn, to a new location further up the River Hayes, since another Company ship, which arrived before their departure had wintered on site. Jean-Baptiste Des Groseilliers had therefore decided it was prudent to relocate his settlement just beyond a configuration of powerful rapids to take cover from any surprise, for the Amerindian allies of both camps at times threatened and even attacked their respective adversaries. Thanks to a second message, Radisson learned where the fort was located; and so, he sent for his nephew with the help of a group of Amerindians he had just encountered, one of whom claimed to be Des Groseilliers' adopted father. Despite supposedly solid relations with the French, this adopted Father apologized to Radisson for having traded his furs with the English, who had offered him a better price, even though Radisson had formally prohibited such activity before leaving the Bay, the preceding summer. Radisson reassured him by telling him that he had made "peace with the English, through love of you; you, they and myself, henceforth, we shall be but one – embrace this Captain [designating an English interpreter who was accompanying him], and me, as a token of peace, for he is your new brother, and as to your son [Jean-Baptiste Des Groseilliers], go bring to him this news and these symbols of peace without further delay" (Raw: 114).

Des Groseilliers junior joined Radisson at the old French fort the following day. The Company's interpreter was present when they met, a measure of precaution in the interest of all the parties involved. However, Radisson explained the situation to his nephew in private; he, in turn, showed surprise at his uncle's abrupt realignment. Radisson gave him the strongest arguments possible to convince him to submit to his authority. He formally pledged to defend the interests of the eight Frenchmen who had stayed behind at the Bay while he and his group were travelling to England; and he reminded him that he had been *ordered* to force him to serve the English. He further pointed out that they were blood relatives and that he saw in his nephew many fine qualities: "I know that you have much courage and determination" yet, he concluded by speaking words of affection tinged with threatening implications: "never forget the injuries that the French dealt to him who gave you life; and remember that you are in my power" (Raw: 117-118). Apparently, Des Groseilliers did not seek to better understand the whys and wherefores, nor to contest his uncle's will; rather, he surrendered to Radisson all the authority he needed to order the other Frenchmen to also throw in their lot with him, then to load their furs on the vessels of the English Company. Radisson and Des Groseilliers confirmed before all the Frenchmen assembled that henceforth Radisson would take the reins at Nelson River on behalf of the Hudson's Bay Company; and, if they were to place their trust in him, they would lack for nothing, neither here, nor when they reached London (Raw: 118-119).

To speed up collecting the furs, Radisson promised a double ration of food to those Amerindians who helped the Frenchmen to bring the furs out of the bush where they were hidden, then to carry them down below the rapids which protected Des Groseilliers' fort, "where they loaded them on canoes, which brought them to the row boats, which, in turn, conveyed them to the small frigate, for their removal to the ships" (Raw: 147). During this operation, Radisson is often quick to point out the hard work and unstinting cooperation of the Frenchmen, even though the furs in question ultimately belonged to them (Raw: 127). Radisson even went as far as formulating a detailed clarification as to his own and the Frenchmens' right to claim this manna, almost as if he had anticipated the Company's refusal to pay them any compensation whatsoever for these furs:

> I was unable to contain my joyful feelings at the realization that I had succeeded in my undertaking, […] [which would oblige the Company] to respect my interests and those of the other Frenchmen just as I had promised them, the just reward for their long and arduous labor (Raw: 130).

Over the weeks that followed, Radisson managed to convince Jean-Baptiste Des Groseilliers and one other Frenchman to remain on site for one or two more years, the time he felt they needed to strengthen the alliance with their Amerindian partners who knew and respected his nephew. In the course of a public meeting, several Amerindian chiefs ostensibly gave their word: "that they would always consider him [Jean-Baptiste Des Groseilliers] as the nephew of the man who had brought peace to the nations [Radisson] by uniting the English and the French making them withal, brothers to one another" (Raw: 148). Des Groseilliers had also received the support of the Governor, John Abraham, who had taken up office at Nelson that same year (Rich, 1958: 166) (Oldmixon, 1708: 399); but only a few short hours before the departure of the ships. Abraham, now the hierarchical senior at Nelson, reversed Radisson's decision once the furs were safely on board the vessels,[4]

---

4. Radisson held a plenipotentiary mandate at Nelson which was to last until the "recapture" of the post and up to such time as all the furs had been loaded on the ships. Only then could the Governor, John Abraham, take over and remain on site.

proposing, at a special assembly, that all the Frenchmen without exception be dispatched to London. To boot, since he feared they might disobey his order, he had them forcibly removed to the ships and kept under constant guard like prisoners[5] (Raw: 156-157).

The *Happy Return* thus carried all the Frenchmen to England, in October 1684, and Radisson, who had much to prove and many backers to appease, immediately set out on horseback for London. On arrival in the middle of the night, he contacted Squire Yonge, who took him, the next morning, to meet with the King and the Duke of York. These two congratulated him for his dedication and his successes and they "commanded" the Company to look after him. Such insistence, as we have seen, when coupled with the "command" of the Duke of York, angered certain shareholders and members of the Steering Committee, who already deplored York's having become a capricious Governor, one much less useful than had been anticipated. But, in the end, the shareholders had very little to reproach Radisson as he had brought back the fruits of a highly successful trading venture; he had also scrupulously kept his promises and this time provoked hardly any stir at the Bay. Then too, since Radisson affirmed his desire to continue faithfully serving the Company, placing the exceptional experience he had acquired at their service, the Steering Committee renewed his contract for two years – from 1685 to 1687 – as Director of Trade, at the Nelson River.

The "French way"

Over many years, a number of Company shareholders and retainers had noted that certain French Canadians possessed an incomparable expertise on issues relating to the Amerindians.[6] Since the time of Étienne Brûlé, whom Champlain had sent out to live among the Hurons in 1608, the arbiters,

---

5. In this way, the Englishmen of the Company repaid Radisson and his Frenchmen for the insult they had served them the preceding year, when they made Governor Bridgar their prisoner, and conducted him forcibly as far as Québec.

6. "The next thing in course is that we send some of our men [...] with some presents to treat the Indians withall in the most friendly maner we can, that thereby we may drawe down a trade, and learne the way the fransh-men use amongst them" (Governor Nixon to the Company, 1982, in HBRS-8: 254). A number of authors attest to French expertise in the area of Amerindian relations, the French often having shared the existence of their native partners (Jennings, 1984: 167); (Rich, 1958: 179); (Trudel, 1997: 579).

interpreters and coureurs de bois of Canada spent at least part of the year living with their Amerindian allies. The Jesuits strengthened this tradition by locating themselves within the communities they wanted to convert, learning the native languages and intervening in community affairs, at both public and private levels, just as Radisson and Des Groseilliers would do later on. The "French way" that Radisson promotes in his last two narratives represents an often extreme mode of sharing the material and cultural existence of the Amerindians. However, this mode of existence would snowball as of the end of the XVIIth century, giving birth to the Métis nation. The French way or mode was therefore widespread, provoking in certain individuals a very intimate fusion of the two cultures.

Although Radisson quit the Amerindian world at an early age, his travel narratives leave no doubt as to the deep-seated and far-reaching ties which united the early French voyagers with their Amerindian guides, partners and allies. In the fifth and sixth narratives Radisson extends to other Frenchmen the detailed observations that he had related thus far about his own bicultural experience as a coureur de bois.

Under the orders of Radisson

Virtually all the Frenchmen on the voyage of 1682-1683 appear to be good hunters, for many engaged almost continually in this activity. Radisson's comments on his own experience as well as on that of the veteran Frenchmen shed light on the sort of apprenticeship a coureur de bois required to practice his art. Jean-Baptiste Des Groseilliers for example, "having spent his entire life in native lands" (Raw: 14), was quite able to relocate his fort at a place "difficult to reach for any who were not raised like us among the savages;" because he knew, as did they, how to surmount daunting hurdles and cover immense distances. He had made it his business to know intimately the American territory and its main resources (Raw: 136). Does Radisson exaggerate when he speaks of the particular talents of these few Frenchmen?[7] I think not.

In the depths of the subarctic winter, Radisson, Des Groseilliers and, indeed, a few other Frenchmen were able to accompany, over several weeks'

---

7. "The English being surprised to see with what liberty and familiarity I lived with these savages" (Raw: 67).

time, a band of Amerindians; they covered great distances with them, forging alliances with the nations they encountered by offering them presents, by endlessly parleying with them in their language and by inviting them to join in the trade (Raw: 33-34 and 64-65). In my view, the testimony of Jean-Baptiste Des Groseilliers, who, at that point, had never been to Europe, ingenuously reveals the level of integration in the Amerindian culture that the most seasoned French coureurs de bois could achieve.[8] He relates how he and seven French companions spent the winter of 1683-1684 in the midst of some fifteen Amerindians whom they had wanted to keep close to hand for reasons of safety, after an incident during which two of their number encountered a native band of the New Severn region who were in transit; they had invited them to come to the French fort to smoke their favorite tobacco. But one of the Amerindians had first paid a visit to the English, who apparently encouraged him to assassinate Des Groseilliers junior in exchange for a hefty reward. Jean-Baptiste Des Groseilliers easily staved off the attack of this Amerindian, deciding most generously to let him live, "hoping by this generosity, and in giving life to their Chief, that I do offer marks of my courage, and (evidence) that I apprehend neither the English, nor them"[9] (Raw: 134).

Nonetheless, Des Groseilliers wasted no time in alerting his native allies by sending up smoke signals.[10] Once informed, his allies took several ini-

---

8. There can be no doubt about the native ability of Jean-Baptiste Des Groseilleirs as a coureur de bois and intermediary between the Europeans and the Amerindians since the authorities of France and of New France, once they learned that he had gone over to the English, sought to persuade him to return to the service of the French. De La Chesnaye, who hoped to hire him for his Company of the North, also praised his merits to Governor Denonville: "he shall convince them of this truth [that Jean-Baptiste Des Groseilliers was taken away "from them and from the French"] all the more easily in that he has, among these savages, adopted relatives with whom he has been trading for seven years, and who hold, to his favor, that there exists no braver man; he is so clever in tempering their spirits by his experience in their ways, that he can persuade them in all matters" (letter of La Chesnaye to Denonville, 10-04-1685, ANQ). See the exchanges of letters among Governor Denonville, the Minister Comporté and J.-B. Des Groseilleirs in 1685-1686 (in C-11A, vol.7, f.28-29, 255-257 and vol.8, f.42-47v).

9. Des Groseilliers senior had also developed towards his Amerindian partners, or perhaps inherited from them, an attitude that consisted in defending oneself by attacking first: "the genius of the savages being never to await the enemy but, on the contrary, to go in search of him" (Jean-Baptiste Des Groseilliers, as written by Radisson, Raw: 143).

10. "A few days later, our native allies and good friends, warned by the smoke from our fires, our usual signal, arrived at our habitation" (Raw: 134).

tiatives unknown to the French, most importantly, that of confronting the chief who had assailed Des Groseilliers. Realizing that this Chief was only waiting for the opportunity to finish the deed, they killed him then and there, before attacking the English fort, after which they assured Des Groseilliers "that they were prepared to sacrifice their lives in his service" (Raw: 136). The Frenchmen spent the remainder of the winter in the company of this band, whose Chief Des Groseilliers had taken as his adopted father. Later, another hostile Amerindian shot one of the Frenchmen in the shoulder; the wounded man cried out "that he had been killed and that it was up to the men who loved the French to avenge his death (Raw: 138); in this way would he obtain the immediate assistance he needed. As a result of that incident, Radisson's adopted father (the very first Amerindian he had encountered on the Hayes River) left two young children with the French as a guarantee of his loyalty (Raw: 139).

What I find singularly telling and, indeed, most astonishing, is the attitude of Jean-Baptiste Des Groseilliers during a meeting he had organized with the English, through the intervention of the Amerindians. He hoped thereby to discover their intentions so as to better face the events: "I paid them a visit with one of my Frenchmen who carried the presents that I wanted to offer them *in the manner of the Savages* and who also received presents from them for me, as is the custom" (Raw: 140). Des Groseilliers thus elected to negotiate and parley "in the native way" with other Europeans who also responded to him in the same way… as if the Amerindian practices had become the norm for these Europeans, plunged as they were into an environment almost entirely foreign to their own culture.

Radisson's new relations with the Amerindians

Nowhere does Radisson explain the strategy he pursued at the Nelson River; but his game plan can be easily deduced from the negotiations and happenings that he has described. His strategy is quite like that which he and Des Groseilliers had adopted at Lake Superior, in 1659-1660, particularly since Radisson was still trying to set up a trading post *in a zone of conflict among Amerindian bands*. The distribution of trade goods on the continent since the turn of the century had provoked many conflicts among rival bands and nations in the vicinity of the Great Lakes, and an identical dynamic prevailed at Hudson's Bay. To succeed in establishing a permanent post at Nelson River, Radisson sought first to forge an intimate alliance with a band

living in the immediate area; he saw such alliance as paramount if he wanted
to safeguard that post against the envy, the coercion, even the attacks of
rival bands encamped in the shore areas or located farther afield.[11]

   One of the negotiations with the Amerindians, as described by Radisson,
illustrates, for me, the spirit in which the two brothers-in-law had been op-
erating at Hudson's Bay, probably since their arrival there, in 1668 and in
1670. The negotiation in question (which transpired in 1683) clearly seeks
to impose a balance of power that favors the European merchants, based on
a rate of exchange furs/goods largely profitable to the Company (the famous
Standard of Trade which Radisson continued to promote). Radisson explains
as well how he was obliged to repair the errors of the English governors who
had preceded him at Nelson, for example, by discarding their "misguided
habit" of being the first in offering presents to the Amerindians, for this was
construed as a grave offense to the deference which the natives were expected
to observe in regard to Company representatives (Raw: 122). Radisson also
resolved to reply decisively to the natives' recriminations about their pov-
erty, the hardships they endured in coming to trade and the difficulty of
killing beaver as well as to their insinuations about the generous presents
given to them by the French of Canada and the good prices accorded them
by the "English from the far end of the Bay" (James Bay) (Raw: 122).
Radisson answered that he felt compassion for them and that he would do
all he could to bring them relief; but he reaffirmed that the Amerindians
must first offer presents to him because he came from a country more distant than their own. To conclude, he added that it was of little consequence
to him that a dissatisfied element journeyed south to trade at the tip of the
Bay, in that he counted as his friends and allies several nations who had already been trading with him for thirty years, and, moreover, that he was quite
prepared

> to advise them that I would assemble all the surrounding nations to give them
> the responsibility of my goods, that the advantage rendered them by this suc-
> cor would make them powerful, and quite able to block the passage of all the

---

11. The contrary was also true. The native bands living in the immediate region of a post
could count on obtaining supplies more regularly and have the assurance of a formidable
defense mechanism: the fort, its cannons and its rifles; the Amerindians were also reassured
to see that the whitemen occupying these installations were not only brave, but also as resolute in the defense of their allies as they were in protecting themselves.

savages living on these lands, that because of this, they themselves would be forced to lead a fallow existence, to witness their women and their children die in war, or of hunger and privation; from all this, even their most powerful allies could not save them, because I would have proclaimed that they had neither knives nor guns (Raw: 123-124).

Both in the coastal areas and in the interior of the North American content, it seems clear that the introduction of Europeans goods was contingent on military priorities. Radisson's last two narratives demonstrate this in convincing fashion. With his first negotiation at the Nelson River, in spring 1683, Radisson had decided to assert himself as a Warrior Chief in the presence of a group of Amerindians from a distant region, who were demanding that he accord them rates comparable to those to be had at the English trading posts of James Bay.[12] Radisson remained silent for a long while before hurling this scathing reply at those who would contest his authority: "I told the savage who was exhorting me to speak, to whom do you want me to reply? I heard a dog [howl]." Then, his knife drawn, Radisson seized his adopted father by the hair and queried him: "who are you? He replied to me your father, very well said I to him, if you are my father, if you love me and if you are the Chief, speak out for me, you are the master of my goods, that dog who just spoke, what purpose has he here? Let him go to his brothers, the English, at the far end of the Bay" (Raw: 81). Radisson then challenged this malcontent of a Chief and his band to confront the perils and distress of the long voyage, concluding that inevitably "it is more advantageous to trade with us than with the others" (Raw: 81). Radisson explains his intransigence thusly: "I was obliged to speak in such way, during this encounter, or else our trading venture would have come to naught, for when one yields to the savages, be it only once, they never return" (Raw: 81).

It is certain that Radisson's earliest and closest allies appreciated the qualities of Warrior Chief which he manifested on that occasion: "I wanted to withdraw with my brother-in-law (Médard Chouart Des Groseilliers), but we two were stopped by the Chief who encouraged us, telling us that we were real men, that we compelled no one, the each of us was free, and that he and

---

12. "You men who claim to give us life, you really want us to die; you know what the beaver is worth; you know how difficult it is to trap him; you call yourselves our brothers, and yet, you are unwilling to give us that which those who have no such pretensions readily give us" (Raw: 80).

his nation wanted to remain united with us" (Raw: 82). Radisson and Des Groseilliers had just gained the undivided support of a band living in the immediate region, but at the same time they were as good as declaring war on a nation encamped higher up on the Nelson River and whose Chief had negotiated obdurately to secure parity with the English prices that could be obtained at the far end of the Bay. This unidentified nation was certainly also in a position to act as a go-between, since their Chief retorted to Radisson "that he would slaughter the Assiniboines if they came down in our direction, as for me, I answered him – I will repair to your country to eat *sagamité* in the skull of your grandmother: this is a potent threat among the savages, the most offensive that could be hurled at them" (Raw: 82).

Although the negotiations to achieve an alliance and to promote trading, which Radisson conducted briefly during summer 1684, were less arduous owing to the peace that transpired between French and English traders at the Nelson River, the events of the preceding winter, as reported by Jean-Baptiste Des Groseilliers, illustrate the singular importance of firearms in establishing and developing the fur trade at Hudson's Bay. Not that these weapons dominated the exchanges, but they alone could guarantee the effective control of bartered goods in front of bands and individuals who were armed. Firearms thus constituted a strategic necessity for the bands who wanted to acquire and keep European goods. Jean-Baptiste Des Groseilliers recounts that the French were unable to satisfy a band of Amerindians who had come up from the south for the particular purpose of trading guns; and so, off they went to procure firearms from the English, who seized the opportunity to recruit them and pit them against the French (Raw: 137).[13] The need for guns was just as compelling among the allies of the French, who had to abandon then and there all thought of avenging the attempt to assassinate Des Groseilliers, "not having enough guns to undertake such a portentous deed" (Raw: 139). Radisson confirms this fact (Raw: 146).

However, tenacity – albeit an essential quality – did not suffice to gain the affection or the respect of the "savages;" it was also imperative "to boast about our courage and influence, about our being in a position to assist them, to protect them from their enemies, yet as well to make it clear to them

---

13. "It was important that I have enough (firearms) in order to prevent the savages, who were coming down from the highlands to trade, from turning towards the English" (Raw: 140-141).

that we espouse their interests out of consideration for them and, most importantly, want to give them many presents" (Raw: 21). Once he had demonstrated his strength, Radisson also had to prove his generosity; in this he never failed, particularly in regard to his adopted father. Prior to his departure in 1683, for example, Radisson had him brought on board the *Bachelor's Delight* with a written ordinance on his part that he was to be given presents and offered food;[14] his adopted father was more than surprised and indeed overjoyed by such marks of esteem. And Radisson made yet another seemingly indulgent gesture in 1684 when, after having negotiated rigorously with his partners, he consented to a small premium:

> That discourse forced the savages to submit to my every wish (...) I told them that since they had an extreme need of knives and muskets, I would give them ten knives for one beaver, even though the master of the earth, the King, my Sovereign Lord, had ordered me to give only five, and in regard to the muskets, I would give them one for twelve beaver (Raw: 124).

According to the Standard of Trade, as reproduced by Oldmixon (Oldmixon, 1708: 380-381), which appears to be in line with what the Company was suggesting in 1684 (HBRS-9: 237), Radisson actually offered them the knives at reduced rates, but not the muskets, which were offered at the regular price, hence, a rather steep one.[15]

The other means Radisson employs to establish his authority "over the spirit of these nations" (Raw: 120) is quite typical of the French approach; he becomes actively involved in community life and takes sides in Amerindian affairs. In 1683, just before his departure, Radisson learned that his adopted father had been on the run for several months when he first encountered him, this because he had assassinated a rival lover whose family had been angling for revenge ever since. Since Radisson's interests were at immediate issue, he spared neither attention nor generosity in attempting to settle this affair (Raw: 86); and he tried to promote a peaceful resolution

---

14. "He was to be so well received by my nephew that a cannon shot would mark his arrival, that he would also be served food and offered biscuits and two sheaves of tobacco as presents" (Raw: 84).

15. The Oldmixon Standard mentions "6 great Knives, or 8 Jack Knives" per beaver, and in compliance with a letter of May 1684 from the Committee, the maximum price for long muskets is set at twelve beaver, and at 10, 9, or even 8 beaver for the shortest muskets or for those of inferior quality.

of the conflict by offering his father presents which would compensate for
the murder of his rival. He offered him: "a musket, two large buckets, three
jerkins, four sword blades, four cleavers, six scrapers, six dozen knives, ten
hachets, ten sheaves of tobacco, two blankets for women, three bonnets,
gunpowder and lead" (Raw 87), enjoining two emissaries to summon at once
the injured family to a great feast of bonding, where they would be exhorted
to accept these presents of reconciliation. Unfortunately, Radisson had to
leave before their gathering took place. Moreover, later events indicate that
this conflict, or some other, persisted, since his adopted father spent all of
the following summer on the warpath. When Radisson finally saw him again,
immediately prior to his departure in 1684, he learned of the death of a
number of his father's allies and close relatives and of the existence of other
conflicts that again he tried to arbitrate (Raw: 154-155). Since Radisson remained active at Nelson until 1687, he must have been able to pursue his
diplomatic efforts with some successes, since Nelson was straightaway prosperous, hence at relative peace.

During that period, Radisson was no longer, strictly speaking, a woods-
man; his mind was entirely occupied by the Company, the English economy
and by European values. He was totally absorbed by his responsibilities and
his advancement, as well as mindful of Company directives. Even though he
still knew how to deal with the Amerindians, how to negotiate, hunt and feast
with them, the Amerindian chapter of his life had closed forever.

Radisson enjoyed a major advantage in the Amerindian world, where
family ties often represented the main social structure. He belonged to a
family who had been trading with the Amerindians for many decades: since
Médard Chouart Des Groseilliers, from the 1640s to the 1680s, not forgetting Radisson, and then Jean-Baptiste Des Groseilliers who played an important role at the Nelson River in the 1680s. The abiding relations between
the Des-Groseilliers-Radisson family and the Amerindian traders and warriors of several nations – and even more importantly, the crucial times when
certain of these encounters occurred, such as when they were the first to
arrive at the southern end of Lake Michigan, the first to journey west of Lake
Superior, or again, the first to reach James Bay and the Nelson River – these
many feats worked in Radisson's favor, for he could prove his attachment
to the Amerindians over the long haul, even if certain natives questioned his
claim of being their "brother" (Raw: 22, 113, 141-142 and 148). It cannot
be denied that Radisson and Des Groseilliers worked mainly in their own

interest and that they did not always behave as "brothers" towards the Amerindians; nonetheless, it is just as obvious that they *ably served* the cause and the interests of the Amerindians, even at the risk of their life, by delivering the European goods their partners coveted there where these were most needed. The role they assumed amid the Amerindians is not unequivocal, neither all black, nor all white; it is paradoxical.

What did the Amerindians of Hudson's Bay expect from the fur trade?

Even though the utterances recounted by Radisson could never be entirely faithful to the Amerindian mind-set, the extract of a harangue pronounced by a Chief, who had come to trade in 1684, seems to reveal the essence of Amerindian expectations:

> Men and women, youths and children, even those who suckle, recognize this man here (Radisson) as your father; he is worthier than the sun which warms you; you shall find in him always a protector who will assist you in your every need, and console you in your afflictions; men, know that he gives you firearms each and every year for your defense against your enemies, and to slay the animals that feed you and your families; women, consider that he gives you hatchets and knives with which you banish hunger from your land; young girls and children, from now on, fear nothing since he, who is your father, loves you always and gives you *from time to time* all that is necessary for assuring your subsistence (Raw: 150).

Radisson's adopted father had reacted in a very similar way in 1682: "youths, you have nothing further to fear, the sun looks favorably on us, our enemies shall fear us" (Raw: 21), a reaction all the more understandable in that he was on the run; as well, this providential encounter with European traders would give him the power to defend himself and the opportunity to make himself known in the region, especially after all he had surely heard say about weapons and French goods.

Trade therefore came to be intimately associated with pre-existent conflicts, in this instance with a conflict between two rival lovers. The nomadic Crees of James Bay and of the western shore of Hudson's Bay had yearly contacts with the nations to the south; and they too suffered the repercussions of the numerous upheavals that had been agitating the regions both of the Saint Lawrence River and the Great Lakes. In any event, it is clear that the geopolitical tension in the region before the whiteman's arrival meant that the earliest trading posts at Hudson's Bay were set up in an atmosphere of confrontation. The institution of the English posts, the French reprisal from the inland regions and the long-standing Franco-British competition in the region only served to exacerbate and polarize all pre-existent tensions. Jean-Baptiste Des Groseilliers recounts as follows the words of his would-be assassin: "telling me that I was worth nothing because I did not like the English, that I had failed to give presents to pay for possessing the country I inhabited, to him who was the Chief of all the nations and friend of the English at the far end of the Bay" (Raw: 132-133).[16] If Jean-Baptiste Des Groseilliers is faithfully reporting the words of this Chief, his comments detail at least two major transformations that had occurred shortly before at Hudson's Bay. The first of these is the permutation of the Franco-British conflict in the Amerindian world, by the interplay of alliances and competition. The second involves a specifically Amerindian problem which consists in knowing who is "the Chief of all the nations," consequently, to whom are the Europeans expected to pay tribute when they settle in a territory – lands often contested by many different tribes. The will of the Amerindians to see their nation, their band or their family get the better of all others is a recurring phenomenon, one which Radisson noted throughout his lengthy career in America; moreover, it is all but certain that the Amerindians did not inherit this widespread attitude from the Europeans alone, in only a few short decades.

Their own ambitions, strategies, interests and lifestyles constituted the motor propelling their actions, even though they rapidly adapted to the presence of the whiteman and came to count on him thereafter in so many ways. Hence, the declaration of this "Chief of all the nations" and friend of the James Bay English implies a vital inference; it should read as follows: "I

---

16. A noteworthy evolution regarding the offering of presents had been in the works for some time. Traditionally, the presents offered sealed an alliance between Amerindians, atoned for an insult or accorded a right of passage or permission to use a given territory, for a specified length of time; whereas now appears the notion of *owning* a territory, and the presents, at least to English eyes, represent a "price of purchase" which grants them henceforth the exclusive property rights on the territory or territories they covet. This shift in the Amerindian discourse is thus recent and points to the dynamism with which certain individuals or certain nations attempted to adapt to the new order – obviously without yet assessing the full meaning the Europeans gave to the word – *ownership*.

can claim to be the Chief of all the nations, because I am a friend of the English at the far end of the Bay who supply me with weapons and various implements..." Despite the ever growing need for the Amerindian bands at Hudson's Bay to ally with one or another group of Europeans, particularly to increase their fire power, the Amerindian acts and decisions that Radisson describes in his last two narratives may be qualified as autonomous. The allies of Jean-Baptiste Des Groseilliers thus conduct their own inquiry into the attempt to assassinate him and they alone decide to execute the guilty party, even though Des Groseilliers had elected to spare his life (Raw: 124-135). These same allies would also take the initiative of attacking the English, no doubt because they believed that such an act could strengthen their alliance with the French, hence their position in the region; and so, they announced the news to Des Groseilliers with great pride (Raw: 140).

A band of some two hundred Assiniboines came north from a far-off nation to trade at the Nelson post and to meet with Radisson and Médard Chouart Des Groseilliers, whose exploits had been related to them by their Cree allies; this group of Amerindians would manifest the most conspicuous signs of self-determination. Over the summer of 1684, the Chief of this band multiplied the acts of devotion towards the French to the point that Jean-Baptiste Des Groseilliers, who at first had mistrusted them, came to be entirely convinced of their desire to ally with the French, from whom that Chief had already received presents on his home ground, through intermediaries. Following a series of decisions, which, at times, *ran counter* to what Des Groseilliers wanted, this Assiniboine Chief announced to him that he had resolved to attack a gang of prowlers who had been seen in the immediate vicinity and who were thought to be enemies. The Chief gave him these directives:

> He ordered all his men to take up their bow and arrows, and having summoned us (the French), he placed them in battle formation, and told them – my plan is to cross the river with two of the bravest [among his men] [...] to go forth to attack the enemy, and to deploy you in such way that you shall be able to assist me or protect me, while the French shall make up the reserve force, and our women shall load all their possessions onto the canoes, then shall they torch their habitation, if needs be, [...] this brave Chief instructed us to encamp at the edge of the bush, with our muskets at the ready to prevent the enemy from approaching (Raw: 144).

At this stage, it might well be reasonable to question whether or not the traditional values underlying Radisson's personal authority were not disintegrating under all sorts of pressures and new ideas. For example, he attached the greatest importance to respect for the word given: "for the first time, I was found to be a liar by these savages, which was of perilous consequences, for these nations hold this vice in abomination" (Raw: 153). If Radisson is right, it must be recognized that the Europeans to be found at Hudson's Bay very quickly demonstrated to their native partners that their word had but little value; indeed, that it was of scant use to cultivate this practice any further, since clearly, it brought them next to nothing, in comparison with the game of competition, which practice they took up most successfully. Radisson alone serves as a good example of this phenomenon. In spring 1683, he declared to a group of Amerindians, whom his nephew had just brought back from the midlands, that he would deal with them "in better fashion than the English at the far end of the Bay" (Raw: 66). Nevertheless, that same year, the two brothers-in-law would refuse categorically to trade their goods at the price fixed by the English of James Bay (Raw: 79-82). Again in 1684, despite Radisson's talent for expatiating on the Franco-British reconciliation at the Nelson River, the geopolitical reality elsewhere at the Bay accentuated the tensions between the French and the English; indeed, the abrupt shift in discourse and as concerns the promises of alliance made by Radisson probably caused a greater stir and provoked much more skepticism among his partners than his narrative cares to admit.

The different Governors and English traders who followed one another at Nelson and at James Bay, such as Bridgar, Abraham, Bailey and Nixon, men who had no experience with the Amerindians and who, to boot, were at each other's throats because of envy and crass competition, must also have held to a devious discourse and made unreliable promises, the whole dependent on a situation that was evolving rapidly, as much at London as at Hudson's Bay, that bleak and isolated outpost. It appears that for such reasons an Amerindian Chief reproached Governor Abraham, who had claimed that Des Groseilliers was dead and that Radisson was his prisoner: "That Chief of the savages [...] said loud and clear that this one [Abraham] was unworthy of his friendship as were their former brothers, who had begun to settle amongst them while telling them lies" (Raw: 120). In light of the Company's rather anarchic organization, coupled with the schemes of the French – including those of Radisson and Des Groseilliers – and the soon-to-come Franco-British wars at Hudson's Bay, which last would see the trading posts passed from one camp to another over many years, thereby perturbing the supplying of European goods to the Amerindians, it is safe to conclude that Europeans must have *sorely disappointed* the native peoples over the entire XVIIth century, as concerns respect for promises made and pledges given.

Radisson's final voyage to Hudson's Bay

Radisson's success at Hudson's Bay in 1684 failed to bring him as many dividends as he had hoped to realize in the Company, among other reasons because of his alliance with the Duke of York. In fact, during winter 1684-1685, he was forced to intensify his efforts to convince the Steering Committee to entrust him with the consolidation and development of the Nelson River post.[17] Penning the sixth travel narrative represented one of these efforts; it provides very specific information about the project and about Radisson's state of mind that particular winter.

Obviously, Radisson continued to enjoy critical support within the Company, with Hayes as Director and Yonge on the Steering Committee. Moreover, Radisson appeared to be in top form, sure of himself, lucid and responsible. He did not hesitate to denounce the incompetence of acting Governor Abraham, who was demoted, while emphasizing the need to surround any skillful leader with men of talent and valor (Raw: 152). Radisson also tried to sell his "business" capabilities to the Steering Committee, to make them realize that he has a keen sense of responsibility and that he knows how to remain his own master. Finally, he offered them unequaled guarantees of success in dealing with the Amerindians, promised to respect the Company's hierarchic order and their directives, stressing that he had the ability to impose his authority on tough men at work in a far-off location. Nonetheless, the negotiations proved long and difficult between the Company, Radisson and the other Frenchmen back from the Bay, who, without exception, hoped to obtain the right to trade for their own profit. Radisson was the first to give in on this issue, after being assured that Bridgar would not serve as Governor at Nelson (Rich, 1958: 180). The election of a new Governor of the Company, namely, Churchill, Duke of Marlborough, a man favorable to Radisson (HBRS-11: 138), and the imminent departure

---

17. "I resolved [...] to return to England, where my presence was absolutely necessary to advise the gentlemen of the Company, how we must act to fully profit from the solid establishment I had just accomplished, and as to the things that it was indispensable to have in that country to facilitate trading with the savages, and to prevent them from trading with [...] the French of Canada" (Raw: 149).

towards Hudson's Bay prompted a settlement. Four Frenchmen, including Jean-Baptiste Des Groseilliers, committed themselves to serving the Company for four years; as for Radisson, he was engaged as Superintendant and Director of Trade at Nelson for two years. To make sure that the French agents conducted themselves in an acceptable way and, more importantly, to restrain their "natural" penchant for engaging in private trading, Radisson and his four companions were obliged to leave a deposit of some £5000 – a quite substantial amount – at London (Rich, 1958, 178-179).

However, Radisson had obtained exactly what he wanted: the power to direct both diplomatic and commercial relations with the Amerindians at the Nelson post. Radisson's final proposals were submitted to the Steering Committee, in writing, then accepted, and finally, ratified by the new Governor, Lord Churchill (Nute, 1935: 47). The orders drafted by the Committee reminded Radisson that they were placing great hope in him while granting him the considerable favor of placing him "in an eminent position – we therefore expect you to bring us extraordinary success and to make use of the four Frenchmen [...] in such a way that we find every advantage in having hired them, which, in turn, will prompt us to reward you in proportion" (HBRS-11: 147). During that same year, Radisson had no choice other than to act in compliance with the other Company officers at Nelson River, or at the very least to advise them as to his intentions. How did Radisson and the other Frenchmen conduct themselves with the English present at Nelson? The question cannot be answered. But it is certain that Radisson, Jean-Baptiste Des Groseilliers and Elie Grimard[18] were active among the Amerindians, convincing many of their number to come trade at Nelson.

While Jean-Baptiste Des Groseilliers was journeying inland with a group of Amerindians, Radisson was taking great pains to satisfy his clients by having corn flour and birch bark fetched to the Nelson post, and by insisting that he be supplied only goods of the finest quality (HBRS-11: 180 and 195):

> Our muskets are all of English make, replied the Committee to Radisson's letters, they are the finest and the most costly [...] and our tobacco [...] the very good sort of tobacco from Brazil that they (the Amerindians) covet so. We have also sent you [...] everything that you requested and we have taken care

---

18. The other two Frenchmen hired by the Company were captured when their vessel was seized by a French competitor with the Compagnie du Nord (Company of the North). Ultimately, these two Frenchmen returned to Canada.

to furnish you in every way. Our gunpowder is also the very best, as are our cartridges, buckets and all sorts of commodities which, we hope, will please you (letter of the Committee to Radisson, May 20, 1686, HBRS-11: 198).

Ever constant in his great vigilance, Radisson also proposed a number of improvements to better defend the fort: "to comply with your counsel, we have sent out two large cannons [...] and enough cannonballs [...] to better secure the fort" (HBRS-11: 198). It transpired that Radisson carried off highly successful trading ventures as of 1685 (Rich, 1958: 185), thanks to the precautions he had taken the previous year and, it seems clear, thanks in no small way to the opportunism and skill of the English who had remained at Nelson. The Company was more than satisfied and, in their orders of 1686, accorded even greater power to Radisson, who, this time, no longer had to depend on anyone in matters of trade or relations with the Amerindians.[19]

This promotion is all the more significant in that James Hayes had relinquished his position of Director to one Edward Dering, a man who, ostensibly, also appreciated Radissons efforts (Rich, 1958: 185). Nonetheless, at Nelson, as of 1685, the new Governor, Thomas Phipps, became envious of the powers Radisson had secured; and so, he wrote to the Steering Committee to complain, demanding that his stipend be doubled to bring him £200 per annum, just like Radisson and the other Governors – or so he believed. The Committee denied that such a sizeable stipend was ever accorded to anyone, all the while trying to mollify the ill will Phipps harbored against Radisson (HBRS-11: 192-193). But, by 1686, Radisson having obtained virtually every power, Thomas Phipps and his assistant George Geyer began to wage war on him.

By concentrating power in Radisson's bands, the Company again expected him to repay the confidence they were according him by making exceptional profits for them. Since the price of furs had dropped throughout

---

19. "For the trading parte at Port Nellson, and all circumstances which may conduce to the Improvemt. or Conduct of it, *We doe expressly order & Command that it be left supremly and chiefly to Mr. Radison,* whose skill that way & knowledge of the Indians, we have a particuler assurance, as well as an intire confidence in his Integrity & faithfullness. [...] In all the Designes & methods which he shall project or lay for the carrying on of our Trade *no man whatsoever shall oppose or controule him,* so long as consistes with the apparent safety & preservation of our Fort & Factorey (letter of the Steering Committee to the Governor of Port Nelson, Thomas Phipps, May 20, 1686), (HBRS-11: 194).

Europe, the Company was asking him to increase his exchange rates without losing the confidence of the Amerindians (HBRS-11: 197). They were also asking him to lure the distant nations and those who possessed the very best furs. Of course, the Company expected Radisson to send them "a bumper cargo;" they also reminded him that the Committee "would have no one else to blame but yourself should we fail to boast a splendid trade," adding that Radisson would be well rewarded if he succeeded.[20] Lastly, the Committee reassured him as to his position in the Company: "We believe it useful to remind you that your particular interest is certain and stable here, at London" (HBRS-11: 200).

Final return

In summer 1687, the Steering Committee sent orders to Governor Phipps to the effect that Radisson was to have use of the main cabin and be treated "with respect and courtesy over the entire (return) voyage to London" (HBRS-11: 235). Unfortunately, Radisson was unable to enjoy this special treatment because the struggle between the French clan and that of Phipps-Geyer had prompted the Governor to once again make him a prisoner, during the time of the crossing. Then at London, Phipps lodged a serious complaint against Radisson with the Steering Committee (Nute, 1935: 44); it transpired that Radisson would have great difficulty defending himself since another Thomas Phipps, a cousin to the first, had become a member of the Committee, the year before, and was actively supporting his cousin's malevolent efforts (Nute, 1935: 44); (HBERS-11: 382 and 387). The Directors decided that same year to keep Radisson in England, in part, no doubt, owing to Phipps' complaints, but also because the French of Canada had just seized three of the James Bay posts; hence, Radisson's "Frenchness" was more than ever a problem. Nonetheless, Radisson continued to benefit from solid support within the Company; thanks to which he enjoyed an allowance of £50 per annum (a gratuity) which was added to the pension of £50 that the Company was already paying him, "until such time as he obtain employment by favor of His Majesty or by some other means" (Nute, 1935: 48); (Rich, 1958: 283).

---

20. "We shall alwaies enlarge our selves towards you in such waies of acknowlidgment as shall be fitting & Due to your prudence & Industrey" (HBRS-11: 199).

7. Radisson's Expeditions to Hudson Bay

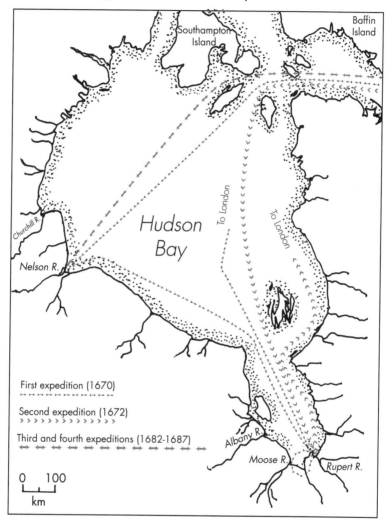

First expedition (1670)

Second expedition (1672)

Third and fourth expeditions (1682-1687)

0   100

km

Radisson made four expeditions to Hudson Bay. He began by making two brief trips, each lasting one year, in 1670 and in 1672, both times returning as soon as possible to London for the summers of 1671 and 1673. The first of these expeditions was for exploration. Radisson established a camp on the Nelson River, wintered on the Rupert River and traveled by foot during the winter to Moose River. He returned to Hudson Bay again in 1682, on the Nelson River, accompanied by Des Grosseilliers. Both stayed for only the few months necessary to trade and returned to London in 1683. Radisson went on to spend two more years on the Nelson River as trade manager, between 1685 and 1687 (based on a map published by *The Beaver* magazine, in 1936).

It may be concluded that between 1684 and 1687, Radisson accomplished important work in developing commerce at the Nelson River, by establishing stable contacts with a large number of Amerindian bands and nations, but also by knowing how to cope with so many particular conditions and exigencies created by the difficult geographical situation of Nelson in regard to climate and vegetation. Over a few short years, Radisson, Jean-Baptiste Des Groseilliers and a handful of other Frenchmen, like Médard Chouart Des Groseilliers and Élie Grimard, spared no effort in making Nelson one of the pivotal fur trading posts in America, as the two brothers-in-law had always believed possible, based on their information from the Amerindians.[21] In 1686 and in 1687, 20 000 beaver pelts were traded at Nelson, 21 000 in 1688 and 27 000 in 1689 (Rich, 1958: 232), reaching a high point in 1692, when "the Company was able to manage quite nicely with no more than the furs from Nelson; the Committee was duly advised that since the year when Radisson had taken over the Nelson post on the Company's behalf, in 1684, such post had been successful in trading to the tune of approximately £100 000 in furs" (Rich, 1958: 293). It was not therefore because Radisson was a bad employee that the Company no longer retained his services after 1687, but more owing to the fact that since England was again in the throes of great political turmoil and Radisson's political beliefs were in step with the social status he was demanding – that of a gentleman – his opponents had all the ammunition they needed to thwart his ambitions.[22]

---

21. The Governor, one Denonville, was convinced that the best way to harm the English and Radisson was to repatriate all the Canadians who were working for them "being important to take away from Radisson all those in the Colony whom he may have debauched or supported to keep under his control, for without their presence (if he were) with the English alone, he would have difficulty in successfully accomplishing what he had determined to do [at Nelson]" (Denonville to the Minister, BNQ, C-11A, vol.7, f.28v).

22. "Indeed, the culture that specified who was and who was not a gentleman laid great emphasis on how individuals were placed *vis-à-vis* wealth, work, and the production of goods and services. Recognition, authority, and the political rights of spokesmanship flowed locally from the control of land and the disposition of labor on that land," "it was recognized that gentlemen were [...] being made by informal processes which were [... not always] adequately justified by principles of legitimacy [...] social mobility made the distinction between gentlemen, on the one hand, and yeomen and mercantile citizens, on the other, both much contested and much insisted upon" (Shapin, 1994: 48 and 46).

The bittersweet "Glorious Revolution"

The death of Charles II came much too early for many Englishmen; and he was succeeded by the Duke of York in February 1685. Lord Churchill, the new Governor of the Hudson's Bay Company, was one of the first to openly support the legitimate succession of York, who became James II. The new King surprised no one when he espoused absolutism and promoted Catholicism; but in less than two years, James II, a mediocre politician, had alienated virtually all his allies, including Churchill, who was now in favor of his out-and-out expulsion from England. Since a majority of Englishmen had devoted their efforts over the first fifty years of the century to combatting absolutism, through considerable sociopolitical turmoil and many sacrifices, very soon there emerged from the British population and the elites a widespread desire, to be followed by a specific project for removing James II from the throne of England and replacing him by a royal couple comprising Mary Stuart, a daughter of James II, and her spouse, William III of Orange, who was the Stathouder[23] of Holland and a sworn enemy of Louis XIV.

The will of a vast majority of Englishmen, of all walks of life, to refuse to cede under absolutist pressures of any sort allowed for rallying a critical coalition so that the change of government could, in some way, be decided by plebiscite, with James II and his partisans having no choice other than to beat a retreat before William III of Orange, who landed on British soil with a large army, in autumn 1688. William III of Orange enjoyed enough popular support to take power at London, without a hitch, a few weeks later. Three fundamental elements rallied a majority of Englishmen behind this new revolution, widely called "glorious," or even the "Revolution of the Roses," since it transpired without bloodshed.

Since the regicide of Charles I, the English had come to realize that on balance, they appreciated the monarchy and that resorting to regicide was a somewhat radical way of controlling the power of kings. They wanted to entrust the task of governing to Parliament, once the existence, the powers and the influence of that body were guaranteed; they were even prepared to accept the tradition of hereditary succession proper to the Monarchy, as long as such was reserved for Protestants only. The "revolutionary" solution of 1687-1688 respected to some extent these rules of succession since efforts

---

23. The Chief Executive of the United Provinces (today's Holland, roughly speaking).

were expended to put Mary Stuart on the throne, as she was a daughter of James II, and a confirmed Protestant. But the guiding strategy behind this maneuver, which served to strengthen the will of the British majority, was to empower William of Orange, a man as fiercely opposed to the absolutisms of Rome and Paris as were his British subjects. The entire political arrangement was novel, subtle, almost legal, and ardently desired by Englishmen of all stripes, including those involved in trade and finance.

The City had played a major role in financing and organizing the grand movement of protest known as the Exclusion Crisis – which had ended in a victory for York and Charles II. But the deep-rooted Whig movement, the first political bloc in modern parliamentary history had a "program." The Whigs wanted to open the stock market to a wider public, thereby enabling more investors to participate in the now considerable maritime trade or in other projects requiring substantial amounts of start-up capital. Since the Whigs had devoted much energy to procuring widespread popular support, they spoke as well of social justice and equity – but not however of equality; they accorded a particular insistence to the rights of ownership, a key element in the eyes of businessmen who were anxious to avoid at all cost the random expropriations and transfers that had accompanied the Revolution of the 1640s. The influential Whigs therefore demanded that the rights and powers of Parliament be solemnly guaranteed by William III of Orange and his spouse, before their accession to the throne of England.

To better establish by law this new "contestable" social order – or so thought James II and his partisans, who again attempted to seize power in 1689-1690, on landing in Catholic Ireland – the English hastened to put in writing the new rules governing power-sharing, which now constituted the primary law of the land. The great colonialists like Shaftesbury were past masters in the art of drafting the basic rules for assuring order and justice in the new colonies. Moreover, the expertise developed by the English in the colonial sector even allowed them to go one step further, albeit in England, by drafting a document complementary to the Constitution, to wit, the first *Bill of Rights*, which specified that a certain number of individual and collective rights were to be viewed as sacred, in the "new" English society.

The fact that this revolution transpired without a clash and almost without violence indicates that the root principles of the English collectivity had never budged in any real way. A reaction to the absolutist penchants of James II, the Revolution of the Roses appears to have been more the end result of the principal demands made over recent decades than a sudden shift in social forces. In all likelihood, the audacity and novelty of the solution adopted by the English cast a "revolutionary" light on the events of 1688, since at that point these would inaugurate an entirely new form of social contract. And yet, the hierarchical structure of English society remained intact. All powers, all privileges, were still reserved for an elite whose members believed that they alone merited it. It is clear that England was still far from being democratic; but, in contrast to France, she was inclining towards a more transparent form of government, believing, as she did, in the need to entrust management of the country to a larger, more diversified, less aristocratic, but wealthier elite; it was less refined, but more enterprising than the French peers, yet was subject to the same stringent code of ethics, education and conduct of the gentleman.

In concrete terms, these political changes had a determining impact on Radisson's career as he had been overeager to support the Duke of York. A new wind was blowing over England and on the Company; it would also blow away Radisson's career.

Radisson's career comes to an end

James Hayes had to relinquish his position as Deputy Governor in 1686, to be replaced by Edward Dering; but his star continued to wane in the Company because he was suspected of having abused his powers over a period of several years. It was thus in a recriminatory climate that he sold his remaining shares and left the Company definitively, in January 1688 (Rich, 1958: 229). With Hayes gone, the only shareholder left who had knowledge of the fundamental role played by the two Frenchmen was Squire Yonge. Moreover, the departure of Hayes, then the abrupt shift of the Governor, Churchill, in favor of an exclusively Protestant succession,[24] coupled with the ever-waxing influence of many of the City's leading businessmen and financiers within the Company, all led to the Steering Committee's radical change of political heart when they embraced the Whigs and deserted the Tories, the latter party being a Royalist stronghold (Rich, 1958: 256).

---

24. "The political situation in England was coming to a boil with Churchill deeply involved in the maturing plot to oust James from the throne" (Rich, 1958: 232-233).

In summer 1688, Radisson again tried to prove his fidelity to the Company, or, at least, to foil his enemies, by denouncing George Geyer, the recently appointed Governor at Nelson, as one who engaged in private trade (Rich, 1958: 259). But his accusation fell flat and Missenden, the warehousekeeper whom Radisson had convinced to come to London, to testify against Geyer, was dismissed for having left his post without a valid reason. The Company reappointed Geyer for three years, even though they were aware of his private trading activities, simply because he did his work well; then too, the Company had to contend with many other problems in that period of revolutionary turmoil. In any case, the Steering Committee had no intentions of hiring a Frenchman, even a naturalized Britisher like Radisson. In August 1688, the Committee voted to authorize a new dividend of 50% per share; then, they notified their most prestigious shareholder, King James II, of the happy news, making sure of his appreciation that this was proof of their fidelity and of their attachment to his cause. However, the Company delayed sending him the money; so ultimately, this sum served as an initial mark of allegiance to William III of Orange, in October 1688. It is important to attend the haste with which the Committee sided with William of Orange, well before he was proclaimed King of England (Rich, 1958: 251). Since Churchill, Governor of the Company, participated in the preparations for and in the actual military campaigns that would soon launch England against France (Rich, 1958: 256), the chances of Radisson, who was a Royalist and French, of again being retained by the Company seemed virtually nil after 1688.

It might even be suggested that Radisson was fortunate, in December 1687, to obtain a supplement to his pension of £50, thanks to the intervention of Churchill, Duke of Malborough, who proposed such measure to the Steering Committee. For, despite his change of allegiance in regard to James II, it seems, on the one hand, that Marlborough continued to support Radisson over many years, even though, on the other, he was both favorable and useful to the Company's Whig Steering Committee. Marlborough seems to have backed Radisson in recognition of the services he had rendered to England, in full compliance with that which the Duke of York would have asked him to do, upon relinquishing to him the position of Governor of the Company, when he acceded to the throne. Although Marlborough was unable to have the Company employ Radisson, he was certainly in a position to ensure that he would receive a pension equivalent to the last stipend he had earned in their service (£100 per annum). Then, in the mid-1990s,

Marlborough supported the fight that Radisson undertook against the Company which was no longer paying him the annual supplement of £50, nor the dividends, nor even the profits from the shares he still held.[25]

The radical social and political transformations in England continued to influence the Company (Rich, 1958: 267-268). In 1690, a personal enemy of Deputy Governor Dering, a certain Chambers, who was also on the Steering Committee, realized during an auction sale that a given transaction had been concluded beforehand and that the auction itself was only a front, the Company having rejected the best offer which was his. And yet, Parliament had specifically prohibited the Company from engaging in "private" sales between privileged partners, ever with the intent to offer more business opportunities to a larger number of investors and to let the "laws of the market" prevail (Rich, 1958: 275). At the next meeting of the Steering Committee, the defiant Chambers produced a written accusation against Dering and against all the other members of the Committee, who, at that point, joined forces against the assailant, almost coming to blows. Dering and his associates managed to suppress the affair, expelling Chambers from the Steering Committee. After all this discord, the shareholders believed it best to reaffirm their confidence in the new Deputy Governor, and did so at a general assembly held June 8, 1690: "no further proof is needed as concerns the prudence and good management of the Deputy Governor [Dering] than the huge profit reaped by the Company since he has been at the helm, especially now with shares at so high a rate as '400li per Cent'." According to a periodical of the day, the Hudson's Bay Company was, for that era, one of the few highly successful associations in the realm (quoted in Rich, 1958: 270-271).

One month later, the Steering Committee decided to triple the value of Company shares, without recourse to new money. This spectacular jump represented for each shareholder a premium of 300% on his assets, indeed, more than enough for anyone to indicate satisfaction with the sitting Deputy (Rich, 1958: 272). Then, the Committee's stance hardened against Chambers; they decided to delete the "scandalous" accusations recorded in the

---

25. The fourth rule of courtiers seems to apply here. Certain persons did exist in England (the Duke of York, Hayes, Yonge…) who firmly believed that Radisson, thanks to his talents and his efforts, had increased, in a tangible way, the power and wealth of the British Empire; these few individuals were deeply grateful to him and would continue to support him for many years.

minutes and to deprive him of the remunerations usually granted to Committee members. Next, to better combat their enemies within the Company
itself, "the Committee covered themselves by seizing the right to fine, sus-
pend from the Committee, or prevent the sale of stock of an offending
member" (Rich, 1958: 275). These wider powers instantly affected Radisson,
who found himself the victim of a powerful cliquish mentality and a spirit
of vengefulness that was taking hold of the Committee, slowly but surely.
At a later time, the Company declared in Court that they had decided to
reduce Radisson's pension to £50 per annum, because of the financial difficulties they were undergoing (published in Nute, 1935: 48). Yet, quite to the
contrary, we have just seen that the shareholders deemed their affairs to be
in excellent shape at that juncture, despite the revolutionary changes and adjustments. Hence, the immediate issue involved a sort of harassment directed
specifically against certain enemies of the Steering Committee and against
Radisson, whom the members wanted to exclude as far as possible, or even
to remove, definitively, from the Company.[26]

Interestingly enough, it was this same tyranny rooted in the gamble, in
favoritism and even in collusion that the highminded Whigs, who had just
increased their own power, had specifically denounced in their opponents,
those incurably Royalist and absolutist Catholics. Pushing their segregation
even further, the Committee also sought to exclude Radisson's shares from
the recent increase of 300%, this time, by scrupulously respecting the minutes as recorded and which indicated that he had been offered shares worth
a total of £200, finis (Rich, 1958: 284). After making a few fruitless efforts
to right the situation, Radisson, a man convinced that his case was legitimate,
and one supported by influential persons, set out on a final Hudsonian adventure by demanding in Court that his individual rights be respected by
the powerful Hudson's Bay Company, whose members had decided unilaterally to modify the written agreement all the parties had accepted.

---

26. Harassing Radisson was not a gratuitous gesture, politically speaking, for the taxes
on the major colonial imports, like furs, represented for the King one of his most important
revenues that was independent from Parliament. James II, in particular, counted on the expansion of colonial commerce to hold out against his opponents. To weaken Radisson and
exclude him from the Hudson's Bay Company was one sure way to weaken James II, not by
sapping the fur trade, but rather by removing it, as much as possible, from Royalist control,
as well as by diverting the profits towards the interests of Republican Whigs, far from the
Crown, which many were seeking to fell (Steele, 1980: 16).

The written summary of the plea presented by Radisson to the Court and the Company's rebuttal provide a means to carefully assess of the stakes and strategies of each of the parties (published in Nute, 1935: 41-49).

Radisson in Court against the Hudson's Bay Company

Radisson based his case on two arguments that he believed were very strong. To start, he related the history of the services he had rendered to the Company since its very beginning, insisting on the "debt of honour" which the Company owed him: *"the Company well knowes that if it had not been for your Orator [Radisson] and his Conduct and management there never had been any Hudsons bay Company"*[27] (in Nute, 1935: 44). Radisson then recalled the promises of reward that were made to him: *"the Company well knowes that your Orator [Radisson] would not have undertaken the said Voyage* (1684) had it not been for the promises of great Rewards made to him by them in case of his Successe" (Nute, 1935: 44). Radisson also found the Company "more dishonourable… unjust and ungrateful" (in Nute, 1935: 44) and reproached them for having failed to respect the code of honor that must prevail among *gentlemen* as concerns respect for the word given.[28] But there was even more at stake.

Radisson insisted on one capital issue: everything that he claimed in Court was duly voted on and accepted by the Company's Steering Committee, then recorded in the minutes to which he was refused access, so that Radisson "found himself without legal recourse." However, he intimated that if the Court were to oblige the Company to open their books, the Court would note his "just and reasonable demands" (in Nute, 1935: 45). In this way, Radisson invoked the legality of a duly authorized business decision, one officialized in writing, as opposed to the new discretionary powers that the Steering Committee purported to hold, meaning that *"by one of their Orders they can repeal or make void [a decision] when they please which is very unconscionable in them* (Nute, 1935: 44). In the new "revolutionary" England

---

27. Quite true, if the vital contribution of Médard Chouart Des Groseilliers is also included.

28. "A gentleman's word was his bond. No other bond but that which the gentleman freely imposed upon himself was held to be necessary to guarantee that what he said was the case or to secure his obligation to do what he promised. To require any further surety was to express doubt that he was indeed a gentleman" (Shapin, 1994: 65).

where the written word of law, the Constitution and the *Bill of Rights* would assume an ever-burgeoning importance; in a country where development continued to increase thanks to the participation of a growing number of investors in huge and costly enterprises, it was becoming increasingly intolerable to presume that shares in a Company held by a specific individual could be frozen or voided simply because the direction of that company did not appreciate that shareholder's political bent. Even worse, it was shocking to suppose that an individual depositing funds with the new Bank of England, for example, might see his money "disappear" solely because the Bank's directorate did not like Royalists, or Scots, or even Captains of the Royal Navy.[29] The question raised by Radisson was thus crucial for English society of the day: could a contract, or a business decision between partners, or between employers and employees – once concluded, applied and conserved in writing – remain valid permanently, or could such be unilaterally modified by one or other party, according to the mood or the interests of the moment? In consideration of these many issues, Radisson concluded that the Company "not only for reasons of honour, but also under the law" was obliged to restore to him the supplementary amount of £50 they had granted to him in 1687. To close, he also demanded that he be treated in a manner similar to the other shareholders with respect to the increase of 300% on his shares, and that he receive his just allotment for the furs he had brought back in 1684, of which he had yet to receive even a single penny.

The Company had resolved to pay the smallest possible sum to this man Radisson, whose role as a pioneer they perhaps failed to understand; but they did know that he was French and a Royalist, as well as being a creature of James Hayes, whom all were content to see gone. Nonetheless, even if it was fair play to discredit Radisson in Court, the Company showed just how mean-spirited they could be by calling into question every effort of Radisson's in founding and developing the Company; they even maintained that they had never paid him a stipend of £100 per annum (untrue) and that he had done nothing but create problems at Nelson, between 1684 and 1687 (also untrue). As concerns the gentleman's code of conduct, the Company's defense was dishonest, albeit legal, as the associates did agree to open their books and read aloud in Court the pertinent minutes as recorded. In the

---

29. The Bank of England opened for business in July 1694 and its directors were obliged to swear, before taking up their assignment, that they would be "indifferent and equall to all manner of persons" (Giuseppi, 1966: 12 and 15).

business world, seen as the ethically gray area of the gentleman's ideal, the English appeared to have developed great tolerance for opportunism, in its many guises, along with a taste for strategic abilities; hence, it was not really essential for the prosperous and honorable Hudson's Bay Company to treat Radisson in any particularly "honest" way, if it could be sufficiently shrewd and eloquent to seize control of the situation and win the contest.

The clumsy defense presented by the Company in Court clearly indicated that the associates had failed to respect the decisions taken by their Steering Committee and that they were incapable of explaining in any convincing fashion why they had acted thus. In fact the defense presented an outlandish denial of Radisson's role and abilities, in what appears to be a concerted will to discredit him: for example, the defense stated that the two brothers-in-law had already received more than enough money at that juncture, that Radisson's pension was paid to him as an act of charity, because Marlborough had requested same and not because he deserved it[30] and that, in any cause, there was no question of engaging such a good-for-nothing – "these Defendts (the Company) thinke that the Complt (Radisson is (neither) fitt (n)or capable (n)or in any wayes qualifyed for their Service or employment" (Nute, 1935: 48). Finally, the defense indicated vexation that Radisson would dare contest in Court the decisions taken by the Company, whose associates denied he had any right to even a single hair from the beavers of 1684.[31]

As the hostility was too visible and the stakes too important, Radisson won his case in respect of the annual pension and the shares, namely, the two questions that counted most for the English; however, the Court rendered a decision favorable to the Company in regard to the furs of 1684; and Radisson was never able to recuperate anything at all of the manna he had

---

30. "Being meerly bestowed on the Complt (Radisson) for the present out of charity and at the request and desire of the said Earle of Malbrough and not out of any meritt" (Nute, 1935: 48).

31. "The said Company [...] therefore thinke the Complt (Radisson) to be a very ungrateful and disingenious person to bring this troublous and vexatious Suite against them without any Just ground or cause for the same And these Defendts [the Company] further say as before in this their Answer that they never received any Beavers Skins or any other goods whatsoever of or belonging to the Complt or wherein he had any interest right or clayme whatsoever [...] and these Defendts say that they know not of any promises of any reward that were at any time made to the Complt by the said Company or any of their members" (in Nute, 1935: 49).

stolen from the French. The Company never again tried to confront
Radisson, henceforth paying him his annual pension until the day he died.
Nor did they ever again employ him. For his part, Radisson remained faithful to the Company despite the lengthy controversy, then advanced his point
of view in an 1697 affidavit, in preparation for a new round of negotiations
between France and England on the subject of Hudson's Bay.[32]

In the absence of any new documents about Radisson's professional or
familial activities, it is very difficult to gain even an approximation of the
life he led in England at the end of his days. Nor is there any precise information about the marriages of his children, which would reveal how fully
he had been accepted in English society, since Radisson states in his will that
he had sought to promote the advancement of "my former Wifes Children
being by me according to my ability advanced and preferred to severall
Trades" (published in Nute, 1943: 357). The few indications that are available reveal that Radisson, at least to some extent, renewed his relations,
among others, with one whom he qualifies as "my trusty and beloved
Friend" in his will, to wit, James Heanes, master craftsman (Winnecooper)
of the City of London (Nute, 1943: 356). It seems that he enjoyed a relatively affluent lifestyle, enough at least to retain his rank of Squire, the lowest estate of the well-off and refined milieux within which Radisson sought
to carve out a place alongside such men as Hayes and Yonge who had inspired him.[33] It is known that he had financial difficulties; and it is on a
rather bitter note that he ended his life,[34] when a priest of London recorded
in the death register, June 21, 1710: "Pierre Radisson... a decay'd Gentleman bur[rial]." Radisson had thus acquired and managed to conserve, if
only officially, the social status he had no doubt coveted since his earliest

---

32. This affidavit reproduces the same facts that Radisson recounted in his last two
narratives, except that he adds a Parisian episode, which favors the claims of the Hudson's
Bay Company: a final boon for the enterprise to which he had devoted a large part of his life.

33. At the end of the XVIIth century, "Gregory King [...] estimated the average annual
income of hereditary knights (barons) at £880; simple knights [lowest actual rank of English
nobility] at £650; Squires at £450; and simple gentlemen at £280 (Shapin, 1994: 48). With his
guaranteed annual income of £100, Radisson must have had great difficulty indeed in making ends meet and in maintaining his rank of Squire or even that of mere gentleman.

34. As confirmed by the petition that Radisson presented to Parliament in 1698, as well
as by the remission of debt amounting to £50 consented to him by the will of William Yonge,
in 1708, and, finally, by the requests for assistance that his last wife made to the Hudson's
Bay Company, after his death.

years in England; but he had exhausted his financial resources. At the time of his death, this audacious adventurer was already consigned to history, thanks to the pen of the first historian of the Hudson's Bay Company, Oldmixon, who had recognized the crucial role of the two Frenchmen during the early years. The auspicious unearthing of Radisson's entire six travel narratives provides a fine opportunity to understand and appreciate this hardy, talented and highly adaptable individual, who lived in many cultures brought to the forefront of history by his keen sense of observation.

Portrait of Radisson

RADISSON AND DES GROSEILLIERS ENJOYED CONSIDERABLE AUTHORITY in the Great Lakes region at the end of the years 1650 and at Hudson's Bay in the years 1670-1680; but their influence in France was barely discernible and little more than modest in England, although they certainly left an indelible mark on the Hudson's Bay Company. The two adventurers played the primary role in establishing this Company because the English had no idea of the vital commercial potential of Hudson's Bay and no knowledge of how best to exploit any such potential. The English were inexperienced when it came to forging the necessary alliances with the Amerindians, from the earliest encounters, and did not know how to negotiate with them so as to command their respect and avoid disorder and sharp drops in prices. But most important for increasing the Company's clienteles, Radisson and the other Frenchmen knew how to persuade distant nations to come and trade far from their homelands. In short, those whom the members of the Steering Committee were in the habit of calling "the two Frenchmen," Pierre-Esprit Radisson and Médard Chouart Des Groseilliers, contributed more than anyone else, in England and even at Hudson's Bay, to capitalizing on the economic potential they had been the first to identify so clearly.

From their arrival in England, the objectives of the two brothers-in-law reflected their cardinal attribute: a judicious blend of audacity and prudence. They wanted first to reach James Bay, where they were certain to encounter a number of Amerindians they already knew and who were used to trading with the French. But, once they were convinced that the enterprise was both feasible and profitable, the two brothers-in-law set about establishing a trading post at the Nelson River, each in his turn, in 1670, then in 1673. They had learned from the Crees they had encountered at Lake Superior, in particular, that the Nelson River communicated with several other waterways and that a large number of nations could eventually come to trade their furs in that desolate, sparsely populated region, should a trading post be established at the mouth of it. The two Frenchmen were soon convinced that this location could become one of the most important fur trading centers in America. Starting in 1670, they relentlessly promoted this project in England and in France, until, finally, they were able to establish a trading post at the Nelson River site in 1682. It is now clear that Radisson played the dominant role in founding, developing and consolidating this post, between the years 1682 and 1687. This was the greatest achievement of this dynamic and unusually skillful man, who, on so many occasions, took control of the region, acting as much for France, as for England.

Both England and France needed men of action and adventure, hardy voyagers like Radisson and Des Groseilliers who combined the myriad talents of seafarers, traders, explorers, leaders of men and perceptive observers – all in the interest of developing the colonial empire of their dreams. In such a capacity, Radisson was indispensable, as indeed were many other men of his mettle in that era.

Radisson's multiple transformations blend in countless bursts of energy, with his temperament actually heightening each successive adaptation. Over time, his ambition, intelligence, flair and determination, all combine to weave a singular life. This amazing man's one, yet multiple life reminds me of the invisible mixture of colors to be found in sunlight. We know that the colours of the rainbow are always there in any light but they only appear under certain favorable circumstances, through rainfall or through a prism, or even through the atmosphere, which seems to filter the celestial vault's azure hue, igniting the horizon with orangy tints, especially at dusk. This invisible mixture of colors, always present in white light, is, for me, remarkably like Radisson's complex and fascinating personality.

The Amerindian chronicle

Following a childhood in France about which little is known, the young Radisson will immigrate to New France in 1651. He spent an entire year among the Amerindians native to the vicinity of Trois-Rivieres, in the company of certain members of his family and with other Frenchmen on site, whom they came to know. Throughout his youth, Radisson discovered in the Amerindian customs and culture various aspects that pleased him, that were well-suited to his artless, yet curious, temperament, to his physical strength and to his talents, both as orator and warrior. After having been captured, tortured, then integrated in an Iroquois family, he participated, towards age sixteen, in a guerilla expedition along with a small group of Iroquois. But Radisson never stopped enjoying his life among the Amerindians for whom, as he writes, he felt affection. With them and with a number of French coureurs de bois, between 1653 and 1660, he learned everything about the "savage" life, before becoming the partner of his brother-in-law Médard Chouart Des Groseilliers who showed him that he could also earn a great deal of money, while climbing the social ladder, thanks to his knowledge of the Amerindians. The expedition of 1659-1660 was a commercial success because of the experience, ambition and determination of Des Groseilliers, who had mapped out the approach and fixed the objectives. Radisson would take inspiration from this partnership to become, over time, a highly successful fur trader in his own right.

He loyally followed Des Groseilliers to New England, then to England, where he came to know exactly what it meant to *succeed* in a powerful Western country. Eminent personnages of great influence and distinction backed their projects, supporting them materially; but most important of all, these same people took a keen interest in Radisson, the man, and in all that he had learned and accomplished in America. His first four travel narratives were composed at a turning point, a time when he realized that he could take his place on the European stage; but most of all, the narratives exemplify the decisive transformation of his persona.[1] Therein, Radisson recounts the life he shared with the native peoples of America, both close to them and among them. And yet, that same period, one so important to him, and that he later recalls with great emotion, is already well in the past when he puts it in writing. Henceforth, Radisson seeks to *use* his knowledge and his experience to acquire, in Europe, the property and power that correspond to a new understanding he now has of his merits and his talents, with reference to the cultural standards prevailing in England and in France, far from the Amerindian world. When he renews contact with the natives at Hudson's Bay in 1670, after five years at London, his attitude has changed. In England, Radisson and Des Groseilliers wagered everything on the abundance of the fur trade and the considerable profits they would surely make on behalf of

---

1. "It (the autobiographical narrative) presents the "before" and "after" of individuals who have undergone transformations […]. Autobiography is about change" (Barros, 1992: 1).

their initial backers. There was therefore never any question of them exchanging their commodities at reduced prices, nor would they submit to the ploys or preferences of their Amerindian partners. The two men arrived at Hudson's Bay fully intending to establish their supremacy over one and all; they wanted to direct the trade, give the orders and, above all, make certain that their own interests and those of the shareholders of the Hudson's Bay Company were gratified. At the Nelson River post, between 1682 and 1684, it is quite clear that Radisson sought to impose his will, his plan of action and his price scale on the Amerindian traders.

Radisson's about-face in regard to the Amerindian question is remarkable, to say the least; he shifts from a sort of nonchalant foundness to deliberate exploitation. But, while he was never an unconditional ally of the Amerindians, he kept no secrets from them; and, though at times, he failed to respect the word he had given them, Radisson at least remained an honest trader, one who had their best interests at heart, since he tried to meet their needs in every possible way, particularly by keeping a watchful eye over the commodities he was furnishing them.[2]

It is probable that Radisson's view of the world, his attitudes and his values reflected traces of the Amerindian influence. But this influence is virtually imperceptible in the last two narratives; it would appear that his "savage" youth had lost much attraction for the Radisson of the years 1680-1690, a man who had been living in Europe for more than two decades. However, since certain of his qualities and attitudes, such as self-control, courage and honor of the warrior, eloquence and the ability to lead men, were revered in all the cultures he had come to know, it would appear that the cultural "barriers" were not always as difficult to surmount as might have been the case for anyone other than himself. It would thus be unreasonable to believe that Radisson had to reshape his personality from stem to stern each time he changed cultures. Fundamentally, he was able to stay the same everywhere, while showing boundless energy, enthusiasm, shrewdness and good will – a quasi-universal recipe which he would spice by adding ease in expressing himself and fine manners; finally, he needed to discover the "keys to success," to wit, the attitudes and qualities which could open the doors to the most

---

2. "We are requested by Mr Radison at Port Nelson to give order to the Bottome of the Bay, that the Barke of Burch trees be brought from thence to Port Nellson, to make Canoes with which it seemes in scarce there, and the Indians there have very much sollicited us to have it done" (HBRS-11: 180).

desirable circles in each milieu that he sought to penetrate. Radisson's personality never appears to be "fractured;" quite the opposite, it seems to have been strengthened, consolidated, even heightened, by repeated displacements from one culture to another.

Most of Radisson's cultural adaptations and his voyage through life can be explained by two fundamental characteristics: he possesses a sharp sense of observation and, at least when travelling, he forces himself to be constantly *on guard*. This state of lucid wariness, of availability to the information that can help him discern the right phrase and adopt the proper stance in all circumstances,[3] is a combination of a great many talents and abilities that help him understand the groups and the cultures which he wants to call his own, by seeking out the most useful attitudes, the most coveted qualities and the most appreciated values; and, since he was conditioned by his unique experience among the Iroquois, he accepts, from the outset, the sociocultural parameters to which he feels he must conform.[4] It is again his wariness, but this time turned inward, that allows him to hold onto his identity, his "center," when he shifts from one culture, one lifestyle, to another, always remaining perfectly aware of a process of adaptation that he seems able to direct, to some extent. Thanks to his multicultural experiences, Radisson disposed of many intellectual resources along with a considerable number of spiritual and cultural references which enabled him to remain firmly rooted in all the cultures that he came to know.[5]

---

3. "[The] distinction between action and reaction reveals a more subtle meaning. If we see reality, just as it is, actually speaking, we act; our action is an appropriate response to exactly what the situation demands, including that which is exterior to us, namely, our habitual context, but it also comprises the reality of us, or, as we see ourselves from within" (Desjardins, 1992: 211).

4. At Hudson's Bay, as well, in 1682-1683, Radisson comes to fully understand the strengths and vulnerabilities of his adversaries after only a few visits of a sociable nature, during which he gathers the information he needs to elaborate his own strategy and assess his chances of success. He also seems able to evaluate in his adversaries and his partners precisely the level of tolerance, beyond which a confrontation might arise.

5. The Iroquois and the other Amerindians sought to develop tight control over themselves and their emotions, but in their own peculiar way. The Jesuits tried to impose a very precise direction on their thoughts and their actions, based on the strict rules that governed and structured their missionary order. The English Protestants pursued similar goals but by different means; finally, the aristocratically inspired ideal of the gentleman also imposed a code of conduct and different rules; these were aimed at achieving the same final objective: to take control of oneself and to remain lucid in all circumstances.

The English chronicle

In a number of ways, the English society of Radisson's era was quite similar to the Amerindian communities he had known in America; hence, it is not unusual that he relished his time in England, a country where so many groups and sub-groups enjoyed a measure of independence as shown by, among other phenomena, the many religious confessions. Even more significant, public discourse still played a key role in regulating society in England: in Parliament, in the taverns and coffee-houses, especially in the street, where well-organized demonstrations often lent support to a cause, an argument or a specific political movement. France, at the other end of the spectrum, had virtually abolished all forms of public debate in order to sound the single drumbeat of absolute power. However, the English society known to Radisson encouraged debate, conducted in situations where each individual enjoyed a certain freedom of speech and the possibility of intervening directly in affairs that concerned him. In most instances, this meant getting help from a member of his immediate circle – any person who might be vested with a measure of special influence, having been elected in the municipal or the corporate sphere – or perhaps through the intermediary of commercial networks. Some form of power was always available to any resourceful and well-meaning Englishman. Even the business milieux were more accessible there than in France for anyone who wanted in, provided he was dressed *comme il faut* – for Pepys, a basic precaution – and that he frequented the Exchange, where, each and every day, many hundreds of big and not-so-big businessmen made contact in the persistent hope of gaining the confidence of some prosperous and dynamic partner in waiting.

In any event, Radisson's success or failure, both in England and in France, should not be related to the similarities that existed between the sociocultural climates of those two countries and the Amerindian cultures he had also known, nor even to the respect or contentment that he experienced there. In every situation, Radisson appeared to act with the same determination, the same enthusiasm, the same respect for all social and cultural criteria. Radisson was a success in England because the English needed a man of his mettle to develop energetically the colonial and financial empire of which they dreamed, a yearning that inclined them to respect those who possessed great knowledge of a *practical nature, men of experience*, able "to deliver the goods." Over and above such capacities, Radisson had a cast of mind and certain analytical abilities that tallied, at least to some extent, with the Royal Society's new criteria of excellence – an additional asset. Since Radisson was quite aware of his superiority, he strove to take every advantage of same when he returned to England, in 1684, by demanding full recognition of all the qualities that had made him an *esquire*[6] in other words, a gentleman.

It is obvious that Radisson wholly adapted to the sociocultural environment of England. There, he took three wives. He enjoyed the support, in succession, of three English monarchs. From the very beginning, he found backers for his projects in at least two separate groups of investors; and the story of his many voyages interested a number of influential personages, certain of whom remained attached to him over many years, despite the ups and downs of his career. What we know about Radisson's personality and conduct, after 1680, indicates that he had acquired a great many English virtues: he proved himself to be judicious, temperate and industrious; he attended to his affairs and to those of the Company. He owned a residence in one of the better areas of London; he insisted on the respect due his standing and was actively concerned with the progress of his children. Radisson remained in England until the end of his life as much by choice as by obligation. He had developed roots there and enjoyed a decent guaranteed (almost) income of £100 per annum, to which were probably added the dividends from his shares and perhaps from other revenues, for example, through the intermediary of his friend Haynes the winecooper. In all events, and even if he died "ruined," Radisson was able to lead a rather enjoyable life in England, from the time of his forced retirement until his death. His life in England satisfied him to the extent that he had no desire to effect any drastic change that could mean risking all, especially now that his main assets – an unbridled vivacity and limitless energy – were on the wane.

---

6. Strictly speaking, this title did not constitute the first rung of British nobility, but rather a sort of antechamber, a place of transition or of passage, where one acquired the distinction and recognition needed to achieve full integration in the British aristocracy, whose lowest official title was that of Knight and not that of Esquire, which latter title Radisson held (Stone, 1985: 88).

The French chronicle

Since there exists no documentation about Radisson's childhood, any French influence on him is detectable only after he returns to his country of origin, at midlife – aged forty years, or thereabouts – in 1675. Even if France offered him only a perfunctory welcome because he was not an aristocrat, because his practical abilities were less exclusive, less useful and, ultimately, less prized, than in England – in addition to the fact that he enjoyed no solid backing at Court and that an element of doubt was entertained in high places as to his religious allegiance – Radisson was quite impressed by the France he came to know. The few other details about the French period and the obvious traces of that short sojourn on the fifth and sixth travel narratives indicate that he fully adhered to certain powerful elements of French culture, such as the primacy of reason and the hierarchical order, elegant manners and the demand for clear and well-expressed thought. The splendor and influence of the French Court at that time seems to have fired Radisson's nationalistic pride, since he penned his sixth travel narrative in the French language, even though he was located at London; moreover, he stubbornly insisted that the "cultural gains" he had achieved in France be recognized on his return to England. Radisson did not hesitate to support the Duke of York when he became King James II, not only out of opportunism – it would have been much more astute to curb his enthusiasm, as York had always been a controversial figure since his arrival in England – but also owing to royalist and absolutist convictions, no doubt consolidated by his lengthy stay in France.

An intriguing personality

On a number of occasions over his lifetime, Radisson had to adopt alien values and alien cultural mores. He did so as far as his capabilities allowed and as a function of what he understood about the individuals and the milieux with whom he aspired to consort. Yet, in many ways, Radisson's personality remained constant. He had a gift for discourse and negotiation; he always strove to convince the other by communication and skill rather than by force or denial. Radisson was a pacifist who, to quote the proverb, readied for war to obtain peace; indeed, there are many clear indications of this propensity in each of Radisson's narratives. He was less individualistic and unpredictable than many thought him because of their tendency to confuse his steadfast fidelity towards Des Groseilliers with the remarkable autonomy of the latter individual who would cut, successively, all the social ties he had developed. To all appearances, Des Groseilliers was faithful only to himself and to his young brother-in-law, Radisson, whereas Radisson, for his part, was prepared to risk his career, indeed his life, in support of the persons to whom he was attached, those whom he admired and whom he had resolved to follow, albeit, at times, through self-interest. He dared to confront a number of powerful Englishmen to defend his political opinions and his perception of the interests of the Hudson's Bay Company, for it is true that Radisson had a particular concern for the development and the enduring prosperity of a Company he had helped found and from which he expected an equitable reward for his "precious" services.

A too rational, too linear, view of Radisson's voyage through life, or of his personality, would fail to allow for the shiftings of course and the many detours that fate would impose on him, the resurgences, the predicaments and the hardships, but also the moments of triumph, which were all part and parcel of his persona and his destiny. An overly rational approach would also overlook the shifting weight of the myriad influences that worked on him in unison, or that Radisson sometimes selected individually, in a quite deliberate way, such as upon his return to Hudson's Bay in 1682, after seven years of absence, at which juncture he had no difficulty in renewing friendly relations with the Amerindians, then proceeding to put the Nelson River post on solid footing. Radisson's personality, under a transparent veil of stability, conceals like white light, very diverse resources which will appear, then attract attention with as much display as the circumstances and requirements of the moment may require. Radisson is always free to draw from his vast experience without changing his persona, therein to unearth the inner references and the outer codes, as well as the right attitude and the finest manners in order to understand well and act accordingly in so many contrasting cultural environments.[7]

---

7. Francisco Varela has qualified his research on the human brain in an actual situation that he terms "a study of the way in which the perceiving subject manages to direct his actions in his immediate situation" (Varela, 1993: 235). An American researcher proposes a similar mode for pinpointing the identity which I believe defines Radisson's identity dynamic: "the concrete interactions and social relationships within which identities are constantly renegociated, whereby individuals present one identity as more salient than another, and which allows individuals to achieve some personal sense of continuity and balance among their various sorts of identities" (White, 1992, summarized in Calhoun, 1995: 26).

Radisson's identity was therefore alterable, variable, yet rooted in his ability to perceive with great lucidity the environment to which he had to adapt; hence, he was also able to look upon himself in the act of such adaptation and upon how he mastered his own psyche for the purpose of influencing the social environment that was influencing him.[8] Without pretending to act as a psychologist, I do see Radisson as an individual who is aware that he is in a state of permanent flux, depending upon the milieu and the prevailing circumstances; Radisson's own capabilities limit all transformations and his experience channels them; but primarily, Radisson accepts these transformations seeing them as necessary and beneficial. In the end, his identity hinges less on the permanence of certain character traits than on the dominance of this unusual ability to adapt to so many situations with the greatest ease and to transform himself accordingly, like the proverbial chameleon.

In conclusion, am I able to answer one simple question: did I discover the real Radisson? How can I be sure, since I passed over a number of pertinent documents and excluded many valid points of view, simply because time and space were lacking, or because a specific order and interpretation had to be selected, or because, ultimately, I had to write *a story*, to the exclusion of many others that remain to be told.

Since I was particularly concerned with the evolution of Radisson, the human being, I above all sought to understand him in a perspective that seemed to be his own. Perhaps an historian more attentive to the foreign policy of Louis XIV might not reach the same conclusions as I did as to Radisson's intervention at the Nelson River, even after consulting to the same documents, for it cannot be denied that Radisson's action at that point was uninformed and disquieting in the eyes of Louis XIV. I can also imagine that it would be easy to compile any number of negative comments taken from the correspondence of Radisson's enemies in England, over the years 1686-1688 and 1694-1697, but, lacking time and material resources, I was unable

---

8. "The principal activity of the brain is to produce changes in itself" (Minsky, quoted in Varela, 1993: 199). "The brain utilizes processes which modify themselves; this, in turn, means that these processes cannot be separated from the products they engender. For example, the brain produces memories, which alter our ways of thinking later on" (Minsky, quoted in Varela, 1993: 199). These references to research on the brain may be explained by the fact that I borrowed several methodological tools from this field. The ensuing postface offers more detailed explanations.

to consult these documents which might well shed light on other aspects of Radisson's personality; perhaps too, these would unearth less edifying information about this coureur de bois, who so wanted to become a gentleman, as well as about the Englishmen who adamantly refused to allow this erstwhile French "savage" to enter the "hallowed halls" of their nation's elite.

In the end, each reader will construct his own idea of the Radisson I have tried here to resurrect, so that the *real* Radisson will continue to remain beyond reach. By all accounts, the "historical truth" about this astonishing coureur de bois, about the events that marked his life, his chequered era and the many cultures that he came to know, will gradually emerge from a body of disparate exchanges between documentalists, historians, lovers of history and the wider reading public. Finally, I hope that I have been able to spark an active and enduring interest in Radisson, by contributing to his living memory in a stimulating, well-documented way – one more endeavor, my own, to utilize the knowledge extant to better appreciate the past.

Networks of Meaning and Living Communication

Concepts and consequences

The relational approach that I have adopted in producing this biography, in other words, my systematic analysis of the interactions that create ties and privileged networks, refers to that mass of scattered information which makes up any individual's actual life, and which provides an opportunity to refine a reflection on human phenomena, thanks to specific examples, those provided by a single individual. The relational analysis opens the door to a more substantive, more diversified perception of human reality, and to greater plausibility when analyzing the multiple realities of cultures and personae. In fact, this approach invites the interested person to conceive of, then explore, new realms of thought, by postulating the polysemy common to every historical event for the many actors and observers; yet it also ensures that he never loses his sense of direction in the historical diversities as he attempts to discover the stronger, more stable systems of meaning that link people and communities, companies and nations, cultures and eras.

My project relies on two key concepts: emergent order (Prigogine, 1979) and relational analysis (Varela, 1993)[1] which at present are being applied with success in a number of scientific disciplines, particularly those that examine

---

1. In my view, these concepts seem well adapted to the historico-biographical analysis of Radisson that I wanted to produce; they have been utilized in a large number of fields thus far: "it is clear that emergent properties have been discovered in every field" (Varela, 1933:

living phenomena. A little like Radisson, I wanted to discover an audacious yet reliable method, hoping thereby to better appreciate which more or less disorganized, interactive substratum, which mix of circumstances, means, objectives, individuals, sentiments, oppositions and alliances, perceptions and experience, techniques and mentalities, determined that the course of events would ultimately adopt a specific direction for one man, in particular, at one determinate moment. In view of the limited quantity of data that can be obtained about one person or one historical situation, I realize that any relational analysis often leads to a solid and exact delimitation of a particular zone of probability, of determining tendencies, and less often to a determination of *the specific* causal factor or the singular event which will have provoked a particular evolution; this stage appears to be somewhat fortuitous in an interactive, emergent and relational perspective, one where more importance is attached to the fluctuations and conjunctures that create or perturb resonances and synergies.

Fundaments in history

Micro-historians, such as Carlo Ginsburg, Giovani Levi and Jacques Revel have developed an approach similar to the analysis of complex systems in the natural sciences. They have been taking an active interest in the strategies deployed by social actors in their diverse environments; they have examined the "choice spaces" of individuals and have also endeavored to follow such persons into the "cracks" in a society which they describe as mutable, composed of diverse categories and sundry groups that evolve at different rhythms, according to their intrinsic values and perceptions. In brief, their approach poses questions about the dynamic of adjustments and individual interpretations in the variability and diversity of social rules.[2]

---

136). "These notions (dissipative chaos, emergence) have completely transformed ecology, climatic history and meteorology. They also enrich our view of the world. [...] I believe that we may speak, without exaggerating, of a second revolution à la Copernicus" (Prigogine, 1992: 27); "once more, the importance of emergent properties in complex systems (be these neural, genetic or cellular). [...] The most probing explications resort more and more to the self-regulating properties intrinsic to these systems" (Varela, 1993: 257).

2. The historian, Jacques Revel, believes that it is imperative "to study the social [...] as a series of changing interrelations within constantly mutating configurations," (Levi, preface of Revel, 1989: xii and xxxii). Giovani Levi wrote that he saw "a permanent and reciprocal connection between biography and context; change is precisely the incalculable sum of interrelations" (Levi, 1989: 1334).

Their viewpoint is supported by an observation available to anyone in his own environment, to wit, in the web of values and social relations; any individual nearly always has the possibility of choosing his partners or his degree of adhesion to particular values, customs or rules, or his level of commitment to whatever sub-group, even one which seeks to pursue as radical a goal as overthrowing the established order! Consequently, the individual may, to some extent, organize his own social space.[3]

Much contemporary research work highlights the adjustments that any individual makes according to his interests at a given moment, or to the events he has just experienced or that he anticipates, with more or less intuition or acumen, depending on his age, his level of conviction, his fatigue or his conceptual abilities to react and to learn.[4] The social sciences are rediscovering the plurality of the ego, a reality Montaigne had already observed four centuries ago: "The disparity that exists between us and ourselves is as great as between us and others"(quoted in Gendreau, 1995: p. 28). In any case, investigating an individual like Radisson must begin with an unequivocal recognition of the dynamic nature of the individual identity, supported by the theoretical know-how that will permit conducting such an investigation in an intelligible and rigorous fashion.

---

3. Some researchers say that individual identity cannot be restricted in any way to a heterogeneous collection of values and endlessly reconstructible modes of behavior, according to circumstances alone; and, even if they do agree on the idea of a modifiable identity, they refuse to encourage same as a mere strategic function, "a type of plural identity which allows the interested party to choose, consistent with the diverse situations confronting him, the particular identity best suited to meeting his needs at a given time" (Fuma and Poirier, 1992: 58). "It is undoubtedly a truism – but, at the same time, an indisputable fact – to state that everyman is enlightened thanks to his diversity, but on one condition: that there exists, an entity strong enough to encompass and contain these dissimilar even disparate elements" (Fuma and Poirier, 1992: 61). See also Calhoun (1994: 13-20).

4. "Recent approaches to issues of identity have stressed the incompleteness, fragmentation and contradictions, common to collective and personal existence. They have shown how complex is the relationship among projects of identity, social demands and personal possibilities" (Calhoun, 1994: 14). "The individual [...] must always be considered as a subject who makes a personal synthesis of his cultural fund with reference to his personal experiences, according to his personality and his life-project, in other words, what he wants to become" (Guilbert, 1993: 117). "The identity, or selfhood, is created at the very heart of human interraction" (Friedman and Roy, 1996: 5). See also Amselle (1990) and Gendreau (1995).

From rational analysis to relational analysis[5]

At each moment in a normal human life, a considerable number of factors acquire significance at the same time, in varying proportions and intensity, in comprehensive configurations that are always somewhat different. Because much information, energy, food, mutual assistance and commercial relations, love or amity, are in constant circulation among the elements of any social system, between the individuals, enterprises and institutions that constitute that system, a complementary common "resonance" appears at the heart of the society or the culture, and between individuals, establishing, by contact and by communication, a "comprehensive, interactive and circular causality" which springs from the *exchanges* between the various actors and institutions in a given society and *from what people do when relating to one another rather than from what they are, in and of themselves.* It would thus appear that the intensity and the complementary of the exchanges between the members of a human community are the factors that give same its cohesion and its vitality.[6]

Just recently, a well-known French historian drew researchers' attention to this type of phenomena, to the dynamic exchanges which animate and transform individual identities and the course of history: "each being is [...] provided with a set of more or less stable connections, which he activitates successively or simultaneously according to the context [...]. The identity constitutes a personal history, one related to varying capacities to interiorize or refuse inculcated standards [...], identity is thus always defined on the

---

5. "Once you seize on non-integrable systems (complex systems), you understand [...] that there exists [...] a time of relations between the subjects. An internal time, a mutual time, [...] a relational time. [...] This is also the time of history, the time of relations between human beings" (Prigogine, 1992: 31). The biochemist Ilya Prigogine is one of the principal conceivers of the theoretical context that I have used here. Winner of the Nobel Prize in Chemistry in 1977, for his innovative work on "dissipative structures," today called the phenomena of self-organization, Prigogine discovered this phenomenon of spontaneous complexification in the biochemical reactions at the root of all living phenomena.

6. "Whether we examine a cell or a city, the same observation will be made: not only are systems receptive but they live on this receptivity; they feed on the spate of matter and energy that comes to them from the outside world. [...] we can isolate crystals, but the city and the cell, if cut off from their milieu, die rapidly; they are an integral part of the world that feeds them. They represent a type of local and singular incarnation of the very matter that they never cease to transform" (Prigogine, 1979: 198).

strength of relations and multiple interractions (Gruzinski, 1999: 47-48). Using a theoretical approach similar to that of Gruzinski, but a different method, this historical biography of Radisson follows in the same direction, toward complexity.

Practical application

The following schematic presents the theoretical framework which enabled me to articulate my relational investigation of Radisson. This framework was developed by a researcher in neurophysiology and in artificial intelligence, Francisco Varela; Varela has studied the structure and functioning of the brain as the nucleus of the human being and his conscience.[7] Varela's findings were quite easily applied to my historical investigation in light of their liberal and humanist nature, and because the brain is situated exactly at the cusp between the individual and his natural and social environment.[8] I summarize here in five points the passage where Varela assesses the

---

7. Francisco Varela is Director of Research at the C.N.R.S., in Paris. He works on the human being as an entity and on the brain in actual situations: "The main point that we want to emphasize here is that the emergence of comprehensive configurations in systems formed by interacting elements is neither a particularity of a few isolated cases, nor a characteristic of the neuronic systems alone. In fact, it seems unlikely that a medley connected in a close-knit fashion would fail to present emergent properties; this is why the theories underlying these properties constitute a natural link between the different levels of description of natural and cognitive phenomena. [...] the enaction program [...] seeks to consider the temporality of wide-reaching cognition as a life story, [...] at the level of the individual (ontogenesis), of the species (evolution), or of the social structures (culture)" (Varela, 1993: 136-137 and 288-289).

8. I felt it was all the more relevant to attempt a comparison with the human brain, in order to examine the relational tie linking the individual and society, because the work had already been carried out in reverse by Marvin Minsky, a leader in the field of cognitive sciences in the United States. In his book *The Society of the Mind*, Minsky presents the human brain like a society, composed of diversie agents and agencies, all more or less autonomous, but interconnected by a number of communication channels to comprise a relatively coherent entity (Minsky, 1988). Prigogine also used that comparison, giving it an even wider meaning: basically, nature may be viewed as a gigantic brain in which all the molecules, all the particles are in constant chaotic movement [...] the brain is the very acme of complexity, of instability" (Prigogine, 1992: 33-34)."The functioning of the human personality can be fully appreciated only in terms of the active interrelations between an individual and his own specific universe. In such perspective, the brain acts as "mediator" between the substantial world and that which the individual does in that world, through his acts of thought, his acts of language, his conduct" (Pierre Karli, 1992: 92). See also Varela (1993: 155-156).

knowledge extant about the brain. The following propositions do not pretend to offer a "recipe" for the curious reader, but rather they give him an intelligible synopsis of the relational approach as applied in this study (Varela, 1993: 119, 139-140 and 143).[9]

1) *Emergent properties are essential to the functioning of the brain.* The individual is at the pinnacle of a very high level of biochemical, physiological and ecological complexity; using his brain, he must manage and integrate the quite complicated human organism in a constantly changing environment. These emergent properties are essential to the proper functioning of living organisms because they allow for stability and for the rapid adaptation of organisms, individuals and cultures (within certain limits).

2) *Each neuron presents multiple and mutable responses depending on where it is situated.* When it is transposed to the human level this characteristic serves as a reminder that the individual depends on his ambient milieu, the persons with whom he associates, and the culture that feeds him. Any individual is inspired by and reacts to those who surround him; he responds to that which he perceives to be their expectations while seeking to adopt the right image, and fill a role within a given group. The same individual behaves in different ways depending on where he is – at home, at work, on a trip, among his friends or in the midst of strangers. The human being, his attitudes, behavioral patterns and his development depend upon and are influenced by his milieu.

3) *The brain is [...] a highly cooperative system: cooperative, both locally and comprehensively, one that functions within tiny cerebral sub-systems, while depending on the connections between these sub-systems.* As a rule, every individual associates with many people and knows many milieux. He will no doubt accord priority to his family and his intimate friends, but he will also have to adjust to wider social currents which can affect him directly, such as a change of government or a war, or indirectly, such as

---

9. This approach, when applied to one highly significant example in the study of human phenomena, the brain, effectively meets one increasingly obvious requirement in social sciences, namely, the need to favor at least partially, certain non-linear modes of analysis: "Descriptions and explanations of human communication across cultural boundaries confront the scholar with the limits of a linear notion of history and invite him or her to replace it with a non–linear history" (quoted in Gruzinski, 1999: 51, footnote 55).

the acquaintance of a friend thrice removed who has just obtained an
influential position. This characteristic of the brain reflects the complex
and more or less coherent organization of a given society, made up of
myriad associations and diverse groups that affect in so many ways this
or that particular political, economic or cultural event.

4) *Since each cerebral level reveals strong reciprocal connections that are rami-
fied, the network in its entirety can operate only thanks to a vital resonant
impetus impelled by multiple comparisons of activity levels.* A brain, like
an individual, or a society, cannot live in chaos. By means of communication and contact between the various elements of the social systems
and sub-systems, by a complementary and mutual process of adjust-
ment, one or several orders eventually emerge, one or several vaster
coherences take the lead, in larger or smaller collectivities, for a certain
time. It thus appears that a people, a nation, represents an entity which
exchanges and shares enough goods, connections and information, in
a sufficiently coherent and lasting fashion, to assure the development
and maintenance of bonds that must needs unite their collectivity in a
dynamic way.

5) *Brains are not networks structured in a homogeneous way; [...] the entire
system resembles a patchwork of sub-networks assembled by a complex yet
makeshift process, much more than a system resulting from an irreducible,
clear, straightforward and precise concept.*[10] Such property brings to mind
the point of view of the micro-historians as to the splitting up of the
major social coherences which they tend to break down into "combined
partial constructions." It thus seems preferable to observe the social
phenomena as a constellation of particular cases, sufficiently in tune
with each other to constitute a stable synergetic entity, yet, one that is
not uniform and that is subject to transformations. All the levels of organization, all the micromilieux of a given society are integrated, in one
way or another, in the grand network of global interaction and inter-
dependence which puts everyone in contact, via distortions, delays and
deteriorations, accelerations and sudden appearances. It is through this
patching up, this relative *connecting* between several levels of organization and association, somewhat like a cascade between a number of

---

10. "The behavior of the system, in its entirety, resembles more a conversation in a café
than a chain of command" (Varela, 1993: 143).

intersecting social *cells*, that the individual and the collectivity touch and influence one another, forming a single vast sociocultural system, one that is complex, adaptable and diversified.

Finally, those non-homogeneous structures and those many junctions, cobbled together by the diversity of networks and the multiplicity of circumstances, call for developing an equally non-homogenous approach, one that is multidisciplinary, in order to grasp them all in a manner, both intelligent and germane (Gruzinski, 1999: 38-39); which is exactly what I wanted to do in writing this biography.

APPENDIX 1

Presence of Shareholders at the Meetings and General Assemblies of the Company (According to HBRS-5).

Name of the shareholder	1671 (out of 8 meetings)	1672 (out of 13 meetings)	1673 (out of 16 meetings)	1674 (out of 37 meetings)	Total presence (out of 74 recorded)
John Kirke	8	12	14	16	50
James Hayes	0	5	13	32	50
John Hawkins	0	1	14	32	47
Lord Ashley	2	4	11	26	43
John Robinson	7	17	15	4	43
Dannet Foorthe	0	0	7	28	35
Francis Millington	3	3	5	14	25
John Griffith	1	6	7	7	21
Peter Colleton	5	7	0	0	12
Robert Vyner	7	2	2	2	13
Georges Carteret	1	1	5	5	12
Count Craven	1	5	5	1	12
William Prettyman	0	0	5	6	11
Prince Rupert	2	2	3	2	9
William Yonge	1	3	4	1	9
John Foorthe[1]	3	2	0	4	9
John Portman	4	2	1	0	7
Paul Neile	0	3	3	1	7
Edward Hungerford	0	1	1	0	2

1. John Forth participated in a few Company meetings in 1671, 1672 and 1674; his brother Dannett attended meetings assiduously in 1674. Dannett was reputed to be a shrewd businessman "a man of great ability in busynesse, but as to church affairs, of the same principles as his brother," whereas his brother, John, was viewed as considerably less reputable: "a hasty passionate person; noe lover of the Church of England [...] a man of noe reputation for keeping his word;" John regularly held non-conformist religious offices at home, in a consecrated chapel he had installed at his residence (HBRS-5: 225-226). The names of the brothers Forth are not to be found on any official document of incorporation, a clear indication of the tensions and precautions surrounding the religious allegiance of the shareholders in the years 1660; the former Puritans, or "non-conformists," although many and powerful, were viewed in a rather bad light or blatantly persecuted, in conformance with the times and the circumstances.

Bibliography

Manuscript Sources

ANQ   Archives nationales du Québec

ASQ   Archives du Séminaire de Québec

NAC   National Archives of Canada

BN   Bibliothèque nationale, France

RADISSON, Pierre-Esprit (Raw, 1685) *(Windsor Manuscript), Travel narratives of Sieur Pierre Esprit Radisson, Esquire, in North America, over the years 1682, 1683 and 1684. Executed at LONDON,* in the year 1685; a photocopy of the manuscript, 103 pages in length, was discovered in the library of Windsor Castle, by Jean Radisson, in 1997; Mr Radisson very graciously sent me a copy.

Printed Sources

ADAMS, Arthur T. (1961), ed., *The Explorations* of *Pierre-Esprit Radisson, from the original manuscript in the Bodleian Library and the British Museum, text updated by Loren Kallsen,* Minneapolis, Ross &Haines.

"Adventures of Captain James (1944), [...] extracts from rare books in the library of Hudson's Bay House, Winnipeg," *The Beaver,* outfit # 275, pp. 34-38.

BARBOT, Jean (1978), "Journal d'un voyage de traite en Guinée, à Cayenne et aux Antilles fait par Jean Barbot en 1678-1679, présenté, publié et annoté par Gabriel DEBIEN, Marcel DELAFOSSE et Guy THILMANS," *Bulletin de l'Institut fondamental d'Afrique noire,* T. 40, série B, no 2, pp. 235-395.

BIRCH, Thomas (1968), *The History of the Royal Society of London, for Improving of Natural Knowledge from its Rise,* a facsimile of the London Edition of 1756-1757, vols. 2-3-4, introduction by A. Rupert Hall, New-York and London, Johnson Reprint Corporation.

BOGAERT, Harmen Meyndertsz van der (1988), *A Journey into Mohawk and Oneida Country, 1634-1635. The journal of Harmen Meyndertsz van der Bogaert, C.T.* Gehring and W.A. Starna, trans. and ed.; wordlist and linguistic notes by G. Michelson, Syracuse University Press, Syracuse, 77 pages.

BOUCHER, Pierre (1964), *Histoire véritable et naturelle des moeurs et productions du pays de la Nouvelle-France, vulgairement dite le Canada,* Boucherville, Société historique de Boucherville (fac-similé).

CAMPEAU, Lucien (1996), *Monumenta Novæ Francice. Tome VIII. Au bord de la ruine (1651-1656),* Bellarmin, Montréal, 1 045 pages.

DEBIEN, G., "Engagés pour le Canada au XVIIᵉ siècle," *RHAF,* vol. VI, no 2, septembre 1952, Montréal.

HUDSON'S BAY RECORD SOCIETY, vols. 5, 8, 9 and 11.

-HBRS-5, *Minutes of the Hudson's Bay Company, 1671-1674,* edited by E. E. Rich, introduction by John Clapham, London, The Hudson's Bay Record Society, 1942, 276 pages.

-HBRS-8, *Minutes of the Hudson's Bay Company, 1679-1684, first part, 1679-82,* edited by E.E. Rich, introduction by G.N. Clark, The Champlain Society, London, 1945, 378 pages.

-HBRS-9, *Minutes of the Hudson's Bay Company, 1679-1684, second part 1682-84,* edited by E.E. Rich, introduction by G.N. Clark, London, The Champlain Society, 1946, 368 pages.

-HBRS-11, *Copy-Book of Letters Outward &c, begins 29th May, 1680, ends 5 July, 1687,* edited by E.E. Rich, assisted by A. M. Johnson, introduction by E. G. R. Taylor, London, The Champlain Society, 1948, 415 pages.

JAMESON, J. F (ed.) (1909), "Narratives of New Netherland, 1609-1664," in *Original Narratives of Early American History,* Scribner's and Sons, New York.

(JR)The Jesuit Relations and Allied Documents (1959), R.G. Twaithes (dir.), Pageant Book Company, New York, 73 volumes.

Le journal des jésuites (1646-1668), (1892), texte établi par Casgrain et Laverdière, J.M. Valois, Montréal, 403 pages.

LA BARRE, Joseph-Antoine de (1993), *La Nouvelle-France sous Joseph-Antoine Lefebvre de La Barre,* textes établis et présentés par Pauline Dubé, Septentrion, Québec.

LA SALLE, Robert Cavelier de, dans MARGRY, Pierre (1974), *Découvertes et établissements des Français dans l'ouest et dans le sud de l'Amérique septentrionale, 1614-1698,* vol. 2, deuxième partie, "Lettres de Cavelier de La Salle et correspondance relative à ses entreprises (1678-1685), Paris; AMS Press (reprint), New York, 1974.

LATHAM, Robert (1978), selected and edited by, *The Illustrated Pepys, Extracts from the Diary,* University of California Press, Berkeley and Los Angeles.

LOYOLA, Saint Ignace de (1963 [1548]), *Exercices spirituels de Saint-Ignace de Loyola,* traduit et annoté par François Courel, Desclée de Brouwer.

MARIE DE L'INCARNATION (1971), *Correspondance,* rassemblée et annotée par Dom Guy Oury, Abbaye Saint-Pierre, Solesmes, 1 071 pages.

MOOD, Fulmer (1936), "Shareholders in the Hudson's Bay Company in 1673 and 1675," *The Beaver,* March, pp. 16-18.

NUTE, Grace Lee (1943), *Caesars of the Wilderness. Médard Chouart, Sieur Des Groseilliers and Pierre Esprit Radisson, 1618-1710,* D. Appleton-Century Company, New York-London, 386 pages.

NUTE, Grace Lee (1935), "Radisson and Groseilliers' Contribution to Geography," *Minnesota History,* Vol. 16, December 1935, no. 4, pp. 414-426.

OLDMIXON ([1708] 1931), "The History of Hudson's Bay Containing an Account of its Discovery and Settlement, the Progress of it, and the Present State; of the Indians, Trade, and Every Thing Else Relating to it," in *Documents Relating to the Early History of Hudson Bay*, J.B. Tyrell ed., The Publications of the Champlain Society, vol.18., Toronto, 1931.

PERROT, Nicolas (1973), *Mémoire sur les moeurs, coustumes et relligion des sauvages de l'Amerique, septentrionale*, édition et annotation par J. Tailhan, Éditions Élysée, Montréal, 341 pages.

PEPYS, Samuel (1987), *Journal*, traduction de Renée Villoteau, Mercure de France, Paris, 486 pages.

PEPYS, Samuel (1985), *The Shorter Pepys*, selected and edited by Robert Latham, University of California Press, Berkeley and, Los Angeles, 1 096 pages.

PEPYS, Samuel (1972), *The Diary of Samuel Pepys*, a new and complete transcription edited by Robert Latham and William Matthews, volume VI, 1665, G. Bell and Sons Ltd, London, 367 pages.

RADISSON, Pierre-Esprit ([1885] 1943), *Voyages of Peter Esprit Radisson, being on count of his travels and experience among the North American Indians, from 1652 to 1684*, reprint of the original edition (Skull, ed.), Smith, New York, 247 pages.

RADISSON, Pierre-Esprit ([1885] 1999), *Les aventures extraordinaires d'un coureur de bois. Récits de voyage au pays des Indiens d'Amérique*, traduit de l'anglais et annoté par Berthe Fouchier-Axelsen, Éditions Nota bene, Québec, 366 pages.

SAGARD, Gabriel (1990), *Le grand voyage du pays des Hurons*, texte établi par Réal Ouellet, introduction et notes par R. Ouellet et Jack Warwick, coll. Bibliothèque québécoise, Montréal, 383 pages.

SKULL, Gedeon D., ed., voir RADISSON, Pierre-Esprit ([1885] 1943).

TALON, Jean (1930-1931), "Correspondance," *Rapport de l'archiviste de la province de Québec, années 1930-1931*, Imprimeur du roi, Québec.

Historial Studies

AMNISTIE INTERNATIONALE *(1974)*, *Rapport sur la torture*, Gallimard, Paris.

APOSTOLIDES, Jean-Marie (1981), *Le roi-machine, spectacle et politique au temps de Louis XIV*, Paris, de Minuit, 164 pages.

ARNOLD, John Cannon Edward (1981), ed., *The Whig Ascendency, Colloquies on Hanoverian England*, London.

BAILYN, Bernard (1979), *The New England Merchants in the 17th. Century*, Harvard University Press, Cambridge, 245 pages.

BEAULIEU, Alain (1992), *Ne faire qu'un seul peuple? Iroquois et Français à l'"âge héroïque" de la Nouvelle-France (1600-1660)*, thèse de doctorat, département d'histoire, Université Laval.

BIAGIOLI, Mario (1995), "Le prince et les savants. La civilité scientifique au 17ᵉ siècle," *Annales HSS*, novembre-décembre 1995, no 6, pp. 1417-1453.

BORINS, Edward H. (1968), *La compagnie du Nord, 1682-1700*, Thesis, Master of Art, History Department, McGill University, unpublished.

BOSHER, J. F. (1995), "Huguenot Merchants and the Protestant International in the Seventeenth Century," *The William and Mary Quarterly,* 3rd Series, vol. LII, no. 1, January 1995, pp. 77-102.

BOSHER, J. F. (1993a), "The Imperial Environment of French Trade with Canada, 1665-1685," *The English Historical Review,* vol. CVIII, no. 426, January 1993, Oxford University Press, pp. 50-81.

BOSHER, J. F. (1993b), "The Political and Religious Origins of La Rochelle's Primacy in Trade with New France, 1627-1685, *French History,* vol. 7, no. 3, pp. 286-312.

BOUSSIN, Fabienne (1997), *Rencontres el rituels diplomatiques entre Français et Iroquois au Canada dans la première moitié du XVIIe siècle,* mémoire de maîtrise, Département d'histoire, Université Bordeaux III, Bordeaux, 103 pages.

BURLET, Françoise-Laure (1996), *Un rêve aristocratique en Nouvelle-France, la demeure de Charles Aubert de La Chesnaye,* Septentrion, Québec, 126 pages.

CALLOWAY, Colin G. (1997), New Worlds for All. Indians, Europeans, and the Remaking of Early America, John Hopkins University Press, Baltimore.

CAMPEAU, Lucien (1995), "La Condition économique des Jésuites dans une Nouvelle-France pionnière, (1625-1670)," *Les Cahiers des dix,* no 50, La Société des dix/éd. Laliberté, Québec, pp. 23-53.

CAMPEAU, Lucien (1994), "La Route commerciale de l'Ouest au dix-septième siècle," *Les Cahiers des dix,* no 49, La Société des dix/éd. Laliberté, Québec, pp. 21-49.

CAMPEAU, Lucien (1992), "Les Cartes relatives à la découverte du Mississipi par le P. Jacques Marquette et Louis Jolliet," *Les Cahiers des dix,* no 47, La Société des dix/éd. Laliberté, Québec, pp. 41-90.

CAMPEAU, Lucien (1983), *Gannentaha, première mission iroquoise (1653-1665),* Bellarmin, Montréal.

Le castor fait tout, choix de textes présentés à la 5e conférence nord-américaine sur la traite des fourrures (l987), sous la dir. de B.G. Trigger, T. Morantz et L. Dechêne, Montréal, 653 pages.

CLERMONT, Norman (1988), "Le pouvoir spirituel chez les Iroquoiens de la période du contact," *Recherches amérindiennes au Québec,* vol XVIII, nos 2-3, 1988, Montréal, pp. 61-68.

CODIGNOLA, Luca (1990), "Laurens Van Heemskerk's Pretended Expeditions to the Arctic, 1668-1672: A Note," in *The International History Review,* vol. XII, no. 3, August 1990, pp. 514-527.

COTTRET, Bernard (1986), "Le roi, les Lords et les communes. Monarchie mixte et états du royaume en Angleterre (XVIe-XVIIIe siècles)," *Annales ESC,* janvier-février 1986, no 1, pp.127-150.

DAINVILLE, François de (1978), *L'éducation des jésuites (16e-18e siècles),* textes réunis et présentés par M.-M. Compère, de Minuit, Paris.

DECHÈNE, Louise (l974), *Habitants et marchands de Montréal au XVIIe siècle,* Plon, Paris.

DE KREY, Gary Stuart (1985), *A fractured Society, the Politics of London in the First Age of Party, 1688-1715,* Clarendon Press, Oxford.

DELAGE, Denys (1992), "Les premiers contacts, selon un choix de récits amérindiens publiés aux XIXe et XXe siècles," *Recherches amérindiennes au Québec,* vol. XXII, nos 2-3, 1992, pp. l01-115.

DELAGE, Denys (1991), "La religion dans l'alliance franco-amérindienne," *Anthropologie et Sociétés,* vol. 15, no 1, 1991, pp. 55-87.

DELAGE, Denys (1988), en collaboration avec PARENT, Sylvie, compte-rendu de *Parole et pouvoir. Figure du chef amérindien en Nouvelle-France, dans Recherches amérindiennes au Québec,* vol. XVIII, nos 2-3, 1988, pp. 159-161.

DELAGE, Denys (1985), *Le pays renversé. Amérindiens et Européens en Amérique du Nord-Est, 1600-1664,* Boréal Express, Montréal, 416 pages.

DESJARDINS, Arnaud (1992), La voie et ses pièges, de Table ronde, Paris, 237 pages.

DESSERT, Daniel (1984), *Argent, pouvoir et société au Grand Siècle,* Fayard, Paris, 824 pages.

DEYON, Solange (1976), *Du loyalisme au refus, les protestants français et leur député général entre la Fronde et la Révocation,* Publications de l'université de Lille III, Lille, 200 pages.

(DBC) *Dictionnaire biographique du Canada (Dictionary of Canadian Biography)* (1966), vols. 1 et 2, W. Brown et M. Trudel (dir.), Presses de l'université Laval and University of Toronto Press Québec/Toronto.

DIONNE, Narcisse-Eutrope (1910), *Chouart et Radisson: odyssée de deux Canadiens-Français au XVIIe siècle,* Laflamme et Proulx, Québec, 212 pages.

DOIRON, Normand (1988), "L'art de voyager. Pour une définition du récit de voyage à l'époque classique." *Poétique,* no 73, pp. 83-108.

DOMINIQUE, Richard (1989), *Le langage de la chasse. Récit autobiographique de Michel Grégoire, Montagnais de Natashquan,* Presses de l'université du Québec, Sillery, 206 pages.

DUBÉ, Jean-Claude (1984), *Les intendants de la Nouvelle-France*, Fides, Montréal, 327 pages.

ECCLES, William J. (1964), *Canada under Louis XIV, 1663-1701,* McClelland and Stewart, Toronto, 275 pages.

FOURNIER, Martin (1998), "Le voyage de Radisson et Des Groseilliers au lac Supérieur, 1659-1660: un événement marquant dans la consolidation des relations franco-amérindiennes," *Revue d'histoire de l'Amérique française,* vol. 52, no 2, pp. 159-187.

FOURNIER, Martin (1996a), *Pierre-Esprit Radisson, coureur de bois et homme du monde (1652-1685),* Nuit Blanche éditeur, Québec, 125 pages.

FOURNIER, Martin (1995), "Paul Lejeune et Gabriel Sagard: deux visions du monde et des Amérindiens," *Canadian Folklore Canadien,* vol l7, no l, pp. 85-101.

FOX, Paul W. (1960), "Louis XIV and the theories of absolutism and divine right," *Canadian Journal of Economics and Political Science,* vol. 26, no. 1, February, pp. l28-142.

FRANCIS, Daniel and MORANTZ, Tody (1983), Partners in Furs: A History of the Fur Trade in Eastern James Bay, 1660-1870, McGill/Queen's University Press, Kingston/Montréal, 203 pages.

FRASER, Antonia (1993), *Charles II, His Life and Times,* (picture research: Julia Brown), Weidenfeld and Nicolson, London, 264 pages.

FRÉMONT, Donatien (1937), *Pierre Radisson. Roi des coureurs de bois,* édition Liberté, Winnipeg, 266 pages.

GABOURY, Lorraine (1992), *La noblesse de Nouvelle-France, familles et alliances*, HMH, Montréal.

GARNEAU, François-Xavier (1944-1946), *Histoire du Canada*, 8ᵉ édition, édition de l'Arbre, Montréal, 9 volumes.

GIUSEPPI, John (1966), *The Bank of England. A history from its foundation in 1694*, Evans Brothers Limited, London, 215 pages.

GIVEN, Brian J. (1994), *A Most Pernicious Thing. Gun Trading and Native Warfare in the Early Contact Period*, Carleton University Press, Ottawa, 138 pages.

GRABOWSKI, Jan (1994), "Les Amérindiens domiciliés et la "contrebande" des fourrures en Nouvelle-France," *Recherches amérindiennes au Québec*, vol. XXIV, no 3, pp. 45-52.

GUILLET, Diane (1997), *Les "Radisson" de l'historiographie revus et corrigés*, mémoire de maîtrise en histoire, Université de Montréal, 180 pages.

HALEY, K.H.D. (1968), *The First Earl of Shaftesbury*, Clarendon Press, Oxford, 767 pages.

(H.N.A.I.) *Handbook of North American Indians*, STURTEVANT, William, ed., vol. 15, Smithsonian Institute, Washington.

HARRIS, Tim (1993), *London Crowds in the Reign of Charles II, Propaganda and Politics from the Restoration until the Exclusion Crisis*, Cambridge, Cambridge University Press, 264 pages.

HAVARD, Gilles (1992), *La grande paix de Montréal de 1701. Les voies de la diplomatie franco-amérindienne*, Recherches amérindiennes au Québec, Montréal, 222 pages.

HEIDENREICH, Conrad (1997), "Early French Exploration in the North American Interior," in *North American Exploration, volume 2*, J. L. Allan ed., University of Nebraska Press, London, pp. 65-148.

HICKERSON, Harold (1960), "The Feast of the Dead Among the Seventeenth Century Algonkians of the Upper Great Lakes," *American Anthropologist*, vol. 62, no. 1, February 1960, pp. 81-107.

HNAI: see Handbook of North American Indians.

HORGUELIN, Christophe (1997), *La prétendue république. Pouvoir et société au Canada, 1644-1675*, Septentrion, Québec, 169 pages.

INNIS, Harold (1956), *The Fur Trade in Canada: an introduction to Canadian economic history*, University of Toronto Press, Toronto, 463 pages.

JACQUES, André (1994), *L'interdit ou la torture en procès*, préface de Paul Ricoeur, du Cerf, Paris.

JACQUIN, Philippe (1987), *Les indiens blancs*, Payot, Paris, 310 pages.

JENNINGS, Francis (1984), *The Ambiguous Iroquois Empire. The Covenant Chain Confederation of Indian Tribes with English Colonies*, W. W. Norton and Company, New York, 438 pages.

JETTEN, Marc (1994), *Enclaves amérindiennes: les "réductions" du Canada, 1637-1701*, Septentrion, Québec, 155 pages.

JOHNSON, Alice M. (1946), "Early Ships in Hudson's Bay," in *The Beaver*, outfit 277, June 1946, pp. 10-13.

JOHNSON, Alice M. (1945), "First Governor on the Bay," in *The Beaver*, outfit 276, June 1945, pp. 22-25.

JOHNSON, Laurence, et MARTIJN, Charles A. C. 1994), Les Malécites et la traite des fourrures," *Recherches amérindiennes au Québec,* vol. XXIV, no 3, pp. 25-42.

JOUANNA, Arlette (1989), *Le devoir de révolte. La noblesse française et la gestation de l'État moderne, 1559-1661,* Fayard, Paris, 498 pages.

LE BER, Marc (1992), *Charles Le Moyne, seigneur de Longueuil. Histoire d'une réussite commerciale* Société historique de Marigot, Longueuil, 85 pages.

LYTWYN, Victor P. (1994), "Pleinement conscients de leur propre importance." Les Cris des basses terres de la baie d'Hudson et la chasse aux oies (XVIIIe siècle)," *Recherches amérindiennes au Québec,* Vol. XXIV no 3 1994, pp. 53-65.

MAC FARLANE (1945), "Prince Rupert, first Governor," in *The Beaver,* outfit 276, June 1945, pp. 19-21.

MARTIN, A. Lynn (1988), *The Jesuit Mind. The Mentality of an Elite in Early Modern France,* Cornell University Press, London, 256 pages.

MATHIEU, Jacques (1991), *La Nouvelle-France. Les Français en Amérique du Nord, 16e-18e siècles,* P.U.L./Belin, Québec/Paris, 254 pages.

MERLIN, Hélène (1994), "Langue et souveraineté en France au XVIIe siècle. La production autonome d'un corps de langage," *Annales HSS,* mars-avril 1994, no 2, pp. 369-394.

MERWICK, Dona (1990), *Possessing Albany, 1630-1710. The Dutch and English Experiences,* Cambridge University Press, Cambridge.

MOOD, Fulmer (1945), "Adventurers of 1670," *The Beaver,* outfit 276, June 1945, p. 48-530.

MORGAN, K. O. (ed.) (1984), *The Oxford History of Britain,* Oxford, Oxford University Press (Paperback revised edition of 1988).

MORTON, William L. (1963), *The Kingdom of Canada: A general history from earliest times,* McClelland and Stewart, Toronto, 556 pages.

MOUSNIER, Roland (sous la dir. de) (1988), *Un nouveau Colbert,* Sedes, Paris.

MUHLSTEIN, Anka (1992), *Cavelier de La Salle, l'homme qui offrit l'Amérique à Louis XIV,* Grasset, Paris.

NATALY, Jean-Paul (1993), *Catalogue de l'exposition multidisciplinaire sur la douleur,* Paris.

NUTE, Grace Lee (1943), *Caesars of the Wilderness. Médard Chouart, Sieur Des Groseilliers and Pierre Esprit Radisson, 1618-1710,* D. Appleton-Century Company, New York-London, 386 pages.

NUTE, Grace Lee (1935), "Radisson and Groseilliers' Contribution to Geography," *Minnesota History,* Vol. 16, December 1935, no. 4, pp. 414-426.

Old Trails and New Directions: Papers of the 3rd North American Fur Trade Conference, C.M. Judd and A.J. Ray ed., University of Toronto Press, Toronto, 337 pages.

OUELLET, Réal, (1993a), "Qu'est-ce qu'une relation de voyage?" *La recherche littéraire au Québec objets et méthodes,* sous la dir. de C. Duchet et S. Vachon, XYZ éditeur. Montréal.

OUELLET, Réal, (1993b), sous la dir. de, *Rhétorique et conquête missionnaire: le jésuite Paul Lejeune.* Septentrion/Célat, Québec, 137 pages.

OUELLET, Réal, (1989), "Le statut du réel dans la relation de voyage," *Littératures classiques,* no 11, janvier 1989, pp. 259-272.

PONSONBY, Arthur (1972[1928]), *Samuel Pepys,* Kennikat Press, London.

PROULX, Jean-René (1988), "Acquisition de pouvoirs et tente tremblante chez les Montagnais. Documents tirés de *Mémoire battante* d'Arthur Lamothe," *Recherches amérindiennes au Québec,* vol. XVIII, nos 2-3, 1988, pp 51-59.

PURVER, Margery (1967), *The Royal Society: Concept and Creation,* Routledge and Kegan Paul, London 246 pages.

RATELLE, Maurice (1993), "La localisation des Algonquins de 1534 à 1650," *Recherches Amérindiennes au Québec,* vol. XXIII, nos 2-3, pp. 25-38.

RAWLYK, George A. (1973), *Nova Scotia's Massachusetts, a Study of Massachusetts-Nova Scotia Relations, 1630 to 1784,* McGill-Queen's University Press, Montreal and London.

REID, John G. (1981), *Acadia, Maine and New Scotland, Marginal Colonies in the 17th. Century,* University of Toronto Press, Toronto, 293 pages.

REID, John G. (1977), *Maine, Charles II and Massachusetts, Governmental Relationships in Early Northern New England,* Maine Historical Society, Portland.

RICH, E. E. (1958), *The History of the Hudson's Bay Company, volume 1:1670-1763,* London, Hudson's Bay Record Society, vol. XXI, 687 pages.

RICH, E. E. (1960), "Trade Habits and Economic Motivation among the Indians of North America," *Canadian Journal of Economics and Political Science,* vol. 26, no. 1 February 1960, pp. 35-53.

RICHARDT, Aimé (1990), *Louvois,* Erti Éditeur, Paris, 1990, 287 pages.

RICHTER, Daniel K. (1992), *The Ordeal of the Longhouse. The Peoples of the Iroquois League in the Era of European Colonization,* University of North Carolina Press, Chapel Hill, 436 pages.

RICHTER, Daniel K. (1985), "Iroquois Versus Iroquois: Jesuit Missions and Christianity in Village Politics, 1642-1686," *Ethnohistory,* vol. 32, no.1, pp. 1-16.

RICHTER, Daniel K. (1983), "War and Culture: The Iroquois Experience," *William and Mary Quarterly,* vol. XL, no. 4, pp. 528-559.

RONCIÈRE de la, Charles (1934), *Histoire de la marine française,* tome V, Plon, Paris.

ROUSSEAU et ROY (1950), "La mission politique du père Albanel à la baie d'Hudson," *BRH,* vol. 56, printemps 1950, nos 4-5-6, pp.71-77.

ROY, J.-Edmond (1884), *Guillaume Couture, premier colon de la Pointe-Lévy,* Mercier, Québec, 160 pages.

RUMILY, Robert (1981), *L'Acadie française (1497-1713),* Fides, Montréal.

SAINT-YVES, M. G. (1899), "Les campagnes de Jean d'Estrées dans la mer des Antilles, 1676-1678," *Bulletin de géographie historique et descriptive,* vol. 2, pp. 217-246.

SAVARD, Rémi (1996), *L'Algonquin Tessouat et la fondation de Montréal. Diplomatie franco-amérindienne en Nouvelle-France,* L'Hexagone, Montréal, 185 pages.

SCHWOERER, Lois G. (ed.) (1992), *The Revolution of 1688-1689, changing perspectives,* Cambridge University Press, Cambridge, 288 pages.

SCOTT, Colin (1992), "La rencontre avec les Blancs d'après les récits historiques et mythiques des Cris la baie James," *Recherches amérindiennes au Québec,* vol. XXII, nos 2-3, pp. 47-62.

SHAPIN, Steven (1994), *A Social History of Truth. Civility and Science in Seventeenth-Century England*, University of Chicago Press, Chicago and London, 483 pages.

SHAPIN, Steven (1998[1996]), *The Scientific Revolution*, University of Chicago Press, Chicago and London, 218 pages.

SPILLER, Michael R.G. (1980), *'Concerning Natural Experimental Philosophie,' Meric Casaubon and the Royal Society*, La Haye, Martinus Nijhoff Publishers, 232 pages.

ST-ARNAUD, Daniel (1998), *Pierre Millet en Iroquoisie au XVIIe siècle. Le sachem portait la soutane*, Septentrion, Québec, 203 pages.

STEARNS, R. P. (1945), "The Royal Society and the Company," in *The Beaver*, outfit 276, June 1945, pp. 8-12.

STEELE, I.K. (1980), "The Empire and the Provincial Elites: An Interpretation of some Recent Writings on the Anglish Atlantic, 1675-1740," in *The British Atlantic Empire Before the American Revolution*, Frank Cass, Londres, pp. 2-32.

STONE, Lawrence (1985), "L'Angleterre de 1540 à 1880: pays de noblesse ouverte," *Annales ESC*, jan.-fév. 1985, no 1, p.71-94.

SUE, Eugène (1845), *Histoire de la marine française*, 2e édition, tome troisième, Paris.

TAYLOR, Charles (1989), *Sources of the Self. The Making of the Modern Identity*, Harvard University Press, Cambridge, 593 pages.

TOOKER, Elisabeth (1987), *Ethnographie des Hurons, 1615-1649*, Recherches Amérindiennes au Québec, Montréal, 215 pages.

TRIGGER, Bruce, G. (1976), *The Children of Aataentsic. A History of the Huron People to 1660*, 2 volumes, McGill-Queen's University Press, Montréal and London.

TRUDEL, Marcel (1997), *Histoire de la Nouvelle-France, IV. La seigneurie de la compagnie des Indes occidentales, 1663-1674*, Fides, Montréal, 894 pages.

TRUDEL, Marcel (1983a), *Histoire de la Nouvelle-France, III. La seigneurie des Cent-Associés, 1627-1663l, II, la société*, Fides, Montréal, 669 pages.

TRUDEL, Marcel (1983b), *Catalogue des immigrants, 1632-1662*, Hurtubise HMH, Montréal.

TRUDEL, Marcel (1980), "Jean Nicollet dans le lac Supérieur et non dans le lac Michigan," *RHAF*, vol. 34, no 2, septembre 1980, pp. 183-196.

TRUDEL, Marcel (1979), *Histoire de la Nouvelle-France, III. La seigneurie des Cent-Associés, 1627-1663, tome I, les événements*, Fides, Montréal, 489 pages.

TURGEON, Laurier, FITZGERALD, William et AUGER, Réginald (1992), "Les objets des échanges entre Français et Amérindiens au XVIe siècle," *Recherches amérindiennes au Québec*, vol. XXII, nos 2-3, pp. 152-166.

VAILLANCOURT, Daniel (1986), *Des récits de voyages de Pierre-Esprit Radisson: une traduction*, mémoire de maîtrise en études littéraires, Université du Québec à Montréal, 130 pages.

VAILLANCOURT, Daniel (1987), "Figures de Radisson: de la cour aux bois," *Recherches amérindiennes au Québec*, nos 17, 3, 1987, pp. 23-30.

VECSEY, Christopher (1983), *Traditionnal Ojibwa Religion and its Historical Changes*, The American Philosophical Society, Philadelphia, 233 pages.

VIAU, Roland (1994), *Enfants du néant et mangeurs d'âmes: guerre, culture et société, en Iroquoisie l'époque de la colonisation européenne,* thèse de doctorat, département d'anthropologie, université de Montréal; publié depuis chez Hurtubise HMH, Montréal, en 1997.

VINCENT, Marguerite (1984), *La nation huronne: son histoire, sa culture, son esprit,* éditions du Pélican, Québec, 507 pages.

WARKENTIN, Germaine (1996a), "Discovering Radisson: a Renaissance Adventurer Between Two Worlds," in *Reading Beyond Words: Contexts for Native History,* Broadview Press, Peterborough.

WARKENTIN, Germaine (1996b), "Radisson's Journals: an Editorial Puzzle," paper given at the Hakluyt Society, London, in November 1996 (of which I was kindly given a copy).

WARKENTIN, Germaine (1993), "Pierre-Esprit Radisson (c1640-1710)," in *Canadian Exploration Literature, an anthology,* Oxford University Press, Toronto.

WESTERN, J.R. (1972), *Monarchy and Revolution, the English State in the 1980s,* Brandford Press, London, 406 pages.

WHITE, Richard (1991), *The Middle Ground,* Cambridge University Press, Cambridge.

WIEN, Thomas (1998), "Le Pérou éphémère: termes d'échange et éclatement du commerce franco-amérindien 1645-1670," dans *Vingt ans après, habitants et marchands. Lectures de l'histoire des XVIIᵉ et XVIIIᵉ siècles canadiens,* sous la dir. de S. Dépatie, C. Desbarats, D. Gauvreau, M. Lalancette et T. Wien, McGill-Queen's University Press, Montréal et Kingston, pp. 160-188.

WYKOFF, M. William (1995), "The Land of the Eres in 1653: An Analysis of Radisson's Captivity Voyage," *Terrae Incognitae,* no. 27, 1995, pp. 15-45.

ZOOK, George Frederick, (1919), *The Company of Royal Adventurers trading into Africa,* Lancaster, Press of the New Era Printing Company, 105 pages.

Theoretical and Methodological Considerations

Over close to two decades, biography has become the designated venue for retracing the life of a particular individual, quite apart from the surroundings that he knew or from all the people who came in contact with him (including the researcher). Guided in particular by such micro-historians as Giovani Levi and Jacques Revel, whose work has sought to isolate the diversity of individual perceptions, interpretations and actions in a given micro-milieu, such as the village, I have attempted in this biography to develop a *dynamic* approach to the subject matter, one that would incorporate a goodly number of determining influences, for example, specific circumstances, a given era or the disparate sociocultural surroundings which may have shaped, then altered, the character of a particular individual – in this instance, Pierre-Esprit Radisson – while affecting in like manner his values and his deeds. To best meet my objective, I took inspiration from the natural sciences that consider certain complex phenomena, those for which the conjuction of multiple causes may provoke unforeseen consequences; for my purposes, these had me seize upon certain concepts and methods which, in turn, enabled me to carry out my study, then present the results, in ways that reflect the interdependent relations and interactions between Radisson, the evolutionary man and the changing sociocultural milieux he knew so intimately.

My attempts to understand Radisson and to interpret his existential path are rooted most notably in an analysis of the interactions which seem to have created his closest ties and most privileged networks; these last would prove stronger, more stable and more meaningful, as evidenced by the passel of information and of disparate exploits which, in a body, made up Radisson's life as lived. Indeed, thanks to such a wealth of details about Radisson's personal energy, his relationships involving mutual assistance or trade, as well as about the love or friendship that continued to exist between himself and others, indeed, even about the food he ate, all these, despite or because of the different customs, enterprises and institutions that he came to know, so clearly brought to the fore over time a multitude of "resonances," at once complementary and willingly shared. These same helped shape a multi-faceted, existential path, one that relied above all on exchanges between the various actors involved, as well as on the way in *which individuals act and react, one towards the other*, rather than on *what they are, in and of themselves*. This is how I thought best to define the evolution and the intimate nature of such a complex figure.

An essay presenting the details of these theoretical and methodological considerations is now in preparation; the following list enumerates the principal documents which helped me write this biography of Radisson from a specifically *relational* perspective.

AMSELLE, Jean-Loup (1990), *Logiques métisses*, Payot, Paris.

AUGÉ, Marc (1992), *Non-lieux. Introduction à une anthropologie de la sur-modernité*, Seuil, Paris, 149 pages.

BAREL, Yves (1977), *La ville médiévale; système social, système urbain*, Presses universitaires de Grenoble, Grenoble.

BARROS, Carolyn A. (1992), "Figura, Persona, Dynamis: Autobiography and Change," *Biography*, Vol. 15, no. 1, Winter 1992, pp. 1-28.

BOURDIEU, Pierre (1986), "L'illusion biographique," *Actes de la recherche en sciences sociales*, nos 62-63, janvier 1986, pp. 69-72.

CALHOUN, Creg (1994) (ed.), *Social Theory and the Politics of Identity*, Blackwell, Oxford, 350 pages.

DRAY, Dominique (1994), "L'agression physique, une "peur" irréparable," *Terrain*, no. 22, mars 1994, pp. 35-50.

FOURNIER, Martin (1996b), "Analyse d'un phénomène complexe et plurudisciplinarité: le cas Radisson," dans *Canadian Folklore Canadien*, vol. 18, no 2, pp. 91-109.

FUMA, Sudel, et POIRIER, Jean (1992), "Métissages, hétéroculture et identité culturelle. Le "défi" réunnionnais," dans *Métissages, linguistique et anthopologie*, tome 2, l'Harmattan, Paris.

GENDREAU, Andrée (sous la dir. de) (1995), *La différence*, Fides/Musée de la Civilisation, Montréal/Québec.

GRUZINSKI, Serge (1999), *La pensée métisse*, Fayard, Paris, 345 pages.

LE GOFF, Jacques (] 996), *Saint Louis*, Gallimard, Paris.

LÉTOURNEAU, Jocelyn (sous la dir. de) (1995), *La question identitaire au Canada francophone. Récits, parcours, enjeux, hors-lieux*, P.U.L., Québec.

LEVl, Giovanni (1989a), "Les usages de la biographie," *Annales ESC*, vol. 44, no 6, p.1325-1336.

LEVI, Giovanni (1989b), *Le pouvoir au village,* préface de Jacques Revel, Gallimard, Paris.

POPPER, Carl (1986), *La quête inachevée, autobiographie intellectuelle,* Presses-Pocket, coll. Agora, Paris, 350 pages.

PRIGOGINE, llya, STENGERS, Isabelle (1979), *La nouvelle alliance, métamorphose de la science,* Gallimard, coll. Folio-essais, Paris, 439 pages.

PRIGOGINE, Ilya (1992), *dans L'homme face à la science. Un enjeu pour la planète?* collectif sous la dir. d'llya Prigogine, Centurion, Paris, 240 pages, pp. 21-36. *La science du désordre,* numéro spécial de la revue *La Recherche,* mai 1991.

VARELA, Francisco, Evans THOMPSON et Eleanor ROSCH (1993), *L'inscription corporelle de l'esprit, sciences cognitives et expérience humaine,* Seuil, Paris, 377 pages.